explanation be reconciled with the belief that miracles are exclusively spiritual phenomena? Rogo's conclusions are challenging and provide some surprising theories about the nature of supernatural involvement in the miraculous.

For the student of the paranormal or the general reader who is curious about these little-understood events, *Miracles* is compelling reading, a thorough and accessible inquiry that promises to become the standard general reference on an astonishing subject.

D. SCOTT ROGO has written nearly twenty books and over a hundred magazine and journal articles on psychic phenomena and related subjects. He served as a visiting research consultant for the Durham, North Carolina-based Psychical Research Foundation in 1973 and in 1975 was both a visiting researcher at the Maimonides Medical Center's division of parapsychology and psychophysics (in Brooklyn, New York) and director of research for the Society of Psychic Research in Beverly Hills, California. Since 1979 he has been a lecturer in parapsychology at John F. Kennedy University in Orinda, California. He is also consulting editor of *Fate* magazine.

Mr. Rogo is a lifelong resident of Los Angeles, where he makes his present home.

ALSO BY D. SCOTT ROGO

Books
NAD, a study of some unusual "other world" experiences
A Psychic Study of the "Music of the Spheres"
Methods and Models for Education in Parapsychology
The Welcoming Silence
An Experience of Phantoms
Parapsychology: A Century of Inquiry
In Search of the Unknown
Exploring Psychic Phenomena
The Haunted Universe
Minds and Motion
The Haunted House Handbook
The Poltergeist Experience

Anthologies
Mind Beyond the Body
UFO Abductions

Co-author
Phone Calls from the Dead (with Raymond Bayless)
Earth's Secret Inhabitants (with Jerome Clark)
The Tujunga Canyon Contacts (with Ann Druffel)

MIRACLES

MIRACLES
A Parascientific Inquiry
into
Wondrous Phenomena

D. SCOTT ROGO

THE DIAL PRESS · NEW YORK

105815

Published by
The Dial Press
1 Dag Hammarskjold Plaza
New York, New York 10017

Acknowledgments

The author would like to thank the following authors and publishers for allowing use of copyrighted material:

From *The Apparitions of Garabandal,* by F. Sanchez-Ventura y Pascual. Copyright © 1966 by Peter Klein. Reprinted by permission of San Miguel Publishing Company (Detroit, Michigan).

From *Our Lady Comes to Garabandal,* by Joseph Pelletier. Copyright © 1971 by Joseph Pelletier. Reprinted by permission of Assumption Publications (Worcester, Massachusetts).

From *Teresa Helena Higginson—Servant of God,* by Cecil Kerr. Copyright © 1978 by Tan Books and Publishers. Reprinted by permission of Tan Books and Publishers.

From *Miracle,* by Des Hickey and Gus Smith. Copyright © 1978 by Des Hickey and Gus Smith. Reprinted by permission of Hodder & Stoughton.

From *Our Lady Returns to Egypt,* by Jerome Palmer. Copyright © 1969 by Culligan Publications. Reprinted by permission of the author and Tan Books and Publishers.

From *Possessed by Satan,* by Adolf Rodewyk. Copyright © 1975 by Doubleday & Company, Inc. Reprinted by permission of Doubleday & Company, Inc.

From *Psychic Nexus,* by Berthold Schwarz, M.D. Copyright © 1980 by Litton Educational Publishing Inc. Reprinted with the permission of Van Nostrand Reinhold Company.

Portions of Chapter 8 originally appeared as an article in *Fate* magazine and are adapted here with the special permission of the editors.

Manufactured in the United States of America
First printing
Design by Nancy Dale Muldoon

Library of Congress Cataloging in Publication Data

Rogo, D. Scott.
    Miracles, a parascientific inquiry into wondrous
phenomena.

    Bibliography: p. 315
    Includes index.
    1. Miracles. 2. Psychical research. I. Title.
BT97.2.R63   231.7'3   81-17329
ISBN 0-385-27202-2   AACR2

CONTENTS

PREFACE

My INTENTION in writing this book is modest. It is meant basically as an introduction to the study of religious miracles from a critical and, I hope, scientific viewpoint. I have not attempted to write an authoritative volume on the subject. Such an endeavor would take a lifetime of research, and the results would fill more than a dozen books. What I have done instead is to document the existence of the miraculous by exploring several representative genres and examples of these awesome events. My general goal is to present the scientific rather than the religious case for the miraculous. In no way is this approach meant to diminish the purely religious significance of these events, however.

My strategy throughout this volume will be to compare and contrast the miracles of Christianity to miracles recorded in other religious traditions and to miracles that have, on rare occasions, been produced by gifted individuals in the course of their secular lives. Clues about the nature of these events can be gleaned from many recent findings in parapsychology and Fortean studies as well.

Writing this book has been one of the most difficult challenges I have confronted in my professional career as a parapsychologist. I am therefore very indebted to several individuals who aided me. I owe a great debt of gratitude to my long-time friend and collaborator Raymond Bayless, who first introduced me to many of the topics covered and who first suggested to me that they fell within the purview of psychic studies. In addition, he provided me with leads and information pertinent to many of the topics discussed herein. I am also extremely indebted to George Zorab and Kent Ward, two keen students of the psychic field, who willingly and laboriously translated French source material I desperately needed, and to Carlos Alvarado, one of our students at John F. Kennedy

University, who directed me to Spanish language source material and duly translated it for me as well.

Thanks are also due to several others who helped provide me with material, including the Reverend Gordon Melton, Mr. Stewart Robb, Mr. Tom Malone, and many others who answered my queries and letters. Special thanks are also due to Father Jerome Palmer, O.S.B., who thoughtfully provided me with extremely valuable material on the Zeitoun miracles, and to R.J.M. Rickard, the editor of the *Fortean Times,* for helping me track down photo sources. For help in processing some of the photos used in this book, I am indebted to Richard Nazarian.

Finally, every writer on the subject of miracles is indebted to the late Father Herbert Thurston, an eminent priest, scholar, and insightful expert on psychical research, who devoted years to studying the psychic side of miracles. His two posthumously published books, *The Physical Phenomena of Mysticism* (1952) and *Surprising Mystics* (1955), serve as nearly definitive sources on the Church's findings pertinent to the psychic and supernatural gifts of her members. I have drawn on these exhaustive volumes frequently in Part One.

D. Scott Rogo
Graduate School of Consciousness Studies
John F. Kennedy University
Orinda, California

Northridge, California
June 1981

MIRACLES

∽ I ∼
SCIENCE, PSI, AND
THE MIRACULOUS

TO DISCOVER *how* miracles occur, *when* they occur, and *why* they occur are empirical questions which should be answerable (or at least explorable) through the application of scientific examination. We have hundreds of facts about miracles at hand, including accounts of people such as saints, yogis, psychics who have levitated spontaneously into the air, holy men who have been seen in two places at the same time, statues and icons that have bled human blood, and healings that seem to defy all medical and physiological laws. Although these strange occurrences are real events occurring in the real world, very few conventional scientists have chosen to study them. One reason for this neglect is that miracles are exceedingly rare—so rare, in fact, that most people either refuse to believe that they happen, or have simply never been exposed to the evidence substantiating their existence.

Few scientists have dared try to naturalize the supernatural. Those who do try usually end up ostracized by their peers, ridiculed by the scientific establishment, or embarrassed into keeping their interest secret or inchoate. One might say that science has "pushed" the study of miracles back into the arms of religion and religious apologists.

This tendency on the part of the scientific world has been so perennial that Charles Fort (1874–1932), an iconoclastic American writer of around the turn of the century, deliberately alluded to it in the title of his first book, *The Book of the Damned.* This volume assembled over a thousand reports from eyewitnesses all over the world who had seen strange objects flying through the skies, fish or other uninvited guests falling from the heavens, and houses bombarded by volleys of stones.* It also documented reports of people with strange abilities or those who simply vanished from the face of the earth. These events were damned, explained Fort, not because they were evil, but because science (or, more properly, *scientists*) had refused to acknowledge their existence.

You might say that just as nature abhors a vacuum, science abhors anomaly. Modern science seems threatened by anything that tends to upset the fragile view of the world that old-fashioned Newtonian physics prescribes for us. This is a world where such things as psychic forces, ghosts, and miracles can't exist. Even the challenging findings of quantum physics, which have totally disrupted our cause-and-effect view of the universe, have not done much to disturb our everyday view of the "real world" in which we live. It is just a little too disquieting for most of us to realize that the universe isn't as predictable, friendly, or cooperative as we would like it to be.

But "conventional science" has now been disrupted. New facts and new findings have started to cause a rift in the scientific establishment. One might say that science has now splintered into "normal science"—the conventional study of the physical, biological, and social sciences—and what has recently been labeled "unconventional science,"[1] which studies anomalies. The latter includes the study of mysteries of nature, such as those Fort compiled (often called "anomalistic science"), and the study of unrecognized faculties in man, such as telepathy and mind-over-matter (which can be called "psychic science" or, more properly, parapsychology). The study of miracles would seem to fall in between these two categories, since it investigates both occurrences in which the laws of nature are interrupted or overridden and people with wondrous powers.

Contrary to what many people believe, parapsychologists do not spend most of their time sleeping in haunted houses, trying to photograph the human aura, or casting horoscopes. Parapsychology is a highly specialized field that uniquely combines elements

---

*For instance, in November 1962, a cabin in Big Bear City, California, became the scene of one of these attacks. For weeks it was bombarded by rains of stones, often falling slowly from the sky. They struck several times a day, even as local sheriff's deputies swarmed over the area in hopes of finding some spry teen-ager armed with a hidden catapult! None was ever found, and the mystery remains unsolved.

of both natural and experimental science. A parapsychologist may, for example, investigate and attempt to verify such phenomena as telepathy and precognition (seeing the future) either by interviewing people who have had these experiences or by asking them to demonstrate their uncanny powers in the scientific laboratory. But collecting and studying accounts of ESP is only one branch of parapsychology, and many feel it is the least important branch. Parapsychology today is basically an experimental science, more concerned with finding out the hows and whys of ESP and mind-over-matter (collectively called *psi* or *psi phenomena*) than with merely gathering more evidence that these powers exist. Through the application of the scientific method—extrapolating hypotheses about psychic phenomena and then testing them out experimentally in labs with both gifted psychics and unselected volunteer subjects—parapsychologists have been able to learn a great deal about psi phenomena. They now know, for instance, that people with certain personality characteristics tend to make good ESP subjects, and that people are prone to display ESP when they enter into certain altered states of mind. Many such startling findings have been made in the field over the last sixty years or so.

Parapsychologists basically study only two major *types* of scientific anomalies. These are ESP (a blanket term that includes telepathy, clairvoyance, and precognition) and psychokinesis (or PK), which is a category covering a wide range of psychic phenomena, including the power to make objects move by merely concentrating on them, and healing. A few parapsychologists have also examined such phenomena as extrasensory contact with the dead, hauntings, out-of-body travel, and other more bizarre powers of the mind. Because these phenomena are hard to isolate and investigate in the laboratory, they are not widely pursued, and are certainly not as commonly studied today as they were eighty years ago, when parapsychology was an infant science still trying to verify the very existence of its subject matter.

The world of the miraculous may seem a little less enigmatic and exasperating to us if viewed in the light of parapsychology. To illustrate this point, let me cite just one of the many miracles allegedly performed by St. Francis of Paolo (1416–1507), an Italian friar whose life has recently been examined in a full-length biography.[2] The incident occurred while the saint was helping to build a monastery near the city of Paolo in 1435. A furnace had been set up at the site to help in the construction. According to St. Francis's biographers:

Perhaps the most amazing of all the miracles during the building of this monastery was one of the first, related to the furnace built to prepare lime for mortar. Shortly after it was completed, workers noticed that some of the stones making up the wall had come loose, either from faulty construction or from the tremendous heat of the fire. Alarmed, the workmen tending the furnace ran to tell Francis, expressing fear that the furnace would collapse. Francis examined the damage and advised the workers to be of good spirit and to trust in the help of God. When all the workers had left for lunch, Francis stood in front of the furnace entrance, lifted his arms in prayer, made the Sign of the Cross over it, then entered into the roaring flames. He assessed the condition of the furnace, then calmly walked back out, his clothes completely unharmed by the fire. The furnace's imperfections were repaired instantaneously.

We can, of course, just dismiss this story as an apocryphal tale. Yet in 1519, when canonization hearings were held to consider the case of St. Francis, no fewer than eight eyewitnesses testified to the authenticity of the incident. (The furnace, by the way, still stands by the monastery.) This was not a unique incident in the saint's life. Years before, while a friar at St. Mark's Monastery in the town of Argentano, he had given another display of fire immunity. While assisting at Mass, Francis was asked to bring a flame by which to ignite an incense burner. The only available source was some burning embers in the monastery kitchen. Not having anything to hold them with, St. Francis merely picked them up in his hands, wrapped them in his tunic, and brought them to the church. Neither his hands nor his clothing was burned.

We have here two miracles, attested to by several witnesses, to contend with—the facts that St. Francis was not burned and, perhaps even more astonishing, that his clothes were not scorched on either occasion. Yet we do not have to suggest that St. Francis was under some sort of divine protection when he produced these miracles. The eyewitnesses to these events may have been observing a form of psychic phenomenon known in a very different context to parapsychologists today in the spectacular fire-immunity displays that are regularly practiced by certain Holiness pentecostals in many rural American locations.

The Free Pentecostal Holiness Church is a fundamentalist sect with churches in Kentucky, Tennessee, Virginia, and North Carolina. Being strict literalists of the Bible, they take the Gospel at face value when it states that those who trust in God can defy serpents, poison, and fire. So as part of their religious observances, which often resemble old-fashioned revival meetings, members of the congregation will openly handle rattlesnakes without being bitten, drink solutions of strychnine with no harmful effects, and perform sometimes remarkable exhibitions of fire immunity. They invariably perform such feats in states of ecstasy or trance. While these exhibitions have been reported for years, it wasn't until 1959 that a scientific investigation into them was made by Dr. Berthold Schwarz, a New Jersey psychiatrist.[3] During several visits to Tennessee, he was able to watch church members light makeshift kerosene lamps and hold them to their hands and feet for up to fifteen seconds without discomfort, burning, or blistering. Sometimes a flame applied to little pools of kerosene they held in their hands would not cause the liquid to ignite. And, as with St. Francis, the fire immunity would sometimes extend to the handler's clothing.

As Schwarz reports about one of his field trips:

On three occasions, three different women held the blaze to their chests, so that the flames were in intimate contact with their cotton dresses, exposed necks, faces and hair. This lasted for longer than a few seconds. Twice, at separate times, one of the "most faithful of the saints" slowly moved the palmar and lateral aspects of one hand and the fifth finger in the midpoint tip of an acetylene flame (produced by the reaction of calcium carbide and water in a miner's headlamp). He did this for more than four seconds, and then repeated the procedure, using the other hand. Later that same evening, he alternately applied each hand again to the acetylene flame for slightly longer periods. Once this saint, when in a relatively calm mood, turned to a coal fire of an hour's duration, picked up a flaming "stone coal" the size of a hen's egg and held it in the palms of his hands for sixty-five seconds while he walked among the congregation. As a control, the author could not touch a piece of burning charcoal for less than one second without developing a painful blister.

There is simply no medical explanation for this type of "miracle," which is known to just about every religion in the world. Analogies to St. Francis's feats and to the Holiness displays can be found in the fire-walking ceremonies practiced in Fiji, Hawaii, Thailand, Japan, Roumania, and Sicily, and by shamans in many primitive cultures.*

It should also be noted that fire immunity can occur in a secular as well as a sacred context. On September 7, 1871, the New York *Herald* reported that several prominent citizens of Easton, Maryland, had tested a local blacksmith, Nathan Cohen, who was apparently immune to fire. The city commission watched as, under their direction, Cohen placed a white-hot shovel directly to his naked feet, swished molten buckshot in his mouth, and held red-hot coals. And Mircea Eliade, an anthropologist at the University of Chicago, alludes to several similar cases occurring among primitive people in his classic book on shamanism.[4]

There are even several cases on record where fire handlers have conferred their amazing ability on onlookers. Merely by touching them, they can apparently make even casual spectators immune to fire for short periods of time. This phenomenon is also sometimes practiced by Holiness fire handlers.

The point of all this discussion is that what we call "miracles" seem to be widespread. They are not the exclusive domain of any one religion or belief system. Although this book will focus on the traditional miracles authenticated by the Catholic Church, it will also show that these miracles have non-Christian and even totally secular analogues as well. Whatever their nature, then, miracles do not seem to be exclusively divine as such, but extensions of some sort of psychic talent possessed by the practitioners themselves.

But let's return to St. Francis and the burning-furnace inci-

---

*Not all fire walking is miraculous, however. Many forms of it, especially as practiced in India and Sicily, can be quite normally explained. The walker is in contact with the burning embers for only short periods of time and walks steadily, raising each foot off the fire as he steps. Burning does not have a chance to take place, and anyone can learn the trick. Some forms of the fire walk *are* paranormal, especially as practiced in Japan and Roumania, where witnesses have seen the walkers actually stop and stand in the embers, with flames licking their feet, for several seconds. (For more information on how most fire walking can be explained, see my book *In Search of the Unknown* [New York: Taplinger, 1976, pp. 143–4]. See also a brief report on fire walking in *Human Behavior* magazine, September 1978.)

dent. It indeed seems miraculous that he could have walked completely into a furnace without doing harm to himself or his clothing. Yet, in view of what parapsychologists have learned about fire immunity through fire-walking rituals and through Schwarz's field investigations, we have no right to automatically reject this sort of reported miracle merely because of its inherent implausibility. It is quite possible to accept this account as genuine if we do not view it as a miracle at all, but as merely a radical extension of similar phenomena being witnessed today by scientific observers. Miracles seem impossible to us only because those who have chronicled them (and modern religious writers are the worst offenders in this regard) have tended to isolate them from similar feats reported in parapsychology. If we accept Schwarz's observations as valid, we must assume at least the possibility that St. Francis did exactly what those eight eyewitnesses in 1519 claimed he had done.

The idea that miracles are forms of psychic phenomena is not original. There is a sizable amount of literature on the subject of Biblical miracles, showing how they can be explained as psychic rather than miraculous events.[5] These books, however, usually ignore the fact that at least some Biblical miracles are allegories which have perfectly obvious meanings to anyone versed in Judaic symbolism.* A similar explanation was offered by the great Harvard psychologist William McDougall, who casually suggested back in the 1920s that religious miracles might in fact occur via the collective psychic powers of whole *groups* of worshipers.

If miracles do represent a different order of psychic phenomena from what is normally studied in parapsychology, then what actually constitutes a miracle? How exactly does one define the difference between the paranormal and the miraculous at all? This is an important distinction, since it is crucial to defining the subject matter that will concern us in this book.

One definition of the miraculous has been offered by Red-

---

*For instance, many psychically oriented writers have dubbed Christ's ability to walk on water as an instance of levitation. But this story is most easily explained as an allegory. Water is the biblical symbol for chaos, which signifies all that is bad in the world. Christ's walking on the waves symbolizes his control over chaos, thus indicating his divinity. It should be noted, though, that at least one modern saint, St. Zachary of Russia (d. 1936), was seen to perform this feat.

mond Mullin, an authority on miracles, who has suggested that "what I mean by 'miracle' is an extraordinary and inexplicable event, beyond the scope of the ordinary natural causes, which is therefore attributed to supernatural or preternatural powers."[6] This definition is unsatisfactory, though, since any form of psychic phenomenon—from simple telepathy to psychically affecting the roll of dice—could be considered as a miracle. We might therefore say that a miracle is any extraordinary and inexplicable event beyond the scope of ordinary or *recognized* paranormal causes. Recognized paranormal causes are those types of psychic phenomena (such as telepathy, clairvoyance, precognition, etc.) that seem directly linked to the human psyche. Miracles are therefore events that are qualitatively different from those we can observe in a laboratory setting and which seem to indicate the intervention of some supernatural force into the affairs of human life.

The dichotomy between the paranormal and the miraculous has long been a key issue in the writings of traditional church theorists. It was addressed fully by Prospero Lambertini (later Pope Benedict XIV) in the 1730s, when he wrote his dissertation on miracles, *De canonizatione,* which is still the official Church authority on the subject. Lambertini wrote his book as a guide for papal authorities who were often asked to examine the miraculous deeds of saintly people during the long process of canonization. Cardinal Lambertini was very aware of the fact that some allegedly "miraculous" events could easily be linked to the human mind, and as such had nothing to do with anything divine. Only by separating the paranormal from the truly miraculous, believed Lambertini, could one determine if an event was genuinely produced by God. He therefore rejected such phenomena as clairvoyance, telepathy, and most healing as not being of divine origin, though he felt that some forms of prophecy could come through the will of God. He defined a miracle, to quote from Renée Haynes, Lambertini's biographer, as an "event brought about by the supernatural order within the physical world."[7]

Lambertini's definition allows inclusion of such phenomena as the stigmata, bilocation (the physical duplication of the human body so that it can appear in two places at once), involuntary levitation, and some miraculous healings not produced by traditional psychic healing practitioners. It also allows for several miracles of nature, such as incorruptibility (the failure of the body to putrefy after death), the odor of sanctity (wondrous perfumes that emanate from or herald the presence of saintly people), and divine images of Christ or others that have appeared on such physical objects as walls and pieces of cloth. Finally, it includes cases of Marian apparitions (appearances of the Virgin Mary) if seen by more than one person at the same time.

I consider the critical difference between a paranormal event and a psychic event to be that a psychic phenomenon usually occurs through an act of conscious or unconscious intention by the witness. We try to "send" a telepathic message; we carry out the laying on of hands when we try to heal; and our minds produce precognitive dreams when, for some reason, it is necessary for us to get a glimpse of the future. In the case of miracles, though, some alien intelligence does in fact seem to be directly interacting with the affairs of human life. The witness has no inclination that his own mind or powers may be involved in the occurrence. (This "ego-alien" nature of miracles is one of their most mysterious aspects. While I do believe miracles occur through the agency of the human mind and its psychic capabilities, I leave open the question of whether or not some other intelligence might not be behind them in some way. This is a problem that I'll address in the last chapter.)

But is there really evidence that such events occur, and are occurring, in the world today?

David Hume, the famous nineteenth-century Scottish philosopher, wrote a famous dictum against the existence of miracles in *An Enquiry Concerning Human Understanding:*

> A miracle is a violation of the laws of nature; and as a firm and unalterable experience has established these laws, the proof against a miracle, from the very nature of the fact is as entire as any argument from experience can possibly be imagined . . . . no testimony is sufficient to establish a miracle unless the testimony be of such a kind that its falsehood would be more miraculous than the fact which it endeavors to establish.

It is my hope to show in this book that the evidence authenticating the existence of miracles is indeed so strong that its collective falsehood would be, quite literally, miraculous.

Part One

~⌒⌒~

MIRACULOUS TALENTS

Miracles can occur within the framework of nature or they can occur through people. In this section, we will examine what might be called "miraculous talents"—the abilities some mystics within both Christian and Eastern traditions possess to produce wonders that defy every known law of the physical world. Just *why* these individuals are endowed with these gifts, or how their powers are a reflection of their lives of austerity and spirituality, are issues too abstract and delicate to speculate upon. More pertinent to the critical study of the miraculous are two fundamental issues: First, can the wonders these very special people produce be scientifically documented, and second, what physical and psychic factors seem to predicate such talents?

Many different types of miraculous talents have been recorded in the lives of the saints, ascetics, and holy men, regardless of the religions to which these gifted individuals have adhered. In the following chapters we will be concerned with both historical and contemporary accounts of three of these great talents.

∾ II ∾
LEVITATION

LEVITATION can be defined as the paranormal suspension of the human body in midair. The word *levitation* is, however, actually a generic term, since it doesn't really refer to one specific type of phenomenon. For example, "simple" levitations are instances in which a saint or holy man will become buoyant and will suddenly float up into the air, often against his will. Accounts have also come down to us describing the "spiritual flights" of levitating mystics and yogis who, after becoming airborne, have found themselves whizzing through the sky. There are also cases on record of deliberately induced levitation, a phenomenon most often produced by yogis.

Whatever the truth or fiction of these accounts, stories about human levitation are not rare. It can purportedly be produced by the shamans of Asia, and also occurs during cases of "demonic" possession. It is perhaps the most commonly mentioned miracle in yogic and Tibetan Buddhist literature and in the lore of the Roman Catholic saints. In his book *The Wonders of the Saints,* the Reverend F. Fielding-Ould, an Anglican priest and an expert on psychic phenomena, notes that:

When we turn to the records of the Church, we find the same phenomenon observed in many instances. St Ignatius Loyola [d. 1556], the founder of the Society of Jesus, was, while at prayer, seen by one John Pascal to be raised more than a foot above the ground. St Philip Neri [d. 1595] was levitated "about a palm" from his sickbed, in full view of his attendants. St Joseph of Copertino [d. 1663], while celebrating the Mysteries in 1649 before the Duke of Brunswick, was bodily raised a hand's-breadth above the level of the altar, and remained there six or seven minutes. St James of Illyricum [d. 1485] was levitated while at prayer; St Dominic [d. 1221] at the Holy Communion, a cubit from the ground. Much the same thing is told of St Dunstan, St Philip Benite, St Cajetan,

St Albert of Sicily, and St Bernard Ptolomaei. St Richard, his chancellor, testifies that he saw St Edmund, Archbishop of Canterbury, "raised high in the air with knees bent and arms stretched out."

Fielding-Ould goes on to mention the better-known levitational feats of St. Thomas Aquinas (1225–1274) and St. Teresa of Avila (1515–1582), as well as a few cases known to have occurred in non-Christian settings.[1]

An actual count of just how many Catholic saints allegedly experienced levitation is hard to compile. In his *Die Christliche Mystik* (1842), J. J. von Görres, an authority on Catholic mysticism, lists seventy-two levitating saints. An extensive compilation naming dozens of levitating saints was published in the January 1875 issue of the *Quarterly Journal of Science*. A similar list was made out by Dr. A. Imbert-Gourbeyre, a French authority on miracles, in his book *La Stigmatisation* (1894). An additional twenty cases *not* mentioned by Dr. Imbert-Gourbeyre are given by Father Herbert Thurston, an English priest who wrote several volumes on miracles, in his exhaustive, posthumously published book *The Physical Phenomena of Mysticism* (1952). Finally, Olivier Leroy, a Catholic writer whose classic *La Lévitation* is an authoritative book on the subject, cites some two hundred cases.

Although there is obviously no dearth of material on this fascinating subject, scholars disagree about the value of unsubstantiated *tales* of levitation as opposed to those relatively fewer well-documented reports of the phenomenon. Thurston, for example, argues that many accounts were the apocryphal inventions of overeager biographers. While studying the lives of many saints and ascetics who purportedly manifested this miracle, in several cases he couldn't find any firsthand reports written by contemporaries of these saints, nor adequately documented references in the Church records that led to their canonizations.* In many other instances eyewitness reports were apparently placed on record many years after the miracles had occurred. By this time the witnesses had grown old and feeble, and probably no longer clearly recalled the

---

*Before an ascetic is canonized, the Church sets up a commission whose duty it is to study all records and testimony pertaining to any miracles the ascetic performed either before or after death. Many of the cases reported in this book are taken from these records and archives.

incidents they had observed so many years before. Thurston's conclusions were that "in the imperfect and limited inquiry which I have had time to make, I have taken note of the names of something over two hundred persons alleged to have been physically lifted free from the ground in ecstasy. In about one third of these cases there seems to be evidence which, if not conclusive, is to say the least respectable." [2]

Despite these problems, at least a few excellent accounts of Christian levitation have been recorded, both in the writings of the levitators and by eyewitnesses. But why, if levitation is so commonly reported, are trustworthy first-person accounts so rare?

The answer to this question seems to lie in how the Catholic saints viewed and experienced levitation. Because of their humility and fear of publicity, most Christian ascetics attempted to keep their supernatural gifts secret. They were more embarrassed than pleased about the powers bestowed upon them, and expressly attempted to see to it that their psychic talents *were not* observed by anyone else. It is almost amusing to read how St. Teresa of Avila would rush everyone out of her convent church when she felt a levitation coming on! The mystics of the Church were so diligent in their desire to be alone with their divine gifts that we are lucky to have had *any* firsthand accounts come down to us.

Despite their desire for privacy, several saints have left us detailed descriptions of their levitations. These accounts appear in their private diaries, autobiographies, and in letters to their confessors and advisors. Although these sources are admittedly weak evidence, since we have to take the accounts purely at face value, there seems little reason to doubt their sincerity. These individuals lived lives of such nearly superhuman honesty and virtue that any act of deceit would seem to be quite beyond their moral capabilities. Teresa Higginson (1844–1905), for instance, an English schoolmistress and ascetic, suffered attacks of guilty conscience all her life because of a single childhood incidence of lying to her parents! Similar examples could be cited from the lives of other mystics of the Church.

A typical autobiographical account of a spontaneous levitation was recorded by Sister Maria Villani, a seventeenth-century Dominican nun who lived in a small convent in Italy. Her report, extracted below from a statement she made in a letter to her spiritual director, originally appeared in D. M. Marchese's *Vita della V. Serva di Dio Suor Maria Villani,* published in Naples in 1717:

> On one occasion when I was in my cell I was conscious of a new experience. I felt myself seized and ravished out of my senses, and that so powerfully that I found myself lifted up completely by the very soles of my feet, just as the magnet draws up a fragment of iron, but with a gentleness that was marvellous and most delightful. At first I felt much fear, but afterwards I remained in the greatest possible contentment and joy of spirit. Though I was quite beside myself, still, in spite of that, I knew that I was raised some distance above the earth, my whole body being suspended for a considerable space of time. Down to last Christmas eve (1628) this happened to me on five different occasions.

Perhaps the most famous—and impressive—accounts of spontaneous human levitation have been preserved in the writings of St. Teresa of Avila, which are notable for several reasons. First, her levitations were witnessed by independent observers, so we don't have to rely only upon her own word when trying to evaluate them. Second, because St. Teresa was a brilliant woman—a devout religious ascetic gifted with ecstasies and paranormal gifts, yet so practical that she was able to administer a convent with ease, deliberation, and firmness—her accounts are especially detailed and intelligently written. Third, the original documents (as opposed to secondary sources) pertinent to her levitations are still on record.

Born in Avila, Spain, in 1515, St. Teresa displayed few religious virtues as a child. She planned a life of marriage, and used to immerse herself in books devoted to tales of chivalry. It was because of her secular preoccupations, in fact, that Teresa's father placed her under the care of an order of Augustinian nuns in 1531. There she was educated, not in religion, but for secular life. Through the influence of one of the nuns, however, Teresa began to develop an interest in spiritual matters, an interest that was furthered by a devoutly religious uncle after her return home. Her eventual decision to become a nun was met with little enthusiasm by her family, and her father objected so strenuously to the idea that Teresa had to flee her home to devote herself to a religious life. She joined a Carmelite order in 1535, but was compelled to leave it because of constant problems with her health. She remained a partial invalid for several years, during which her health gradually returned. After her recovery, Teresa began plans to found her own convent, which was built in her hometown of Avila in 1562. This motherhouse eventually spawned sixteen additional convents. Teresa spent the remainder of her life traveling between these houses and overseeing their operations. She died in 1582, leaving several accounts of her life and philosophy.

In her autobiographical writings, St. Teresa does not cite many specific examples of levitation, admitting that it was not a frequent occurrence during her life. Instead, she offers deeply introspective accounts of her experiences, interspersed with several firsthand anecdotes about them. She also mentions a number of incidents that caused her extreme embarrassment. Once, while she was preparing to approach the altar of the convent chapel, she was suddenly lifted from the ground in full view of several nuns who were present. She was so disconcerted by the incident that she later forbade any of the witnesses to speak about the event. On another occasion she felt a levitation coming on during a church service, and though she threw herself to the floor, she floated up from the ground nonetheless. Luckily, several nuns had the presence of mind to surround her so that the levitation would not be seen publicly.[3] Her levitations were so annoying that Teresa often prayed for them to cease. Her prayers were apparently answered, since she had relatively few of them toward the end of her life.

St. Teresa was one of the few mystics who took care to write detailed accounts of the actual *internal experience* of levitation. In the following passage, for instance, she explains how it felt to be elevated into the air:

I repeat it; you feel and see yourself carried away you know not whither. For though we feel how delicious it is, yet the weakness of our nature makes us afraid at first . . . so trying is it that I would very often resist and exert all my strength, particularly at those times when the rapture was coming on me in public. I did so, too, very often when I was alone, because I was afraid of delusions. Occasionally I was able, by great efforts, to make a slight resistance, but afterwards I was worn out, like a person who had been contending with a strong giant; at other times it was impossible to resist at all; my soul was carried away, and almost always my head with it—I had no power over it—and now and then the whole body as well, so that it was lifted up from the ground.

Later she writes in greater detail: *

It seemed to me, when I tried to make some resistance, as if a great force beneath my feet lifted me up. . . . I confess that it threw me into great fear, very great indeed at first; for in seeing one's body thus lifted up from the earth, though the spirit draws it upwards after itself (and that with great sweetness, if unresisted), the senses are not lost; at least I was so much myself as to be able to see that I was being lifted up. . . . After the rapture was over, I have to say that my body seemed frequently to be buoyant, as if all weight had departed from it, so much so that now and then I scarcely knew that my feet touched the ground.

Fortunately, the process leading to Teresa's canonization was begun only thirteen years after her death, so that additional evidence pertaining to her levitations comes from witnesses who probably recalled them in vivid detail. One of the most straightforward of these reports is that of a nun who was a resident in a Teresian convent in Segovia. Under oath she told a Church inquiry investigating Teresa's life how she had seen one of the levitations while coming upon the ascetic at prayer in the convent chapel. "As I was looking on," told Sister Anne, "she was raised about half a yard from the ground, without her feet touching it." The nun was terrified at the sight, but approached St. Teresa in order to inspect the miracle at close range. "I moved to where she was," she continues, "and I put my hands under her feet, over which I remained weeping for something like half an hour while the ecstasy lasted. Then suddenly she sank down and rested on her feet." [4] When she regained consciousness, Teresa was confused, and on learning that she had been observed during her ecstasy, ordered Sister Anne never to reveal what she had seen.

Nine additional firsthand witnesses placed their testimony on record during the canonization hearings. One saw the saint levitate

---

* Both of these passages appear, with minor differences of translation, in many different editions of her writings and in various books about her. I have deliberately used Herbert Thurston's versions, adopted from his *The Physical Phenomena of Mysticism*, since they were checked for accuracy against St. Teresa's original handwritten accounts.

in church after receiving communion, and watched her desperately clutch a nearby grille in an attempt to remain grounded. This same witness also saw Teresa levitate while she was standing in a choir with several other nuns. He observed her grasp at some floor mats to anchor herself to the ground, but she rose into the air nonetheless—with the mats held firmly in her hands!

As far as I am aware, there has been only one attempt to discount St. Teresa's levitations. In his book *Comparative Miracles* (1965), Father Robert Smith, a Catholic priest, critically rejects the evidence documenting the existence of miracles. He argues that belief in miracles is not a matter of Catholic dogma, and so each Catholic is free to accept or reject evidence of these wondrous happenings. Father Smith clearly feels one should reject it. Specifically, he believes that we can dismiss the evidence documenting St. Teresa's levitations on the basis of the following points:

(1) None of Teresa's levitations occurred in public, but only before her own order and friends.

(2) While individual witnesses testified to seeing the levitations, we have no documented examples of levitations seen by more than one person at any given time.

(3) St. Teresa's passion for secrecy would indicate that her levitations were not well known and thus could not have been well witnessed.

(4) The Church officials who transcribed eyewitness reports about the levitations kept their records confidential and presumably did not allow their informants to check over the accounts for accuracy.

(5) Many accounts of St. Teresa's levitations are contradictory, and some of the witnesses altered their accounts at various times when they retold their stories.

(6) St. Teresa's own accounts are suspect, because the saint experienced her levitations while in an altered state of consciousness brought on by ecstasy. She may not, therefore, have been aware of exactly what was happening to her.

However, Smith's criticisms, valid as they appear, fail to make a serious case against St. Teresa's levitations, and each of his arguments can be easily rebutted.

First, the fact that St. Teresa had no public levitations seems to be inconsequential and certainly not odd. She usually experienced her levitations during religious observances and while in pri-

vate prayer, so one could not really expect them to occur in public. It is possible, however, that at least some outsiders did observe
her levitations. In one of her accounts, St. Teresa specifically mentions that "some great ladies" (probably referring to noblewomen
or to the wives of prominent Avilan citizens, who were known to
attend services at her convent chapel) were present when she
underwent one of her levitations.

Father Smith's second point—that we have no collectively
witnessed accounts of St. Teresa's levitations to evaluate—is not a
convincing one either. While the evidence *would* be stronger if
such cases had been on record, it is hard even in their absence to
dismiss such private observations as those carefully recorded by
Sister Anne, who was able to study one of St. Teresa's levitations
at close range for almost an hour. One must finally decide whether
Sister Anne (and many others) were hallucinating, lying, or genuinely saw what they claimed they did. Neither of the first two theories seems very plausible.

Father Smith's third point, which is addressed to St. Teresa's
insistence on secrecy, seems based on a total non sequitur. Her
habit of ordering the accidental witnesses to her levitations to
silence in no way implies that her feats were not well known nor
well attested to. We know from her own writings that Teresa
shunned her gift of miracles for several valid reasons: She did not
wish the other nuns in her order to look upon her as in any way
special or holy; she felt unworthy of her gift; and she didn't want
convent life disrupted. It is plausible to assume that St. Teresa did
not want specific stories or accounts of her levitations to be
repeated because they tended to feed the fire of interest already
rife in the convent over her miracles.

The fourth point Smith raises is equally questionable. Anyone
familiar with the lives of the saints knows that the Church is very
conservative in its documentation of miracles. Church inquiries are
usually designed to expose tales of the miraculous rather than to
substantiate them. It is hard to believe that those Church officials
charged with collecting testimony pertinent to Teresa's levitations
would misrecord the accounts they had heard in order to make
them sound more impressive. It could also be charged that Smith's
point is clearly in error. Bishop Yepes, who personally knew the
saint well, gives his *own* account of two eyewitnessed levitations in

his book *Vida, virtudes, y milagros,* so these reports must be considered accurate.

Smith's fifth argument against St. Teresa's levitations can be similarly rejected. The contradictions that appear in the written records are either totally inconsequential or attributable to errors in translation.*

Finally, Father Smith's last point—that St. Teresa could not critically evaluate what was happening to her—can be challenged on several different grounds. First, the objection is based on pure speculation. It can be argued that at least some of Teresa's levitations occurred against her will and when she was entirely lucid. How else would she have had the presence of mind to try to prevent them as she so often did? Second, her own accounts are fully consistent with the testimony of the few witnesses who observed her levitations. And last, her accounts are similar to those placed on record by other levitating mystics.

The inherent plausibility of the case of St. Teresa is also supported by the existence of other saints whose levitations were witnessed. One especially impressive account concerns the seventeenth-century mystic St. Bernardino Realino, who died in 1616 in the town of Lecce in southern Italy. St. Bernardino was not a "levitating" saint in the manner of St. Teresa. He apparently had only one such experience, or else he was able to keep his talent hidden from his friends and Church authorities. However, at least one witness, Tobias da Ponte, was able to observe St. Bernardino quite carefully during a levitation. A prominent citizen of a nearby town, da Ponte had gone to the saint's monastery in Lecce in 1608 to ask the saint for spiritual advice. While waiting in the lobby by his room for Bernardino to emerge, da Ponte noted a bright illumination streaming out from the sides of the door, which had been left slightly ajar. His first thought was that a fire had broken out in the room. Peeking in, he saw Bernardino floating about two and a half feet off the ground. The saint was still in a kneeling position and was whispering in prayer as he hovered. Light was radiating from him. Da Ponte was so overcome by the

---

*For example, Smith argues that one witness first stated that he saw St. Teresa levitate just after communion had been given. Later, the same witness wrote that the miracle occurred *during* communion. Although the witness indeed altered his account, he never changed that portion of his testimony specifically dealing with the levitation itself.

numinism of the scene that he left the monastery with the feeling that he had trespassed on the saint's privacy.

In 1621, da Ponte described this event to a Church inquiry studying Bernardino's purported miracles. He told the commission that he had seen the priest "raised from the ground as unmistakably as I now see your Illustrious Lordships."[5]

Another eyewitnessed and carefully recorded levitation was that of Francis Suarez (1548–1617), a Spanish priest, theologian, and teacher who in 1597 became a professor of divinity at the University of Coimbra by the direct appointment of King Philip II. His levitation was witnessed by a fellow priest, Jerome de Silva, and occurred while Suarez was teaching theology at the University of Salamanca. De Silva had been sent to fetch Suarez from his room by their superiors. He was stunned by what he saw:

Across the door of his room I found the stick which the Father usually placed there when he did not wish to be interrupted. Owing, however, to the order I had received I removed the stick and entered. The outer room was in darkness. I called the Father but he made no answer. As the curtain which shut off his working room was drawn, I saw through the space left between the curtain and the jambs of the door a very great brightness. I pushed aside the curtain and entered from the inner apartment. Then I noticed that a blinding light was coming from the crucifix, so intense that it was like the reflection of the sun from glass windows, and I felt that I could not have remained looking at it without being completely dazzled. This light streamed from the crucifix upon the face and breast of Father Suarez and in this brightness I saw him in a kneeling position in front of the crucifix, his head uncovered, his hands joined, and his body in the air lifted three feet above the floor on a level with the table on which the crucifix stood. On seeing this I withdrew, but before quitting the room I stopped bewildered, and as it were beside myself, leaning against the door-post for the space of three Credos.

De Silva soon heard Suarez moving about the room, and so entered and approached him. Immediately realizing that his levitation had been seen, Suarez grabbed de Silva and made him promise never to reveal what he had witnessed.

The case for levitation does not rely solely on three-hundred-year-old accounts, though. An especially good nineteenth-century case of levitation recounted by Leroy concerns St. Seraphim de

Serov, a Russian mystic who died in 1833. Leroy cites the first-hand report of a man who had seen the saint levitate while praying at the witness's sickbed. The saint had told the witness that he would recover only if he never told anyone what he had seen. Relatively recent levitations are documented in biographies of Sister Marie Baourdie, a Carmelite nun of Syrian birth who lived in Bethlehem and died in 1878. Levitations often plagued St. Gemma Galgani, an Italian nun who died in 1913, and were noted to occur during the life of Padre Pio, a priest in Foggia, Italy, who became a legend in his own lifetime before his death in 1968. Before his death in 1936, St. Zachary of Russia was seen to "walk on water."

Perhaps the most unbelievable, yet excellently substantiated, case of a levitating saint recorded in Western literature is that of St. Joseph of Copertino (1603–1663) who, during his life, became known as "the flying friar." St. Joseph experienced numerous spectacular levitations over the course of many years. Sometimes the experiences were brief, while at other times they would last for several minutes or even for hours. Sometimes Joseph was lifted only a few inches into the air; at other times he was seen to glide through the air several feet above the ground.

At face value, the case seems so outlandish that even Thurston glosses over it in embarrassment, and Smith considers that the accounts of the friar's aerial flights are "in some cases . . . ridiculous." But Dr. Eric Dingwall, a British anthropologist and authority on psychic phenomena who is one of parapsychology's most respected scholars, has collected, translated, and evaluated many of the original accounts testifying to St. Joseph's levitations and spiritual flights.[6] In his book *Some Human Oddities* (1947), he cites over one hundred references to St. Joseph and his talents.

St. Joseph was born in Copertino, where his father was a carpenter. From earliest childhood he showed an inclination toward a religious life, and he was experiencing religious ecstasies by the time he was eight years old. He decided to enter the priesthood when still a teen-ager, and although he had not had much formal education up to this time, he was accepted into a Capuchin order as a lay brother in 1620. Because of his absentmindedness and rather erratic mentality, Joseph was quickly ejected, and he traveled about for several months before eventually entering a

monastic order in a town a mile from Copertino. There he practiced such austerities as wearing a hair shirt and flagellating himself. He was eventually received as a cleric in the order of St.
Francis in Altamura and finally attained the priesthood in 1628.

It was at about this time that St. Joseph first began experiencing levitations. He had traveled to Naples to stand before a Church
commission on a charge of heresy, and while saying Mass at the
monastery where he was staying, he suddenly levitated from a
corner of the church and flew across the chapel to the church altar.
No sooner had he alighted than his body was borne aloft once
again. He then floated back to the other end of the building,
where he landed. The incident was witnessed by several nuns and
by St. Joseph's traveling companion. Soon after the experience in
Naples, St. Joseph traveled to Rome, where he spontaneously levitated as he knelt to kiss the feet of Pope Urban III.

From Rome, St. Joseph went to Assisi, where one of his most
remarkable and most frequently cited levitations occurred. According to several firsthand accounts, no sooner had St. Joseph
entered the basilica of a monastery where he had gone to pray
than he levitated at the sight of a painting of the Virgin Mary that
had been placed near the altar. He levitated and floated some
fifteen feet *over* an entire group of worshipers, so that he could
kiss it. Dozens of onlookers witnessed the event.

Many eyewitness accounts of Joseph's levitations were preserved by D. Bernino, and several were included in his book *Vita
del P. Fra Giuseppe da Copertino* (1753). Dingwall, who studied
Bernino's volume, writes:

> The flights and levitations of Joseph did not always occur inside
> buildings, but sometimes out of doors. For instance, it is recorded that
> one day a priest, Antonio Chiarello, who was walking with him in the
> kitchen-garden, remarked how beautiful was the heaven which God had
> made. Thereupon Joseph, as if these words were an invitation to him
> from above, uttered a shriek, sprang from the ground and flew into the
> air, only coming to rest on the top of an olive tree where he remained in
> a kneeling position for half an hour. It was noticed with wonder at the
> time that the branch on which he rested only shook slightly as if a bird
> had been sitting upon it. It appears that in this case Joseph came to his
> senses whilst still on the tree, as the Rev. Antonio had to go to fetch a
> ladder to get him down.

Another feature of St. Joseph's levitations was that onlookers who tried to restrain the saint as he levitated would often be hoisted into the air along with him. Again, to quote Dingwall's summary of one of Bernino's accounts:

In the Church of Santa Chiara in Copertino a festival was once in progress in honour of the clothing of some novitiates. Joseph was present, and was on his knees in a corner of the church, when the words *Veni Sponsa Cristi* (Come, Bride of Christ) were being intoned. Giving his accustomed cry, he ran towards the convent's father confessor, a priest from Secli, a village not far off, and who was attending the service and, seizing him, grasped him by the hand and . . . finally both rose into the air in an ecstasy, the one borne aloft by Joseph and the other by God Himself, both being sons of St. Francis, the one being beside himself with fear but the other with sanctity.

Unlike the levitations of St. Teresa of Avila, those of St. Joseph were witnessed by a number of outside observers. Several notable intellectuals of the day, even skeptics and non-Catholics, testified to the genuineness of his levitations. One such witness was Johann Friedrich, the duke of Brunswick and the patron of G. W. Leibniz, the great German philosopher. Friedrich traveled to Assisi in 1651 with the deliberate intention of seeing one of Joseph's levitations. After considerable political maneuvering, Friedrich was allowed to hide with two companions by a doorway leading to a chapel where Joseph often said Mass. (None of the three men was Catholic.) As they watched, Joseph entered the church, knelt before the altar, and began to pray. Suddenly he gave a cry, lifted into the air, floated several feet backward, and after floating toward the altar, was then returned to the ground. The next day Friedrich was able to observe the saint levitating for fifteen minutes. He was so overwhelmed by what he had seen that he converted to Catholicism. His two Lutheran companions, though not renouncing their own faith, left Assisi deeply disconcerted.

Among other notable witnesses of St. Joseph's levitations during these same years was the daughter of Carlo Emmanuel the Great, duke of Savoy; Juan Alfonso Henriquez de Cabrera, Spain's ambassador to Rome; and the son of Cosimo II of Austria, who eventually became a cardinal under Pope Clement IX and who was a pioneer in the development of Italy's educational system.

In 1653 Joseph was ordered to leave for Urbino, where he took up residence in a Capuchin monastery. By then he was so famous that people flocked to wherever he said Mass, hoping to see one of his levitations. His health finally gave way, and in 1663, even as he lay dying, his doctors frequently witnessed their patient's uncanny flotations. Only a few months before his death, the friar's surgeon, Francesco Pierpauli, was able to see several such displays. Pierpauli later testified to Church officials that he was once examining Joseph's leg while the saint sat calmly in a chair. The saint entered ecstasy and suddenly lifted three feet over the chair during a spontaneous trance. Pierpauli explained to the officials how he had tried to pull the saint back down to the chair by his leg, but Joseph's body remained rigidly suspended in space. Two fellow surgeons who were in attendance also saw the miracle. Over the next several days, Pierpauli saw two additional levitations.

The evidence authenticating St. Joseph's levitations is awesome. They were publicly observed by both his friends and total strangers; we have numerous firsthand accounts of them; they were not secret events but often occurred in public places; and they do not rest merely on St. Joseph's own word. In short, the testimony pertinent to St. Joseph's levitations is a perfect rebuttal to the types of criticism to which St. Teresa's levitations are prone. He was even beatified (in 1753) during the pontificate of Pope Benedict XIV, who, as Cardinal Lambertini, had become the Church's leading authority on human testimony and on the nature of miracles. Benedict was fully familiar with the evidence supporting the authenticity of St. Joseph's miracles, and in his *De serverum Dei beatificatione* he stated that the case deserved merit and acceptance. This is an impressive admission, since Benedict XIV was not easily swayed by tales of the miraculous.

Despite the strength of available evidence, Robert Smith presents the skeptic's case against St. Joseph's levitations in his *Comparative Miracles*. His arguments here, however, are even weaker than those against the validity of St. Teresa's feats:

(1) The records of the inquiry leading to St. Joseph's canonization are no longer available to us and cannot therefore be objectively evaluated.

(2) Some of the eyewitness reports contradict each other.

(3) Considerable time elapsed between the time the levitations were observed and the time they were placed on permanent record.

(4) There is some evidence that St. Joseph was extremely agile. Some of his levitations could therefore have been gymnastic feats.

In response to Smith's first point, it seems of little consequence that the actual documents that the Church used during St. Joseph's canonization process are no longer available. The original Church commission that studied the case was able to interview and cross-examine the eyewitnesses at first hand. This is something we certainly can't do today. Thus the opinion of these original evaluators was undoubtedly more astute than any conclusions we might reach now. Benedict's acceptance of the testimony concerning St. Joseph's levitations is also compelling, since his *De canonizatione* reveals that he had a remarkably critical mind when it came to such matters.

Smith's second point appears more challenging than it actually is. When one is dealing with human testimony, there are always going to be contradictions in the evidence: it is quite impossible to get two witnesses to agree on *everything* they might have observed. Smith correctly points out that mutual witnesses to St. Joseph's levitations often disagreed about how high he ascended, how long he stayed suspended, or how far he flew during his "spiritual flights." But these contradictions are just the type one would expect when two onlookers are recalling such an extraordinary event. This in no way undermines the fact that the witnesses always agreed that St. Joseph had *indeed* levitated.

Smith's only valid objection is that many of St. Joseph's levitations were not permanently recorded until years after the events in question took place. While this argument cannot be used to dispose of the matter, since many accounts (such as Pierpauli's) were obviously placed on record soon after the levitations had occurred, it must be considered seriously since it can conceivably invalidate many accounts of mystic levitation. Thurston, for instance, rejected several otherwise dependable levitation reports that he cites in *The Physical Phenomena of Mysticism* on this basis alone. As with Smith, he believed that a witness's memory of a miraculous event is subject to disintegration over time, and that an event recollected some twenty years after it occurred could not therefore serve as first-class evidence for the authenticity of a miracle.

Yet both Smith and Thurston may have been rash in subscribing to this principle. The problem of human memory, and whether it declines in accuracy over time, is a very old one in parapsychology and a few parapsychologists have even attempted to study the dependability of memory experimentally.

The first to do so was Walter F. Prince, who at one time was the chief investigations officer of the New York–based American Society for Psychical Research. He once recorded a psychic dream he had about an accident in 1902. He told his wife about it and she wrote out an account. Eight years later, she rewrote it from memory. The two accounts were compared and found to be virtually identical.[7] This little experiment was recently replicated by the late Rosalind Heywood, a well-known British psychic and psychic investigator. Some years ago she wrote out an account of a dramatic personal psychic experience she had had, and wrote it again from memory ten years later. There were no material differences between the accounts.[8]

The results of these tests suggest that when an individual has witnessed something extraordinary, he tends to remember it vividly enough so that his recollections remain extremely accurate even after many years.

In the end, most people—Catholics and agnostics alike— would probably tend to reject the tales of St. Joseph's levitations simply because, as Smith points out, they sound so blatantly ridiculous. Yet if, as the cases of St. Teresa of Avila and Sister Maria Villani suggest, the body can transport itself into the air, why couldn't it fly through the air as well? If one accepts the evidence for one *order* of miracle, one cannot justifiably reject the evidence documenting the other.

It is not true, as Thurston and Smith claim, that the case of St. Joseph of Copertino is truly unprecedented, however. Similar cases, though perhaps not as theatrical, are on record. One that parallels the feats of St. Joseph is that of Sister Marie Baourdie, a Syrian nun who lived in Bethlehem in the nineteenth century and whose levitations were briefly mentioned earlier. Accounts of no fewer than eight levitations she experienced in public between 1873–4 have been adequately documented. The nun would often levitate (or would "fly") when out of doors to the top of a tree she loved to tend.

Also similar are the levitations apparently experienced by Anne Catherine Emmerich (1774–1824), a German stigmatic and visionary. As she told her biographer:

When I was doing my work as vestry nun, I was often lifted up suddenly into the air, and I climbed up and stood on the higher parts of the church, such as windows, sculptured ornaments, jutting stones; I would clean and arrange everything in places where it was humanly possible. I felt myself lifted and supported in the air, and I was not afraid in the least, for I had been accustomed from a child to being assisted by my guardian angel.

This statement is quoted by Father K. G. Schomöger in his *Life of Anne Catherine Emmerich,* which he wrote soon after the mystic's death. Father Schomöger was personally familiar with all the documents pertinent to the case.

For a more direct parallel to St. Joseph's spiritual flights, however, we have to turn away from Catholic hagiography and look eastward. According to the biographers of Milarepa, a Tibetan holy man who lived from 1052 to 1135, this Buddhist saint was equally at home in the air and on the ground. Although no eyewitness reports of his powers have come down to us—psychic phenomena are taken for granted in Tibet, so no one is too concerned about documenting miraculous events when they occur—we do have statements purportedly made by Milarepa himself. In his autobiographic notes, which were recorded by one of his disciples, Milarepa spoke of his ability to levitate and fly over great distances. He claimed that he suddenly became endowed with this supernatural gift as a result of his yogic training. One of Milarepa's delightful stories recounts his flight over the home and fields of a distant relative. The man's son, who was ploughing a field at the time, spotted the levitating monk and called to his father to stop work and observe the miracle. Milarepa's relative looked up, saw the levitating holy man, and firmly instructed his son to ignore that "good-for-nothing" and get back to work![9] Milarepa eventually decided to give up his aerobatics in order to dedicate his life to more spiritual matters.

The case of Milarepa has not been cited here to provide evidence, but to indicate how widespread belief in the phenomenon of levitation is noted and accepted within Eastern religious traditions. "The Saints of the Roman Catholic church are not the only ones who are credited with these powers," writes Dingwall in his biographical notes on St. Joseph of Copertino. "Holy men and ascetics in India and the Far East have many times been levitated, and the idea is not unknown among so-called savage tribes."[10] Leroy makes a similar observation.

Yogic traditions speak of many practices that are said to help induce levitation, and there is ample evidence that these and similar practices might even work. No one knows exactly when the practice of yoga first evolved. According to tradition, its basic tenets may have been taught in India as long ago as five thousand years. As we know it today—consisting as it does chiefly of detailed methods for body control, breathing, and meditation—yoga was first systematized in the *Yoga Sutras* of Patanjali, an Indian scholar of the third and second centuries B.C. Most scholars agree, though, that Patanjali edited and structured his material from a vast oral tradition that predated him by at least one thousand years.

At first glance, there doesn't seem to be anything too mysterious or arcane about yogic practices, and the *Yoga Sutras* refer very little to anything so strange as paranormal abilities or how they might be developed. But there is a more mystical and supernatural side to even these traditional yogic teachings. Later Hindu writings, such as the twelfth-century *Hatha Yoga Pradipika,* discuss such psychic phenomena as ESP, mind over matter, and astral projection in great detail, and teach that one automatically acquires supernatural powers through proper mastery of yoga. For instance, certain forms of yoga (such as Kundalini yoga) that had their greatest developments in both India and Tibet hold that a dormant energy rests within all of us at the base of the spine. If properly aroused, this energy has the power to travel up the spine and awaken various psychic centers in its path. The "awakening" of these centers (or *chakras*) allegedly gives the yogi specific psychic abilities. Different types of psychic powers (or *siddhis*) are related to each of the different centers.

According to these same teachings, levitation can be induced through certain breathing exercises. One must learn to control how one breathes, to regulate the rate of oxygen intake, and length of retention, and to control certain methods for exhaling. Proper mastery of these methods results in two physiological effects that herald actual levitation. First, the body breaks out in perspiration, and second, the mind blacks out momentarily. Then, the body—if the practitioner is seated on the ground cross-legged in customary yogic style—will begin to hop about the ground involuntarily. If the body is properly "balanced" by the intake of oxygen, this hopping phenomenon is supposed to convert into true levitation.

In May 1977 there was quite a stir in the popular press when the Maharishi Mahesh Yogi, the founder of the TM (Transcendental Meditation) movement, announced that his techniques could actually help people learn to levitate and develop other *siddhis*. As reported in the June 13, 1977 issue of *Newsweek*, Robert Oates, the Maharishi's biographer and a spokesman for the TM movement, told the press that several TM teachers had already learned to master these supernatural abilities.

It is a moot point, though, whether these claims were made because TM practitioners were actually reporting such phenomena or whether, as some critics have claimed, the move was a publicity stunt used to recruit new members to the movement. In either case the announcement backfired badly. To date, not one TMer has publicly levitated, though several challenges have been made to TM officials at the Los Angeles–based International Meditation Center and the Swiss-based Maharishi European Research University, the two official centers dedicated to the furtherance of the Maharishi's teachings. TM officials have also constantly refused to sanction such demonstrations. Photographs of alleged levitations have emerged from various TM sources, but these have been uniformly impossible to analyze. A few secondhand and/or anonymous reports have been included by D. W. Orme-Johnson and J. T. Farrow in their anthology *Scientific Research in the TM Program* (1977). Despite its academic title, however, this volume was published by the Maharishi European Research University itself and so can hardly be considered an unbiased source of information.

Though the TM claims appear to be nothing more than a rather badly planned hoax, spokesmen for the movement have based their assertions on a very genuine tradition. This will be obvious to anyone who has carefully read the claims Orme-Johnson and Farrow make in their book and compared them to those of traditional yogic literature. But for eyewitness accounts of levitating gurus and swamis we must look elsewhere.

Perhaps the most impressive firsthand report documenting a yogic levitation was recorded by Louis Jacolliot, a highly intelligent French official who traveled extensively in Asia during the 1860s. Jacolliot was not a cheap miraclemonger. He was a judge, a scholar, and a dedicated student of Eastern religion. He was also a pioneer in the study of anthropological sexology.

Jacolliot's travel memoir, *Occult Science in India and Among the Ancients* (1884), still ranks today, despite its popular style and appeal, as one of the most important volumes ever written on the psychic tradition of yoga.[11] Most of Jacolliot's book is devoted to explaining the hidden psychic teachings behind yoga. During his stay in India, though, he met and became friendly with a fakir named Covindasamy. The fakir was apparently well endowed with psychic ability and visited Jacolliot's residence frequently, often giving the judge demonstrations of his psychic talents. In 1866, Jacolliot decided to conduct several scientific tests with him. In the course of these Jacolliot witnessed two full levitations in broad daylight. The more impressive one occurred after Jacolliot and the fakir had finished a long series of experiments and were ready to break for lunch. Covindasamy was leaving the room when, according to Jacolliot:

. . . the fakir stopped in the doorway opening from the terrace into the back-stairs, and folding his arms, he was lifted—or so it seemed to me—gradually without visible support, about one foot above the ground. I could determine the exact height, thanks to a landing mark upon which I fixed my eyes during the short time the phenomenon lasted. Behind the fakir hung a silk curtain with red, golden and white stripes of equal breadth, and I noticed that the fakir's feet were as high as the sixth stripe. When I saw the rising begin, I took my watch out. From the time when the magician began to be lifted until he came down to earth again, about ten minutes elapsed. He remained about five minutes suspended without motion.

While this eyewitness report is certainly as persuasive as anything documented in Roman Catholic literature, the case unfortunately rests solely on Jacolliot's word, which has led some skeptics (including Leroy) to argue that the Frenchman merely fabricated the story. But this accusation is not consistent with what we know about Jacolliot's life and character.

A very different type of levitation that fakirs in India are also known to perform is what might be called an "elevation," during which the fakir will levitate his body while resting his hand on the top of a cane or stick. Not only have elevations been publicly performed many times in India, but one was even photographed in 1936. A report on the incident, as well as the photographs, was published in the June 6, 1936 issue of the *Illustrated London News*. The story was written by a British news reporter, P. T. Plunkett, who was present at the event.

According to Plunkett's account, the actual demonstration, which was seen by dozens of spectators, took place in a compound on a plantation owned by a friend of his. It was held at twelve thirty in the afternoon under a tent supported by four poles. Before levitating himself, the yogi marked out a circular area under the tent, forbade anyone to enter it, stepped inside, braced one hand on his walking stick, and then—right before the eyes of the startled onlookers—rose laterally up into the air so that ultimately he was floating on his side without any visible brace other than his stick. This he touched only lightly with his outstretched hand. The yogi allowed bystanders to walk around and examine him and then slowly descended back to the ground.

Plunkett was impressed enough by the display that he wrote in his *London News* story, ". . . as I have witnessed the performance with several of my planters, I am quite convinced of the total absence of trickery."

However, this demonstration may have appeared more extraordinary than it actually was. In his report, Plunkett admits that even after the stunt was over the yogi's body was still extremely rigid. This suggests that the "levitation" might have been nothing more than a clever balancing act which the yogi had mastered through phenomenal muscular strength and control, or that the walking stick he used to support himself may have been a trick device.

If this feat was actually a trick, though, its modus operandi is not apparent from the photographs. Several were taken at close range and it does not look as if the fakir's hand is gripping the cane. Nor is there any sign of stress in the yogi's hand or arm muscles.

What is curious about the levitation is that it has been performed—always in *exactly* the same manner—by many different fakirs and yogis in India. John Keel, an American magazine writer who traveled extensively in India during the 1950s, watched an identical performance, which he describes in his entertaining book *Jadoo* (1957), and even Jacolliot observed Covindasamy perform the stunt in the 1860s. Jacolliot tells how one day, in the course of some experiments, the yogi had reached for a cane that was in the room:

> Leaning upon the cane with one hand, the Fakir rose gradually about two feet from the ground. His legs were crossed beneath him, and he made no change in his position, which was very like that of those bronze statues of Buddha that all tourists bring from the Far East, without a suspicion that most of them come originally from English foundries.
>
> For more than twenty minutes I tried to see how Covindasamy could thus fly in the face and eyes of all the known laws of gravity; it was entirely beyond my comprehension; the stick gave him no visible support, and there was no apparent contact between that and his body, except through his right hand.

Jacolliot could never decide whether he had seen a genuine levitation or a bizarre balancing act.

It is difficult to make a judgment about the authenticity of these elevations. On one hand, the very consistency in the way the feat is performed suggests that it is a trick. On the other hand, since Covindasamy was apparently truly capable of levitating himself, this incident may well have been truly miraculous.

The case for the genuineness of paranormal elevation becomes a little more plausible if we reexamine the levitations of Sister Marie Baourdie. One of her best-witnessed levitations occurred while she was caring for a lemon tree on her convent grounds. A lay sister watched in surprise as the nun took hold of a fragile branch and began to float to the top of the tree. She was able to see that Sister Marie's feet were floating without support, and also noticed that the nun seemed to be sustaining the levitation by touching (though not grasping) small branches of the tree as she floated upward.* For some reason, then, certain forms of levitation may be possible only when the performer somehow maintains contact with a physical object attached to the ground.

Another type of levitation feat has been recorded by Swami Rama, a contemporary Indian yogi who has recently made several visits to the United States.† In his autobiography, Rama tells a remarkable story concerning a yogic master who had just died near the banks of the Ganges. Although the body had become so heavy that it could not be moved, it suddenly "rose in the air, apparently of its own accord, and moved slowly towards the Ganges." [12] Rama claims that he himself witnessed this miracle, but because he does not give the names of the other witnesses or provide their accounts, his report can only be considered an anecdote in the worst sense of the word.

Well-witnessed examples of yogic levitations by Western observers are, in fact, quite rare—so rare that one can easily comprehend Leroy's argument that the evidence for yogic levitations is vastly inferior to the evidence the Church has collected authenticating the levitations of its saints and ascetics.

One scientifically trained observer who *has* witnessed some-

---

*Dingwall has written of this incident: "These accounts compel us, I think, to suspect that Sister Marie was never levitated at all, but was merely remarkable and agile in climbing trees, an activity which was probably accentuated and assisted by the dissociated state in which she passed many hours of her life" (*Some Human Oddities*, p. 166). But Dingwall's theory cannot explain several of the eyewitness reports that M. Estrate included in his *La Vie de Marie de Jésus Crucifié* (1913). The lay sister whose account was summarized above clearly saw the nun floating and only touching, not gripping, the branches of the tree. She especially noted that the branches did not bend when touched.

†Rama's testimony is especially valuable since, unlike most self-proclaimed "holy men" from the East, he has actually allowed his powers to be scientifically examined. Several pioneering tests were conducted by Dr. Elmer Green, an authority on biofeedback training, in 1970 at the Menninger Foundation in Topeka, Kansas. Rama was able to demonstrate that he had perfect control over several automatic functions of the body and gave two displays of his psychokinetic abilities. In one of these instances he was able to move a knitting needle balanced on an axle while sitting several feet away from it.
See Elmer and Alyce Green, *Beyond Biofeedback* (New York: Delacorte, 1977).

thing akin to levitation, however, is Dr. David Read Barker, who until recently was an anthropologist at the University of Virginia, where he worked in the school's division of parapsychology. Barker conducted his doctoral research in Nepal, where he lived from 1970 to 1973. He had gone there to study the culture of the Tibetan refugees who had set up communities in Nepal and northern India in 1954 after fleeing from the Communist takeover of their homeland. Barker witnessed several presumably psychic feats there and gave a report on his research to the twenty-first annual convention of the Parapsychological Association in 1978. He described, during breaks at the meeting, how he had witnessed aged lamas scaling mountains, even extremely steep slopes, with such ease and swiftness that their performances verged on the paranormal. He went on to suggest that these ascensions could well have been a form of levitation.

A virtually identical phenomenon was described by Father Cepari, the biographer and confessor to St. Mary Magdalen de' Pazzi, a sixteenth-century Italian ascetic. Cepari reported in his *Vita di S. Maddalena de' Pazzi* that the nun would sometimes go "with incredible swiftness from one place to another, mounting and descending the stairs [of her convent] with such agility that she seemed rather to fly than to touch the earth with her feet." The saint could also "spring securely onto the most dangerous places" after jumping thirty feet or more with one bound.

A more recent account of this same phenomenon has been recorded by the Reverend L. A. Fontana, the biographer of Sister Mary of the Passion, an Italian nun who died in 1912. Father Fontana, who was Sister Mary's confessor, provided several firsthand reports of her miracles, which included the stigmata and supernatural fasting, in his *Vita de la Serva di Dio, Suor Maria della Passione* (1917). One of the nuns in Sister Mary's order gave the following account in 1913:

I was still a novice and on those last occasions when Suor Maria della Passione was able to come down to the choir to receive Holy Communion, the Reverend Mother Superior bade me take her back to her cell, because, as she was so ill, she had to return to bed almost immediately after Communion was given her. Well, no sooner had we left the choir together than I noticed that the servant of God, though she was in a most suffering state, mounted the stairs in an instant, as if she flew on wings, while I, who was in perfect health, could not keep pace with her; so much so that it seemed to me that she never touched the ground but that she really flew up the flight of stairs which led to her cell.

As is true of so many of the miracles of the saints, levitation resembles various forms of psychic phenomena known to parapsychologists. Many psychics in the late nineteenth and early twentieth centuries claimed to be able to perform this feat. This era was the heyday of popular Spiritualism, a religious movement that originated in the United States in 1848. Spiritualism teaches that the living can contact the dead. One method the early Spiritualists commonly employed to make such contact was table tilting. In a typical table tilting or "table turning" session a group of people would sit around a wooden table in a darkened room while trying to maintain a cheerful frame of mind. They would place their hands lightly on its surface, and soon the table would begin to rock. Codes were invented whereby, through certain motions, the table could answer questions or spell out messages sent, it was believed, directly from the departed friends and relatives of the participants. Spiritualistic practices eventually became more varied and complex. Sometimes the table was seen not only to rock about, but to lift into the air; the sitters would become entranced and spirits of the dead would speak through them; and one of the participants might even be levitated as well.*

Perhaps the best-known medium of the period was Daniel Dunglas Home (1833−86). Scottish by birth but American by upbringing, Home was famous for his levitations. A number of accounts of his astonishing levitations, which occurred both during dark-room seances and in full light, were published by Lord Adare, a young British nobleman who was Home's traveling companion from 1867 to 1869.[13]

Adare reports how the medium was levitated out of his seat for several moments in full view of the sitters during a table-tilting séance he had with Home on December 20, 1868. On another

---

*There are several general histories of the Spiritualistic movement available. See, for instance, G. K. Nelson's *Spiritualism and Society* (London: Routledge and Kegan Paul, 1969) and R. Laurence Moore's *In Search of White Crows* (New York: Oxford University Press, 1977). For a more popular treatment, refer to Slater Brown's entertaining *The Heyday of Spiritualism* (New York: Hawthorn, 1970) or to Sir Arthur Conan Doyle's two-volume *History of Spiritualism* (London: Cassell, 1926).

occasion, Adare, his father, and Home were visiting a London church when the medium suddenly became semientranced and walked out of the building and over to a ruined wall that faced it. "Presently we all saw him approaching," writes Adare, "and eventually raised off the ground, for he floated in front of us." Home continued to float, over the ruined wall, which was about two feet high, and for a distance of about ten or twelve feet, before returning to the ground and coming out of his trance. On a different occasion, Adare and two of his friends saw Home levitate during a séance in London, float out a third-storey window, and hover over the street below.

In 1871 Home collaborated with Professor (later Sir) William Crookes, a famous British chemist of his day, in a series of experiments in London. Crookes described his experiments and several of Home's levitations in the *Quarterly Journal of Science,* a journal he edited. One of the most impressive of these levitations occurred in Crookes's own home. He had been sitting with Home at a table. While attempting to levitate it Home "went to a clear part of the room. After standing quietly for a minute, he told us he was rising. I saw him slowly rise up with a continuous gliding movement and remain about six inches off the ground for several seconds, when he slowly descended." During another séance Crookes saw Home levitate three feet off the ground.

Home rarely produced his levitations in total darkness. He preferred to work in a moderate amount of light so that observers would have the opportunity to study his displays critically. It was not rare for him to levitate all the way to the ceiling and float over the heads of the sitters during these demonstrations.

Another levitating medium who came to the attention of scientists and investigators of the supernatural at the turn of the century was Eusapia Palladino (1854–1918), an Italian medium who began her career in Naples. From 1891 to 1916 she was tested by some of the most eminent scientists in Europe, including Cesare Lombroso, the founder of modern criminology and a psychiatrist at the University of Turin, and Charles Richet, a physiologist at the Faculté du Médicin in Paris and later a Nobel prizewinner. Even Mme Curie attended some experiments with her at the Institute Général Psychologique in 1908. During her séances, Palladino would be seated in a darkened room before a wooden table. The experimenters would also sit around the table and would hold her hands and feet. Even with these restrictions it was not unusual for both the medium and her chair to rise into the air and be carefully set down on the table. Both Lombroso and Richet saw at least one of these startling levitations during a series of séances they had with Palladino in Milan in 1892. She was also able to produce table levitations, move objects without touching them, and perform a variety of other telekinetic phenomena.

At least one levitating psychic, a contemporary of Palladino, has left us with photographic evidence of his ability. Amedee Zuccarini was a state employee in Bologna, Italy, where his psychic abilities were studied in great depth by Dr. L. Patrizi, a physiologist from the University of Modena, and Professor Oreste Murani of the Milan Polytechnic Institute. With the aid of magnesium flash photography they were able to take photographs of the psychic while he levitated during his darkroom séances. These pictures, along with a detailed report on how they were taken, were published in the *Annales des sciences psychiques* in 1908. They clearly show the medium suspended in the air, his hands held by the experimenters. Some of his levitations would last from twelve to fourteen seconds.

As these brief summaries reveal, the miracle of levitation has been performed by psychics, Catholic saints, and the holy men of the East. But are these levitations all of the same nature, or do they differ in some significant respect?

There is some evidence that psychic levitation is not the same type of phenomenon as true mystic levitation. Olivier Leroy discusses this issue in great depth in his *La Lévitation*. Writing from a Catholic viewpoint, Leroy argues that while saintly levitations are of a divine nature, psychic levitations are most often due to diabolic forces.* To demonstrate his contention, Leroy points out several differences between the phenomena:

---

*Leroy's views should not, however, be considered representative of Catholic thought in general. While acknowledging that some spiritistic phenomena may be diabolical in nature, the Church has never officially made a pronouncement on the nature of these occurrences. The Church has also suggested that spiritistic phenomena may be communications from intelligences belonging to a separate "order of creation" yet unknown to us.

(1) Mystical levitations are achieved through weightlessness, while psychics are hoisted into the air by some sort of invisible system of support.

(2) The mystics of the Church often radiate light while levitating. This is never true of psychics.

(3) The mystics of the Church can levitate anywhere, while mediums can induce the phenomenon only through indoor preparations.

(4) Mystical levitation may occur in broad daylight, while psychics levitate only in the dark.

(5) While saints and mystics have been known to levitate even during an illness, psychics cannot perform when their health is impaired.

(6) Mystics levitate during spontaneous ecstasies, while psychics must invoke trance deliberately before they can produce the feat.

(7) The saints and ascetics of the Church levitate only in private, while psychics give public performances.

(8) The saints' ability to levitate is apparently due to their possession of personal grace, while psychic abilities seem to be an inherited gift.

While Leroy is correct in distinguishing between these two types of phenomena, the difference between psychic and mystical levitation is certainly not as clear-cut as he suggests. First, some of Leroy's differentiations are unfounded. For example, although it was a view widely held by French parapsychologists at the time Leroy wrote his book, there is no formal evidence that psychic abilities are inherited. Second, there are notable exceptions to many of Leroy's generalizations. D. D. Home was often seen to glow while levitating, could lift into the air both indoors and outdoors, and would sometimes levitate spontaneously. On the other hand, St. Joseph of Copertino's levitations were hardly private affairs and, though they were certainly not planned as such, might even be considered "public" performances. Finally, Leroy's argument that divine levitation is performed through weightlessness is also contestable. In his *Die Christliche Mystik,* von Görres tells how levitating saints often remain rigidly fixed in the air, even if attempts are made to pull them back to earth.

In general, most of Leroy's points are valid to some extent. There do seem to be basic (though not unequivocal) differences between psychic and mystical levitations, which suggests that they may indeed be two separate orders of psychic phenomena.

Though Leroy biasedly ascribes psychic levitation to diabolic forces, some of the best-documented levitations have in fact taken place within the context of cases of so-called "demonic" possession. William Peter Blatty's bestselling novel *The Exorcist* gives a fairly accurate, though exaggerated, picture of the syndrome, including a graphic description of a levitation closely resembling one that has been documented in a genuine case.

Demonic possession is not a myth. Although many forms of mental and physical illness—such as classical hysteria or Gilles de la Tourette's syndrome*—can show some of the same symptoms, a true demonic possession syndrome exists as well. During a typical case of possession, the victim (usually an adolescent or young adult) will at first manifest symptoms indistinguishable from those of mental illness. Convulsions will set in, a "secondary personality" will speak through the victim's mouth, and so on. These symptoms will then be followed by supernatural ones. The sufferer will display clairvoyant and prophetic gifts and might even speak and/or understand a foreign language he or she has never formally learned. Spontaneous psychokinesis will break out in his or her presence, and sometimes the victim will levitate in full light.

Many instances of possession have been recorded in the twentieth century. Perhaps the best-known example occurred in Georgetown, near Washington, D.C., in 1949. (This is also the case on which Blatty based his novel.) The original facts had long been kept fairly confidential by Church authorities, but the true story slowly leaked out after the case was fictionalized. One authoritative source of information about the affair is John Nicola's *Diabolical Possession and Exorcism*. Nicola, a Catholic priest and expert on demonic possession, was able to examine the original documents pertaining to the matter, including the diaries of the priests who exorcised the victim. He was also able to speak personally with at least one witness.

The actual victim of the possession was a thirteen-year-old

---

*Gilles de la Tourette's syndrome is an illness that causes the victim to suffer tics, convulsions, and compulsive bouts of obscene swearing. The disorder seems remotely related to some forms of psychomotor epilepsy, and may have a genetic basis. The precise etiology of the disease is, however, not understood. Some drugs, such as the tranquilizer Haldol, seem to alleviate the symptoms, but there is no known cure. The syndrome was first identified as a disease by Gilles de la Tourette, a student of J. M. Charcot, a French physician who pioneered the study of mental and nervous diseases at the Salpêtrière in France during the last century.

Lutheran boy, identified as "Roland Doe" in all the official reports, who lived in a middle-class Georgetown home with his parents and grandmother. The first indications of a demonic attack occurred on January 15, 1949, when weird scratching and knocking sounds were heard in the house. The family attributed the disturbance to the soul of a recently deceased relative, Roland's aunt, who had taught the boy how to play with a Ouija board. After the sounds abated, small household items began to dematerialize and reappear in odd places, furniture moved by itself, and paintings began rattling on the walls. The poltergeistery erupted in the boy's schoolroom as well. Only after several weeks of this initial manifestation did symptoms of possession first become noticeable in the boy—he began to talk in his sleep and shout obscenities.

It was at about this time that Roland's family saw the first of what would be several levitations. One night when they were awakened by the boy's screams they ran to his room and watched in horror as their son and his mattress levitated and remained suspended in the air for several moments. To quote Nicola, this performance was "in the weeks to follow . . . repeated several times in different beds, both in private homes and in the hospital."[14] Realizing by this time that they needed religious guidance, Roland's parents asked their minister to look into the case. The clergyman spent a night in Roland's room and saw the same levitation performance that the boy's parents had seen a few nights earlier.

The actual possession followed the onset of the levitations. Roland now had violent seizures, a "secondary personality" would control his body and speak through his mouth, and his entire personality began to disintegrate. His parents were by now so alarmed by the seriousness of the boy's condition that they petitioned for a formal Roman Catholic exorcism as their only hope.

In March the boy was removed from Georgetown to a Catholic hospital located in St. Louis where the exorcism rites were to be conducted. The priests chosen to administer the ritual were Father Raymond Bishop, Father F. Bowdern, who had originally looked into the case at its earlier stage in Georgetown, and Father Lawrence Kenny, a local cleric. A detailed diary was kept of the supernatural events that took place during the exorcism. During the proceedings the boy would often break away with superhuman strength from the attendants holding him to his bed, was often able to read the minds of the exorcists, understood Latin when addressed in that language, and levitated several times. The room in which the rite was held would also become icy cold.

These levitations were witnessed not only by the exorcists but also by several other priests who acted as onlookers to the rites. One of these was Father Charles O'Hara, a teacher at Marquette University in Milwaukee. It is not clear from the records how many sessions he attended, but O'Hara later told Father Eugene Gallagher, a teacher at Georgetown University (and the first to introduce Blatty, who was his student, to the facts of the case), that during the rituals the boy was sometimes able to break free from his attendants and fly through the air:

One night the boy brushed off his handlers and soared through the air at Father Bowdern standing at some distance from his bed [with] the ritual in his hands. Presumably, Father was about to be attacked but the boy got no further than the book. And when his hand hit that—I assure you I saw this with my own eyes—he didn't tear the book, he dissolved it. The book vaporized into confetti and fell in small fine pieces to the floor."[15]

Roland Doe was delivered from his tragic ordeal only after several weeks of exorcisms.

Unfortunately, a large portion of the diary kept by Roland's exorcists is now lost. The case report written by the priests was in the possession of Father Gallagher until 1950, at which time he lent it to a colleague. Somehow a number of its sixteen pages were misplaced at that time. However, many of the original witnesses who took part in the case, in both St. Louis and Georgetown, are still alive. Father Bowdern has appeared on television several times, though few people realize his connection to the Georgetown case.

There are many other instances on record every bit as spectacular as the Georgetown possession. There is, for instance, a 1928 case reported from Earling, Iowa, which involved a middle-aged woman who had been brought out from Milwaukee expressly so that the exorcisms could be done privately. But the circumstances of the affair became so dramatic that soon the whole town knew about them. The rites were conducted over a three-month period in the rectory of St. Joseph's Church by Father Theophilus Riesinger, a priest from Marathon, Wisconsin, who had discovered the case in Milwaukee some years earlier. Father Joseph Steiger, the pastor of St. Joseph's Church and a highly respected member of the community, served as a witness to the proceedings. Both men are now dead, but their testimony was collected and published in a privately printed booklet, *Begone Satan!*, shortly after the events had transpired. The author was Father Carl Vogt, who had clearly spoken with the witnesses personally. The accuracy of Vogt's account was attested to in a signed affidavit supplied by Teresa Wegener, Father Steiger's housekeeper, who also observed some of the doings. Vogt's report is also consistent with the statements Father Riesinger himself made during several sermons he gave on possession before his death.

The subject of the exorcism, whose identity has never been revealed, had suffered attacks of possession for most of her life. She first fell victim to demonic attack in her hometown of Milwaukee in 1908, when she was twenty-six years old. Father Riesinger exorcised her at that time, but there is no information available on the matter. The possession eventually recurred, and in 1928 Riesinger had her moved to Earling, where exorcisms were held in the rectory in August, September, and December.

During the ritual the woman was continually seized by convulsions and displayed extraordinary extrasensory powers. Raps and disembodied voices were also heard in the church. Although only one levitation took place during the proceedings, it was an extraordinary one. It occurred on the very first day of the rite, as Father Riesinger was beginning the formula of exorcism. The victim lay contorting on her bed in the rectory while attendants tried to hold her still. Her body suddenly tore away from the attendants, literally flew across the room, and lodged itself on the wall space over the entry. She stuck there as if glued and finally had to be wrenched down.

Although Father Riesinger never wrote out a public account of the Iowa case, he did admit during an interview he granted *True Mystics* magazine in 1939 that he had seen several levitations among the twenty-two possession cases he had exorcised.

Another well-documented case of demonic levitation was

reported from Natal, Africa, in 1907. The victim was a Bantu native girl, Claire-Germaine Cèle, who had been brought up by nuns in an African mission. Her possession began when she was a teen-ager, shortly after her first communion. She would be thrown into convulsions, speak and understand languages she had never learned, and would display other psychic gifts. The girl could also read the minds of the attending priests, and often a "demon" would speak through her, mocking and castigating them. The exorcist in this case was the local bishop.

The most remarkable feature of this possession, however, was Claire-Germaine's full levitations. These were witnessed by many visitors to and residents of the mission. On one occasion the girl levitated six feet over her bed during the reading of the rituals and then challenged the exorcist to join her! According to a report drawn up by the exorcists, these levitations took place frequently and were always astonishing:

Germana [sic] floated often three, four, and up to five feet high in the air, sometimes vertically, with her feet downward, and at other times horizontally, with her whole body floating above her head. She was in a rigid position. Even her clothing did not fall downward, as would have been normal; instead, her dresses remained tightly attached to her body and legs. If she was sprinkled with holy water, she moved down immediately, and her clothing fell loosely onto her bed. This type of phenomenon took place in the presence of different witnesses, including outsiders. Even in church, where she could be seen by everyone, she floated above her seat. Some people tried to pull her down forcibly, holding on to her feet, but it proved to be impossible.[16]

The failure of Germaine's clothing to drape down normally (and according to the laws of gravity) when she levitated is a phenomenon that exactly parallels a phenomenon mentioned in a possession reported from France circa 1590 which was written up in a pamphlet entitled *Original d'un procès-verbal, faire pour le délivrer d'une fille possédée.* The young victim of the possession would often levitate when religious rites were administered to her. The spectators noted that on some occasions her clothing would cling to her body as she levitated and floated about the room.

A final example of diabolic levitation, and a most dramatic one, is drawn from an account sent by a missionary who traveled in Indochina in 1738 to his superiors in France of a possession case he had uncovered. The following is his description of one of the levitations he observed during the exorcism he performed?[17]

While engaged in my exorcism, I suddenly had the idea to ask the Devil in Latin to move the possessed to the ceiling of the church. Specifically, this was to be done with feet upwards and head pointing down. Immediately the body became rigid, and the possessed was unable to use his limbs. He was propelled to a pillar in the middle of the church and, with his feet close together, pushed with his back toward the pillar. All this occurred while his hands remained out of use. He was transported to the ceiling, much like a weight that is forcibly pulled upward. Throughout all this, the man remained seemingly passive. He hung from the ceiling, his feet flat up against it, his head downwards. . . . I kept him, in this manner, up in the air for more than half an hour, but I did not have the persistence to leave him there any longer. I was, in any event, very frightened by what I had observed. I ordered the Devil to put the possessed back on his feet without any damage whatever. . . . He immediately tossed him down, like a package of dirty laundry, completely unharmed.

Leroy believed that psychic levitation was actually diabolic in nature because its characteristics were so different from those of saintly levitation. Yet the features of a truly diabolic possession appear to be much more similar to those of a mystical levitation than to those of a psychic levitation! Both diabolic and mystical levitations can be maintained for long periods of time and occur in broad daylight, in any location, when the victim is healthy or ill, and in public as well as privately. Both are usually spontaneous in nature.

Mystical, demonic, and psychic levitations all seem to represent an *order* of psychic phenomenon, and so fall more into the realm of parapsychology than that of religion. There is little justification, therefore, to assume that the physical *force* that produces the phenomenon is necessarily either divine or demonic. The ability to levitate may well be a psychic potential we all possess, since parapsychologists have learned that everyone seems to be endowed with at least minute amounts of psychokinetic powers.

But what is the nature of the force that produces telekinetic action, and how does this force produce levitation? There are basically three theories that can explain the mystery of levitation. The first is that it is not a physical phenomenon at all, but actually a hallucination—albeit of a very special kind. This is Leroy's theory, which he discusses at great length in his book on the subject. He concludes that levitation is a "non-objective phenomenon"—a "divine hallucination" whereby God allows the mystic to *perceive* himself levitated, and grants any happenchance observer similar perceptions.

A correlated and secularized version of this explanation would state that the levitating person does not really levitate at all, but telepathically hypnotizes his audience and himself into hallucinating the feat.

Many objections can be raised to rebut this type of theory. For instance, if we assume for the moment that levitation is actually an illusion produced by divine intervention, isn't it equally feasible that an all-powerful being could just as easily levitate a person physically? Leroy's interpretation also does not take into account the physical evidence that seems to establish levitation as an objective phenomenon. Photographs attesting to the genuineness of the phenomenon do exist. Nor can the hallucination theory explain the levitations of such saints as Joseph of Copertino or Sister Marie Baourdie. Both would occasionally be levitated to the tops of trees or other high places, where they would find themselves after their ecstasies ended. At times they even had to be helped down!

Similar arguments could disprove the "collective hypnosis" theory as well. There is actually no basis for the existence of "mass hypnosis," much less mass *psychic* hypnosis.*

A more viable theory is that levitation occurs through an induced weightlessness, so that the body lifts into the air somewhat

---

*This theory was popular in some psychic circles in the 1930s when it was reported that a German college professor had filmed the celebrated Indian rope trick. According to this report, the professor and several witnesses watched a swami sit in an open field with a rope and an assistant at his side. After the swami meditated, the rope floated into the air and the assistant climbed it. Later, when the film was developed, the scientist was astounded to see that nothing had actually happened. The swami had merely sat quietly, concentrating on his audience. The professor concluded that he and the other spectators had been telepathically hypnotized into seeing the trick. This convincing explanation appeared in many books on the powers of the mind published in the 1930s and 1950s. Actually, the story is a total fabrication, originally invented by a newspaper reporter in the 1890s, but resurrected from time to time.

like a helium balloon. Leroy, especially, notes that the bodies of levitated saints appeared to float freely in space. Much impressive evidence could be cited in support of this idea. For instance, in his narrative of the life of Maria Coronel de Agreda, a seventeenth-century Spanish nun, Thurston relates that "the nuns found that if they blew in her direction her [levitating] body swayed with their breath, just as a feather or leaf might have done." [18] Similar observations were made by those who witnessed the levitations of Sister Beatrice Mary of Jesus (1632–1712). The life of this Spanish nun was chronicled by Father Tomas de Montalvo in his book *Vida prodigiosa de la extática y venerable Madre Sor Beatriz Maria de Jesus* (1719). Sister Beatrice would often levitate while kneeling in prayer before the altar of the convent chapel. The other nuns noticed that any current of air entering the chapel would cause her floating body to swing. It might also be pointed out that St. Joseph of Copertino and Sister Marie Baourdie, who were sometimes levitated to the tops of trees, never seemed to bend the branches on which they were set.

Although there is no scientific evidence that the human body can become weightless, several researchers in the Soviet Union have proposed that it may have an inherent ability to levitate itself through such a process. Their principle of "biogravitation" is based on a hypothesis that each cell of the body gives off "gravitational waves" that can be focused out and away from the body so that an artificial antigravitational field forms around it. The existence of such a force could explain such biological anomalies as why chromosomes of different weights and sizes move uniformly during cell division. It might also be suggested that levitation occurs when the body is subjected to such a field, which might offset the normal laws of gravity. Unfortunately, the biogravitational theory *is* only a theory, and no one has yet been able either to prove or to disprove it.

Still, the notion that levitation occurs when a psychic field is created around the body, or affects the physical area surrounding the levitator, is an intriguing possibility. Recent experimentation has determined that a psychic can alter the energy level of a small area of space and can reorder the free energy that normally exists in any body of air. There is even some indication that psychics can extract small amounts of energy from the air and redirect them to other locations.* A similar process might be the principle underlying levitation—i.e., the mind of the levitator somehow physically alters the area about him so that the laws of gravity are temporarily suspended and weightlessness ensues. Such a theory can explain the apparent weightlessness of some saints and can also account for those rare instances when onlookers trying to restrain levitating saints were lifted into the air along with them.

Levitation might also be similarly explained through some principles drawn from quantum physics. Dr. Richard Mattuck, a physicist at the University of Copenhagen, and Evan Harris Walker, an eminent American physicist at Johns Hopkins University, have both proposed what they call a "thermal noise" theory of psychokinesis. They suggest that a physical object could be made to "move by itself" if some force (such as the human mind) could interfere with the random movement of the subatomic particles within it. Every physical object is a collection of atoms, and every atom is a mass of subatomic particles shooting about in random directions and at random time intervals. If, however, some energy were able to arrange these particles so that they would move uniformly and in the same direction, the object they comprise would move in the corresponding direction. Levitation could occur if the ordering process somehow interfered with the atoms composing the human body.

Leroy's claim that all levitating saints displayed weightlessness is, however, open to dispute. In his *Die Christliche Mystik,* von Görres cites several instances where saints remained so rigidly fixed in space after their initial levitations that spectators were often unable to pull them to the ground. (A similar phenomenon also occurs during demonic levitation, as was true of the Earling, Iowa case.) This type of levitation also resembles certain phenomena that occur during table tilting. Many researchers have noted that once a table has been tilted up on two legs, *it sometimes cannot*

---

*These findings were made by Dr. Gertrude Schmeidler during some experiments she conducted with Ingo Swann, a well-known New York psychic, at the City College of the City University of New York in 1972. Schmeidler was testing to see if Swann could alter the temperature readings of small thermistors attached to pieces of bakelite and graphite merely by concentrating on them. She discovered that each time Swann altered a thermistor, there were corresponding temperature shifts—but in the opposite direction—in the air spaces near, but not directly around, it.

be pressed back to the floor. Professor Marc Thury, a scientist at the University of Geneva, first observed this phenomenon in the 1850s. A group of experimenters in Toronto recently encountered the effect while conducting some table-tilting experiments under the auspices of the Toronto Society for Psychical Research. (They report on this research in their book, *Conjuring Up Philip* [1976], which recounts the history of their tests.) Both Thury and the Philip group also documented another interesting phenomenon— objects placed on top of the table would not slide off as the table tilted, but would remain rigidly in place, defying the laws of gravity. This phenomenon seems related to that in which clothing of levitating demoniacs fails to drape down normally during their flights.

So a third theory of levitation is that some invisible force actually leaves the body when the miracle takes place and produces a psychic support system.

These theories are only tentative conjectures which have been cautiously extrapolated from a few recent findings made by parapsychologists both in this country and abroad. But these rough ideas may eventually provide material for a formal theory about the nature of levitation. It is also quite conceivable that there isn't any *one* process by which levitation takes place. As was stressed at the beginning of this chapter, levitation is a generic term encompassing many different types of effects. Different forms of levitation may rely on different operative mechanisms.

Any breakthrough in our understanding of this phenomenon will come only when the scientific community can observe and study levitation at first hand. Unfortunately, there are no contemporary psychics who seem capable of performing this feat, and it is unlikely that any Catholic nun, priest, or ascetic who has recently experienced levitation would be willing to reveal his or her ability and submit to laboratory research. Perhaps our only alternative lies in the East, with some yogic master who would be willing to levitate himself under careful scientific scrutiny. Then . . . and only then . . . will this wondrous mystery be solved within our lifetime.

❧ III ❧
THE STIGMATA

IF LEVITATION is the most often mentioned miracle in Christian hagiography, then the stigmata are probably the most complex and controversial. According to the *Reader's Digest Encyclopedic Dictionary,* the stigmata can be defined as "the wounds that Christ received during the Passion and Crucifixion; also marks on the body corresponding to these wounds, said to be miraculously impressed on certain persons." This chapter will be concerned with the second definition of the term. But this miracle is actually a multifaceted mystery, and a simple definition does not do justice to the incredible diversity of effects collectively labeled "the stigmata." Since no two Christian ascetics who have been miraculously impressed with the wounds of Christ have manifested them in quite the same way, the stigmata are probably the most controversial of all religious miracles. They are also a uniquely Christian phenomenon, for despite the fact that the historical Christ was only one of several religious leaders who suffered crucifixion, Christianity alone has evolved the tradition of the stigmata.

Impression with the stigmata may even be a more common miracle than levitation. According to Dr. A. Imbert-Gourbeyre, a French physician and authority on the subject, 312 appearances* can be traced from the beginning of Christianity up to the end of the nineteenth century. He discusses these cases in his monumen-

---

*This figure is open to question. Imbert-Gourbeyre based his calculation on cases of both visible stigmata and invisible stigmata (i.e., cases in which the sufferer felt the pain of the Passion wounds but never developed any visual lesions or bleeding), and it is debatable whether the latter cases can be considered truly miraculous. On the other hand, Thurston points out in *The Physical Phenomena of Mysticism* that Imbert-Gourbeyre overlooked several historical cases when compiling his study. A true count of how many saints and ascetics manifested the stigmata may therefore be impossible to determine. Of the stigmatics of the Church, most have been women and only about forty have been men. To date, only about sixty stigmatics have been beatified or canonized.

tal two-volume study, *La Stigmatisation* (1894), which still ranks as an authoritative work on the subject.

Most church scholars maintain that the first ascetic to exhibit the stigmata was St. Francis of Assisi (1181–1226).* The son of a wealthy merchant, Francis was a rambunctious and frivolous youth and adopted a more austere way of life only after suffering various illnesses and witnessing the horrors of the civil war that was ravaging Italy at the time. After experiencing a vision while praying in a church in the town of San Damiano in 1207, he became a roving preacher and eventually founded two friaries, one in the city of Maria degli Angeli (near Assisi) and the other at Bologna. Although he was never actually ordained a priest, Francis did attempt to become a missionary and traveled to Egypt for that purpose. Failing to make any impact there, however, he returned to Italy soon afterward. By 1217, when Francis's movement began to develop into a formal religious order, he resigned from its leadership.

St. Francis received the stigmata in 1224, only two years before his death. On September 14, in the middle of a forty-day retreat to Mount Alvenia in the Apennines, he had a vision while praying outside a cave. The figure of Christ on the cross appeared to him, and wounds simultaneously opened on Francis's hands, feet, and side. They were not simple lesions, but exactly simulated the wounds of Christ. They were never to leave him.

Many detailed descriptions of St. Francis's stigmata were recorded by his contemporaries. Most of these witnesses specifically noted that the saint's stigmata had two distinguishing features. First, the wounds themselves never healed or became inflamed. They simply remained on his body until his death, and even afterward. Second, actual protuberances resembling nail heads formed in the middle of the wounds. They seemed to be composed of hardened flesh supernaturally molded so that the lesions precisely matched those of the Crucifixion. "No power of autosuggestion, no abnormal pathological conditions could

---

*There is some debate about whether St. Francis was actually the first stigmatic of the Church, as a few cases nearly contemporary to his have been reported. Even St. Paul claimed (Galatians 6:17) that he bore "the stigmata of Jesus in my body." For many years ecclesiastic writers merely assumed that St. Paul was speaking figuratively, and not literally. Opinion on this matter has changed since the thirteenth century.

enable a contemplative to evolve from the flesh of his hands and feet four horny excrescences in the form of nails piercing his extremities and clinched in the back," writes Thurston. "Such a manifestation, if it occurs, must surely be miraculous."

One eyewitness account of St. Francis's stigmata was related by Thomas of Celano, a friend of the saint's, who wrote Francis's biography at the direct behest of Pope Gregory IX: [1]

His hands and feet seemed pierced in the midst by nails, the heads of the nails appearing in the inner part of the hands and in the upper part of the feet and their points over against them. Now these marks were round on the inner side of the hands and elongated on the outer side, and certain small pieces of flesh were seen like the ends of nails bent and driven back, projecting from the rest of the flesh. So also the marks of nails were imprinted in his feet, and raised above the rest of the flesh. Moreover his right side, as it had been pierced by a lance, was overlaid with a scar, and often shed forth blood so that his tunic and drawers were many times sprinkled with the sacred blood.

Celano also tells how the stigmata could be seen even after the saint's death:

His sinews were not contracted as those of the dead are wont to be, his skin was not hardened, his limbs were not stiffened, but turned this way and that as they were placed. And while he shone with such wondrous beauty in the sight of all, and his flesh had become still more radiant, it was wonderful to see amid his hands and feet, not the prints of the nails but the nails themselves formed out of his flesh and retaining the blackness of iron, and his right side reddened with blood.

In a later book, Celano described how the naillike protuberances in St. Francis's wounds were "implanted in the flesh itself, in such wise that if they were pressed in on either side they straightway, as if they were one of sinew, projected on the other." The representation was not based only on visual impressions: "We who recount these things ourselves witnessed them, we felt them with the same hands with which we now write."

Thomas of Celano's account was corroborated by St. Bonaventura (1221–74), an Italian bishop and theologian who became head of the Franciscan order in 1257. He, too, wrote a biography of St. Francis, in which he told how the saint's hands and feet "were pressed through the midst with nails, the heads whereof were on the palms of the hands and on the soles of the feet, outside the flesh, and the points came out through the back of the hands and of the feet, where they were showed bent back and clinched." [2] St. Bonaventura also noted that the nail heads were composed of blackened material and were so clearly defined within the wounds that one could slip a finger under them and *into* the stigmata.

Although some skeptics (including Thurston) have disputed the phenomenon of the nail heads, believing them to have been misperceptions on the writers' part, it is clear from Celano's account that he had inspected the wounds at very close range. It is also true that St. Francis's stigmata are not unique in this respect, for other contemplatives have been impressed with the same nail formations as part of their wounds.

Several characteristics of St. Francis's stigmata refute any theory that would ascribe the formation of the wounds to autosuggestion. No medical explanation can account for the fact that they were deep fissures within his hands, feet, and side, and not merely bleeding patches of skin. In other words, the stigmata resulted only when Francis's flesh *physically* opened to allow the bleeding. Similarly, no medical principles can demonstrate why these wounds never closed or became infected; nor can medicine explain the process by which the horny protuberances formed within them.

With St. Francis we see the beginning of a virtual *tradition* of the stigmata, a tradition that has asserted itself countless times during the course of the last seven hundred years. During the centuries following the saint's death, the appearance of the wounds began to be associated with an increasingly complex ideology. One of the first of these variations occurred in the midthirteenth century, when the stigmata became identified with the visionary, ecstatic reliving of the Passion. In 1275 a biography of a Cistercian nun and stigmatic named Elizabeth, who lived in Herkenrode, near Liège, was published. It described how the nun would enter a trance in which she would seem to be witnessing the Passion and Crucifixion of Christ. During these vivid ecstasies her stigmata would bleed. Elizabeth of Herkenrode may also have been the first stigmatic to bleed from the forehead, where small wounds imitating the lesions caused by Christ's "crown of thorns" would form during her trance.

Another tradition which developed during this period was the phenomenon of the periodic (as opposed to the continuous) bleeding of the wounds. This version of the miracle was apparently first exhibited by a nun named Lukandis (1276–1309), who lived in a convent in Oberweimar, Germany. (A biography of her appears in Volume XVIII of the *Analecta Bollandiana.**) Like Elizabeth of Herkenrode, Lukandis was a visionary. During her reenactment of the Passion she would often flog herself, and for this reason some historians believe that her stigmata may have been accidentally self-inflicted. But this theory cannot explain the odd periodic nature of the bleedings, which were copious only on Fridays and which would vanish altogether during Easter, only to reappear afterward.

The first manifestation of *internal* stigmata occurred during the seventeenth century. This phenomenon, in which the stigmata affect the internal organs of the body, most notably afflicted St. Veronica Giuliani (1660–1727).

Much of what we know of Veronica's life is derived from a lengthy book, *Un tesoro nascosto ossia diario di S. Veronica Giuliani* (1895), which contains the saint's own testimony. She was mistress of novices and later abbess at a convent in Città di Castello in Umbria, Italy. She was known for her levelheadedness and efficiency, though inwardly she was an intense ascetic. Her stigmata were extremely well observed.

St. Veronica was first impressed with the stigmata in April 1697. After three years, the stigmata in her hands and feet disappeared, but the wound in her side persisted. The bleeding of this wound could be controlled by her confessor and religious superiors, and would mysteriously open and close at their commands. She also bore a wound on her shoulder representing the bruise that formed where Christ had to support the cross as he carried it

---

*Founded in the seventeenth century, the Bollandists are a society of Jesuit scholars devoted to the study of the saints from a critical historical perspective. Headquartered in Brussels, they have pioneered the field of hagiography. The Bollandists publish annotated historical texts, one of which is the *Analecta Bollandiana.* They have also published a multivolumed encyclopedia, *Acta Sanctorum,* on the lives of the saints.

to Calvary. This wound was in the form of a physical depression so deep that two surgeons who inspected it after the saint's death were unable to understand how she had retained the use of her right hand.

The most unusual feature of Veronica's stigmata was the effect they had on her internal organs. During the last years of her life, she believed that insignias of the stigmata—in the shapes of a cross, a crown of thorns, three nails, swords, a letter, and so on—had been stamped directly onto her heart. She even drew several diagrams of her heart, showing the locations of these emblems and how they altered their positions. After her death, an autopsy revealed that the emblems were indeed impressed on her heart, just as she had sketched them in her last diagram. The two doctors who examined her subsequently drew up a formal statement of their findings.

Many of the saints and ascetics who have suffered the stigmata have also had marks impressed on their hearts, though none of the imprints were as complex as those of St. Veronica. St. Teresa of Avila describes in her confessions how an angel once appeared to her in a vision and thrust a sword into her heart. After the saint's death in 1582, a deep, abnormal fissure was found there. Her heart is now on display as a relic in the city of Alba de Tormes (Spain), and the fissure is still quite evident. Caterina Savelli of Sezza, a stigmatist who died in 1691, was stamped with the wounds of the Passion while taking communion in 1659. Only the wound in her side bled. After her death, a fissure was found impressed into her heart. Blessed Charles of Sezza, who died some thirty years before Caterina Savelli, had a similar internal wound. An autopsy found that his heart had been completely pierced, and was also stamped with emblems of a cross and a nail.

During the seventeenth and eighteenth centuries, it also became apparent that many stigmatics seemed to share a certain kind of *personality*, which had many of the same characteristics of abnormal behavior that J. M. Charcot and other pioneering physicians of the mid-nineteenth century would eventually diagnose as *hysteria*. This is not to say that all these stigmatists were merely hysterical individuals, but only that a certain *type* of person appears to be stigmata-prone. Virtually every serious student of the stigmata, including Thurston, has acknowledged this fact, even while maintaining that the stigmata may in fact be a preternatural phenomenon.

The dual nature of the stigmata is best illustrated by the strange case of Domenica Lazzari, whose life was recounted in two books that appeared in the mid-nineteenth century: *L'Extatique et les stigmatisées du Tyrol* (1846) and the less complete *Geschichte der zwei tyroler Jungfrauen Maria Mörl und Domenica Lazzari* (1843). According to Thurston, "No case is better attested. The witnesses were men of high position, quite independent of each other, and their reports, which are in absolute accord regarding the main features of the case, cover a period of more than ten years."[3] Lazzari's is a classic history of a hysteric, complete with childhood traumas, repressed fears, and mysterious illness—as well as a number of supernatural elements.*

Domenica lived most of her life in Capriana in the Tyrol. She was pious as a child, but gave little indication that she would eventually reject secular life completely. After her father died when she was thirteen, she fasted continually for several days and became ill, which presumably marked the onset of her hysteria. Her stability was further threatened in 1833, when, as a girl of eighteen, she was stranded in a mill where she spent a terrifying night. Nine days later Domenica suffered a mysterious seizure. From that point until 1848, the year of her death, she was bedridden. During these years she developed two further hysterical traits: a distaste for eating (*anorexia nervosa*) and an inability to be touched without suffering severe pain (hysterical *hyperasthesia*). If she was forced to eat or if a bright light was flashed on her, convulsions would set in. Domenica's aversion to food eventually took on a supernatural nature when in 1834 she gave up eating completely. She apparently ate nothing whatsoever until her death, yet lived a relatively healthy life. This phenomenon, called *inedia* (the paranormal ability to live without nourishment), is a miracle that often accompanies the stigmata.

Domenica was first impressed with the stigmata in July 1837,

---

*The term *hysteria* is used here according to its proper medical definition. Hysteria refers to a group of disorders that are manifested in the form of such physical conversion symptoms as blindness, paralysis, tics that have no organic basis. The symptoms are usually brought about by the sufferer's own mind, often as a reaction to psychological trauma. Women seem to be much more prone to the disorder than men.

seven years after she had become bedridden. Dr. Dei Cloche, who had been the woman's physician before he left Capriana, made several trips to the town to attend his former patient. Like many stigmatists, Domenica bled periodically on Friday. Cloche himself witnessed a number of these bleedings, and later reported:

. . . I could hear piercing cries which came from the window of her room looking out upon the road, and as I drew near I could distinguish the words, repeated again and again, "O God come to my assistance." At ten o'clock the unfortunate sufferer was still repeating the same invocation in vibrant tones. Now and again she returned laconic answers to questions addressed to her, but at once resumed her distressing ejaculation. . . . At four o'clock in the afternoon, though the blood had then ceased to flow from the stigmata, she continued to utter her piteous cry with unabated energy. When asked why she never stopped this clamour, "It is," she answered, "because I never cease feeling intense pain all over my body and particularly in the places of the wounds, and I find relief in crying as I do."

The flows were so prolific that her entire face would sometimes be covered with the blood that dripped from her stigmatic "crown of thorns."

Though one might be tempted to explain Domenica's bleeding as a manifestation of her hysteric disorder, the flows of blood from her wounds often exhibited a most unusual effect—they defied gravity! This phenomenon was witnessed by her doctors and by the many travelers who journeyed to Capriana to observe the stigmata. Lord Shrewsbury, an English visitor, testified in 1842 that he had seen the flows of blood from Domenica's feet supernaturally run against all gravitational laws. Since Domenica was bedridden, her feet were always extended horizontally when her stigmata erupted. Any blood issuing from the wounds should therefore have flowed down the side of her foot after forming little pools. Yet in his *Letters,* Shrewsbury states that "instead of taking its normal course, the blood flowed upwards and over the toes, as it would do were she suspended over a cross." In his book *Journey into France and Italy* (1849), J. H. Wynee, another British traveler, claimed that Domenica's doctor once told him that he had seen her blood flowing upward and over the toes many times.

The case of Domenica Lazzari presents the student of the stigmata with a series of formidable paradoxes. To what extent were her wounds psychological in nature and to what extent were they supernatural? Domenica does not seem to have been especially religious, and she was certainly not a true ascetic. She experienced neither ecstasies nor visions, nor did she display any apparent supernatural gifts apart from her stigmata and inedia. On the other hand, there is little doubt that the woman was mentally ill. Even her doctors agreed that psychological and not physical factors were the basis of her illness. She had all the symptoms of classical hysteria, including self-masochism, hyperesthesia, psychogenic catalepsy, anorexia nervosa, and bleeding through the skin.

Yet these psychological components of Domenica's condition were complicated by genuinely paranormal factors. Although her inedia would probably be diagnosed today as anorexia nervosa by any competent psychiatrist, we know that Domenica did not suffer from a *simple* case of this disorder. Victims of anorexia nervosa lose weight, grow weak, and can even starve to death. Domenica, however, suffered no detrimental effects from her anorexia, though she neither ate nor drank anything for over ten years. The matter of her bleeding is equally inexplicable. While the human body is capable of "sweating blood," no psychological explanation can account for why Domenica's blood flowed counter to gravity.

In some cases of stigmata, then, it appears that the real miracle is not the development of the wounds themselves but the manner in which paranormal factors are able to intensify what is basically a psychological phenomenon.

The theory that the stigmata are at least in part a psychogenic phenomenon has even been subjected to experimentation. At the turn of the century, several physicians in France and Germany attempted to artificially induce classical stigmata on their patients through hypnosis. Charcot and several others claimed that they had been able to reproduce these wounds and so believed that the stigmata of the saints were in no way divine or even paranormal. But all that these physicians were really able to accomplish was *to cause their subjects to produce red marks or splotches on their skin in the same areas in which the stigmata usually appeared.* They were *not* able to elicit the production of open wounds or actual flows of blood.

A major controversy over the implications of this form of artificially induced stigmata arose again in 1933, when Dr. Alfred Lechler, a German physician, claimed that he had produced the Passion wounds in a hysterical subject he was treating with hypnosis. In his book *Das Rätsel von Konnersreuth im Lichte eines neuer Falles von Stigmatisation,* Lechler describes how with hypnosis he had trained a Protestant patient, Elizabeth K., to develop the stigmata at will through autosuggestion. However, Elizabeth K.'s stigmata, which included marks on the hands, feet, shoulder, and forehead, differed from true mystical stigmata in several respects. Her wounds were only reddened, inflamed patches of skin through which a drop or two of blood would seep. They were not open lesions such as many ascetics of the Church exhibited. Unlike the mystical stigmata, which are usually carried for life, Elizabeth K.'s wounds would disappear within a day or two. In short, Lechler had been able to produce an effect that only slightly resembled the true phenomenon.

Imbert-Gourbeyre was also concerned with the issue and summarized the differences between hypnotically induced stigmata and genuine mystical stigmata in his *La Stigmatisation:*

(1) Many genuine stigmatics possess wide fissures in their skin. In cases of hypnotic stigmata, no true wound opens; the blood—if it appears at all—merely seeps through the flesh.

(2) Mystical stigmata bleed either periodically or perpetually. Hypnotic stigmata are transient effects.

(3) The wounds of the genuine stigmata never heal, nor *can* they be healed. Hypnotic stigmata clear up naturally and of their own accord.

(4) Sufferers of the true stigmata usually experience intense pain brought about by the bleeding. Hypnotic stigmata is apparently painless.

(5) Divine stigmata always appear first when the ascetic is undergoing an ecstasy or vision. Hypnotic subjects can produce the phenomenon only while in an artificially induced trance.

(6) The tissue around the true stigmata never decays, becomes fetid, or shows any sign of deterioration. Hypnotic effects follow a normal medical course of healing.

Genuine stigmata are also endowed with a number of peculiar properties. The blood that flows from the wounds occasionally exudes a sweet scent, and often it doesn't coagulate and dry normally. "It is known," writes Montague Summers in his *The Physi-*

cal Phenomena of Mysticism (1950), "that in not a few instances where the blood flowing from the wounds of a stigmatic has been collected and preserved in a glass phial . . . the blood from time to time has been observed to liquefy [after becoming dry] and assume a ruby red color as though full of life and vital." [4] There are even reported instances of fresh blood flowing from the corpse of a stigmatic.

The actual wounds of the stigmata also present some mysteries. There can be little doubt that some of the wounds are deep fissures. Those of Venerable Giovanna Maria Solimani (d. 1758), an Italian nun, were so deep that her confessor was able to press a small key into her left palm to a depth of half an inch. Yet sometimes these clefts will close up completely, leaving no scars, only to reopen later!

This effect was witnessed many times by those doctors and priests who were able to study the stigmata of St. Gemma Galgani (1878–1903). A biography of this extraordinary young woman, *The Life of Gemma Galgani,* was written by her confessor, Padre Germano di S. Stanisloa.

Gemma was born in Camigliani, Italy, and remained a lay person all her life. She was left an orphan when she was nineteen, whereupon she became a domestic servant in the town of Lucca. Although she passionately desired to become a nun, she had been struck by tuberculosis at an early age. She was later miraculously healed of this disease, and as a result, she became so devoutly religious that she developed the stigmata, clairvoyant talents, and the ability to see apparitions.

A description of St. Gemma's stigmata is given by Germano in his biography: [5]

. . . The phenomenon continued to repeat itself on the same day every week, namely on Thursday evening about eight o'clock, and continued until three o'clock on Friday afternoon. No preparation preceded it; no sense of pain or impression in those parts of the body affected by it; nothing announced its approach except the recollection of spirit that preceded the ecstasy. Scarcely had this come as a forerunner than red marks showed themselves on the backs and palms of both hands; and under the epidermis a rent in the flesh was seen to open by degrees: *this was oblong on the backs of the hands and irregularly round in the palms.* After a little the membrane burst and on those innocent hands were seen marks of flesh wounds. *The diameter of these in the palms was about half an inch, and on the backs of the hands the wound was about five-eighths of an inch long by one-eighth wide.*

Sometimes the laceration appeared to be only on the surface; at other times it was scarcely perceptible with the naked eye; but as a rule it was very deep, and seemed to pass through the hand—the openings on both sides reaching each other. I say seemed to pass, because those cavities were full of blood, partly flowing and partly congealed, and when the blood ceased to flow they closed immediately, so that it was not easy to sound them without a probe. Now this instrument was never used; both because of the reverential delicacy inspired by the Ecstatic in her mysterious state, and because the violence of the pain made her keep her hands convulsively closed, also because the wounds in the palms of her hands were covered by a swelling that at first looked like clotted blood, whereas it was found to be fleshy, hard and like the head of a nail raised and detached and about an inch in diameter. In her feet, besides the wounds being large and livid around the edges, their size in an inverse sense differed from those of her hands; that is, there was a larger diameter on the instep and a smaller one on the sole; furthermore, the wound in the instep of the right foot was as large as that in the sole of the left.

These severe wounds would often *totally vanish* just as mysteriously:

As soon as the ecstasy on Friday was over the flow of blood from all five wounds ceased immediately; the raw flesh healed; the lacerated tissues healed too, and the following day, or at latest on Sunday, not a vestige remained of those deep cavities, neither at their centres, nor around their edges; the skin having grown quite uniformly with that of the uninjured part. In colour, however, there remained whitish marks.

Though Gemma's stigmata were undoubtedly supernatural, they were also at least partially psychogenic in nature. Her wounds appeared in the same places and in the same proportion as those on the crucifix before which she loved to pray.

Not all the classic stigmatists developed open wounds in their hands. Louise Lateau, a contemporary of Gemma Galgani, was prone to a somewhat different manner of affliction. She was born in 1850 to a French peasant family that lived in the town of Bois d'Haute. As a child she had been trampled by a cow, and by 1867 further medical complications almost caused her death. She was spontaneously healed at the height of her crisis, but became ill again three weeks later. This second illness was accompanied by religious visions, and Lateau also began suffering intense pain at the sites of the traditional stigmata. In April 1868 the full stigmata finally developed, and bled periodically on Fridays. She began to have an aversion to food at about the same time, and she ceased eating altogether in 1871. Even swallowing a spoonful of water would cause her to vomit.

The case became widely discussed, and a fierce debate arose over Lateau's inedia in the pages of the *Bulletin de l'Académie royale de médicine* in 1876. Yet even as cautious a researcher as Thurston agrees that "it is admitted by practically all the many medical men, some friendly and some hostile, who concerned themselves with the case, that no fragment of positive evidence has ever been produced which can throw doubt upon the statement made by Louise, her sisters, and confessors, that during all these years she took no food." [6] Her stigmata were nearly as controversial, for unlike Gemma Galgani's wounds, Lateau's never actually formed open lesions.

Dr. Gerald Molloy, the rector of University College of Dublin, was able to make a detailed study of her wounds and published his observations in a short book, *A Visit to Louise Lateau* (1873). He described how Louise's palm would be found unwounded when the blood of her stigmata was wiped away:

> The nature of the stigmata was then more distinctly seen. They are oval marks of a bright red hue, appearing on the back and palm of each hand about the centre. Speaking roughly, each stigma is about an inch in length and somewhat more than half an inch in breadth. There is no wound properly so-called, but the blood seemed to force its way through the unbroken skin. In a very short time, sufficient blood had flowed again to gratify the devotion of other pilgrims, who applied their handkerchiefs as had been done before, until all the blood had been wiped away a second time. This process was repeated several times during the course of our visit.

Perhaps the most bizarre case of stigmata reported in relatively recent times is that of Palma Matarelli (1825–1888), an Italian peasant woman whose stigmata were personally studied by

Imbert-Gourbeyre and described in *Les Stigmatisées.* Matarelli
received the stigmata in 1857, and they remained for eight years.
She also suffered from a variety of other supernatural afflictions.
Sometimes her body would become so hot that burn marks would
appear on her skin. She would repeatedly vomit undigested hosts,
even though she had not taken communion recently, and she
often fell into trances during which a host would miraculously
materialize in her open mouth. Her stigmata were most commonly
impressed on her forehead in a "crown of thorns" configuration.
If cloth was applied to her wounds, the resulting blood stains
would fashion into the shapes of hearts, swords, and other religious emblems!

The unusual nature of the Matarelli case caused a good deal
of uneasiness within ecclesiastic circles. Officials at the Vatican
were of the opinion that the miracles were either fraudulent or
diabolic in nature. Imbert-Gourbeyre eventually bowed to ecclesiastic pressure and underplayed the affair in his work, *La Stigmatisation,* but he never recanted a word that he had previously
written.

No general history of the stigmata would be complete without
some mention of Anne Catherine Emmerich, the famous German
visionary. Emmerich was a poor peasant girl who lived in West-
phalia. She became an Augustinian nun while she was young, and
is best remembered today for her frequent and elaborate religious
visions, accounts of which are still in print and fill several volumes.
Her stigmata first appeared in 1812. Both ecclesiastic officials and
medical authorities were able to examine her wounds, despite the
fact that she herself continually attempted to keep them secret.
Her stigmata closed permanently in 1818. Emmerich also exhibited a unique series of small wounds in the form of crosses which
were sometimes impressed on her body. One was permanently
branded on her breast and bled every Wednesday. Yet the skin
never actually opened to allow the blood to flow freely. The blood
merely seeped through the tissue.

The stigmata are not a miracle of the past; cases are still being
reported today. Many stigmatists of the twentieth century have
been subject to the very same symptoms as afflicted the historical
mystics that have been discussed above. Such phenomena as inedia, the supernormal opening of holes in the flesh, miraculous

communions—all these wonders have been reported by reliable witnesses within the last few decades. These modern cases help to establish the accuracy of older accounts of the stigmata, for they indicate that the priests and medical men of ages past were probably not mistaken about what they had seen.

The best-known modern stigmatic was probably Therese Neumann (1898–1962), a peasant who lived her entire life in Konnersreuth, a small Bavarian village situated close to the Czech border. Her stigmata (which she bore most of her life) and her other miracles (including bilocation and divine inedia) were examined by doctors and theologians, skeptics and believers. By the end of her life, thousands of visitors had traveled to Konnersreuth to assemble before her house, hoping to be allowed to enter and meet her, see her stigmata, or watch her ecstasies.

Neumann had a basically happy childhood. Her family was poor, but not destitute, and devoutly Catholic. She often worked on neighboring farms doing either domestic or farming chores in order to help supplement the family income. She was a healthy girl and a good worker, and her goal was to become an African missionary. But in 1918, her plans were interrupted by a string of serious illnesses which heralded the onset of her religious asceticism.

Injured while helping to fight a fire on a nearby farm on March 10, Neumann was forced to take to her bed. She attempted to return to work several times over the next few days, but found it impossible to do so. In early April she fell down a flight of stairs while in a neighbor's home and injured her head. She entered a hospital on April 23, suffering from violent convulsions and internal injuries, and was released on June 10 in no better health. By August her eyesight began to fail as well, and by the end of the year Neumann had become a bedridden, blind invalid. Even when bedridden she suffered severe convulsions, often violent enough to throw her out of bed. Bedsores broke out over her body, and she soon found it impossible to retain solid food.

Neumann's invalidism lasted for several years, until suddenly, one by one, her physical disabilities were "miraculously" cured. She was deeply devoted at the time to St. Thérèse of Lisieux (1873–1897), a young French nun whose life served as a model for all who knew her. Though Thérèse was not canonized until

1925, Neumann had adopted her as a spiritual patroness early in life. On April 29, 1925—the very day Thérèse of Lisieux was beatified—Neumann was spontaneously healed of her blindness. A few days later her left foot, which had become decayed from lack of use, regenerated new skin after rose leaves from St. Thérèse's grave were placed under its bandages. On May 17, 1925—the date of Thérèse of Lisieux's formal canonization—Neumann's paralysis immediately disappeared. And on September 10, the anniversary of St. Thérèse's death, Neumann found her strength so revitalized that she could leave her bed without aid.

To the villagers of Konnersreuth, Neumann had been the recipient of divine healing. But a more reasonable explanation would be that there was really nothing wrong with her originally. In retrospect, it is highly likely that her condition was basically psychogenic in nature. Her various symptoms—blindness, convulsions, and paralysis—were never diagnosed as due to a specific physical malady and would seem to be telltale signs of hysteria. The only mystery about her "healings" was the regeneration of tissue on her foot, since such a cure cannot be considered psychosomatic.

Neumann's stigmata first appeared during Lent in 1926 in the form of the five classic wounds of the Passion. She was alone one night, lying in bed in deep contemplation, when she saw a vision of Christ before her. As she stared at the figure, she felt an intense pain in her side and a warm liquid trickling down her body. When she came out of her ecstasy, she found blood flowing from a wound that had opened there. The wound continued to bleed all through the next day, leaving her exhausted. Similar religious visions began to appear to her on consecutive Fridays, and each one presaged the onset of further bleeding.

Neumann at first attempted to keep her stigmata a secret, and recruited the aid of her sister in washing her bloodstained clothing and bedding. But her family discovered the truth when linen soiled with blood was found in her room. On Good Friday she entered into an ecstasy once again, and her entire family saw blood flowing from the backs of her hands, her feet, and her side, while tears of blood fell from her eyes. The stigmata had not yet appeared on her palms.

Neumann described her sensation of the stigmata to her parish priest, Father Naber, in 1926:

The five wounds hurt me constantly, although I have already become accustomed to pain. It is as though something is penetrating into my hands and feet. The wound in the side seems to be really one in the heart. I feel it at every word I utter. If I draw a deep breath when speaking forcibly or hurrying, I feel a stabbing pain in my heart. If I keep quiet, I don't notice this. But I suffer this pain willingly. Actually, the wounds close up during the week. The real pain lies much deeper inside. An accidental pressure on the back of my hand or the instep of my foot I feel far less than one on the palm or sole. Because of this, I cannot use any stick, nor even stand on the soles of my feet much less walk.

The wound on my side is in a different place from where I see it on Jesus. In my case it is just above the heart where the heart beats. It is on the left side, but only slightly sideways. I am told that learned people have discussed this from every point of view, but I can only say what is, and what I see, even if others would prefer to hear what suits them.

The stigmata so intensified toward the close of 1926 that on Friday, November 19, eight small wounds opened around Neumann's forehead, representing the crown of thorns. By 1927 the wounds in her hands had opened into holes extending completely through them. According to one eyewitness, "the wounds on her hands and feet worked their way through from the back and instep inwards and broke through the palms and soles." [7] Her side wound deepened as well, so that it formed into a fissure extending deep into her body. At times, the stigmata even glowed. (This mysterious phenomenon was photographed on May 17, 1927, while Neumann was praying at her village church.) The final wound developed on March 8, 1928, when a blood lesion opened on her shoulder.

By 1930, Neumann's stigmata had begun to imitate those of St. Francis of Assisi. Protuberances resembling nail heads slowly appeared within the wounds on her hands. These naillike structures, apparently formed from hardened skin, were examined by several doctors and priests. They passed completely through her feet and hands, taking up most of the area of the wounds. The "nails" could be seen on the backs of her hands, bent to the sides of her palms, and also on her feet. A soft, membranelike tissue surrounded them. During her ecstasies this membrane would break to allow blood to flow.

Neumann's stigmata bled periodically and usually accompanied her frequent visionary experiences. On Fridays she would enter deep trance, during which she would reenact the entire Passion as though she were witnessing the event, and would only revive hours later. Blood would flow copiously from her hands, feet, forehead, shoulder, and eyes during these visions, and bandages had to be continually applied to soak up the blood. (Oddly, normal dressings seemed to aggravate the wounds.) These ecstasies eventually became so common that the Konnersreuth townsfolk would devoutly assemble before her family home every Friday hoping to be allowed entrance.

After the fall of the Third Reich in 1945, many American servicemen stationed in Germany traveled to Konnersreuth to visit the famous stigmatist.* In 1952, Radio Free Europe, then based in Munich, did an on-the-spot documentary about her.

Therese Neumann, like many ascetics, was endowed with other miraculous powers in addition to the classical stigmata. She was widely recognized as a healer, and it is said that she had bilocated on a few occasions. She became extremely clairvoyant while entranced, and sometimes predicted the future. But apart from her stigmata, her most famous miracle was her inedia. In 1927 she had a vision in which she was told that she would no longer need to rely upon earthly food. From that date onward, she neither ate nor drank anything; yet she was able to maintain her health, never lost any weight, and apparently enjoyed a normal physical life.

Neumann's inedia was also critically tested. In 1927, when her inedia was first manifested, the local bishop in Regensburg asked Neumann's father if a commission could be assigned to the Neumann household to ascertain the paranormal nature of her fast. Herr Neumann agreed, and from July 14 to July 28 four nuns were stationed in the cottage to keep Neumann under constant observation. They remained in her presence no matter where she

---

*A moving description of these visits, and Neumann's graciousness in meeting with her visitors, is given in Albert Schinberg's biography, *The Story of Therese Neumann*. (Milwaukee, Wisconsin: Bruce Publishing Co., 1947).

went and even bathed her to make certain she drank no bath water. If she rinsed her mouth, the wash had to be measured before and afterward to verify that none of it was swallowed. Neumann survived the ordeal with no loss of energy or weight. This test seems conclusive, for while the human body can live without food for fourteen days, it cannot do without water for so long a period of time.

Neumann also enjoyed divine communions. As she knelt before the altar of the village church to receive communion from her priest, the host would sometimes fly from the priest's hand and float through the air into her mouth.[8] (On one occasion a photograph of this miracle was taken.) At other times, a host placed on her tongue would simply dematerialize before she could swallow it.* During a number of ecstasies at her home, she would fall to her knees and stretch out her tongue, whereupon a host would mysteriously appear there.

Lastly, even the blood flows from Neumann's wounds were miraculous. Like those of Domenica Lazzari, Neumann's wounds would bleed counter to gravity. This phenomenon was well witnessed on July 8, 1927, when a reporter from the *Berliner Hefte* visited the stigmatic at her home. He was escorted to her room, where he watched her enact the Passion while sitting upright in bed.

"Soon a drop of blood which increased in size formed at one of the foot stigmata," he reported. "It grew and grew in size until finally it dropped from the wound. Gravity would have commanded that the drop of blood flow downwards. But it didn't. It flowed almost directly upward, towards the toes, exactly as happened almost 2,000 years ago on the cross of Christ."[9]

After a careful examination of this case, there seems little doubt that Therese Neumann's stigmata were both hysterical *and* supernatural in nature. She certainly possessed the premorbid and fragile personality structure so typical of many stigmatists. Like most writers on this subject, Professor Jean Lhermitte of the Paris Faculty of Medicine believes that Neumann's phenomena "are of an hysterical nature and must not be considered therefore super-

---

*Again, this miracle is not unique to Neumann. Thurston devoted an entire chapter in *The Physical Phenomena of Mysticism* to similar accounts.

natural."* But he also warns that "the fact that the stigmatist has been affected by hysteria is not necessarily a barrier to her being favored with impulses, a certain fervor of devotion and authentic mystical gifts." [10] Even Thurston, while ultimately taking no position on the nature of Therese Neumann's stigmata, reminds us often in his writings that an ascetic's suffering from hysteria does not preclude him or her from being genuinely devout and favored with supernatural gifts.

The case of Therese Neumann is, in short, impossible to evaluate today. Her stigmata cannot be isolated from her other psychic gifts, and any theory that attempts to explain the nature of her stigmata must also be able to explain all her mystical powers; including her clairvoyance, bilocations, and ability to heal. There seems little doubt, though, that the stigmatist of Konnersreuth was a true ascetic and miracle worker in the tradition of St. Gemma Galgani, Anne Catherine Emmerich, and many others.

In 1918, however, a case of stigmata came to light that would be at the center of scientific and religious attention for half a century to come—and which can only be considered exclusively paranormal.

Francesco Forgione, who would later be known simply as Padre Pio, was born to a poor family in Pietrelcina, Italy on May 25, 1887. Like so many other stigmatists and miracle workers, he was religious at an early age, even though his parents were no more so than most Italians at the turn of the century. The boy's first major tutor was an elderly village priest, and by the time he entered the Italian equivalent of high school, Francesco, too, had decided to become a friar. He entered a monastery in a neighboring town when he was fifteen years old and adopted the name of Brother Pio. Because of his extreme austerities while serving there, including long fasts, his health broke down completely, and he had to be nursed back to health by his mother. He nevertheless returned to the monastery in 1910, where he was eventually ordained a priest. Shortly afterward he entered the monastery at San Giovanni Rotondo in Foggia, where he remained for most of the remainder of his life.

---

*The word *supernatural*, in this context, is not synonymous with *paranormal*, but means a God-given grace.

There is some evidence that Padre Pio suffered the pains of the invisible stigmata as early as 1915. During a visit home in September of that year his family noticed that he seemed to have difficulty using his hands. However, the actual wounds of the stigmata opened during an ecstasy he experienced in 1918 after saying Mass at the monastery. He was kneeling at one of the wooden church benches when a figure of Christ appeared before him.

"I was terrified when I saw him," Padre Pio later wrote to his advisor. "What I felt at that time I cannot explain. I felt as if I were going to die, and would have died if my Lord had not intervened and sustained my heart, which I felt was pounding its way right out of my chest. The vision of the person faded away, and I noticed that my hands and feet and chest had been pierced and were bleeding profusely."

He also told how he felt a "shaft of iron entering at the bottom of my heart and penetrating through the lower part of my right shoulder," which caused him excruciating pain. Padre Pio's chest wound was the most serious of the several he received that day, and would continue to bleed periodically from Thursday evening until Saturday for years to come.

The stigmata were only one of many spiritual gifts Padre Pio received at this time. He also developed the powers of bilocation, healing, and prophecy and the ability to read minds. It was even reported that he was able to control the local weather.* Sometimes wondrous perfumes would fill the air when he entered a room, similar to the odors that emanated from his stigmata or objects that he touched.†

Padre Pio at first tried to conceal his stigmata by wearing gloves; but soon several physicians were summoned by monastery officials at San Giovanni Rotondo to examine the wounds when the priest couldn't hide them any longer. They almost unanimously agreed that Padre Pio's stigmata were not ordinary

---

*Although many saints have apparently been endowed with the ability to control the weather, this miraculous ability is rarely mentioned by hagiographers. Neither Thurston nor Summers mentions it in his writings. A few cases have been collected and published by the present author as an article in the July 1980 issue of Fate magazine.

†Case histories documenting all of these miracles are included in most biographies of Padre Pio, such as Charles Carty's Padre Pio—the Stigmatist (St. Paul, Minnesota: Radio Replies Press, 1955) and John Schug's Padre Pio (Huntington, Indiana: Our Sunday Visitor, 1976).

wounds. No conventional medical treatment healed them, and they extended completely through his hands.

Between 1918 and 1920 Padre Pio's stigmata were studied in depth by Dr. Luigi Romanelli, the chief of staff of the City Hospital of Barletta, Italy, at the request of monastery officials. Dr. Romanelli made a total of five examinations of the stigmata and submitted a report in November 1920. His conclusions read in part: [11]

Padre Pio has a very deep cut in the fifth intercostal space on the left side, 7 or 8 cms. long (about 2¾ or 3 inches), parallel to the ribs. The depth is great, but it is very difficult to ascertain. On his hand, there is an abundance of arterial blood. The borders of the wounds are not inflamed. They are very sensitive to the least pressure. The lesions in his hands are covered with a dark red membrane, but there is neither any edema (swelling) or any inflammation. When I pressed with my fingers on the palm and back of his hand there was a sensation of empty space. By pressing like that you cannot tell whether the wounds (on the front and back of the hands) are joined together, because the strong pressure causes the subject intense pain. However, I repeated the painful experiment several times, in the morning and in the evening, and I must admit that each time I came to the same conclusion.

The lesions of the feet have the same characteristics as those of the hands, but because of the thickness of the foot, it was difficult to experiment as accurately on the feet as on the hands.

I have examined Padre Pio five times in the course of fifteen months, and while I have sometimes noted some modifications in the lesions, I have never been able to classify them in any known clinical order.

Padre Pio's religious superiors verified that the wounds were apparently caused by fissures that penetrated directly through his hands. The head of the monastery even testified that, on occasions, he could actually see *through* Padre Pio's hand by staring into the wounds when they had stopped bleeding.

Another medical examination was made by Dr. Giorgio Festa, a physician from Rome, in October 1919. Festa found that the wounds in the priest's hands and feet, while resistant to normal healing, would become covered with a crusty scab which would periodically dissolve to permit blood flows. A new scab would then form over the open wound.

Festa also noted that the stigmata wounds passed entirely through Padre Pio's hands: "If I were to be interrogated by superior authorities on this particular question I would have to answer and confirm under oath, so much is the certitude of the impression received, that I would be able to read something or to see an object if it were placed behind the hand." [12]

Padre Alessio, a friar at San Giovanni Rotondo who was Padre Pio's assistant at the time of his death in 1968, was able to examine the stigmata as he helped Padre Pio to dress and undress, and even had to wash them on occasion. "The wounds were about as big as a penny," he later testified. "The wounds were very deep and they were covered with half-coagulated blood." Padre Alessio also corroborated that the wounds would often seal themselves with clotted blood.

The priest's personal physician for many years, Dr. Geuseppe Sala, subjected his patient to several blood tests, but was unable to find anything unusual about the blood or arrive at any explanation for the wonderful odor that so often perfumed it. He told the Reverend John Schug, an American priest and Padre Pio's biographer, that the wounds could not be considered psychogenic in nature, and that despite the fact that Padre Pio lost the equivalent of a cup of blood each day, he never showed any sign of anemia.

Padre Pio bore the stigmata until his death on September 23, 1968—three days after the fiftieth anniversary of his receiving the wounds. Although copious blood flows had issued from them for most of his life, the stigmata became less active at the very end of his life, when a thick serum would ooze from them instead of fresh blood.

Because the stigmata are a religious miracle, the Church has advanced a number of its own theories to explain their cause and nature. One proposal is that the stigmata are a "charism"—a sign given to an especially holy person in order to edify others spiritually. Another theory is that the miracle is granted to an ascetic to aid him, through the suffering the wounds bring, in his spiritual growth. A third explanation, and one rejected by many conservative Church leaders, is that the stigmata result from "mystical contemplation"—i.e., that they are basically an autosuggestive effect caused by deep religious fervor.

Plausible as these theories sound, none of them provide a truly convincing explanation for the stigmata. Neither of the first two takes into account the acknowledged relationship between the stigmata and hysterical personality disorders. A more serious objection is that if the stigmata were indeed a God-given wonder, one would expect that the location of the wounds on a stigmatic's body would correspond to the placement of Christ's own wounds. But in fact, they open in the *traditional* location of the Passion wounds. It is customary to portray the crucified Christ as being nailed to the cross through his feet and hands—the very areas from which all stigmatists bleed. Yet we know now that Christ was probably secured to the cross by nails inserted through his *wrists*. It was Roman practice to crucify criminals in this manner and skeletal remains dating from the time of Christ bear this out. Nails inserted through the palms of the hands cannot support the weight of a body suspended on a cross, and would simply rip through the flesh. Rather than a genuine impression of the Passion wounds, the stigmata therefore seem more accurately to be a stylized representation of them. This phenomenon is especially apparent in the case of Gemma Galgani, whose stigmata seemed to imitate the Passion wounds on the crucifix before which she prayed.

The "mystical contemplation" hypothesis was first proposed several decades ago by Dom Alois Mager, a Salzburg priest. Mager developed this theory on the premise that the mystical stigmata are in no way a preternatural event, but are similar to the false stigmata inducible through hypnosis and autosuggestion. As discussed earlier, however, this premise is extremely questionable, for whatever their nature, the stigmata are at least partially attributable to paranormal causes. Suggestion cannot produce holes to open in the hands, perfumes to emanate from blood, or blood to flow counter to gravity. Mager's theory *could* be tenable if we assumed that such an autosuggestive effect might take on a psychic dimension. This theory will be discussed at greater length later in this chapter.

Probably the most authoritative arguments against the divine nature of the stigmata were presented by Herbert Thurston, who rejected a purely religious interpretation of the miracle for the following reasons:

First, the stigmata were unknown to Christianity until the thirteenth century, when St. Francis of Assisi exhibited them. All cases of stigmata dating from that time must therefore be imitative in nature.

Second, the stigmata wounds do not appear in a consistent size, shape, or location. This would suggest that they are an auto-suggestive effect.

Third, the stigmata appear linked to hysteria.

Fourth, the wounds usually develop only after the sufferer has undergone several purgative illnesses that appear to be disorders of the central nervous system.

Fifth, although most stigmatists are also visionaries, a cross-subject comparison of their visions shows little consistency. Most of these visions are simply reenactments of traditional Passion stories and present no evidence that they are divine in nature.

Because many modern writers have misinterpreted Thurston, it should be stressed that he did *not* argue that the stigmata were a solvable mystery, but only tried to disprove the notion that the miracle had a divine etiology.

Thurston's general view—that the stigmata are the product of the sufferer's mind—has recently been reformulated by R. J. M. Rickard, a British authority on scientific anomalies and the editor of the *Fortean Times,* a periodical devoted to this subject. Rickard believes that possessing a hysterical personality may be only a pre-disposing factor leading to the development of the stigmata. The functional determinant in the appearance of the wounds, he suggests, is actually an extreme religious suggestibility.[13] The stigmata result, proposes Rickard, from a trauma "triggered by some profound conflict between bodily 'weakness' and the ideals of religious life." In other words, Rickard believes that the stigmatic wounds may be psychosomatically self-inflicted as a punishment when the sufferer cannot reconcile his own sexual urges or physical inability to adapt to the rigors of ascetic life with his perceived ideals of Christian living. Rickard admits, however, that his theory can explain only the psychological aspects of the stigmata, and while acknowledging that the phenomenon is complicated by genuinely paranormal elements, he has never attempted to explain their modus operandi or how they might interact with normal factors.

Rickard's idea also does not account for the fact that the stigmata are occasionally seen in people who are not genuinely ascetic and in some pathologically disturbed religious fanatics. The following two cases illustrate these variations.

The highly publicized case of Clorette Robinson, a ten-year-old black girl from Oakland, California, involved one of the very few Protestants who have borne the stigmata. The story was first reported by UPI on March 24, 1972. Clorette seems to have been a religious girl and was a member of the local New Light Baptist Church when the stigmata first appeared. The actual bleeding began on September 13, 1971, while she was attending her class at Santa Fe Elementary School. The school nurse later told reporters that Clorette came to her office that day complaining that she was bleeding from her palms. No cut was apparent, and the blood seemed to be seeping through the skin in the customary locations of the Passion wounds.

Clorette was then taken to Oakland's Kaiser Foundation Hospital. She was examined there by Dr. Ella Collier, a staff pediatrician, who later told reporters:

I wrapped Clorette's hand in a "boxing glove dressing." There was no way she could undo that bandage or slip anything inside to make her hand bleed. When I unwrapped it 18 hours later, there was blood all over the inside of the bandage. I cleaned her hand. Then as I watched, blood began to appear again. It started in a small pool the size of a pea and spread over the palm.[14]

Clorette was also examined by Dr. Joseph E. Lifschutz, a San Francisco Bay area psychiatrist. Neither he nor Dr. Collier could discover any signs of abnormality in Clorette's personality.

The symptoms intensified a few days later while Clorette was attending choir practice. Blood suddenly started flowing from her hands, feet, side, and forehead. Her parents rushed her to a local hospital, but the emergency room staff could do nothing to stop the bleeding, nor could they discover the source of the flows. The bleeding finally stopped altogether on March 31, and has apparently never resumed. Subsequent investigation has shown, though, that Clorette had been reading about the Crucifixion at the time the stigmata first appeared.

A second, more controversial case of stigmata has recently been reported from Spain. The sufferer, Clemente Dominguez, seems more a religious fanatic than a genuine contemplative. Dominguez currently lives in the town of Polmar de Troya, near Seville. He had religious aspirations as a youth and attended seminary school, but was never ordained, apparently because of his erratic personality and sexual promiscuity. He began to experience trances during which he claimed that the Blessed Virgin Mary appeared to him, and soon afterward founded his own version of a Catholic church.

Unlike Clorette's stigmata, Dominguez's wounds periodically open at the five traditional locations of the stigmata as well as from a ring of lesions impressed on his forehead. His stigmata appeared about the time his visions began and have been photographed on several occasions. Several photographs that have been published in England (see the Autumn 1979 issue of the *Fortean Times*) clearly show that the wound in his side is a deep fissure.

The subsequent history of Clemente Dominguez is certainly colorful. In 1973 he traveled to Rome, where his stigmata and visionary experiences impressed Father Petrus Ngo-dinh-Thue, an archbishop from Vietnam, so favorably that he ordained Dominguez a priest and, later, consecrated him a bishop! (This investiture was carried out in strict accordance with the canons of the Church.) On returning to Spain, Dominguez boasted of his ordination to the local bishop, who had refused to sanction his priesthood years earlier. Upon learning of the truth of Dominguez's situation, the Vatican was so shocked that they immediately excommunicated him.

Since that time, Dominguez has built up a considerable following in Polmar de Troya. Though recently blinded in an automobile accident, he still wears the vestments of a Catholic priest and celebrates Mass in his church. He has also ordained over three hundred priests. His stigmata appear now and then, usually when Dominguez enters his trances and while he is receiving "divine revelations" from the angelic ambassadors he claims to communicate with. The wounds close and disappear totally after each of these manifestations.

While the renegade bishop seems to be in some sense genuinely pious, his theatricality and flamboyance place him in a long line of hysterics whose personal idiosyncrasies have manifested themselves within a religious (and perhaps psychic) context.

In addition to these two anomalous examples, several other cases of stigmata have appeared during the past decade. Teresa Musco, a poor Italian seamstress who died in 1977, bore the stigmata for seven years, was subject to trances in the course of which she spoke strange languages, and even predicted the time of her own death. Teresa's stigmata mainly wounded her hands, and small holes extended completely through them. Additional holes later appeared in her feet. No rigor mortis set in after her death, and the stigmata wounds remained visible on her hands.

Another non-Catholic afflicted with the stigmata was Lucy Rael of Questa, New Mexico, who suddenly developed the wounds while attending a revival meeting in San Antonio in 1974. A convert to a Pentecostal church from Catholicism, Rael bled directly through the skin of her palms and feet, and suffered extreme pain. Doctors at Lutheran General Hospital in San Antonio have studied her wounds, but have been unable to find any medical cause for the bleeding.

A third case of modern-day stigmata is that of Sister Susan Kuruvilla, a fifty-year-old nun of the Orthodox Syrian Church of the East who currently lives in India. She has borne the stigmata on her palms, feet, and right breast since she was thirteen. The wounds, which are actual fissures in her flesh, bleed periodically on Tuesdays and Fridays and have never closed.

The case histories that have been presented in this chapter illustrate that, while the stigmata have a different physical appearance from person to person, the miracle does conform to certain stereotypical patterns in no matter what era or geographical location the miracle occurs. The student of the miraculous may not therefore really have to try to determine whether the stigmata is a psychological or a parapsychological phenomenon. It seems clear that it is a wonder that combines both psychological and psychic elements.

While the stigmata are a uniquely Christian miracle, they are in all likelihood not a God-given gift. A more acceptable explanation for this miracle can be formulated by combining elements from the views of Thurston, Mager, and Rickard. Each of these theorists has made notable contributions to our understanding of the stigmata, though none of them have arrived at a totally satisfactory solution to the mystery. Thurston was correct in believing that the stigmata are inherently psychogenic, at least to some extent; Rickard rightly proposed that a relationship exists between hysteria and the stigmata; and Mager provided an important clue when he proposed that the mystical stigmata are an autosuggestive effect brought about by intense contemplation.

The fact that the stigmata are most often impressed onto genuinely religious people who have devoted their lives to meditation and religious asceticism indicates that these individuals may suffer from what Thurston once called a "crucifixion complex." They are literally obsessed with the image of the crucified Christ. Through their own desire for suffering in the hope of spiritual growth, they literally *identify* themselves with the holy figure. This desire may well be the source of the mysterious and perhaps psychologically mediated illnesses so many stigmatists experience during their preparation for the religious life. Thus, individuals who are prone to hysteria (a disorder marked by the victims' unconscious desires for suffering) yet at the same time genuinely devout may be prime candidates for eventual stigmatization.

This interpretation suggests that the basic etiology of *simple* stigmata—i.e., those cases in which blood simply oozes through the skin—is in itself not miraculous. New discoveries in the fields of biofeedback and autogenic control have proved that the mind can control the body to a much greater degree than psychology has hitherto conceded. Through proper training, almost anyone can learn to alter the electrical conductivity of the skin, body temperature, and a number of other autonomic functions of the body. It therefore seems reasonable to assume that an ascetic in mystical contemplation, identifying with the crucified Christ figure, could, through unconscious autogenic control, cause small blood vessels under the skin to swell and break and induce superficial bleeding through the skin.

But such a process would constitute only the first step in the formation of the stigmata, which would develop when this purely psychological phenomenon took on a genuinely psychic cast. Most great stigmatics—such as Padre Pio, Therese Neumann, Gemma Galgani—have also possessed remarkable ESP and psychokinetic abilities. Could it be that they used their psychic abilities to *intensify* a basically psychogenic process, and in so doing form stigmata genuinely supernatural in nature?

In short, cases of classic (i.e., complex and supernatural) stigmata are most likely to occur when the victim is a contemplative who is prone to hysteria, but who also possesses great psychic powers. After the stigmata first appear, owing to the contemplative's intense identification with the crucified Christ figure, the sufferer literally directs psychokinesis onto his own body. This forces lesions to open in the flesh. Such a process might also cause the blood to flow counter to gravity and induce it to exude wondrous perfumes.

This theory can also explain why so many stigmatics exhibit supernatural inedia. Because of their hysterical dispositions, individuals such as Therese Neumann, Louise Lateau, and Domenica Lazzari probably suffered from anorexia nervosa, but through some psychic means affected the disorder so that it became genuinely miraculous and supernatural.

As was pointed out before, any explanation of the stigmata must be able to account for both its psychological and parapsychological dimensions. No theory based solely on religious apologetics or on academic psychology can do the job. As the science of parapsychology advances and as we learn more about man's psychic potentials, perhaps the mystery of the stigmata will become less enigmatic.

❧ IV ❧
BILOCATION

ON SEPTEMBER 22, 1774, Alfonso de Liguori was meditating and fasting in his cell at the Palace of Sant' Agata dei Goti in Arezzo, Italy. After several hours of contemplation he roused himself and announced to his fellow residents that Pope Clement XIV had just died. His story was naturally greeted with skepticism, since Rome was over a day's journey away and Alfonso hadn't left his cell. But soon afterward news arrived of Pope Clement's death, along with a report of how Alfonso had been seen at the bedside of the dying pontiff participating in prayer services.

This incident, which is mentioned in most biographies of St. Alfonso de Liguori (1696–1787), constitutes an example of bilocation—the supernatural gift possessed by some holy men to be in two places simultaneously. It shouldn't be presumed, though, that bilocating saints are sending only some apparitional or ethereal *representations* of themselves to far-off places during the production of this miracle. For according to traditional mystical lore, this "second self" is able to eat, drink, and carry out any physical act the body is capable of performing. In fact, according to Church doctrine, during the process of bilocation the human body is actually *duplicated* through the grace of God.

As is true of most miracles, bilocation is the subject of many anecdotes scattered throughout the lives of the saints. For example, St. Anthony of Padua (1195–1231) was preaching in the Church of St. Pierre du Queyroix at Limoges on Holy Thursday in 1226 when he remembered that he was obligated to conduct some services at a monastery on the other side of town. He knelt down and prayed, while his audience waited with due reverence. Meanwhile, across town, the monks at the monastery saw Anthony step forward from his stall, read the proper services, and retreat back into the shadows of the chapel. He thereupon arose from his prayers at Limoges and finished his sermon. Similar stories highlight the lives of St. Severus of Milan (d. 420), St. Ambrose (d. 397), and St. Clement (d. 97), all of whom were seen in their cells or at prayer while simultaneously appearing at funerals or deathbeds miles away.

Evidence documenting the existence of bilocation can be found in two different bodies of literature—the autobiographic accounts of those saints and ascetics who could produce the miracle, and the testimony of those witnesses who were present at the scenes of these visitations. Both sources, however, present unusual problems for the investigator. Self-delusion may well be a factor in the former, and eyewitness accounts by witnesses to the miracles are hard to come by. Thurston barely mentions bilocation in his otherwise authoritative *The Physical Phenomena of Mysticism;* while the late Montague Summers devotes only a few short paragraphs to the subject in his book of the same title.[1]

Despite these formidable obstacles, accounts of bilocation do appear in the canonization proceedings of many Catholic saints. Bilocation was a common feature, for instance, of the life of St. Martin de Porres. Born in 1579, he was first disavowed by his father, a Spanish general, because he had inherited the Negroid features of his mother. Later, however, his father saw to his education and Martin began work as a highly successful barber and physician. The call to religious life was too strong, however, and after only a few years Martin gave up his secular work to enter the monastery of the Holy Rosary in Lima, Peru, where he served as a *donado,* or lay helper. He rejected any formal study for the priesthood, since he wanted to live a life of ultimate humility by serving God in the most menial way possible. He lived at the monastery until his death in 1639, during which time numerous priests and monastery workers witnessed the miracles he performed. In addition to bilocation, these included healing and levitation.

An inquiry into Martin's miracles was begun in 1664 by a commission especially appointed by the archbishop of Lima. On the first day of hearings the commission recorded the testimony of sixty-six witnesses! Eleven more depositions were taken later in the year, and in 1678 delegates were sent to Peru from Rome to look into the matter further. The original documents containing these eyewitness testimonies of the saint's miracles include the *Processus ordinaria auctoritate fabricatus super sanctitae vitae, virtutibus heroicis et miraculis* (1664) and the *Beatificationis et canonizationis Servei Dei Fratis Martine Porres* (1712), both of which are housed in the archives of the Order of Friars Preachers, Santa Sabina, in Rome. Another source of information on the saint's bilocations is the *Responsio ad novas animadversiones R.P.D. fidei promotis super dubio an constet de virtutibus ecc.* issued in Rome in 1742. Also useful are the official volumes on St. Martin's beatification and canonization processes published in Italy in 1960 and 1962 respectively. (Martin de Porres was canonized only in 1957, though he had been popularly revered as a saint in Peru for years.)

St. Martin's feats of bilocation can be divided into two categories. The first would consist of his bilocations in and around Lima; the second, of those cases in which he appeared in distant countries. The *Responsio,* for example, cites several instances of his putative appearances in Japan and China, where a mysterious mulatto friar was seen teaching catechism to groups of children and distributing religious gifts and candy. The description of "the dark brother" matched that of Martin de Porres, who had often expressed a desire to travel to the Orient as a missionary, and even hoped to die there as a martyr.

One of the more unusual cases of bilocation in the *Responsio* concerns a Spanish traveler who had been imprisoned in Algiers by the Turks. On a visit to Lima he was shocked to encounter St. Martin at the monastery of the Holy Rosary. He was overwhelmed, for he recognized the mulatto as the mysterious apparition he had often seen in his locked prison cell and who frequently brought him food and money. The Spaniard even claimed that he had been able to pay off his ransom with the money the brother had supplied.

Martin de Porres's bilocations in and around Lima are even better documented. One of his friends, Brother Francis, had been suffering from a severe illness, which today would probably be diagnosed as pleurisy. One day, as the brother later testified, he suddenly became aware of St. Martin's presence in the room, although the door had been securely locked. The lay helper emerged from the shadows, bringing with him hot coals for a fire and a clean tunic. The figure remained quiet and responded very little when questioned; yet he sponged the ill man's body, remade his bed, and finally disappeared in a shadowy corner of the room.

Other members of the monastery of the Holy Rosary testified that when they would mentally summon Martin to their sickbeds, the apparition of the saint would attend them almost instantaneously. The apparition often brought medicines or uttered a few consoling words, usually about what prognosis to expect.

The most thoroughly documented of St. Martin's bilocations was chiefly witnessed by Martin's sister, Joan, though several other members of the de Porres family were present as well. The scene of the bilocation was a family reunion at the home of Joan and her husband. The festivities had been interrupted by a domestic squabble when Martin suddenly appeared at the door, laden with wine, cake, and fruit. On entering the house, he gathered all his relatives around him and to their amazement proceeded to summarize the argument that had just taken place and suggest how it might be resolved. The problem was settled amicably and the party was able to continue. Martin remained with his family for the night and left for Lima the next day. Joan herself traveled to Lima a few days later and told some of the monastery friars about her brother's timely appearance. They were astounded, for due to a large number of patients in the infirmary during the day in question, Martin had never left the monastery.

Although the testimony concerning St. Martin's bilocations in Lima seems more plausible than that supporting his long-distance appearances, the latter should not be understimated. Transcontinental bilocation is a recurring theme in the lore of this miracle. One continually reads in the lives of the great saints virtually identical accounts of how their apparitions were suddenly seen in some remote place, teaching catechism or distributing religious gifts, only to disappear just as quickly.

A typical example of this phenomenon is seen in the biography of the seventeenth-century Spanish nun Suor Maria Coronel de Agreda, whose levitations were briefly mentioned in Chapter Two. Her life was examined by Thurston in an article in the May 1939 issue of *The Month,* a Catholic magazine published in Great Britain. (This material was later incorporated into his posthumously published book *Surprising Mystics.*)[2]

Suor Maria was the abbess of the Franciscan convent of the Immaculate Conception at Agreda, where she served until her death in 1665. She was born in 1602 to a middle-class family in Agreda. Her brothers, and eventually even her father, became Franciscan friars, so she spent most of her childhood with her sister and mother. As a child she had visions and suffered a host of illnesses allegedly brought on by demonic attack; while she experienced ecstasies as a teen-ager. Maria also practiced the most rigid austerities, such as perpetual fasting, self-flagellation, and sleep deprivation. Her lifelong gift of visions encouraged her to write *The Mystical City of God* (1637–43), which is still considered a classic of mystical literature.

Suor Maria is said to have possessed three very different psychic abilities. She was highly telepathic, and would often respond to the mental commands of people around her, especially those of her religious superiors. She was also able to levitate. But her third talent, bilocation, is perhaps the most unusual. She apparently underwent some five hundred such experiences, which were thoroughly documented by Father Ximenes Samaniego, a friend who wrote a biography of her life, *Vida de la Ven. Madre Maria de Jesus.*

Many of Suor Maria's bilocations followed the same pattern. While praying in her convent cell, she would suddenly be transported to Mexico, where she would find herself instructing the local natives in the Catholic faith. During one of her bilocations she somehow became aware that a band of Franciscan missionaries was giving instruction in another location in Mexico. She thereupon directed the natives to them so that they could receive formal baptism. Ten years later, in 1630, Father Alonzo de Benavides, who was in charge of Catholic missionary activities in Mexico, returned to Spain with the strange story of how a group of Indians had sought him out. They told him that a mysterious woman had appeared to them, given them instruction, and urged them to seek baptism. Father Benavides later met Suor Maria and was soon convinced that she had been this woman. The priest received corroborative evidence directly from the nun, who was able to describe many areas of Mexico with which he himself was familiar. The priest recounts the story himself in his *Revised Memorial of 1634,* so this is no mere undocumented anecdote.

Suor Maria was, however, doubtful about the authenticity of her gift, fearing that her bilocations might actually be hallucinations, and so decided to "test" her experiences. After coming out of an ecstasy, she recalled how she had distributed rosaries to the Mexican natives. She searched her room only to find that her stock of rosaries had been depleted.

The bilocations of Suor Maria Coronel de Agreda are remarkably similar to those of Teresa Higginson, an English ascetic who lived two hundred years later.

Teresa Higginson is unique among mystics in that she led a secular, though devout, life. She was born in Lincolnshire, England, in 1844 and attended a convent school in Nottingham, which she left at the age of twenty-one to take up a vocation of teaching. She traveled from school to school for most of her life before settling at St. Catherine's Convent in Edinburgh, where she continued her work as an educator.

Although to her charges and most of her co-workers Higginson seemed to be a pleasant and "grandmotherly" schoolmistress, few realized that she led an intensely mystical private life. She suffered the stigmata, had many ecstatic visions, and was often the victim of demonic attacks of poltergeistery. What we know of her miracles comes through the testimony of her roommates, from the few fellow teachers who were lucky enough to develop close bonds of affection with her, and through the many letters she sent to her spiritual advisors at their bidding. These letters, written at great length and in minute detail, were sent over the course of her life and represent an almost continuous autobiographical account of the inner life of a mystic. Much of her correspondence was collected by Cecil Kerr, who used them to construct his biography *Teresa Helena Higginson—Servant of God* (1926).

Higginson described her bilocations in two lengthy letters written in January 1882 to Father Edward Powell, the rector of St. Alexander's, Bottle, who was her spiritual advisor from 1879 to 1883. Like Suor Maria Coronel de Agreda, Higginson was often confused about the nature of her bilocations. "At first she tried to persuade herself that she was being deluded," writes Kerr, "and never spoke of her strange experiences, but at last their reality impressed itself so deeply on her mind that she felt bound by her obedience to relate them to her director." [3]

In her first letter, Higginson described what she believed had been a bilocation to Africa and gave a touching account of her experience during the miracle:

Well for some length of time I have from time to time found myself among the negroes, but how I am transported thither I really cannot say—I mean that I do not feel myself going (just as a person might close their eyes and when they opened them again they found themselves in a different place) not in spirit but personally present. I find myself with them whom it pleases our dear Divine Lord I shall assist, and yet I am able to continue where I was and go on with the duties I was performing here. I have all along tried to persuade myself that I was deceived and yet I feel so positive of what I did. It is not always the same place that I visit nor the same people, though I have (been) most of all with a tribe whose chief is lately deceased, and whose name is Jaampooda. He and his people were savages and lived by hunting I should imagine, by the furs and ivory which they possessed in great abundance. It is now over four years since I first visited these people and they were stricken down by a sickness which turned their bodies purple and black, and of which many of them died; then I did all I could to relieve their bodily suffering, and I was instructed to gather some bark off a tree which grew commonly there and make a beverage for them and which I understand they call bitter waters and waters of life.

Later in this same letter, Higginson related her puzzlement upon realizing that she could communicate with the natives even though she could not (normally) speak their language, nor they hers: "This has astonished me a little that I perfectly understand all that they wish to communicate to me, and they comprehend all that I say to them of the dear, good God."

She also tells of her presence at the death of the tribe's chief:

It is about three weeks since the chief of whom I have before spoken, died, and I felt that he needed help and I asked my dear good angel to comfort him in my name, and on the Monday evening I said a special prayer for him, for I felt that he was dying or in great need, and I presently found myself by his side. I heard him distinctly call me and beg of God through that infinite Wisdom enshrined in his adorable Head to guide me to his side; and when I took out the crucifix, he took hold of it and pressed it with reverential love to his heart . . . and I tried to comfort his people and console him and he asked me to leave him his sign for man's redemption till he should stand before that Jesus whom it represents dying in ignominy and shame. And then I hardly knew what to do, I mean I did not like to refuse him and still I felt that I had only the use of it and I should ask of you before I did so. Then the thought came that this would be some sort of a proof to me whether it was a reality or if I was being deceived, for although things that happened seemed to me to be so strange yet I could not but believe them to be realities. So I left him the crucifix and on Wednesday I again found myself with Jaampooda and I stayed with him till he died.

There is an interesting sequel to this story which tentatively substantiates it. Higginson was disturbed about leaving the cross, because although it had been offered to her as a gift by a priest, she had accepted it only as a loan. Although Higginson was in the habit of saying nothing about her bilocations, a fellow teacher who was living with her at the time later testified that one Wednesday night at dinner Higginson, radiant with joy, whispered to her, "I have got back my crucifix." The teacher had no idea what she meant, but it would seem that Higginson had miraculously recovered the crucifix she had left in Africa via bilocation a few days before.

In a second letter to Powell, Higginson told of giving instruction to a savage race of primitive people in some unknown wilderness. (She was later able to ascertain that she had visited a Hottentot tribe in Africa.) There she watched a human sacrifice, but also baptized several children. In another series of bilocations, she goes on to explain, she found herself aiding the dying or taking part in religious services:

I have on several occasions taken the most holy Sacrament to the dying, twice to nuns and once to a poor priest who communicated himself, and twice to young people. I have taken the ciborium from churches where the sacred particles were consecrated by sacrilegious hands (I think in Germany) and taken it where I have been instructed. I don't know how the others received, I mean by whose hands, but in each case I stayed with them till they died, and I have always been careful about replacing the sacred vessel. I have been often at death-beds and joined with the good angel in helping the struggling soul to defeat its archenemy. And God sent me once by night into a prison to a young man who was praying that his innocence might be proved and that he might be restored to his friends, and God told me to tell him that He had heard his prayer, and would graciously grant his petition.

The experiences of these Christian ascetics do not stand alone as evidence documenting the existence of bilocation. This phenomenon is equally known in Hindu, Buddhist, and Tantric literature, where the bilocating feats of the great swamis and yogis parallel the miracles of the saints to a remarkable degree.

A recent attempt to verify the phenomenon of yogic bilocation took place in the early 1970s, when two researchers from the New York–based American Society for Psychical Research, Karlis Osis and Erlendur Haraldsson, undertook a series of field trips to India to explore the range and frequency of psychic phenomena there.[4] During one of their trips, Osis and Haraldsson were able to document at least one well-witnessed bilocation feat of Satya Sai Baba, then a forty-nine-year-old religious leader living in southern India. Baba, whose life story has been told by a number of Western biographers,* is best known for his alleged ability to materialize small objects out of thin air during his public appearances and to produce holy ash from an empty bowl. He can also purportedly read the minds of his followers and, of course, claims the ability to bilocate himself.

The incident Osis and Haraldsson studied occurred in 1965. The bilocation took place at the home of a Mr. Ram Mohan Rao, the director of a technical school in Manjeree, Kerala, many miles away from where Baba was staying at the time. One day Sai Baba appeared at Rao's door and bade him invite his neighbors over. "A sadhu who looked like Sai Baba (whom they had seen only in pictures) was present in the school director's house for over an hour," the two investigators report, "sang some Sai Baba songs with them, produced holy ash in the way characteristic of Sai Baba, handled objects and gave presents which the hosts still have. A few months after this incident a local investigator showed a picture of Sai Baba to a high school girl who had been present and asked, 'Who is this man?' With no hesitancy she answered that she had seen him at the school director's house."

---

*See, for instance, A. Schulman's *Baba* (New York: Viking Press, 1971) and Howard Murphet's *Sai Baba, Man of Miracles* (London: Frederick Muller, 1971).

After hearing this story, Osis and Haraldsson tried to track down any available witnesses. They were eventually able to locate eight observers, three of whom were children at the time of the miracle. Although the incident had occurred ten years earlier, and the accounts of the witnesses were somewhat inconsistent, the researchers claimed that they were able to establish that at the time of his supposed visit to Rao, Sai Baba was on the other side of the Indian peninsula at the palace of Vankatagiri, where records verified his visit.

Despite the convincing nature of the evidence collected, the case for Baba's bilocation is not unassailable. Even Osis and Haraldsson admit that at least two of the witnesses at Rao's residence doubted that the strange visitor really was Sai Baba. There is, in addition, some indication that Sai Baba often deliberately fakes his purported miracles. (When films taken of some of his exhibitions are slowed down, it is clear that he is quite an expert at sleight-of-hand.) It therefore seems possible that Sai Baba may have hired a confederate to pose as himself in Kerala. Since none of Rao's neighbors had previously seen or met Baba, such a stunt could have come off rather easily, and the Hindu miracle worker could count on it to generate added publicity and new converts.

Osis and Haraldsson were able to document a much more impressive example of bilocation while examining the purported abilities of a mystic who calls himself Dadaji. Though not as well known in the West as Sai Baba, Dadaji, too, is venerated as a saint by his large group of followers in southern India. Dadaji began his public career as a singer and businessman, but left these worldly occupations to study yoga in an ashram in the Himalayas. He reappeared in public life some time later under the assumed name of Dadaji, which means "elder brother."

Early in 1970 Dadaji visited Allahabad, a city four hundred miles from his home, where he stayed with a family of devotees. After spending a period of time alone in the prayer room of the house, he told his followers that he had bilocated to Calcutta. He then instructed his hostess to contact her sister-in-law (who lived there) to confirm his story, giving her the address of the house to which he had bilocated.

In due course it was discovered that the family in question had indeed witnessed the bilocation. They reported that at the time of Dadaji's meditation, several of them had seen a mysterious apparition in their house. The chief observer was the daughter of the family, Roma Mukherjee, who was a devotee of Dadaji. She personally told Osis and Haraldsson that she had been in the study reading a book when Dadaji's apparition first became visible. Initially he was partially transparent, but then he solidified. Mukherjee screamed, which immediately alerted her brother and mother. Dadaji motioned her to remain quiet and to bring him a cup of tea.

When she returned to the study with the tea [reported Osis and Haraldsson] Roma was followed by her mother and physician brother. She reached in through the partly opened door and gave Dadaji the tea and a biscuit. The mother, through a crack in the door, saw Dadaji; the brother, standing in a different position, only saw Roma's hand reach in through the opening and come back without the tea. There was no place she could have set the cup without entering the room. Then the father, a bank director, came home from doing the morning shopping at the bazaar. He didn't believe what they told him and, brushing away their objections, peeked in through the crack in the door and saw a man's figure sitting on a chair.

The family remained in the living room, but kept the study within view. When they heard a noise from within they entered, only to find Dadaji gone. Half the tea and biscuit had been consumed, and a half-burned cigarette—Dadaji's favorite brand—was found on a table.

Osis and Haraldsson interviewed all the individuals involved in the case and found that their testimonies were reasonably consistent. It is also worth noting that while Roma was a follower of Dadaji, the rest of the family was not. For this reason a collective hoax seems unlikely.

Yogic and Catholic doctrine differ, however, on the matter of the mechanics of bilocation. The latter teaches that the human body is physically duplicated during the miracle. (This idea was perhaps best expressed in a famous statement purportedly made by St. Martin de Porres in response to a question about his bilocation: "If God can multiply the loaves and fishes, why couldn't he duplicate me?") Tantric and yogic literature, however, takes a more complicated view, basing its explanation of the phenomenon on the existence of an ethereal "double" that is housed within the body and can be exteriorized through practice. Once liberated, the "soul body" (*Linga Sharira*) can travel about to distant locations and even make itself visible. The concept of the *Linga Sharira* is an ancient doctrine, and even Patanjali mentioned its ability to leave the body in his *Yoga Sutras*. Later yogic texts detail rigorous breathing exercises through which the *Linga Sharira* can be physically ejected.

The soul body or human "double" is not exclusively a Hindu concept, for it in fact resembles an entire set of phenomena that parapsychologists have collectively labeled the out-of-body experience, or the OBE.

When undergoing an OBE, an individual will find that his mind or consciousness has left his body and is functioning independently of it. He might be resting in bed on the verge of sleep, for instance, when he will suddenly realize that he is cataleptic. A moment later he will find himself "floating" over his bed and looking down at his body. If the experience continues, he will often be able to move about the room and even travel to nearby locations. While out of body, the individual will generally perceive himself as an apparition. If, however, another person actually sees this "double," one might say that a bilocation has taken place. This theory seems to be borne out by a number of reports of instances in which a person undergoing an OBE was indeed visible to the people he attempted to visit.

An interesting case of this very type was published in 1963 in the *Journal* of the Society for Psychical Research, a London-based organization devoted to the study of psychic phenomena.[5] Lucian Landau, an English inventor and industrialist, is married to a woman who is peculiarly prone to having OBEs. Landau first became interested in these experiences when he discovered that they occasionally contained a veridical element:

I knew my wife, Eileen, for quite a number of years before we were married and she frequently used to talk to me about her out-of-body experiences. These were of the usual kind and on some occasions I was able to verify that something paranormal had, in fact, occurred. For example, she went to bed one afternoon, saying that she would see what our friend, who was on a holiday in Cornwall, was doing. When she woke up, she was able to give an accurate description of a rock plant, which our friend was photographing, the details of the surroundings, also of a gentleman who was with him. All this was subsequently confirmed.

Landau was further impressed when he learned that their friend had had an "impression" of a presence passing him at the time of the psychic visit.

In September 1955 Eileen paid an extended visit to her future husband. He had fallen ill and she wished to care for him, so she stayed in a guest room across a verandah from his own. Since she claimed that at night she would find herself projecting to his room from her own, they decided to conduct an experiment. Landau wanted to determine if Eileen could bring a physical object with her when she induced her next OBE.

The night of the experiment, Landau awoke suddenly. It was almost dawn, and light was beginning to come in through the windows. He then realized that an apparition of Eileen was in the room with him:

The figure was moving slowly backward toward the door, but it was otherwise quite motionless; it was not walking. When the figure, progressing at the rate of about one foot per five seconds, reached [the landing] I got out of bed and followed. I could then clearly see the moving figure, which was quite opaque and looking like a living person, but for the extreme pallor of the face, and at the same time the head of Eileen, asleep in her bed, the bedclothes rising and falling as she breathed. I followed the figure, which moved all the time backward, looking straight ahead, but apparently not seeing me. I kept my distance and ultimately stood in the door of the spare bedroom, when the figure, now having reached a position inside the doorway, suddenly vanished. There was no visible effect on Eileen, who did not stir, and whose rhythm of breathing remained unchanged.

On returning to his room Landau found a rubber dog on the floor by his bed. The toy normally rested on a chest in the room across the verandah.

While Landau was observing her passage through the house, Eileen was indeed undergoing an OBE. As she later testified:

I remember getting out of bed (but do not recall exactly how), going over to my desk, and seeing the diary. As a child, I had been told never to handle other people's letters or diaries, so probably for this reason I did not want to touch this one. Instead, I lifted my rubber toy dog, and I remember taking it through the door, across the landing, to the other room, but do not remember actually *walking*. I did not find the dog heavy, or difficult to hold. I have no recollection of what I finally did with it. I remember seeing Lucian asleep and breathing normally. I felt very tired and wanted to go back to bed. Up to this moment my consciousness appeared to me normal, and so did my ability to see my surroundings, which also appeared normal to me. I do not remember anything about going backward to my room, or entering my bed.

This case demonstrates that the out-of-body self can transport physical objects as it travels. Eileen Landau's OBE therefore lends support to the bilocations of Teresa Higginson and Maria Coronel de Agreda, who apparently carried religious items with them as they traveled to their destinations.

This incident has been specifically cited since the present author has corresponded with Mr. Landau for several years. His good faith and his ability to meticulously evaluate both his own psychic experiences and those told to him by others have been obvious during these interchanges.

There are other evidential cases of bilocation-type OBEs throughout the literature of psychical research, some of which seem almost indistinguishable from the classic bilocations of the saints. The most famous of these is the S. R. Wilmot case, which occurred in 1863.

Wilmot was sailing from Liverpool to New York when a fierce storm broke out in the Atlantic. It lasted over a week, and was so savage that it continually threatened the safety of the ship. It was during this harrowing time that Wilmot had a strange "dream" in which he saw his wife visit him. As he testified in his SPR (Society for Psychical Research) deposition:

Upon the night following the eighth day of the storm the tempest moderated a little, and for the first time since leaving port I enjoyed refreshing sleep. Toward morning I dreamed that I saw my wife, whom I had left in the United States, come to the door of my stateroom, clad in her night-dress. At the door she seemed to discover that I was not the only occupant of the room, hesitated a little, then advanced to my side, stooped down and kissed me, and after gently caressing me for a few moments, quietly withdrew.

Upon waking I was surprised to see my fellow-passenger, whose berth was above mine, but not directly over it—owing to the fact that our room was at the stern of the vessel—leaning upon his elbow, and looking fixedly at me. "You're a pretty fellow," said he at length, "to have a lady come and visit you in this way." I pressed him for an explanation, which he at first declined to give, but at length related what he had seen while wide awake, lying in his berth. It exactly corresponded with my dream. . . .

The day after landing I went by rail to Watertown, Conn., where my children and my wife had been for some time, visiting her parents. Almost her first question when we were alone together was, "Did you receive a visit from me a week ago Tuesday?" "A visit from you?" said I. "We were more than a thousand miles at sea." "I know it," she replied, "but it seemed to me that I visited you." "It would be impossible," said I. "Tell me what makes you think so."

My wife then told me that on account of the severity of the weather and the reported loss of the *Africa,* which sailed for Boston on the same day that we left Liverpool for New York, and had gone ashore at Cape Race, she had been extremely anxious about me. On the night previous, the same night when, as mentioned above, the storm had just begun to abate, she had lain awake for a long time thinking of me, and about four o'clock in the morning it seemed to her that she went out to seek me. Crossing the wide and stormy sea, she came at length to a low, black steamship, whose side she went up, and then descending into the cabin, passed through it to the stern until she came to my stateroom. "Tell me," said she, "do they ever have staterooms like the one I saw, where the upper berth extends further back than the under one? A man was in the upper berth, looking right at me, and for a moment I was afraid to go in, but soon I went up to the side of your berth, bent down and kissed you, and embraced you, and then went away."

The description given by my wife of the steamship was correct in all particulars, though she had never seen it. I find by my sister's diary that we sailed October 4th; the day we reached New York, 22nd; home, 23rd.

An account of the case was published in the *Proceedings* of the Society for Psychical Research along with Wilmot's testimony from his sister, who had accompanied him on the trip and who recalled how Wilmot's cabin mate had questioned her about the incident directly after it had happened. A description by Mrs. Wilmot of her OBE was also included.[6]

There can be no doubt that veridical OBEs do take place. But the key issue at stake is whether the classical OBE and saintly bilocation can be considered analogous phenomena. This is a debatable point, since there are several differences between them:

(1) A bilocation experience can last for a lengthy period of time. OBEs are of rather brief duration.

(2) During a bilocation, the mystic is able to converse, interact, carry physical objects, and perform physical acts (such as making beds). During an OBE, the experiencer usually cannot either communicate well, if at all, or interact with his environment.

(3) Bilocators usually find themselves instantaneously translocated to their points of destination. OBE voyagers most often have a sense of traveling after first finding themselves liberated from their bodies.

(4) Bilocators never actually experience "leaving the body." People undergoing OBEs almost always do.

(5) The witnesses to a bilocation miracle usually have the impression that they are interacting with a real person. People who have seen OBE apparitions often note that the figure is partially immaterial.

Despite the fact that these phenomena seem to possess distinctive sets of characteristics, some psychics who can deliberately induce the OBE can often also produce bilocation-type effects as a consequence of their projection attempts. A number of these effects indicate that these psychics are in some sense actually *materially* present in two locations at the same time during their experiences.

This "dual material presence" was demonstrated during a series of experimental explorations of the OBE conducted by the Psychical Research Foundation in Durham, North Carolina, in 1973. The Foundation was, at the time, a research institute housed in three small buildings situated next to one of the two Duke University campuses. It was founded in 1960 by C. E. Ozanne, a wealthy businessman who was interested in determining whether parapsychology could solve the mystery of life after death, with the proviso that it dedicate itself to studying those psychic phenomena that are directly related to this question. Over the past two decades the institute has chiefly researched apparitions, hauntings, mediumistic communications, and similar phenomena. The long-time project director of the foundations is W. G.

Roll, a Danish-born but British-educated parapsychologist who has had a long-time interest in the issue of survival after death.

In 1973 the foundation received a sizable grant to study the OBE, and was able to conduct two years of research with a twenty-year-old Duke undergraduate named S. Keith Harary, who claimed that he could induce OBEs at will. "Blue," as Harary was known to his friends, eventually demonstrated that he could OBE himself to distant buildings and see who was there, correctly read letters written on posters hung on the walls, and make animals react to his presence.[7]

The animal reactions actually came closest to proving that Blue could become materially located in two places simultaneously. These experiments were designed by Dr. Robert Morris, who was PRF's director of research at the time, to test Blue's claim that he could make animals "see" his out-of-body self while he was having his OBEs. The "kitten experiments," as they have come to be known, were run as follows:

Blue would be taken to a location about a half-mile from the foundation headquarters—usually to a room at Duke University where an isolation booth had been set up. He would be instructed to enter the booth, relax, and then induce an OBE when asked to do so by an experimenter stationed with him. He was then to project himself to PRF headquarters and to a special lab room where his pet kitten was being observed. This room contained an oblong board ($30'' \times 80''$) marked off into 24 ten-inch squares. Before the test began, the kitten was placed on the board and an experimenter kept track of how many squares it stepped across and how many times it vocalized. These measurements constituted a base-line "animal activity rate" for the kitten. During each run of the experiment, which lasted approximately an hour, a phone in the lab would ring four times. Each ring alerted the experimenter to the possibility that Blue might be projecting himself to the cat. In actuality, though, Blue only made two OBE attempts per experiment. The other two segments were used as control periods. The goal of the tests was to see if Blue's presence would be detected by his pet, which—it was thought—would alter its behavior rate when being visited.

This test was conducted several times. After the series was

completed, the experimenters compared the kitten's preexperimental base-line activity rate to (1) the control periods when Blue was not projecting himself to the cat and (2) those test periods when Blue reported that he had bilocated to his pet.

The results were startling. During the control and base-line periods the kitten was frisky and would dart about the board and meow often. But each time Blue projected to it, the animal would become calm, move very little, and purr quietly—the same reactions it would have when Blue *physically* approached it.

That Blue was somehow *physically present* in the PRF lab when he projected to the cat was also suggested by a number of other observations made during the tests. Several of the experimenters could often *feel* Blue's presence in the room during his projections, and one even claimed that he actually had seen Blue's apparition. His apparition was once even visible on a closed-circuit TV that was monitoring an experiment!

Blue's apparent ability to physically project some aspect of his mind during his OBEs suggests that bilocation may indeed be an extremely enhanced form of OBE that gifted psychics can occasionally produce. The bilocations of Padre Pio provide further convincing support for this theory.

Along with his stigmata, Padre Pio's bilocation talents were probably his best-known miracles. Many letters and reports testifying to them are on file at San Giovanni Rotondo. One biographer of the Capuchin priest claims that his bilocating double was seen at various times in his life throughout Italy, in Austria, in Uruguay, and even in Milwaukee, Wisconsin.

Padre Pio's bilocations took a variety of forms. Some resembled conventional OBEs in that only the priest's "spiritual presence" was felt by the individuals to whom he was projecting. Yet others involved actual appearances of Padre Pio's double. And, as in the following instance, he seemed to have possessed St. Martin de Porres's ability to serve physically at the bedside of the sick and infirm.

One of Padre Pio's most devoted followers was Monsignor Damiani, vicar general of the diocese of Salto, Uruguay. In 1929 he visited Foggia and entreated Padre Pio to promise to attend his bedside when it was time for him to die. Padre Pio agreed, but warned Monsignor Damiani that he would die in Uruguay, and not in Italy as he expected. Padre Pio's promise and prophecy were not to be fulfilled until 1942. One of the witnesses to the strange drama that took place in Uruguay that year was Antonio Maria Barbiere, the archbishop of Montevideo, Uruguay, who writes:

In 1942 Bishop Alfredo Viola of Salto celebrated his Silver Sacerdotal Jubilee and at the same time had the laying of the cornerstone of his minor seminary. The Apostolic delegate and five Bishops lodged in the episcopal residence. On the vigil of the Jubilee, about midnight, I was awakened by a knocking at my door. The door was open about a foot. I saw a Capuchin pass by and heard a voice: "Go to the room of Msgr. Damiani; he is dying." I arose, put on my cassock, called the other Bishops and some priests, and we went to the room of the Monsignor. On his night table I found a slip of paper written by Msgr. Damiani: "Padre Pio came."

Monsignor Damiani had indeed suffered an attack of angina pectoris, from which he later died.

In 1949 the archbishop himself traveled to Foggia with thirty-eight members of his diocese. During his trip he had an audience with Padre Pio and made confession. As he later reported:

"Now today, when I spoke to Padre Pio after confession a little while ago," he subsequently reported, "I asked him: 'Padre Pio, were you the Capuchin whom I saw in the residence of the Bishop of Salto, the night Msgr. Damiani died?' Padre Pio was embarrassed and did not answer although he easily could have said, No. When I insisted and he still would not answer I laughed and said: 'I understand.' Padre Pio nodded and answered: 'Yes, you understood.' "[8]

Many people who lived in or around Foggia have testified to Padre Pio's bilocations. Many of these visitations were apparently prompted by letters from his parishioners, who often begged him to heal their sick relatives. One such case was reported by Signora Ersilia Magurna, who had written Padre Pio in February 1947, asking him to help cure her husband of a flu attack that had been so aggravated by complications that the man was now in a coma. Signora Magurna sent a telegram on February 27 repeating her request. At seven thirty the next morning, her husband awoke cured. He claimed that Padre Pio, whom he had never met in the flesh, had "just left the room" with the apparition of another monk. They had informed Magurna that his fever would ebb and that he would be cured in a few days. Signora Magurna testified that a strong scent of violets gradually pervaded the room as her husband related his story. She interpreted this as a sure sign that Padre Pio had been there, since a similar odor was known to emanate from his stigmata.

The Magurnas made a journey to Foggia that July, at which time they finally met Padre Pio. Signor Magurna immediately recognized him as the apparition that had appeared in his room. Padre Pio similarly recognized the man whom he had aided.[9]

In several cases, Padre Pio actually left physical traces of his bilocations at the sites of his visitations. A sick woman in the town of Borgomanero once petitioned Padre Pio to cure her, and the priest subsequently bilocated to her bedside. When she asked him to leave her some evidence of his visit, he placed his stigmatized hand on the edge of her bed. Five bloodstains were left impressed on it, each in the shape of a cross. The linen is still on public display in Borgomanero.

Padre Pio's colleagues have also contributed some interesting corroborative testimony concerning his bilocations. Many of his fellow priests often saw him become distracted and almost enter into a trance. He would appear to be giving the last rites or hearing a confession during these phases. Several witnesses to these episodes believed that they were witnessing the terrestrial side of a bilocation.

Padre Pio, unfortunately, spoke very little about his bilocations and left no personal accounts of the process. When once specifically questioned on the subject, he would only say that bilocation occurs through the "extension of the personality."

Another present-day bilocating mystic is Natuzza Evolo, an illiterate Calabrian peasant woman whose remarkable talents also include the abilities to see spirits of the dead and to diagnose illnesses. She is also a stigmatist, whose wounds appear as large cross-shaped indentations on her wrists and feet. She was born in 1924 in the city of Paravati, where she still lives with her husband and five children. Since 1974 her powers have been studied by Professor Valerio Marinelli, a professor of engineering at the University of Calabria, who collected and documented (as far as possible) some fifty-two cases of Natuzza's bilocations. These were published as part of a privately printed booklet, A Study of the Bilocative Phenomena of Natuzza Evolo (1979).

It is clear from Marinelli's study that Natuzza is a devoutly religious Catholic whose powers are quite similar to the "miraculous" talents of the great saints of the Church. As well as possessing the stigmata, which were impressed on her when she was only ten years old, she often experiences visions in which she relives the agony of Christ.

While it can be debated whether her stigmata and visions are in any sense actually paranormal, one phenomenon related to the former certainly ranks as one of the more bizarre variations of the stigmata. Marinelli calls this wonder "hemography," which might be defined as the paranormal patterning of bloodstains on cloth. Marinelli cites several cases which report how Evolo's wounds, when wiped with a cloth or handkerchief, stained the fabric with splotches of blood which then rearranged to form religious emblems, letters, and figures! One eyewitness account of this process was given by Giovanna Chiari, a schoolteacher known to Marinelli:

It was Holy Monday three years ago; Natuzza was at Catanzaro at my house, and besides myself and her, there were my sisters Nella and Rosetta. All of a sudden we noticed that the wound on Natuzza's wrist was bleeding, so we asked her to produce a hemography for a young man I knew who wanted an example. (Natuzza gives her hemographies to whoever asks her, as long as it forms itself.) For about ten to fifteen minutes Natuzza held to her wrist a white handkerchief I had given to her, with the name of the owner written on it; after that she gave me back the handkerchief. I opened it and saw some bloodstains; I put it on the table, and we all waited for the formation of the design. Slowly, the blood started to move to one side of the handkerchief and vertically spell out the name S. Valeriano Martire. The bloodstain that was left then started to move as well and formed the figure of a saint, which we interpreted to be St. Valeriano. When we read this name, Natuzza exclaimed, "Who is this saint? Does he exist?" When I gave the handkerchief to the owner, I found out that he was devoted to that saint.*

---

*These sections from Marinelli's books have been edited by the present author for clarity.

Because Natuzza is totally illiterate, the intelligent formation of words and letters in the blood must be considered a marvel in its own right.*

During the five years he has known Evolo, Marinelli has collected over fifty firsthand reports (representing fifty-two different cases) from witnesses who have been "visited" by the psychic. Under the rubric of bilocation Marinelli includes a wide assortment of phenomena, which range from simple types of OBEs to actual bilocations. In eighteen cases Evolo's apparition was seen by the witnesses. In eight additional cases, apparitions of the dead accompanied her visual or invisible presence. Evolo's voice was heard, but no apparition seen, in some half-dozen other instances. Evolo's bilocating self carried out physical activities (including such phenomena as pulling the witness's hair, pushing over a vase of flowers, starting a clock, and slamming a door) in thirteen instances. In nine cases the apparition *left bloodstains at the scene of the bilocations.*

These latter examples cannot be easily dismissed as the result of hallucination. The bloodstains either were left behind as a handprint or took on the appearance of religious designs similar to her hemographs. They cannot therefore be discounted as chance marks or stains previously overlooked by the witnesses.

The following is a typical case of one of these visitations, which Marinelli summarizes from the testimony submitted to him by a fellow professor:

In August 1975, Professor Jole Gualtiere was in Sicily, at Castellamare del Golfo, in the district of Trapani.

Waking up one morning, she found bloodstains on the sheet and on the cushion of her bed. They did not seem to her [to be] stains, as she had no wounds. As she knew that Natuzza had the power of leaving bloodstains, she phoned her husband, engineer Leonardo do Romano, who

---

*Imbert-Gourbeyre observed on several occasions a phenomenon virtually identical to Evolo's hemography with his patient Palma Matarelli, who was discussed in the previous chapter. For example, he writes in *La Stigmatisation* (Volume I, p. 567), "I have further seen the blood trickle from the circlet of punctures upon her forehead, and as it was caught in the handkerchief I held under it I watched it trace out emblems. . . ." In a letter to a Catholic newspaper in France (*Voix prophétiques,* fifth edition, Volume II, p. 445) he reported that Matarelli once wiped the blood from her stigmatic wounds and that "this wiping left upon the linen not single blood stains, but emblems clearly outlined, representing inflamed hearts, nails, and swords. This is truly a marvel and I saw it with my own eyes."

was at Vibo Valentia, in Calabria, and told him these precise words: "Go to Natuzza, at Paravati, and ask her to narrate something to you." Jole did not say anything else, because she wanted to see if her hypothesis—that is, that it had been Natuzza—was correct. When Leonardo arrived at Paravati, Natuzza met him at the door saying: "I knew you would come; I have been waiting since this morning. Last night I visited your wife, in Sicily, and left some bloodstains on the bed, and some fingerprints with which I touched the sheet." When Leonardo arrived home, he immediately telephoned his wife, who recognized with amazement the bloody fingerprints, a detail that she had not realized before. Natuzza then explained to Jole that she had visited her with a deceased person, whom Jole identified [from the discription] as her father.

Offering information about her bilocative visit before being informed of a witness's experience seems to be a favorite habit of Evolo's. The following report, which represents another typical example of this pattern, is also a more classic type of bilocative experience. It was given to Marinelli by Father Concezio Galloro, the guardian of the Convent of Minor Friars of San Marco Argentano. Father Concezio was living in Melicucco at the time of the incident, a town some twenty-five kilometers from Evolo's residence in Paravati.

It is some time now since I have completed some research on the history and the location of the antique Basilican churches in Calabria. They are very antique churches dating back to the immediate centuries after Christ, built by the monks of Saint Basilio, who was the founder of the oriental monachism. These monks, of Greek-Byzantine origins, had established themselves during that period in southern Italy. In particular I had identified the location of the Basilican church called Martirion, dating back to the sixth or seventh century, inside the gardens of the Buongiorno Palace at Santa Maria di Capistrano. Inside this garden exists an antique garden basin that I thought was the convent's reservoir. Another thing struck me: The Buongiorno family, owners of the palace, was completely extinct; and to the Vittorio Brizzi family, the subsequent buyer of the palace, befell a series of misfortunes in very little time. I was afraid that there might have been some connection between the mysterious misfortunes and the holiness of the place.

Having heard talk of Natuzza, one day I went to visit her in the month of March, about ten or twelve years ago, together with my friend Father Don Domenico Manfrida. Natuzza did not know how to answer me, but told me that she would have to ask the souls or an angel and she would then let me know something. Time passed and I forgot about my conversation with Natuzza. One morning, at daybreak, I had just woken up and was still in bed when I saw Natuzza in my room at the foot of my bed. Natuzza said to me: "Father Concezio, there are legacies, up and down."

The priest understood Evolo's message, since "legacies" (in the language of canonical right) are posthumous bequests (of either real estate or money) given to a religious order or body in return for prayer, the saying of Masses for the dead, or other religious work.

Father Concezio, however, was not willing to judge his experience with the apparition solely on the basis of his own senses, and devised a method of testing the reality of Evolo's bilocation.

I did not speak of what had happened with anyone and a week later said to Don Domenico Manfrida: "I have not received any news about the question that I asked Natuzza. Would you mind going and asking her?" Don Domenico went then to Paravati and visited Natuzza. Don Domenico had hardly started to talk when Natuzza interrupted him, saying: "I have already been to Father Concezio a few days ago. I found him in bed and I told him that there were legacies, up and down. . . . Excuse me, but what are legacies?"

Perhaps the most valuable information Marinelli acquired in his research was a detailed description of the inner experience of bilocation as provided by Evolo herself. This account is especially interesting in that the great bilocative saints of the Church have traditionally been reluctant to discuss this aspect of their spiritual lives, and so there exist almost no introspective accounts written by them. Only Teresa Higginson has left a personal description of the process.

As Evolo told Marinelli:

The bilocation never happens by my spontaneous will. One or more spirits of the dead, or one or more angels (or angels and spirits), present themselves to me and accompany me to the places where my presence is necessary. Here I can see the place where I am, so that I can describe it, I can speak and be heard by the people present, I can open and close doors, move objects, and produce actions. My vision is not a distant one, like watching a film or the television, but I am plunged into the surroundings visited by me. I remain on the spot only for the time necessary to fulfill my mission, which varies from a few seconds to a few minutes, and then I return to my normal state. I am aware that my physical body is at my home at Paravati. . . .

She also explained that her bilocations occur either at night while she is sleeping or spontaneously while she is awake. In the latter situation she will suddenly find herself in a new environment, as if she had teleported there, and will instantly realize that she has bilocated.

The journey doesn't seem to last at all. I instantly find myself in some place, independently from the distance. When I go to a house, I find myself directly in the room, or more often in a room adjacent to the one where I have to see the person to whom I am bilocating. . . . Sometimes I have been able to convey material objects between the place visited by me in bilocation and my house, where my physical body was. I don't know how this happens, but it has happened.

Eventually, her angelic or spiritual escort will tell her where she is.

Like Padre Pio and St. Martin de Porres, Evolo also believes that she has experienced trilocation:

Sometimes I have been on a trilocation; that is, I saw two places at the same time, apart from the place of the physical body, and I have been seen in the two different places at the same time, by live people. The bilocation can happen even several times a day, and I can visit, in succession, many different places.

Although this chapter has examined a large number of diverse examples of bilocation phenomena, the collected evidence seems to suggest that the OBE and bilocation simply represent opposite sides of a spectrum of similar psychic events. But is it possible to develop a theory that will explain *how* in fact these projections occur?

To the occultist, these phenomena present no great puzzle. Occult theory teaches that all these diverse phenomena can be attributed to the fact that the body possesses a "human double" or "soul body." The double can take on various shades of density, becoming visible as an apparition on some occasions while remaining invisible on others. But this explanation is much too general to account for the many complex elements which complicate the study of the OBE and bilocation. For example, Blue Harary usually perceives himself as an orb of light or as a speck of awareness free-floating in space while undergoing his OBEs. He can produce a body for himself, through a direct effort of will, but he feels that this body is basically illusory. He cannot predict when or where his apparitional body will become visible to the naked eye. Any interpretation of OBEs must therefore include the possibility that the mind simply has the power to *create* a material form for itself during the experience. The traditional "soul body" theory is also unable to explain the fact that both bilocators and out-of-body travelers always appear dressed in their worldly clothes.

Since, on the other hand, both the OBE and bilocation represent the projection of some physical aspect of the self, we are left with only two viable theories that can explain bilocation. Either (1) some superintelligence actually masterminds the physical duplication of the body or (2) bilocation is simultaneously a *partly* objective and *partly* immaterial phenomenon. If, as seems likely from evidence, bilocation is in fact an extended form of the OBE, then the latter view is the more acceptable alternative. A witness to a bilocation may therefore be perceiving the physical but basically *spiritual* presence of the bilocator. This presence may be gifted with the ability *to make itself appear in any form it wishes or which will be acceptable to the viewer,* an effect it perhaps produces by a direct action on the mind of the viewer. Although the bilocator is at least in some sense actually present at the scene of his visitation and may even be able to bring along small physical objects, his visual appearance may probably be more illusory than optically "real."

But even this theory cannot explain all the facts of bilocation. It is difficult to reconcile such a view with the appearances of St. Martin de Porres, whose bilocating self was said to sleep overnight in his sister's house, or those of Maria Coronel de Agreda, who was able to transport dozens of rosaries while bilocating. There is also a widespread story that when Cardinal Mindszenty of Hungary was jailed by the Communists after the freedom-fighter revolt of 1956, Padre Pio often bilocated to him and brought along water, wine, and altar bread and stayed to serve Mass.*

It is difficult to interpret bilocation cases such as these by almost any conventional out-of-body theory. In fact, some bilocations that involve a great deal of physical activity by the subject may actually represent cases of *teleportation,* a miracle in which the physical body is transported instantaneously over space.† This phenomenon, though even more fantastic than bilocation, is not unknown in hagiographic records, and there is at least one good contemporary case documented in the life of Padre Pio. On May 8, 1926, a dozen or so visitors from Bologna were waiting in the hallway that led to the church of the San Giovanni Rotondo monastery. Hoping to meet with Padre Pio as he made his way to hear morning confessions, they had stationed themselves well since the priest had to pass through the hallway on his way to the sanctuary. The group waited for three hours. While holding their vigil they were approached by another priest, who asked what they were doing. He was surprised when they told him that they were waiting for Padre Pio, and explained that the priest had been hearing confession in the sanctuary for some time. Members of the group had checked the confessional earlier and had found it empty, yet the hallway was the only entrance.

Teleportation does not always occur in a religious context. At the turn of the century, Charles Fort cited cases of people who instantaneously "disappeared" from their homes or even from public sidewalks only to reappear miles away with no memory of how they had gotten there. On rare occasion human teleportation has occurred during poltergeist infestations as well. In a classic poltergeist case reported from Germany in 1929, a baby repeatedly teleported from her crib and into various rooms of the afflicted home. On another occasion a one-year-old child disappeared from the house and moments later was found in a stable stall.[10]

---

*Schug tried to question Cardinal Mindszenty about this story while he was being given asylum at the U.S. Embassy and, later, after he had fled to Vienna. The cardinal would only tell Schug that he could not "say anything about that" and refused further comment. Schug claims to have heard the tale from "a reliable source in the Vatican."

†For a more thorough discussion on this topic, see my book *The Haunted Universe* (New York: New American Library, 1977). See also Nandor Fodor, *Mind over Space* (New York: Citadel, 1962).

Teleportation has also been frequently interpreted as a sign of demonic infestation. Two such cases have been documented during the twentieth century.

The first instance was widely publicized at the time of its occurrence (some initial documents pertaining to the case were published in the *Giornale d'Italia* in November 1905), but is hardly known to parapsychologists today. In 1901 Maura Pansini, an Italian mason, moved into a large house in Ruvo, Italy, which soon became subjected to poltergeist antics. Pictures fell from the walls, household knickknacks flung themselves from shelves, and even heavy furniture slid across the floors. Conventional exorcism did nothing to relieve matters. Several days after the infestation began, seven-year-old Alfredo Pansini began developing symptoms of demonic possession. "Angels" spoke through his mouth, and he went into spontaneous trances, suffered bouts of catalepsy, and reported clairvoyant visions. The first teleportations occurred at this time as well. The boy would suddenly disappear from the house and would be found later, usually in a dazed condition, on the other side of town or in neighboring cities. After Alfredo had undergone these teleportations for three years, his younger brother, Paolo, began to experience them as well. The first double teleportation occurred one morning while the boys were at home with their family. They suddenly vanished from the house and were found half an hour later on the grounds of the Capuchin convent in Malfetta, some thirty miles from their home. Their most spectacular teleportation occurred some time later while the boys were having lunch with their parents. At twelve o'clock Paolo was sent to fetch some wine, but he never returned. An hour later Alfredo suddenly vanished as well. Moments after this second disappearance, *both* boys appeared aboard a small fishing boat several miles out at sea near the port of Baletta.

These teleportation attacks lasted until 1904, when Alfredo reached puberty. They were investigated by a number of Italian Church officials, including three bishops, a priest, and one judge. One of the most detailed studies was made by Dr. Joseph Lapponi, a physician who was chief medical advisor to Popes Leo XIII and Pius X. He spoke personally to some of the witnesses in the case before issuing a report in his book *Ipnotismo e spiritismo* (1907). Lapponi tells how on one occasion the boys were locked into their room by Bishop Bernardi Pasquale of Ruvo and Botonto. Even though all the doors and windows to the room were thoroughly sealed, the boys vanished from it within a few minutes.[11]

In 1951, an almost identical series of teleportations began to occur in a home in Manila. The victim was an adolescent boy, Cornelio Closa Jr. Closa reported how he periodically encountered the apparition of a teen-age girl dressed in white, whom only he could see. As soon as he touched her, he would "disappear" from wherever he happened to be and would reappear hours later, sometimes miles away from his home. Several witnesses testified that the boy often miraculously disappeared from his house, from his school room, or even from the street during these weeks. His parents tried locking him into his room, yet he often disappeared nonetheless. They finally had him incarcerated in a mental institution, but they could find nothing wrong with the boy and released him. The Closas finally had him exorcised by an American missionary, and the disappearances stopped altogether. In 1965 Closa was interviewed about his 1951 adventures by Vicente Maliwanag for UPI and maintained the absolute truth of his experiences.[12]

Of all the miracles performed by both holy men and psychics, bilocation is perhaps the most enigmatic. Conventional science has no explanation for human duplication, and even parapsychology can shed only a dim light on the subject. Bilocation, as well as the OBE and teleportation, goes beyond the paranormal. They are all, indeed, supernatural.

Part Two

MIRACULOUS EVENTS

A miraculous event occurs when some Supernatural Intelligence interferes with the normal course of nature. Primitive man believed that any anomaly occurring in the natural world was of supernatural origin, and the Bible is full of accounts of such miracles—from the parting of the Red Sea in the Old Testament to Jesus' ability to control storms as recounted in the Gospels.

Intelligent interference with the natural world is still occurring today. In this section we will look at four types of wondrous events. We will be concerned with holy images that have miraculously appeared on church walls or pieces of cloth; religious paintings that have bled or wept tears; a storm during which hailstones imprinted with the likeness of the Virgin Mary fell to earth; and dried blood that liquefies miraculously.

But just what is this Supernatural Intelligence that seems so eager to intrude upon our world and produce wonders in accordance with our religious beliefs? Is it God Himself? Or are these events related to the minds of the observers who have come face to face with the supernatural? Or might they even be the outcome of a psychic process generated by some Universal Unconscious?

~ V ~
DIVINE IMAGES

ON THE EVENING of May 18, 1975, a miracle occurred in the little town of Holman, New Mexico. Two teen-age boys were wandering about near the Immaculate Heart of Mary Church when their attention was drawn to an odd "shadow" appearing on a wall of the building. Because it was twilight, it was difficult to see. The boys ventured closer and then bolted away from the church in terror when they realized that the "shadow" was actually a figure of Christ's head and shoulders appearing on the wall. The figure resembled a charcoal drawing, but seemed to be formed out of a configuration existing within the texture of the concrete.

Since that night, hundreds of people have flocked to Holman to see the miraculous likeness of Christ. Like many works of art, the image was apparently easier to make out if viewed from a distance, and while it was hard to discern during daylight hours, at dusk it seemed to emerge from patterns directly within the concrete wall. The Reverend Leonard Bayer, a priest at St. Gertrude parish in Mora, publicly described the image as a figure "with a beard and long hair, just as Our Lord appears in some pictures we have of Him." It measured about four feet by two feet and appeared on the wall seven feet above ground level.

The Holman "figure of Christ" is a perfect example of a very unusual type of miracle. Ever since the third century A.D., stories have been recorded of miraculous images of Christ, the Virgin Mary, or other religious figures or emblems, that have suddenly appeared on church walls, windows, or altar cloths. The Holman portrait, despite the incredible media coverage it received, is only a recent example of a miracle that has occurred countless times. Two cases almost identical to it have been reported within the last twenty years alone.

A similar image appeared on a freshly painted wall in the Tabernacle of Glad Tidings in Nassau, the Bahamas, on July 20, 1963. It was first noticed during a regular Sunday service by one of the local parishioners, Mrs. Euna Laine, who began to scream when the image first became visible. Soon other parishioners could also see a figure resembling Jesus' face faintly emerging from the wall of the church. While it was originally much vaguer than the Holman face, over the next few days it became better defined, ultimately resembling a fine charcoal drawing, though it was actually formed from spots appearing within the plaster of the wall. A reporter from the Chicago *Daily News* flew to the Bahamas expressly to investigate the report. By the time he arrived, two additional faces had become visible on the same wall. Indistinct when viewed at close range, they too became better defined as one walked away from them.

The latest case of a miraculous image was reported from Delcambre, Virginia, on March 16, 1980, when the Lafayette *Sunday Advertiser* featured the headline IMAGE OF CHRIST ON SCREEN DRAWS CROWDS TO DELCAMBRE. The Delcambre image began to appear that month on the window screen of a little wooden house at (believe it or not) 406 West Church Street. It was first noticed by the tenant, Mrs. Lois Linden, whose father, the Reverend H. J. Simmons, is a local minister. He, too, was able to see the figure. "Now I've seen it," he told reporters after explaining his initial skepticism, "[and it's] a picture of Christ's face. Like pictures of Him you've always seen. He looks very laborious, like He's worked hard and is tired." The image doesn't seem to be as well defined as the Holman or Nassau wall faces, but that may be due to the unusual medium on which it appeared. Many visitors to Delcambre have been disappointed at the quality of the figure; others, while able to see the image, think it resembles the Virgin Mary or even a demon more than it does Christ.

Despite the publicity these miraculous images have received from the media, few news reporters or even religious writers seem aware that there is a long history within orthodox Christianity that tells of these types of appearances.

The "divine image" miracle probably has its beginnings in the famous legend of Veronica's veil, much beloved by ecclesiastic writers and artists of the Middle Ages. According to tradition, Veronica was a woman of Jerusalem who was busy with her

housework when she heard a crowd screaming in the street outside. Hurrying out, she saw Christ on the road to Calvary being
scourged by Roman soldiers. In a moment of inspiration, so the
legend goes, she fought her way to the front of the crowd and
wiped Jesus' face clean of sweat and blood with her veil. Later
she discovered that a perfect likeness of Christ had been
impressed on the linen.

Despite the fact that no such story appears in the Gospels,
many Christians—especially during the Middle Ages—took the legend of Veronica's veil seriously. According to Ian Wilson, a British
scientist and an authority on artistic depictions of Christ, "So widespread did this story become in Christian mythology that today it
is rare to find a Catholic church that does not have somewhere a
scene depicting Christ, toiling his way to Calvary, impressing the
likeness of his face on Veronica's veil." [1] It is difficult to determine
just when the story of Veronica first arose. Ian Wilson has traced
accounts of the veil back to the twelfth century, and during medi-
eval times several alleged "Veronica veils" were publicly displayed
in churches throughout Europe—each church, of course, claiming
that its own cloth was the original!

Modern church historians tend to dismiss the authenticity of
these veils, since most are clearly the products of deliberate fraud.
The images seem to have resembled scorch marks on cloth, which
would have been easy for an unscrupulous artist to fake. But in
light of the Holman, Nassau, and Delcambre miracles, couldn't
some of these veils actually have contained divine images of Christ
that had spontaneously appeared on altar cloths or on the hand-
kerchiefs of some devout parishioners? Unfortunately, most of
these cloths, including one that was on exhibit in Rome in the
sixteenth century, have been destroyed and so can no longer be
examined. The mystery of the Veronica veils remains just that—a
mystery which even the most astute historical researchers will
never solve.

"Was the whole saga of Veronica [and the] Shroud-like face
on the eventual cloth 'relic' and the long impression of Christ's
features all pure fabrication?" asks Wilson about the Veronica tradition. "However much this might appear implicit from what has
gone before, the answer is no. Those who wrote down traditions
such as that of the Veronica were not charlatans or inventive

geniuses who spun stories out of nothing. Nor was the likeness on the Veronica cloth, as revered during the Middle Ages, the brain-child of one inspired eleventh century Italian artist." [2]

Wilson believes that the Veronica legend was actually imported to Europe from Asia, where a miraculous image of Christ on cloth called the Mandylion had been on display since 944 A.D. in Constantinople, before disappearing when the Frankish army of the Fourth Crusade sacked the city in 1204. The cloth first came to light in Edessa during the seventh century. According to tradition, the figure had been miraculously impressed on the cloth by Jesus himself, who then allegedly sent it to Edessa to cure the ailing King Abgar and to convert him to Christianity. Because the image on the Mandylion bears a striking resemblance to the Veronica veil images as depicted in the art of the Middle Ages, Wilson concludes that the Veronica legend was brought to Europe during the tenth century by travelers returning from Asia, and may thereupon have encouraged artistic forgeries of the Mandylion for European display. The Mandylion is described in early Eastern writings by the Greek word *acheiropoietos,* which translates as "not made by hands."

Though they may have been artistic hoaxes, the existence of the Veronica veil and Mandylion legends proves that there is a rich historical tradition behind such miracles as the Holman face and other similar manifestations. Miracles often seem to be imitative in nature. No other ascetics manifested the stigmata until St. Francis of Assisi was impressed with it in 1224. *Belief* in miracles, in other words, may actually give rise to them. The same holds true for the Veronica veil tradition. Belief in the tradition may have generated the formation of miraculous images on pieces of cloth, church walls, or anywhere else.

The most famous of all "divine image" miracles is that of Our Lady of Guadalupe, in which the divine image of the Virgin Mary appeared on a peasant's cloak in Mexico on December 12, 1531. The cloak, complete with unfaded image, is still on display today at the Basilica of Our Lady of Guadalupe in Villa Madero, a community just a few miles north of Mexico City. Despite the fact that the image is four hundred years old, it has not faded. Nor has the material it appeared on, a rough cloth woven from cactus fiber, disintegrated as it should have done years ago. The miracle of

Guadalupe is one of the great miracles of the Catholic Church and has withstood the tests of time and the scrutiny of modern science. The date of the miracle of Guadalupe is significant. Only ten years earlier, Cortes and his conquistadors had invaded Mexico. This invasion resulted in bloody confrontations between the Spaniards and the native Aztec Indians. By 1531 Mexico was in considerable turmoil, with the Aztec empire cruelly crushed under an unsympathetic Spanish rule. The leader of the colonial government installed by Spain was Nuño de Guzmán, a greedy and corrupt official who exploited the defeated Indian population at every opportunity. He overtaxed them to such an extent that many Indians had to sell their children into slavery in order to pay their levies. This state of affairs often led to public confrontations between Guzmán and Fra Juan de Zumárraga, the humanitarian and kindly bishop of Mexico, who was a staunch supporter of Indian rights. Although Zumárraga eventually won his battle and Guzmán was recalled to Spain in disgrace, the political situation in 1531 was so extreme that the Aztec natives had become factionalized. One element was planning a bloody revolt against the Spanish leadership, while the other was attempting to merge with Spanish culture by adopting Christianity and European ways. The miracle of Guadalupe occurred at the peak of these troubled times.

The protagonist in the story of the miracle was a native Indian, Juan Diego, who had adopted a Spanish name after converting to Catholicism. He was full of enthusiasm for his new faith and would walk every day from his hometown of Quahutitlan, near present-day Mexico City, to Tlatilolco, where he could attend church. He made the journey by way of a road that passed a hill called Tepeyacac (or Tepeyac).

Early on the morning of December 8, 1531, Juan Diego had just reached Tepeyacac when he was distracted by exquisite, almost entrancing birdlike music coming from the top of the hill. The music suddenly stopped, and to Diego's surprise, he heard his name called by a soft feminine voice. On scaling the hill, he was confronted by a radiant and wondrous apparition. The figure was dark complected, like a native, and addressed Diego in Nahuatl, his native dialect. The apparition told him that she was the Blessed Virgin Mary and urged the awe-stricken Indian to inform the bishop that she wished a church built on Tepeyacac in her honor. Diego complied with the request by immediately setting out for Mexico City, where he held vigil at the bishop's residence until he was allowed an audience.

Zumárraga listened to Diego sympathetically, but didn't put too much stock in the story of the apparition. He merely suggested that they meet together at some unspecified later date when they could talk at greater length.

Juan Diego left the city disappointed, since he knew the bishop had not believed him. He went directly back to Tepeyacac, where he found the apparition waiting for him. Once again she urged Diego to place her petition before the bishop.

Diego returned home after this second vision, but made the long walk to Mexico City the very next day. He had to fight his way through servants and guards in order to have an audience with Zumárraga, who again listened attentively to the Indian's story. His interest piqued, Zumárraga now began asking the Indian several questions about the apparition and suggested that Diego ask the figure for a "sign" that would prove her divine nature and mission, to which the Indian agreed. Because he was still suspicious of Juan Diego and his story, Zumárraga ordered his guards to follow him after he left. The guards soon lost him, however, and returned to the capital convinced that the native was merely mad or lying. Meanwhile, Juan Diego met with the apparition at Tepeyacac for the third time, and requested that she provide him with a miraculous sign that he could take back to the bishop. The apparition assented and asked Diego to meet with her on the morrow.

Diego's plan was disrupted when an uncle who lived with him, Juan Bernardino, fell seriously ill. Diego naturally felt that his first duty was to his relative and resolved to find a doctor for the sick man. Knowing his end was near, Bernardino begged his nephew to fetch a priest instead.

The next morning Diego set out to Tlatilolco to find a cleric who would return with him and give his uncle last rites. As he approached Tepeyacac, though, he heard the voice of the apparition calling to him. Diego confronted the Blessed Virgin and explained to her solemnly that he was on a mission for his uncle and could only do her bidding after he had fetched a priest. After listening sympathetically to Diego's story, the apparition gently chided him for his lack of faith, promised that his uncle would recover, and repeated her petition. To this Diego agreed, but asked for the sign that he could take to convince the bishop. Instructed to climb the little hill on which she appeared, Diego saw a wondrous sight at its crest. Instead of the rough weeds and cacti that normally adorned the terrain, a miraculous garden was growing. Flowers of all varieties and colors were in full bloom, even Castilian roses from Spain, and all were out of season. The apparition gathered a bouquet, placed it in the cloak that Juan wore around his neck like an apron, and bade him take the flowers to the bishop as her sign. She also warned him not to open his mantle in the presence of anyone but the bishop himself.

On arriving at the bishop's residence, Diego met with the hostility of the servants and guards, who were still nettled by their failure to trail him two days before. But they were considerably intrigued by the flowers the Indian was trying to hide in his cloak. Juan refused to reveal his precious cache to them and was finally ushered into the presence of Zumárraga. He explained about the apparition, and then opened his mantle so that the flowers would fall to the ground.

But the mantle hid a treasure greater than the flowers. There on the cloak, for all to see, was a perfect full-color image of the Blessed Virgin, as though stamped directly onto it. It was not a painted image, but was impressed directly onto the mantle. When Zumárraga saw the miraculous likeness, he and his attendants fell to their knees in reverence. The bishop immediately begged forgiveness for having doubted the authenticity of the apparition and vowed to build the church as directed.

The church was eventually built,* and Juan Diego's cloak is still on public display there—the impression as thoroughly lifelike as it appeared in 1531. The image, which appears over the entire

---

*The basilica is named after the apparition, who requested that she be known as Santa Maria de Guadalupe. Ecclesiastic writers have long maintained that the apparition wished to be named after the city of Guadalupe, Spain. But several historians now agree that "Guadalupe" may have been a mistake and that the apparition probably said that she wished to be known as Santa Maria Coátlallope. This is a Nahuatl word that means "one who treads on the snake." The "snake" was an Aztec symbol for Quetzalcoatl, their chief god. The apparition may have been making a symbolic allusion to the fact that she had come to "stamp out" the Aztec religion and replace it with Christianity.

cloak, shows a dark-skinned maiden in prayer. The figure stands on a crescent moon supported by an angel. A cape covers her head and shoulders.

The miracle of Guadalupe, which is known to every man, woman, and child in Mexico, is not a legend. Between 1531 and 1648, no fewer than thirty-three documents describing the events of December 1531 were placed on record.[3] As Father José Bravo Ugarte, an expert on Mexican history, states in his *Cuestiones históricas guadalupanas* (1946), there can be little doubt that the story of the Guadalupe miracle rests on firm historical fact. Even Zumárraga apparently wrote out an account of the miracle, though his description was destroyed in 1778 by a fire that struck the archive room of the monastery where it had been deposited. In 1666 the Church officially investigated the miracle, retraced its history, and documented the evidence supporting its authenticity.

The validity of the miracle of Guadalupe rests on scientific testimony as well as on historical proofs. Today, scientists from around the world who have been allowed to study it have noted several factors supporting its supernatural nature. First, though the image appears in full color, it is not a painted figure. There is no evidence that it is composed of brush strokes. There is a rent in the cloak, since it had been sewn together from two pieces of material; yet the portrait appears stamped over it in a way impossible to imitate with paint.

What is even more impressive is that the image refuses to fade, and the cloak itself has not rotted. The paranormal nature of these characteristics is universally accepted by all students of the miracle. In his history of Mexico, *La estrella del norte de Mexico* (1669), Father Florencia was one of the first to recognize these amazing features of the image. He noted that "the permanence of the coarse maguey canvas . . . has lasted more than a hundred years. This is miraculous, since it is as entire and strong as it was the first day; especially when we consider the place in which it is, subject to wind and saline dust and the heat of the candles and the incense which the devout continuously offer—without fading, or darkening or cracking."

Although maguey cactus fiber normally disintegrates after about twenty years, the cloak has shown no sign of wear even after four hundred years. It should also be noted that at the time

Father Florencia wrote about the image, the cloak was merely exhibited over the church altar without any protective covering. Only years later was a glass plate placed over it.

The miracle has recently been investigated, by the Image of Guadalupe Research Project, a group of American scientists headquartered in Florida. In February 1979, Dr. Philip Callahan, a University of Florida biophysicist and an affiliate of the U.S. Department of Agriculture, was able to inspect the Guadalupe image with the aid of special film akin to infrared. His tests showed that the image has no underdrawn blueprint, a requisite had the image been merely painted on the cloak. The photographic analysis has also corroborated the fact that no brush strokes appear on the image itself, thus countering any suggestion that the figure is simply a painting. Callahan agrees with many other students of the miracle that, by all scientific law, candles lit under the cloak in devotion at the basilica should have caused substantial fading or cracking over the years.

Dr. Callahan did discover, however, that the Guadalupe image had been "touched up" at some time in the past by ecclesiastic artists, who painted a sunburst around the figure and affixed stars and a golden border to the figure's cape. Yet these later additions *have* begun to fade, while the original image remains fresh.

Callahan agrees with most experts that the cactus fiber cloak should have rotted sometime back in the 1570s, so he specifically tested it to see if it had ever been sized. (Sizing is a process of varnishing canvas with flour or other material. This clogs the pores of the fabric so that rotting is delayed.) But he found no sign that the Guadalupe cloak had ever been subjected to such a process.

The future may bring new revelations about the Guadalupe image. In July 1980, Monsignor Enrique Salazar, a representative of the Basilica of Our Lady of Guadalupe, agreed to allow researchers from the Center for Applied Research on the Apostate in Washington, D.C., to test the image further. Professor Jody Smith, a philosophy instructor at Pensacola College in Florida and president of the Image of Guadalupe Research Project, hopes that additional tests will provide a scientific explanation for the miraculous preservation of the image. The experiments he envisions seem to be generating a great deal of interest within the scientific community at large. Dr. Donald Lynn, a space scientist at the sprawling Jet Propulsion Laboratory in Pasadena, California, has volunteered to help the team analyze computer-enhanced photographs of the image.

But will the technology of science ever be able to explain what force caused the image to appear on Juan Diego's cloak?

There are actually only two generic explanations for "divine image" miracles. One is that they are a manifestation architectured by some Supernatural Intelligence existing outside the sphere of human life and natural law, but eager to influence our world. In other words, they are produced by God. This explanation, however, can only account for the basic etiology of the miracle, and not the actual modus operandi by which it was brought about. Some chemical alterations must have affected the wall of the Immaculate Heart of Mary Church in Holman so that natural configurations in the concrete modeled themselves into the likeness of Christ. And some constitutional change must have affected the fibers of Juan Diego's mantle so that they do not disintegrate. These are the legitimate concerns of science.

Yet any purely religious or purely scientific solution to either the Holman or the Guadalupe miracle overlooks the fact that they are just as much psychological wonders as they are religious or scientific phenomena. It is interesting that both these images seem to be *imitative* rather than divine—the Holman portrait represents the way Jesus is traditionally portrayed in modern religious art, while the apparition that stopped Juan Diego and that appears on the Guadalupe cloak has definite Indian characteristics. One might therefore conclude that these divine images were (or are) somehow closely related to the minds of the witnesses who first saw them, and in a larger sense, to the cultural consciousness of the times in which they have appeared.

This suggests the second generic theory about these miracles. It may be possible that houses of worship ignite such strong emotions in their members that a form of "psychic blueprint" might build up within these structures. Pooled from storehouses of psychic energy, these blueprints might eventually become—under just the right conditions—psychic realities with the power to break through into the material world.[4] The Holman portrait might therefore have been somewhat akin to a "thought form"—a mass psychic effect produced by the unconscious minds of the parishioners who prayed there. The same goes for the Nassau image.

That these psychic breakthroughs would be allied to especially strong emotions may serve as a clue in the Guadalupe case. On a psychic level, religious emotions were reaching a critical point in the Mexico of 1531; so a mass miraculous effect could well have been in the making. The appearance of the Virgin Mary may have resulted from the intense emotions produced by the factionalization among the native population concerning their European conquerors and (most importantly) their religion. Juan Diego may have been in just the right place at the right time to become the principal in the miraculous drama that followed.

This is, of course, only a germinal theory, and one that will be extended in the concluding chapter. It is not a scientific theory, since it cannot be tested or falsified, so perhaps it should be labeled for now as merely speculation.

Yet strong evidence does exist that certain holy places associated with individuals of great personal power can generate likenesses of those individuals. Any theory about the nature of so-called "divine images" of Christ or the Virgin Mary must take into account the appearance of similar mysterious portraits and images which have occurred in any number of settings—secular as well as sacred.

Perhaps the most famous case of this type is the miraculous portrait of the well-known British preacher Dean Liddell, which gradually formed on a wall of Christchurch Cathedral in Oxford between 1921 and 1923. Liddell, who was for many years dean of the cathedral, died in 1898. The image formed on a wall of the cathedral where Liddell had installed a decorative window in honor of his deceased daughter, and where plaques in honor of the Liddell family had been installed by his faithful parishioners. A white "stain" started to form near the tablets in 1921 and over the next two years it formed into a definite likeness of the dean.

One popular theory for the Liddell image was that it was caused by lichen growing in the plaster of the wall. But lichen usually appears green-gray, brown, yellow, or red in color. The Liddell face seemed formed out of the natural shadings of the white plaster on the wall. Lichen also usually appears on rocks and trees, not in plaster or cement. It seems more likely that the mineral salts in the plaster of the cathedral walls had gradually undergone some form of selective chemical change or manipulation, perhaps similar to the process silver particles undergo on a photographic plate during normal photography.

But the mystery of Christchurch Cathedral did not end with the appearance of Liddell's face. Two other faces gradually became visible, one of which resembled the dean's wife. These portraits were more than just rough configurations. *Cassell's Weekly,* a popular magazine of its day, investigated the Liddell case in 1926 and reported to its readers that the first image was "a faithful likeness of the late Dean" and added that "one does not need to call in play any imaginative faculty to reconstruct the head. It is set perfectly straight upon the wall, as it might have been drawn by the hand of a master artist. Yet it is not etched; neither is it sketched, nor sculptured, but it is there for all eyes to see."

The Liddell portrait also ignited the interest of at least two psychic investigators. Barbara McKenzie, a well-known researcher of her day, visited the cathedral in 1931 and was able to report to the British College of Psychic Science, a Spiritualist organization founded by her husband in 1921, that "the Dean's face is beautifully clear and there certainly seems an emergence of two other outlines close by which bear a resemblance to two human heads."[5]

During her visit to the church, Mrs. McKenzie also discovered that Christchurch Cathedral apparently had a tradition for producing mysterious wall faces! The Liddells' family portrait was, in fact, only the latest in a series of faces that had appeared, now and then, in the building.

Church officials also showed Mrs. McKenzie a gray marble pedestal base that supported a memorial tablet of an earlier date than the Liddell plaques. A patch of white had formed in the marble and had subsequently developed into a clear likeness of a bushy-haired figure with whiskers. The identity of the figure was not known. "Here the appearance is not on an exposed wall but on marble, and there is no apparent explanation for the white patch nor of the human features," writes Mrs. McKenzie. "It may be suggested that damp had arisen from the floor and affected the fixing of the foundations of the pedestal, but it is to be noted that the patch does not reach the ground, and in any case the features are interesting." Yet another wall portrait had appeared at some unknown time behind the organ.

Mrs. McKenzie was lucky that she visited Christchurch when she did. When Nandor Fodor, a Hungarian psychoanalyst and a prominent psychic investigator in London at the time, visited the church in 1932, he found that a new altar had been deliberately erected to cover the image. The Catholic Church, it seems, isn't the only religious body that distrusts miracles!

By studying the history of the Liddell family, however, Fodor did make an interesting discovery which throws added light on the miracle and on the psychic and psychological factors that may have produced it. Prior to the time of the miracle, the Liddell family had been split by an internal feud that had lasted twenty-five years. It was only resolved in 1921. As part of the reconciliation, a marriage celebration was held in Christchurch Cathedral. The wall faces began to form shortly after the festivities. Fodor theorized that the strong emotions of the participants in the ceremony, in conjunction with those of the many parishioners who esteemed their late preacher, may have produced the miracle.

A nearly identical case of a wall image was reported from Llandaff Cathedral in Wales in 1897. Two weeks after the death of John Vaughan, the dean of the cathedral, a damp spot (perhaps caused by minute fungi) appeared on the stone west wall of the church. The spot gradually formed into both a likeness of the dean and the initials *D. V.* The image was even photographed. Though the plate has since been lost, it was examined at the time by Fodor, who turned it over to an expert photographer. The photographer could find no evidence that the image had been artificially enhanced. Judging by the photo, Fodor concluded not only that the image was extremely clear, but that "the letters [were] an integral part of the portrait. There was no sign of superimposition. As if in order to leave no doubt about the meaning on the face on the wall, they had been formed at the same time as the portrait of itself."[6] The stain eventually "dried," and church authorities placed a notice board over the spot.

In another such case, the New York *Sun* reported on January 16, 1929, that a figure of the Virgin Mary had suddenly appeared on an oak door of St. Anne's Roman Catholic Church in Keansburg, New Jersey. "I don't believe that it is a miracle, or that it has anything to do with the supernatural," the Reverend Thomas A. Kearney, pastor of the church, told reporters. "As I see it, it is unquestionably the outline of a human figure, white robed, and emitting light. It is rather like a very thin picture negative that was underexposed, and in which human outlines and details are extremely thin. Yet it seems to be there." Although the pastor didn't think the image was supernatural, he never offered reporters any theory as to *how* he thought the figure got there. *The New York Times* ran a similar story on February 23, 1932, about a Christ figure that had appeared on a marble sanctuary wall of St. Bartholomew's Church in New York. "I consider it a curious and beautiful happening," reported the church's pastor. "I have a weird theory that the force of thought, a dominant thought, may be strong enough to be somehow transferred to stone in its receptive state." One of the most famous of all wall portraits appeared in 1926 on a wall of Bath Abbey in Bath, England, where the figure of a soldier in full marching uniform suddenly formed above a table erected in honor of the Somerset Regiment, which had fought during World War I. The figure eventually faded away as mysteriously as it had appeared.

As is true of most religious miracles, "divinely impressed" images have secular analogues. Mysterious humanlike figures do not appear only on church walls and in other places of devotion and worship. They sometimes appear in private homes.

A classic example of this phenomenon was investigated in 1935 by Barbara McKenzie, who issued a report on it in 1939.[7] In December 1935 she received a letter from a woman living in a small town in western England who claimed that a miraculous portrait had appeared in her home. One day, the woman explained in her letter, as she looked outside her bedroom door at an interior wall that had been covered with plain cream-colored wallpaper, she was shocked to see two figures impressed on it. A dark-complexioned monk holding a cross had begun to form, and beneath it the figure of a dog could be discerned. "It is all in light sepia," the woman wrote, "as though burnt into the wall by sun through the skylight just above it." Eventually another face appeared at the point of the cross, which the woman swore was the perfect likeness of her husband, who had died two years before. She also recognized the dog as a pet she and her husband had once cared for. Later, even more figures became noticeable, including a cat. The identity of the monk remained more puzzling than that of either the dog or the face on the cross. The house in which these fabulous portraits appeared was an old one, which according to local lore was once connected to a monastery nearby. But the legend could not be verified. If it had been, a clue about the identity of the monk might have been forthcoming.

Because the case seemed so promising, Mrs. McKenzie sent a colleague to the house to examine the wall. "The wall is very interesting and the old faces are certainly the clearest," reads the British College's subsequent report as drawn up by Mrs. McKenzie and her colleague. "The wall is an inside wall. There has been a doorway filled in but the only face showing on the new plaster is that of the cat. It seems to me that I was struck, or attracted by the eyes in each case; they seemed to prove a central focus for the images. The impression given is not so much of a photograph or picture as a sculpture. There is a softness in the shading that is very beautiful and gives great depth to the features."

The witness reported that the figures resembled scorch marks, as if they had been burnt into the wallpaper. A possible clue to how these images burned their way into the wall in so strange a fashion may lie in the fact that the figures appear on the portion of the wall illuminated by a skylight. Before the process of glass production was refined a few decades ago, it was quite common for window glass to "warp" or "flow," since solid glass maintains properties of a liquid. These warps often had a magnifying effect on any light passing through them, and many fires still occur in old homes when refracted light passing through warped glass ignites curtains or other flammable material. In this case, it is possible that the witness either influenced the warping of the skylight's glass so that the sun's rays would scorch the paper below it to produce the various forms, or psychically refracted and magnified the light herself so as to create the result. Recent experimental evidence suggests that human minds *can* indeed alter the trajectory of light beams, thus making this theory more credible. (We will return to this ability later in the chapter, in the context of another divine image miracle.)

As these cases have indicated, "wall faces" have a habit of appearing in groups—when one appears, others are bound to follow. Another example of this pattern occurred in 1971 when a rash of spectacular faces began to form on the floor of a little house in the Spanish town of Bélmez de la Moraleda. It is one of the best-documented "wall face" cases in contemporary history, since it was subjected to a thorough parapsychological investigation by Professor Hans Bender, one of Germany's leading parapsychologists and at the time the head of the Institute for the Study of Border Areas of Psychology and Psychohygiene in Freiburg.

The case first came to public attention in August 1971 when Maria Pereira, an Andalusian peasant woman living in Bélmez, discovered that a figure of a woman's face had formed on the hearthstone of her kitchen fireplace. She at first tried to scrub the figure out, but the image appeared to be embedded directly into the concrete. Being very superstitious, Señora Pereira had the hearthstone covered with a new layer of cement. But when it dried the face was still there! Eventually other faces began to form on the kitchen floor at odd intervals. They would sometimes become visible and then vanish, and would occasionally even reappear with different expressions on their faces. New faces might emerge in the same spot, while others remained permanently.

When it leaked out, the story caused a sensation in Bélmez, and the house soon became a tourist attraction. Señora Pereira played up this new development to the hilt—the hearthstone was removed, the face placed on display, and an admittance fee was charged to the local citizens who came to see it. By Easter of 1972 hundreds of people were flocking to the house to see the phantom portrait. But soon the local press charged that Señora Pereira was perpetrating a hoax for financial gain, and it wasn't long before local political and religious authorities forbade any tourist trade at the house.

Fortunately, Professor Bender had already been advised about the case and made two trips to Spain that year to personally investigate it. His second investigation was conducted in cooperation with Professor German de Argumosa, a Spanish psychic investigator who spent two years evaluating the mystery.

It was Bender's plan to determine whether the faces, which were still spontaneously appearing during the time of his visits, were genuine psychic impressions or the product of clever fraud. To test their authenticity, he had a plastic plate sealed over the area of the floor where the faces usually emerged. It was left there for several weeks, and was removed only when condensed water formed under it and obscured a clear view of the floor. New faces did appear under the plastic, but only after Bender had returned to Germany. (It was later revealed that the plate had been removed in the presence of official witnesses. The kitchen was then sealed off while the condensed water evaporated. The new faces were found when the witnesses reentered the room.)

Faces continued to materialize in the house until 1974, and literally dozens emerged during the three-year duration of the case. It is interesting that although Señora Pereira eventually had a new kitchen built onto her house, the images began appearing there as well.

On April 9, 1974, Professor Argumosa was able to witness the formation of one of the faces. He and his colleagues photographed it, but the image faded away completely later that same day. A new face appeared on the same spot a few hours later. This photograph and others dispel any idea that the faces were merely chance configurations or etchings artificially produced on the floor and walls of the house. While a few are only vague sketches formed out of patterns in the concrete floor, many are genuinely artistic in a rather surrealistic or caricaturistic manner. The first hearthstone portrait was perhaps the best defined. It clearly shows the head of a woman with (perhaps) an expression of wonder or surprise on her face. One photograph taken by Bender plainly shows a collage of three well-defined faces which materialized some time after the original hearthstone face first precipitated. It contains the head of a nun beneath a bearded man wearing a monk's cap and above a third male figure. If the collage is viewed upside down, yet another female face appears below the nun's head.

According to a report issued in the November 1976 issue of the Swiss parapsychology journal *Schweizerisches Bulletin für Parapsychologie,* tests were eventually made by Dr. Argumosa and his team to determine whether any artificial coloring had been added to the cement where the faces were manifesting. Scrapings were taken of the faces themselves. The analysis turned up nothing but particles of concrete, ash, and quantities of normal kitchen products—in short, nothing that could account for the mysterious images.

The upshot of the *affaire Bélmez* reads like something out of a Gothic mystery. The local townsfolk eventually dug up the hearth and discovered some human bones buried there. It was later learned that the house had been built on an old cemetery site that held the remains of Christian martyrs killed by the Moors in the eleventh century. After this discovery was made, the faces began appearing even more often.

Some investigators, including Dr. Bender, believe that the Bélmez mystery was caused by Señora Pereira herself, who—possibly a powerful psychic—somehow unconsciously created the disturbance. On the other hand, the discovery of the cemetery beneath the house indicates that the home may have been genuinely haunted, and somehow generated the eerie manifestations that plagued Señora Pereira. Yet the house does not appear to have any history of being haunted. No apparitions have ever appeared there, nor have any other ghostly disturbances plagued it. Another possibility is that the power that gave rise to the Bélmez manifestations was partly contributed by the psychic disposition of the house and somehow catalyzed by Señora Pereira's mind.

Although the Bélmez case is not a religious miracle, the phenomenon that occurred there between 1971 and 1974 is identical in form to the appearances of the miraculous images of Dean Liddell and Dean Vaughan and to the Christ figures which have appeared on various cathedral and church walls throughout history. Any explanation for one order of event must also be able to explain the other.

The fact that "divine image" miracles have both sacred and profane counterparts is only the first clue indicating that this type of miracle may be more a product of the psychic powers of the human mind than the work of a divine intelligence. This theory is also supported by the imitative and epidemic nature of miracles in general. A report of a miracle from one location will often give rise to the occurrence of a similar miracle somewhere else, as though the second event were literally mimicking the first. It often seems that once a group of people (such as a church congregation) in one town hears about a miracle occurring in a neighboring city, they unconsciously produce a similar miracle of their own.

One such epidemic struck Baden-Baden, Germany, in March 1872, when crosses began forming in home windows throughout the town. They would reform if they were washed off, and even acid couldn't burn them off. The window crosses soon spread to the nearby town of Rastadt.

Similar epidemics have cropped up in the United States. According to a report published in *The New York Times,* mysterious images had begun to appear in windows in Cincinnati, Ohio, a year before the Baden-Baden deluge. This epidemic began on January 18, 1871, when homeowners found portraits of unknown people etched onto their windowpanes. These images usually faded and eventually disappeared. A similar plague of window portraits struck Sandusky, Ohio, at about the same time.

The "Great Cross Flap" of 1971 is an example of a rash of mysterious miracles par excellence.[8] It is a modern case of a spate of "imitative miracles" that spread across the United States from California to Florida.

It all began in August when the *Los Angeles Times* ran a story entitled "The Phenomenon on 80th St." It reported that a glowing cross apparently formed by refracted light had begun appearing on a large rear window of the Chapel of Faith Baptist Church in the black ghetto area of downtown Los Angeles. The image had first appeared on August 27 during choir practice. Rehearsal hadn't gone too well that day and Mabel Davis, one of the choir members, was unhappy because she hadn't even been able to find an organist to accompany them. She was just about to leave the church when her daughter, Patricia, spotted the glowing cross. It was so awesome that it frightened her. The cross began appearing daily after August 27, usually at four o'clock in the afternoon, just as the sun positioned itself in a direct line with it. Skeptics naturally assumed that the cross was merely the result of normal refraction. And while this certainly seemed like a logical solution, it didn't satisfy everyone as a complete unraveling of the mystery.

"When I first saw it, it appeared like it was the reflection of the sun in the window," the Reverend Roy Williams of the chapel told the *Los Angeles Times.* "But it is still a mystery to me that I had never seen it before in the six years we've had the church." He preferred to believe that the cross appeared in answer to his prayers for a larger congregation. His prayers were certainly answered; church attendance swelled after news of the miracle spread.

Williams's first point was well taken. *If* the cross was merely a natural phenomenon, why did it only become visible in 1971? The cross was huge and the window faced directly into the congregation room. It simply couldn't have gone unnoticed before.

The Los Angeles report quickly spawned an epidemic of window cross miracles. On September 12 a glowing cross appeared in a window of the First Born Holiness Church in Apalachicola, Florida. The Florida cross didn't possess the stability of the Los Angeles image, and often changed shape and color—from white to orange—over the course of its various appearances. The mystery seemed to be solved when a local scientist, Dr. K. R. Chapman from Florida State University, visited Apalachicola and discovered that the internal surface of the window glass was furrowed so that light projecting through it was abnormally refracted. He also found that an external church light had been installed on the other side of the window and shone directly through it. Yet even Dr. Chapman couldn't explain why the image had only started appearing a year after the windowpane had been installed, since the light had been in position long before that.

On September 22, still another image appeared—this time on a window of the United Methodist Church in Mexico City, Florida. An identical report followed from Panama City, Florida, where a cross of light suddenly gleamed forth on a window of St. John's Baptist Church. And no sooner had that report spread than two more Panama City churches reported that similar lights were appearing in their windows! Officials from one of these churches, the Nazarene Church of Panama City, asserted that their image had suddenly materialized on a ten-year-old window and therefore could not be explained away as a product of natural refraction.

But the most notable glowing cross image was reported from the Paxon Revival Center in Jacksonville, Florida, which was one of three churches that reported the appearance of window crosses during the height of the flap. This light appeared on the outer side of the window and so could not have been due to refracted sunlight. It had never been seen before the flap hit Florida, and was first noticed by two young boys playing outside the church. Dozens of onlookers mobbed the church after news of the manifestation was released by the Florida press, and the image was photographed repeatedly. What is so astounding about the Paxon Revival Center image is that representations of *human hands extending on the crossbeam of the cross appeared on the photographs.*

After news of the Jacksonville crosses became common knowledge, the epidemic spread to Georgia, where more crosses started appearing. The images had little respect for denomination. They struck Seventh-Day Adventist, Methodist, and Baptist churches. Reports were filed from Brunswick, Kingsland, and Savannah.

By November the flap took on a new dimension. The crosses began turning up in the windows of private homes as well as in church windows. The first such account was filed from Darien, Georgia. On November 19 *The New York Times* reported a similar case in New York, where an elaborate cross figure had appeared on the bathroom window of the Bronx apartment of Mrs. Viola Mitchell. A photograph included with the story showed a genuinely artistic cross of light, resembling the traditional Latin cross overlaid with a fourchée. The image was first discovered by Mrs. Mitchell's mother, who was visiting at the time. By coincidence, Mrs. Mitchell was originally a resident of Darien, Georgia, and knew all about the cross epidemic that had been plaguing her home state. The cross caused a sensation in the Bronx. Many heralded it as a miracle and a warning to the growing groups of marauding teen-age street gangs. For, as one witness pointed out to reporters, it is stated in Jeremiah 9:21 that when "death is come up into our windows," the end is near for "the young men of the streets."

No one has ever been able to explain the Great Cross Flap of 1971, which was so reminiscent of the epidemic that plagued Baden-Baden almost precisely one hundred years earlier. The argument most commonly put forward was that *all* these cases were due to light refraction. This theory was given added impetus when the Georgia-based Brunswick Glass Company, which provided the glass used in many Georgia church windows, claimed that the crosses were formed when light passed through tiny vertical lines manufactured in the glass. But this theory cannot explain why the effects didn't show up before 1971 nor why the epidemic spread from one area to another in almost predictable fashion. It also seems highly unlikely that the witnesses who saw the crosses in the various Florida, Georgia, and New York churches and homes had merely failed to notice them until news of the flap came to light. Many of the images were elaborate, rather large, and hardly inconspicuous.

If any solution to the Great Cross Flap is forthcoming, one based on psychic and spiritual factors will probably be the most cogent. These effects do seem to have been caused by refraction to some degree—i.e., they may have indeed been caused by dispersed light rays passing through the windows. But the light was probably not refracted *simply* by the physical properties of the glass. The congregations who witnessed these images may have actually contributed to their production. Each congregation, having heard about the cross flap from reports in the news media, may then have projected a psychic field around a window in its own church so that it, too, could have a window cross of its own. These psychic fields may have "bent" light beams passing through the glass so that they would be refracted in precisely the right way to form the images.

As has been suggested earlier, belief in miracles often produces them. It seems more than coincidental that the Bronx case only precipitated when the apartment was being visited by a woman passingly connected with the previous and similar report from Darien. In his book *The Group Mind* (1920), the great Harvard psychologist William McDougall made a similar proposal. He, too, believed that miracles might in fact be the result of mass PK effects produced by religious worshipers.

McDougall's theory becomes even more convincing when we consider a recent discovery made by a physicist working in Great Britain. There is now strong evidence that the human mind is capable of bending light beams. In a 1974 issue of the *International Journal of Paraphysics,* Benson Herbert reported on his research with Suzanne Padfield, a young British psychic. Herbert is a parapsychologist as well as a physicist and runs the Paraphysical Laboratory in Downton, Wiltshire. Through a series of ingenious experiments he was able to demonstrate that Miss Padfield could directly influence a beam of polarized light by "bending" the beam or rotating the plane of polarization as it passed through a cylinder.[9] She was able to produce the effect repeatedly, even when provided with several different light-projecting devices. This phenomenon has become known as the "Padfield effect," since few other psychics have shown this ability as consistently. Miss Padfield can also produce more conventional PK phenomena, such as making a pendulum swing back and forth in a sealed container.

The Padfield effect may be the clue by which we can solve the riddle of the 1971 cross flap. If a single psychic can alter the path of a beam of light, why couldn't a group of emotionally charged people manipulate rays of sunlight? Once again, the difference between a psychic event and a miraculous one may be more a matter of degree than of nature.

If the mind is indeed capable of producing images on or within physical matter, we also have a possible clue to one of the greatest religious miracles of all times—the famous Shroud of Turin.

No religious controversy has been as heated as that inspired by a mysterious cloth housed at Turin Cathedral which bears a full-length impression of a crucified body. Many people believe that it is the actual shroud in which Jesus was buried after his Crucifixion, and that the image on it is that of Christ Himself. The history of the Shroud is steeped in mystery and can be authoritatively traced back only to the fourteenth century, when it was owned by Geoffrey de Charny, a French knight who died in 1356. It was publicly exhibited first in 1357 and again in 1389 by de Charny's widow. By the fifteenth century the Shroud had temporarily made its way to Italy for more public displays, but it was subsequently returned to France. The Shroud figure was slightly damaged in 1532 when a fire broke out in a chapel in Chambéry, where it was being shown, but the cloth was repaired two years later. The miraculous Shroud was first shown in Turin in 1535 and was permanently deposited there in 1578. In 1694 it was given its current home in the Royal Chapel of Turin Cathedral. Public exhibitions of the Shroud were held in 1804, 1815, 1868, and 1898, when the image was photographed for the first time.

The results of this attempt to photograph the Shroud figure are now famous. The photographer, Secondo Pia, took several exposures of the Shroud and discovered that the image is a perfect (and inexplicable) *negative image of a human face and body.* Pia's discovery caused a sensation within the ecclesiastic establishment of Italy. Now, thanks to his negatives and plates, definite features of the image could be seen more clearly than on the Shroud itself. The Shroud was photographed again during a twenty-one-day exhibition in 1931 with better equipment, and the negative image was even more clearly evident.

The image on the Shroud is a faint yet quite discernible and detailed image of a crucified male around the age of thirty. When the cloth is totally unfolded, two complete images attached at the head are visible. One depicts the front of the body; the other reveals the dorsal end. Each is a full-length impression of a man measuring approximately five feet, eleven inches. Wounds can be seen in the wrists, feet, forehead, and side, and scourge marks appear on the back and legs. Believers in the authenticity of the Shroud claim that the incredible detail portrayed by the wound marks (properly placed according to Roman crucifixion practices) as well as the inexplicable negative quality of the figure guarantee its genuineness. Skeptics, on the other hand, are quick to point out that the failure to trace any history of the Shroud before its appearance in France during the fourteenth century indicates that it is a forgery. Since there were some forty such shrouds shown in Europe during the fourteenth and fifteenth centuries,[10] the Shroud of Turin may not be unique.* But based on several recent scientific reports on the Shroud, the skeptics are going to have a rough time making a case for their cause in the years to come.

Strong evidence now exists that the figure on the Shroud is not an artistic rendition. It is simply too detailed. Dr. David Willis, a physician in England, made an extensive study of the Shroud figure's wounds in the early 1960s. He was able to determine that the figure's eyes were swollen, that its right eyelid had been torn, that the nose had been injured before death, and discovered a host of other minutiae that no art forger would have thought to depict. Dr. Willis's work complemented that of two physicians in the United States. Dr. Anthony Sava and Dr. Robert Bucklin have

---

*Ian Wilson, a British authority on the Shroud, does a credible job of tracing a speculative history of the Shroud back to the sixth century in his book *The Shroud of Turin* (Garden City, New York: Doubleday, 1978). He believes that the Shroud and the Mandylion of Constantinople may have been one and the same.

both studied the wounds on the figure and have shown that they are anatomically consistent with wounds as they affect the human body. Even the tiny flows of blood emanating from the wounds appear to drip in the proper direction, had the body actually been suspended on a cross. The small wounds on the figure's back are detailed to such a degree that the object that produced them can be reconstructed. It was a whiplike instrument of three thongs, each studded with a dumbbell-shaped metal pellet. Such a device was used by Roman soldiers for the purpose of scourging prisoners, and a few remnants of these instruments have actually been unearthed by archaeologists. Dr. Willis was even able to show that the knees of the figure are damaged, as though he fell several times while carrying a large object. This finding is, of course, fully consistent with Gospel narratives.

These findings alone do not prove that the Shroud figure is actually that of Christ; they simply indicate that the Shroud depicts someone who suffered crucifixion. Evidence has now come to light, however, indicating that the Shroud does in fact date back to biblical times.

Cardinal Pellegrino of Turin, under pressure from the U.S. Holy Shroud Guild, allowed the first contemporary scientific examination of the Shroud in 1969. A special team of eleven scientists and experts on the Shroud was chosen by him to serve on the committee. Among these were Professor Enzo Delorenzi, a radiologist from Turin, and Professor Giorgio Frache, a hematologist from the Department of Forensic Medicine of the University of Modena. Professor Silvio Curto of Turin, an expert on early textiles, was also invited to join the team. The commission's job was to examine the Shroud and determine what scientific tests should be carried out on it. The upshot of the commission's recommendations was that several threads were eventually removed from the Shroud and sent to various specialists throughout Europe for analysis.

One of the recipients of the fabric samples was Dr. Gilbert Raes of the Ghent Institute of Textile Technology in Belgium. By analyzing the structure of the thread, Dr. Raes determined that it was a complex weave often used in ancient times. The actual fibers of the thread were constructed from linen and a species of cotton, Gosypium herbaceum, that is common to the Middle East.

An even more provocative analysis of the Shroud was made by Dr. Max Frei, a criminologist who from 1948 to 1972 headed the Zurich police force's research laboratory. In 1973 Dr. Frei noticed that the Shroud was covered with particles of dust, and was eventually able to procure samples of it for analysis. Through microscopic examination Frei identified these particles as hair fragments, plant fibers, bacterial spores, and pollen grains. The latter piqued Frei's interest the most, since pollen is virtually immune to destruction. With today's technology it is also possible to identify a pollen genus even if the samples are very old. After more than a year of work, Frei was able to determine that fifty-nine different pollens contaminated the cloth. Many of the pollens seemed to have been picked up by the Shroud during its travels. But Frei identified one particle as a halophyte pollen, which belongs to a plant that typically grows in Palestine. So at one point in its history the Shroud must have been in what is now Israel, or at least thereabouts.

More evidence documenting the Shroud's authenticity was presented by the forty scientists who met together in Albuquerque, New Mexico, on March 23, 1977, as part of the first U.S. Conference on Research on the Turin Shroud. Several photographic analyses of the Shroud presented there proved that the impression on the cloth was made by a three-dimensional object.

Despite the evidence, there remain several mysteries about the Shroud image that indicate that *it is not a physical impression produced by contact between the cloth and a human figure.* This fact was evident as early as 1902, when Dr. Paul Vignon, a French biologist, made a study of Pia's original photographs. In his subsequent book about this research, *The Shroud of Christ* (1939), he argued that the image was produced by gases emanating from a human body placed at a distance from the Shroud. He thereupon speculated that the image was produced when ammoniacal gases released by a human body at the time of death had acted on the shroud, which had purportedly wrapped it. Vignon even called the Shroud a *vapographic print* and presented detailed chemical and biological explanations of how the image may have been formed.[11]

A more telling point against the physical impression theory is that there doesn't seem to be any real blood on the cloth, even though wounds and stains resembling blood flows spot the image. "Even when viewed with a magnifying glass," writes Ian Wilson, "the wounds in the wrist, and the wound in the side bear no trace of the sort of surface matter one might expect from a cloth that has been in contact with a major injury. Equally inexplicably, they bear no visible trace of any pigment either. The coloring—if coloring you call it—is so thin and flat that they appear as 'portraits' of blood rather than blood itself." [12]

The fact that no blood actually stains the Shroud was proved by analyses of the threads taken from the cloth performed at the University of Modena and the University of Turin. These tests revealed that the visible "stains" appear only on the surface of the linen and did not seep into the texture of the thread as any liquid would do. (No indication that pigments had been used to create the image was discovered either.) Subsequent tests were made to establish more firmly whether the Shroud contained any traces of blood. A standard benzidine test—red blood cells contain a peroxidase that turns blue when in contact with benzidine—turned out negative.

As Ian Wilson suggests, "Whatever created the image would seem to have had no actual substance of its own. It would seem to have been a 'dry' process as from some physical force reacting with the surface fibers of the Shroud's threads." * What, then, was the force that produced the image on the Shroud of Turin? Wilson believes that the actual physical process will eventually be discovered through further scientific examination and testing. He disdains the idea that, to quote his exact words, "it was created by some form of a miracle."

It is odd that no students of the Shroud mystery seem aware that the Turin cloth is only the most famous in a whole tradition of "divine image" miracles. Even Ian Wilson, who is somewhat versed in parapsychology, fails to note the parallels between the Turin figure and other miraculous images. It *is* possible that the

---

*Wilson seems to be describing a process that spontaneously occurs in nature during thunderstorms. There is considerable anecdotal evidence that lightning, when it strikes a physical object, can "imprint" pictures of nearby scenes onto objects (or even people) close by. During the nineteenth century, scientists even coined a name for the phenomenon—keranography; and reports about these strange images appear in the press now and then. For more information, refer to John Michell and R.J.M. Rickard, *Phenomena: A Book of Wonders* (New York: Pantheon, 1977).

Shroud was produced by a miracle—a miracle similar to those that produced Dean Liddell's family portrait on a wall at Christchurch Cathedral, the image of Dean Vaughan at Llandaff Cathedral, and the portraits of Christ that formed on the walls of Holman's Immaculate Heart of Mary Church and of the Tabernacle of Glad Tidings in the Bahamas.

Most people who have seen the Shroud at close range find that the image resembles a scorch mark more than anything else. This characteristic is analogous to the "burn marks" or "charcoal sketches" with which other divine images have been described. The process leading to the production of these various images, including the Shroud, might therefore be the same. Such a theory can also explain why the Shroud image is a negative, a fact no purely physical theory has been able to account for. Just when, and under what conditions, this miraculous image first formed is a mystery that may never be solved. But it may well have appeared long after the actual death of Christ.

What may be the latest case of a "divine image" miracle was recently reported from the small town of Lake Arthur, New Mexico. The *Los Angeles Times* ran a story on July 23, 1978, entitled "Thousands View 'Jesus on a Tortilla.' " The story reported how a local Mexican-American resident, Mrs. Maria Rubio, was frying some tortillas when a perfect likeness of Christ—complete with the marks of his crown of thorns—appeared on one of them. The figure was composed of skillet burns. Since the miracle occurred, thousands of visitors have flocked to the home of Mr. and Mrs. Rubio to see the tortilla, which is now housed in a glass frame and displayed in a little shrine built onto the house. Mrs. Rubio is (most appropriately) a member of Our Lady of Guadalupe Mission in Lake Arthur and even convinced the local priest to bless the tortilla, which even today shows no signs of crumbling—shades of Guadalupe!—as old tortillas are prone to do.

Though he blessed the tortilla, Father J. Elinnigin prefers to think the image is just a coincidence. "I'm not too impressed with that kind of miracle," he told reporters. But most of the visitors who have seen the tortilla disagree.

⌘ VI ⌘
THE
MIRACULOUS HAILSTONES
OF REMIREMONT

REMIREMONT is a small French town about sixty miles from the German border. Its population, like that of so many provincial cities, numbers hardly more than ten thousand people. It is not a tourist attraction, nor is it a bustling metropolitan center. But on May 26, 1907, one of the most startling "divine image" miracles ever documented in the twentieth century occurred there. It hailed "virgins" in the town.

The miracle itself was a relatively simple event. During a hailstorm that struck at five thirty that evening, several stones fell to earth imprinted with the likeness of the Blessed Virgin Mary. These stones were examined (though unfortunately not photographed) by dozens of local residents. But though the event itself was uncomplicated, the occurrence at Remiremont deserves a chapter to itself for one very special reason. The events *surrounding* the incident are so complex and intriguing that they shed light on both the modus operandi and the psychology of miracles.

Any investigation into the miracle of Remiremont must actually concern itself with two related phenomena. The first, of course, is the actual hailstorm of 1907. The second is a miracle that occurred in the town in 1682, which was connected to a mysterious and legendary statue of the Virgin brought to Remiremont by a group of nuns several hundred years earlier.

The background of this legend dates back to the days of Charlemagne (742–814 A.D.), who presented the "Notre Dame du Trésor" (Our Lady of the Treasure)—a cedarwood statue of the Virgin Mary—to a convent in honor of his successful campaigns in Italy. The nuns were forced to flee the convent in 910

A.D. in the face of invading Huns and settled in a community that later became Remiremont. They brought the statue with them, and it has been kept ever since in the town's central church. It wasn't long before the local residents began to believe that the statue possessed supernatural powers and that "exposing" it to public view during religious processions guaranteed good luck to Remiremont. Just how the legend first evolved remains a mystery, and it seems to be little more than a remnant of popular superstition.

The tradition of the statue's beneficence was nonetheless reinforced dramatically in 1682, when on May 12 the town was struck by a major earthquake, which destroyed several homes and damaged the abbey and church. Huge chasms opened in the ground during the catastrophe, and the several aftershocks thoroughly terrified the townspeople. Many of them spent the next several days sleeping in the meadows surrounding the town. It was during this series of violent aftershocks that the "Notre Dame du Trésor" was taken from its shrine and carried through the half-wrecked streets of the village. It was hoped that the procession would deliver the town from what was feared to be imminent destruction.

The devastation ceased at once! In gratitude, the townspeople of Remiremont vowed that each year a procession would be held to commemorate the miracle.

It is, of course, impossible to tell how much truth or fiction is contained in this legend. It is likely that the quakes would have stopped at any time, and that the conjunction of the procession and the end of the calamity was merely coincidental. But whatever the case, at least up until the turn of the century a reenactment of the procession was regularly held in the town in accordance with the pledge made by town officials in 1682. It was a popular celebration, and the residents often made elaborate plans for it.

A description of this ceremony was given in a short booklet, "Notre Dame du Trésor de Remiremont," which appeared in 1750. The following extract provides a rather colorful account of the fête:

On the 12th of May, after vespers, the earthquake procession is conducted, the parochial priest to be present. The canon who reads Mass during that week, and the two ladies who sing in the choir, come to the entrance of the church with the Holy Cross and consecrated water. All the monks, too, have to be present. The procession starts with the singing of the Te Deum, which is sung by the lady singer of the week. After the Te Deum, psalms are sung, which are specially indicated for processions in order to obtain God's Grace. The procession proceeds on its way by leaving the church by the doors facing the town; then it passes along the Rue des Prêtres, and finally re-enters the church by the same doors through which it left.

During the eighteenth and nineteenth centuries the statue maintained its reputation for producing miracles. By the end of the nineteenth century, for example, many of the villagers believed that when displayed publicly for veneration the statue had the power to alleviate droughts, abort earthquakes, avert fires, and so on.

In 1907, the statue became the focus of a heated and emotional controversy which set the scene for the subsequent miracle. Despite the fact that the ceremony in honor of "Notre Dame du Trésor" had been sanctioned by the local cardinal almost two hundred years earlier, it had never received papal approval. Although this situation did not seem to bother Remiremont's citizens, it was somewhat embarrassing to many local priests; so in 1907 the Reverend Archdeacon Vuillemin, an elderly town priest, petitioned Rome to approve veneration of the statue. Vuillemin's lobbying was constant, and later that year Pope Pius X yielded by sending a personal delegate to Remiremont along with a costly crown as a sign of approval of, and blessing for, the statue. The news of papal consent caused a great deal of excitement in Remiremont, and at Vuillemin's suggestion, ecclesiastic authorities in the town decided that the statue would be "crowned" at a public ceremony in the church as part of the annual procession. The celebration was scheduled for May 20 (slightly after the actual date of the yearly procession), and five local bishops agreed to attend the day-long affair. It promised to be one of the most spectacular days in Remiremont's history.

All the plans for the celebration had been made, and the village was eagerly anticipating it. Then, on May 12, the town council refused to approve the procession and canceled it. The decision was based on a sound premise. Remiremont was at the time divided into two factions. While most of the villagers were devout

Catholics, an anti-Catholic and anticlerical movement had recently become vocal, and the council feared that any procession honoring the statue might cause a riot—especially since several important ecclesiastic officials were coming to town for the crowning. They did agree to allow a procession to be held inside the church on May 20, but forbade any public ceremony in the streets.

This decision ignited a storm of controversy. The village council was condemned from the pulpits of local churches, and most of the townsfolk were outraged by the edict. Nonetheless, the mayor and town council stuck to their decision, and for the first time in over a hundred years the public procession in honor of the statue was not held.

And then on May 26 a fierce hailstorm struck Remiremont and several neighboring villages. It had been a sunny day, but late that afternoon a wind arose from the southeast, driving a storm before it. The rain was at first accompanied by small hailstones, and there seemed nothing unusual about the storm. But this first flurry was soon followed by a second hailstorm. Hailstones much larger than those that had fallen earlier—some of them the size of tomatoes—began to fall. Many of them were oval in shape and had a flattened (as opposed to convex) side. These larger stones fell from roughly five thirty to six fifteen; and because of their size, many did not break or otherwise disintegrate but remained on the ground after the storm had ended. A number of them were subsequently collected by curious villagers, who made a fascinating discovery. The stones were impressed with a portrait of the Virgin Mary!

That the hailstones bore this likeness was bizarre enough, but the relationship between the hailstones and the "Notre Dame du Trésor" did not simply end there. In honor of the crowning of the statue, a commemorative medal depicting the Virgin and the Christ Child had been struck. The image on the miraculous hailstones was, according to several witnesses, identical to that on the medallion!

Many of these stones were temporarily preserved by the townsfolk and were examined at close range by believers and skeptics alike. One extremely detailed and impressive account of their weird appearance was given by the Abbé Gueniot, a local priest, in a statement he wrote in 1908. Although Gueniot had not actually seen the stones fall, one of the village women visited him just after the storm had struck and presented him with two of the miracle stones. The priest was at first incredulous.

In order to satisfy her [he told reporters], I glanced carelessly at the hailstones, which she held in her hand. But since I did not want to see anything, and moreover could not do so without my spectacles, I turned to go back to my book. She urged: "I beg of you to put on your glasses." I did so, and saw very distinctly on the front of the hailstones, which were slightly convex in the center, although the edges were somewhat worn, the bust of a woman, with a robe that was turned up at the bottom, like a priest's cope. I should, perhaps, describe it more exactly by saying that it was like the Virgin of the Hermits. The outline of the images was slightly hollow, as if they had been formed with a punch, but were very boldly drawn. Mlle. André asked me to notice certain details of the costume, but I refused to look at it any longer. I was ashamed of my credulity, feeling sure that the Blessed Virgin would hardly concern herself with instantaneous photographs on hailstones. I said, "But do not you see that these hailstones have fallen on vegetables, and received these impressions? Take them away: they are no good to me." I returned to my book, without giving further thought to what had happened. But my mind was disturbed by the singular formation of these hailstones. I picked up three in order to weigh them, without looking closely. They weighed between six and seven ounces. One of them was perfectly round, like balls with which children play, and had a seam all around it, as though it had been cast in a mold.[1]

After reexamining the stones, Gueniot became convinced of their miraculous nature. His subsequent observations corroborated the testimony of others who had seen the hailstones. The depiction of the Virgin Mary seemed impressed onto the side with the freak smooth surface, almost as though snow had formed around a mirror of ice.

Other aspects of the hailstones also indicated something supernatural had happened in Remiremont that day as well. The miraculous stones did not seem to fall from the sky normally, and several eyewitnesses testified that those stones impressed with the portrait seemed to "float" to the ground slowly "as if they were snowflakes," according to one observer. And despite their large size, the stones did *no damage* to any gardens or fields on which they fell. Some of the residents even claimed that the course of the hailstorm followed the historical route used by the nuns who had brought the statue to Remiremont in 910 A.D.

One account attesting to this bizarre feature of the miraculous hailstorm was placed on record in 1908 by Marie Parmetier, a Remiremont resident whose garden had been inundated by the hail:

It was the 26th of May 1907, between five thirty and six o'clock. We had gone to the Toucherie (where the open gardens on the East Canal are) in order to see if our garden had been damaged. When we arrived there we verified that the plants were uninjured and that the hailstones were at least fifty centimeters each. As one of the children had told us that they had seen the image of Our Lady of the Treasure in the hailstones, on the return route we gathered some hailstones and we verified that in fact they contained the image of Our Lady of the Treasure. We were accompanied by Mme Richard, who lives in Moyenmoutier; she, like us, had seen the image. We went by the home of this woman's mother; we showed her a hailstone the size of a hen's egg. She also saw the image, which she described to us through an open window, for we did not enter her house. Our Lady appeared to us as white as the hailstone; she was in the interior (of the hailstone) in the middle. I did not have on such a medal at the time. I have bought several of them since.

Several Paris newspapers soon sent reporters to Remiremont to investigate the strange happening, and most of the stories that subsequently appeared were basically scathing indictments which criticized the "gullibility" of the town residents. Some of the papers even charged that the local clergy had "manufactured" the miracle in order to stir up pro-Catholic sentiment in France.

There were, however, two detailed investigations of the Remiremont affair that deserve closer scrutiny. The first of these was conducted by M. Sage, a French student of psychical research, in 1908. The Society for Psychical Research, an organization based in London that had been founded in 1882 with the goal of scientifically examining reports of psychic phenomena, both funded Sage's probe and published his report in 1908 through an endowment granted to them by one of their French members. It appeared in French with no translation offered.[2]

Sage began his probe in September 1908 by interviewing Archdeacon Vuillemin at his church. On behalf of his bishop, Vuillemin had personally investigated the miracle and had prepared a detailed dossier on the case which Sage wanted to scrutinize. He hoped that it would yield enough eyewitness testimony so that he could evaluate the case from records made right at the time of the event. Father Vuillemin was more than willing to present Sage with a summary of his report, but he could not supply him with a copy of the full dossier, which, he explained, had already been sent to Rome for evaluation. Since the report was now officially out of his hands, he explained, he could not release any material from it without the approval of his superiors. Sage pressed Vuillemin nonetheless, and the priest finally and somewhat reluctantly allowed him to glance over a copy of the dossier and agreed to provide him with the names of several eyewitnesses.

Sage next visited the homes of various Remiremont residents who had witnessed the miracle, and whose names had been given to him by the elderly priest. He found, however, that the townsfolk were reticent about discussing the miracle. The Remiremont townspeople had been the butt of many jibes in the popular press; so they were not talking too keenly to foreigners visiting their town and asking questions. One witness even threatened to throw Sage out of his house!

Nevertheless, Sage was able to collect several brief accounts describing the incident (though considerably fewer than Vuillemin had obtained a year earlier), which provided him with a good amount of material. One witness, Cecile Claude, told him:

I was chatting with a woman in front of our house after the storm. She asked me if I hadn't seen the hailstones containing the image of Our Lady of the Treasure. I answered no. At that same moment a little girl arrived from behind the washhouse and brought me a hailstone to look at; this hailstone was about the size of a pigeon egg. I looked at it and saw the image. Immediately I took it to show my parents. Mama said: "Let's see if we can't find some others." We toured the garden and Mama found some, one sunken in a hole. The image was very distinct. One could see the image in other hailstones, but less distinctly.

The mill had a thousand broken bricks. But no plant in our garden was harmed.

Disturbed by the low intellectual level of the witnesses he had tracked down and unable to find any educated resident of the town other than Father Gueniot who had witnessed the strange events, Sage became more skeptical. He reasoned that since all his sources were essentially simple laborers and farmers, they probably were not dependable informants.*

Sage was also disturbed by his inability to locate anyone who had immediately recognized, spontaneously and independently, the form of "Notre Dame du Trésor" when first seeing the hailstones. Most of the witnesses Sage spoke with affirmed that they had seen a female figure in the hailstones, but had *only later* come to the conclusion that it resembled the figure on the Remiremont medallion. Many told him that they hadn't even gone outdoors to collect the miraculous hailstones until they had been informed by other villagers that the stones were impressed with the figure of the Virgin. Sage's conclusion was that the town had suffered from a mass "collective illusion" brought on by religious hysteria. The townsfolk saw the images on the hailstones, he argued, only because they *expected* to see them—much in the way one tends to see animals and human shapes in Rorschach ink blots. But Sage offers no explanation of *how* the rumor of the miraculous hailstones began, or why only a certain number of hailstones seemed to have been impressed. Nor does he take into account that *some* sort of human figure had obviously appeared in the stones.

Sage also rejected the stories he heard about the uncannily slow trajectory of the hailstones. "It is clear that the alleged slow dropping of the big hailstones should be considered the product of an optical illusion," he writes in his SPR report. "The exact speed of the hailstones' fall could not be measured by anyone. These hailstones dropped down perpendicularly in a calm atmosphere, so one could probably have followed their fall with one's eyes. This would have given the impression that the stones were drop-

---

*In reading over Sage's report, one is forced to question whether he was a very good judge of character. Apart from his obvious élitism, he characterized Father Gueniot, with whom he spoke about the miracle, as "an old man" possessed with "more faith than he has knowledge of human psychology." His basic conclusion was that Gueniot's religious background made him too credulous to be a reliable witness. But as the section of Gueniot's testimony quoted earlier indicates, this was hardly the case. Neither does Sage mention that the priest was himself at first extremely skeptical about the miracle.

ping at a slow speed." His explanation as to why the hailstones
had done no damage to any of the gardens in the town was that
the hail had simply missed them!—a judgment inconsistent with
the testimony of several Remiremont residents who had actually
found hailstones embedded in their gardens. (Oddly, Sage quotes
at least two such personal testimonies in the appendix to his official
report.)

His general appraisal was that nothing unusual had happened
during the hailstorm: "If we sum up the case we shall soon come
to the conclusion that not a scrap of evidence can be brought
forward in favor of this case. Not the slightest proof is available
that would satisfy a somewhat critical-minded person, namely that
the figure of the N. D. du Trésor did appear on the hailstones that
dropped down on Remiremont at the end of May, 1907."

Sage's conclusions should be evaluated with reserve. He was
able to interview only a dozen or so witnesses, who were often
reluctant to talk with him. It also seems evident from the tone of
his report that he was biased against the possibility of the miracle
even before he ever set foot in Remiremont. He also based his
general conclusions on a very arguable premise, to which he alludes consistently throughout his report—i.e., that because his
sources were basically laborers and farmers with very little scientific
background, they could not have been very good witnesses to the
miracle. This may explain why many of his conclusions are totally
inconsistent with the firsthand testimonies he cites in the appendix
to his report.

Were the Remiremont townsfolk reliable witnesses to the hailstorm of 1907? These "peasants" were used to working out of
doors and observing the course of nature. Because they lived off
the land, their survival was contingent on their shrewd ability to
judge weather conditions. They were, in fact, probably very good
witnesses to the miraculous hailstones, and had probably experienced many more hailstorms than Sage or his fellow intellectuals
from Paris had ever even seen!

Sage likewise presents no support for his theory that the slow
descent of the stones was an optical illusion, and poses no explanation of why only those hailstones impressed with the likeness of
"Notre Dame du Trésor" fell in this odd manner. Remember that
the miraculous hailstones were interspersed with normal hail, and

their slow flight was clearly seen by the townsfolk. They were therefore in a perfect position to judge whether the flight of the miraculous hailstones was in any way uncanny.

Finally, Sage omits practically all mention of the favorable conclusions of Father Vuillemin's report—the result of over one hundred interviews, and therefore more extensive than Sage's. Sage's only relevant comment is that Vuillemin was interested in quantity rather than quality while conducting his probe. He uses this argument to dismiss totally its findings! Vuillemin's investigation was addressed to Monsignor Foucault, the bishop of Saint-Die, who issued a summary of it under his own imprimatur.[3] It is obvious from this summary that Vuillemin, while gathering his data, had been keenly interested in determining whether the image on the hailstones was an objective configuration or only an illusion. As his report reads:

I invited all parishioners who had any information to give to come to the presbytery. During several weeks I saw and separately questioned a large number of witnesses, to all of whom I pointed out the gravity and importance of their depositions. The enquiry was conducted with all the rigour which the importance of the subject demanded, and it was closed on July 10 at a sitting presided over by your lordship, accompanied by Canon Chicy, the Vicar-General, by the Curé of Saint-Etienne, and the clergy of the town.

The complete evidence given under oath contains the depositions of 107 witnesses, thus divided:

From Remiremont, men 16, women 26, children 6, total 48; from Saint-Etienne, men 15, women 32, children 1, total 48; from Saint-Nabord, men 1, women 6, children 4, total 11; altogether, men 32, women 64, children 11, or 107 persons in all.

Thus we have the testimony of over a hundred persons who, under oath, state that they saw the image of Our Lady of the Treasure on the hailstones.

What is to be thought of their statements? Was the imprint of the Madonna in their imagination only or in reality on the hailstones, called hailstone medallions because like the Coronation medals, they bore the image of Our Lady of the Treasure?

This question is of great importance; it is the main point of the inquiry. It was therefore necessary to test the value of the statements, so as to set aside illusion and suggestion and bring the authenticity of the hailstones into full relief.

The following are the results:—

1. The observations were simultaneous, concordant, and precise. They were made in the same place, the same day, and the same hour—nearly six o'clock in the evening—and it is not possible to say by whom the first observation was made.

They were concordant; all affirm the presence of the image of Our Lady of the Treasure on the hailstones. The differences are only in minor details, and may be ascribed to the condition of the hailstones when the observations were made.

They were, on the whole, of remarkable precision. It was not a vague form which the witnesses saw, but an absolutely clear effigy, corresponding in every detail with the medal struck in memory of the Coronation.

2. The observations were made at more than twenty different places; at distances apart ranging from some hundreds of yards to two-thirds of a mile.

3. They were nearly all made in the same manner, being due to curiosity. The first witness of the extraordinary occurrence at each place was at first so astounded and enraptured that he hastened to share his joy with others, and to assure himself that he was not deceived, so that in every centre of observation there were from two to nine mutually corroborative witnesses. Many also compared the medals which they wore with these hailstones; the resemblance was perfect. At the same time they threw away the hailstones on which nothing was to be seen—in fact, all which had not the image of the Madonna.

4. The observations resulted in immediately producing in the minds of the witnesses a profound and ineradicable conviction. Your lordship has heard several depositions, and knows with what firmness of conviction they were made. "I would give all my limbs," said one; "even to the last drop of my blood," said another, "rather than say that the image of Our Lady of the Treasure was not on the hailstones, and that I did not see it."

Vuillemin ended his report with a discussion on the intelligence that lay behind the miracle. Like most citizens of Remiremont, he believed that the hailstones were created by a divine intelligence as a "sign" to those who had been robbed of their procession in honor of "Notre Dame du Trésor" a week before.

There can be little doubt that the events of May 26, 1907, constitute a genuine miracle. But, again, it seems more reasonable to assume that it was somehow produced by the minds of the villagers rather than by a divine agency. Somehow the collective "will" of the townspeople acted directly on the weather and psychically produced the miraculous hailstones. In other words, the hailstones were the product of psychically mediated "wish fulfillment" rather than a divine sign from heaven.

There exists strong evidence that the human mind *can* directly interfere with the weather and produce freak effects. Perhaps the most famous historical example of such a psychic weather-control feat was documented during the life of St. Joan of Arc (1412–31). In April 1429 her troops were about to cross the Loire to engage the British. French ships had to be sent upstream to Orléans to procure provisions, but the wind was blowing in the wrong direction. St. Joan began to pray devoutly, and the wind changed direction almost instantaneously.*

Both St. Francis of Paolo and Padre Pio were credited with the ability to influence the elements as well. In his book *Padre Pio—the Stigmatist*, Father Charles Carty cites an eyewitness report from a visitor to San Giovanni Rotondo who once saw Padre Pio control a local rainstorm. An even more remarkable case of psychic weather control was recently reported by Dr. David Read Barker, formerly an anthropologist at the University of Virginia. Speaking before the twenty-first annual convention of the Parapsychological Association, held in St. Louis in August 1978, Dr. Barker described a weather-control experiment he had seen performed on March 10, 1973, in Northern India. He was living that month in a settlement populated by Tibetan refugees, who were preparing for an annual ritual in commemoration of their 1953 flight from invading Chinese troops. A rainstorm threatened to interfere with the celebration, and the Tibetan community called on an elderly lama, Gunsang Rinzing, to clear away the storm. Rinzing prayed the entire night, after which the storm subsided *only in the area of the gathering* for the six hours the ceremony lasted. It continued to rain and hail all *around* the field in which the Tibetans had gathered, but the storm never interfered with the ceremony.[4] (One might also note in this connection that many "rain dance" rituals conducted by American Indian groups and

---

*For an excellent critical evaluation of this miracle and the evidence documenting it, see John Beevers, *St. Joan of Arc* (Garden City, New York: Doubleday, 1959).

shamans have proved efficacious even in areas where no rainfall was expected.*)

Another clue about the nature of the Remiremont hailstones is provided by the manner in which the stones floated down to earth. Because this phenomenon is similar to many manifestations noted during poltergeist attacks, the Remiremont miracle may have actually been a *form* of poltergeist attack on a colossal scale.

A poltergeist (a German word meaning "noisy spirit") is a curious form of haunting that delights in causing violent disturbances in the homes in which it erupts. Poltergeists like to produce knocking sounds inside the house, move furniture around, and cause small household items to fly about mysteriously. In more violent cases, spontaneous fires will break out, and other complex psychokinetic manifestations will sometimes occur.† One of the most common of these is paranormal "stone throwing." Many cases on record report how rocks began "raining down" on the roofs of a poltergeist-ridden house. These rock falls occasionally accompany more traditional poltergeistery, such as object throwings and rappings, and are more rarely the only plan of attack the poltergeist uses against a house. The Big Bear stone-throwing case of 1962 (see page 2) is a good example of the latter. In this instance periodic volleys of stones were seen to fall on a small mountain cabin. The falls, which came every few hours or so, lasted several weeks, but gradually ceased when the residents moved out. Several witnesses to the Big Bear case specifically noted that the stones *fell slowly from the sky* as though floating down to earth.

An interesting variant of the stone-throwing poltergeist took place in 1920, when stones started bombarding a farmhouse in France. (The case is recounted by the famous French astronomer Camille Flammarion in his book *Haunted Houses.*) The poltergeist began its siege in September, when showers of rocks began drop-

---

*See, for instance, Ivan Sanderson, *Investigating the Unexplained* (Englewood Cliffs, New Jersey: Prentice-Hall, 1972).

†The poltergeist received nationwide attention recently when a case broke out in Bridgeport, Connecticut, in March 1974. The eruption plagued the home of Mr. and Mrs. Gerald Goodin. Their TV set kept jumping off its stand, large pieces of furniture would suddenly move by themselves, and pounding noises were heard throughout the house. The events lasted several weeks, and local police investigators could find no normal explanation for them.

ping onto the house from high in the sky. Observers swore that the rocks *fell slowly.* This phenomenon was especially well witnessed by the local priest, who personally investigated the case. The rock falls ceased after a few weeks, but then more traditional poltergeistery broke out inside the farmhouse.

An even better-documented stone-throwing poltergeist struck the little town of Nickelheim, Germany, in 1968, and was investigated by a team of experts from Freiburg University headed by Dr. Hans Bender. The scene of the manifestations was a small home on the outskirts of town. For a period of four months the family complained that odd knocking sounds were erupting in the house and plaguing them day and night. Household items began moving about by themselves soon afterward and would sometimes totally dematerialize, and rocks would often fall on the roof. Eventually the rocks began appearing inside the house as well. They would suddenly materialize out of thin air, and would then fall to the floor. Several witnesses testified that when small household items such as bottles and vials were moved, *they often fell or moved slowly as though floating or being carried.*[5]

Since the turn of the century, not a few psychic investigators have noticed that poltergeist outbreaks generally follow a predictable pattern. They usually erupt in homes in which a young (and often disturbed) person is living and focus on that person—either by attacking him the most violently or occurring only when he is present and awake. (For example, the victim of the Big Bear stone-throwing poltergeist and the primary victim of the Nickelheim disturbance were adolescent daughters of the residents.) If the family moves away, the poltergeist usually follows them wherever they go. On the other hand, though, poltergeist outbreaks are usually brief affairs lasting only a few weeks or months before petering out. They rarely return.

The poltergeist is not merely a diversified and patternless group of psychokinetic phenomena, but a specific *syndrome* which follows a predictable course of action and which is typified by several rather clear-cut characteristics. Because of this semiconsistent pattern, even the first parapsychologists realized that "spirits" of the dead or "demons" had little to do with the phenomenon. They theorized instead that these "poltergeist" children (or agents, since they weren't always children) were somehow actually responsible for the outbreaks, as though they were unconsciously using their own innate *psychokinetic* abilities to produce the disruptions. This theory had some general confirmation when in the 1930s Dr. J. B. Rhine and his colleagues at Duke University discovered through dice-rolling experiments that many people, and not just gifted psychics, seem to possess PK abilities. The theory has had more direct confirmation over the last few decades. With the rise of psychoanalysis and, later, clinical psychology during the period between 1920 and 1940, a few parapsychologists began taking a detailed psychiatric look at these "poltergeist agents." They began to realize that the poltergeist agent is usually a repressed, frustrated individual who is projecting his repressions through the poltergeist.

With the recent refinement of psychodiagnostic testing, this basic theory has been confirmed and extended by parapsychologists working in the United States and Europe. Dr. Hans Bender has been able to make detailed psychological examinations of several poltergeist agents, including the victim of the Nickelheim disturbance, and has found that they usually possess similar personality characteristics. In most cases they seem to be harboring extreme hostilities which they are actively repressing from consciousness. Many appear to be crippled by a total inability to express these hostilities in a verbal or at least socially acceptable way. When confronted with their hostilities, these subjects tend to deny them or rationalize them away. Their anger is most often directed against parents or similar authority figures. Dr. Bender's findings have been confirmed in this country by W. G. Roll, a parapsychologist who heads the Psychical Research Foundation in Durham, North Carolina.

In other words, the poltergeist seems to be a vehicle through which the agent seeks to *express* hostile feelings that have been barred from normal release. The poltergeist, to use a crude metaphor, seems to be like a tea kettle blowing off the steam of excess repression. This theory also accounts for the dynamics of poltergeist behavior. When a child becomes angry, he will invariably pound his fists on the wall, throw things, and act out his anger in other physical ways. The poltergeist carries out the very acts the child, or agent, would like to perform physically but cannot bring himself to do. Of course, the poltergeist is directed by the agent's unconscious mind, and so the agent will usually remain unaware or only dimly cognizant that he is, in fact, producing the outbreak.

These findings are directly relevant to the Remiremont miracle. Here we have what might be called a "poltergeist potential" being shared by the entire town. Its inhabitants were, in effect, manipulated into a psychological situation suspiciously similar to the one in which most poltergeist agents find themselves. They were made to feel hostile, and their anger was directed toward the town authorities. Yet they were in no position to vent this hostility, as they could not strike back at the offending town council.

In such an intensely aggravating situation, something was bound to give. And on May 26 it did. The repressed rage of the Remiremont villagers had undoubtedly grown over the several days following the date on which the ceremony in honor of the "Notre Dame du Trésor" had been scheduled. The hailstorm that broke at five thirty probably became the vehicle for a sublimated expression of this hostility. Most likely some psychic power generated by the collective tensions of the local residents interacted with the storm and psychokinetically produced the miraculous hailstones.

This explanation is supported by the fact that the Remiremont miracle of 1907 is not the only miracle of its kind on record. Several related occurrences, during which the forces of nature were manipulated in times of religious strife or crisis, have been documented. On May 6, 1944, the New York *Sun* reported that a figure of Christ had appeared within a cloud formation over the town of Ipswich, England, during an air raid alert. Hundreds of witnesses saw the image. "His head was bowed and his feet were crossed," reported the Reverend H. G. Green, an army chaplain who investigated the miracle. "All who saw agreed to these details. When it disappeared, it did not drift away like clouds but vanished instantly and entirely."

Is it not possible that this miracle was a psychic effect produced by the Ipswich citizens under the threat of imminent death at the hands of German bombers? Like the miraculous hailstones of Remiremont, the cloud figure of Christ may have been more a case of psychic wish fulfillment than a supernatural sign from heaven.[6]*

A related miracle was reported from the German town of Nuremberg in 1503 by Albrecht Dürer (1471−1528), the great artist and illustrator.[7] An outbreak of plague had struck the city that year and had killed off a large portion of the population. Concomitant with the plague came a series of bizarre red-colored rains. (These rains, which have been reported from all parts of the world, are allegedly produced when rain and airborne red algae interact.) To the generally superstitious inhabitants of plague-stricken Nuremberg, the rains were yet another sign that God had forsaken the city. Soon, though, rumors began to spread that the rain sometimes created a figure of the crucified Christ on clothing or linen left outdoors. Dürer personally saw one of these peculiar stains when a young servant girl who had been caught in one of the storms showed him her linen shift. He was so impressed by the image that he immediately drew a reproduction of it. (This sketch is currently housed in the archives of the Staatliche Museum in Berlin.) Dürer's detailed drawing clearly shows a cross on which appears a human figure. Two additional figures positioned before the crucifixion scene seem to be in adoration. There seems little reason to doubt the accuracy of Dürer's depiction, and it is reasonable to assume that the stain he saw was not the only one of its kind produced during the red rains of 1503.

It is difficult to believe that all the miracles at Remiremont, Ipswich, and Nuremberg were merely the chance products of nature. In each instance the dynamics *leading* to the events were the same. The spiritual concerns of the witnesses seem to have been paranormally reflected in the subsequent productions of nature during times of near religious hysteria.

Could the hailstones that fell in Remiremont on May 26 have been a fluke of nature? When Father Vuillemin initiated his inves-

---

*Some years ago, the Ashland (Kentucky) *Daily Independent* published a photograph showing a figure of Christ formed out of a cloud configuration. Two airplanes can be seen flying near it. The photograph was allegedly taken during the Korean War and supposedly depicts a dogfight. The photograph caused a sensation when it was published, and prints of it are still being distributed by missionaries, evangelists, and Fundamentalist groups in the United States. I am afraid, though, that the photograph and accompanying story have all the earmarks of a hoax.

tigation of the miracle, he was concerned with this very issue. In trying to determine the elements that had given rise to the storm, Vuillemin consulted several university professors and scientists. He wanted to ascertain whether the human figure visible in the hailstones could have been the freak production of nature. All of the scientists with whom the priest conferred agreed that while nature can produce anomalies, chance atmospheric factors could not have produced the direct likeness of a human form. Pierre Duhem, a scientist at the University of Bordeaux, informed the priest that while the normal forces of nature can make water condense into specific forms (such as the rounded forms of hail and the octagonal configuration of snowflakes), it could not produce images within these forms. He therefore tended to agree with Father Vuillemin that the hailstone figures of the virgin could only have been produced by an *intelligence* interfering with the normal course of nature, and not by nature alone.

At the conclusion of his report, Vuillemin states:

The hailstone medallions could not have been struck without the intervention of an *intelligent will*. What is this will? Is it human? Is it devilish? Is it divine? Science and common sense agree in discarding the hypothesis of a human or fraudulent cause, for the reason that a person wishing to deceive could not have foretold the storm, which was entirely unforeseen, strike the effigy of Our Lady of the Treasure on lumps of ice, and cause them to fall in the crowd or mix them with other hailstones falling at the same time at Remiremont, Saint-Etienne and Saint-Nabord.

To state the matter in these terms is evidently to answer this objection. In the conditions set forth the carrying out of such a fraud would be an event more extraordinary than that of the hailstone medallions.

Though it is difficult to believe that the Remiremont miracle was the product of fraud on the part of local residents, it *does* appear that they were instrumental in producing the miraculous hailstones—but in a way too complex for Father Vuillemin to have appreciated.

~ VII ~
BLEEDING STATUES
AND WEEPING MADONNAS

ON THE MORNING of January 3, 1971, Giovanbattista Cordiano, a respected lawyer living in Maropati, Italy, awoke to find that a painting of the Madonna that hung over his bed was dripping blood.

The painting was a thirty-one-inch by forty-three-inch print depicting the Madonna holding the infant Jesus in her arms. Two additional figures kneel beside her. The print had been given to Cordiano and his wife as a present by their son. "For ten years that painting hung above our bed without anything extraordinary happening—until last January 3," Cordiano told reporters. "On that morning I awoke to find spots of blood on the pillow cases. I asked my wife, Katia, if she had cut herself. She looked in the mirror and said no. I checked myself—and found no cuts either." Cordiano attributed the mystery to "cause unknown" and gave little more attention to it.

But then the stains turned up again. "After the blood spots appeared a few more times," Cordiano explained, "I was dumbfounded to discover that they were dripping from under the glass of the painting. The bloodlike liquid was coming from the Madonna's eyes like tears, and from her heart, hands, and feet. It was also dripping from the hands and feet of the two saints kneeling beside her. Some of the red liquid began to form crosses on the white wall below the painting."

Cordiano's observations were soon confirmed by dozens of other witnesses. Alfredo Riva, the Cordianos' neighbor, was able to watch the blood flows when he visited the house soon after the bleeding was noticed. He later told reporters that the blood would rush down the painting from the figure and then drop onto the wall under it after settling at the base of the frame. Once the blood hit the wall, it would mysteriously spread out in the form of a cross. It was "as if a magnet were drawing the blood in four directions at once," Riva stated.

While at first the bleedings came daily, the painting soon dripped blood only every few weeks or so. "There's no warning," testified Filomena Concetti, another neighbor. "Suddenly the spots come and then trickle down. It sometimes lasts a few minutes, but usually the blood stops after about a minute."

The bleeding Madonna of Maropati eventually became a headache for the Cordianos. They had initially tried to keep news of the miracle a secret; but reports of miracles are hard to keep quiet—especially in a family with seven children! Soon throngs of spectators were besieging the Cordianos' home in hopes of getting a peek at the painting. Cordiano, stupefied by the publicity he and the picture were receiving, tried to turn the painting over to local Church authorities. But Church officials in Maropati refused to get involved in the case since the "miracle" had not been authenticated by the Vatican.

Local police officials were called in to investigate when the publicity the painting was receiving threatened to disrupt the entire community. They were quite impressed. "There's no trick," asserted Police Chief Antonio Raia to the press on September 5. "We searched all over the bedroom. There were no tubes, bottles, or holes in back of the painting." The police even took possession of the picture, locked it up in a wooden box, and kept it at their headquarters overnight.

"Next morning we opened the box," reported Raia. "Blood was on the painting."

The sticky liquid flowing from the painting did prove to be blood. Two samples of the liquid were analyzed at the Laboratorio Provinciale d'Igiene e Profilassi di Reggia Cui in Calabria. Dr. Francesco Mollo, head of the laboratory, subsequently issued a report stating that "the chemical examination of the liquid extract has confirmed that it is blood. By using chemical precipitates, it was ascertained that it is human blood." [1]

The case of Maropati's bleeding Madonna is only one example of a type of miracle that has been chronicled repeatedly since

Christianity spread throughout the world. Cases of religious statues, paintings, icons, and other effigies that suddenly begin to bleed or weep have been documented throughout history. Before Rome was sacked in 1527, for instance, a statue of Christ housed in a local monastery wept for several days. When the city of Syracuse in Sicily lay under Spanish siege in 1719, a marble statue of St. Lucy in the city cried continually.

These cases are so commonly reported, especially from such traditionally Catholic countries as Italy and Brazil, that a book could be written about this miracle alone. Bleeding/weeping effigy miracles generally manifest themselves in two basic ways. The more prominent is the "bleeding statue," where sculptured representations of Christ begin to emit human blood. The flows usually emanate from the traditional sites of the crucifixion wounds. The other common form of the miracle is the so-called weeping Madonna, in which paintings or statues of the Virgin Mary cry very real tears.

Cases of the first type do not seem to be contingent on the material composition of the effigy, and instances of bleeding plaster, wooden, marble, and even waxen statues have been reported. A three-hundred-year-old wooden statue of Christ housed in a church in Porto dos Caixas, Brazil, began to bleed in 1968, and still does to this day. The blood drips intermittently from the crucifixion wounds painted on the statue's hands. A limestone crucifix belonging to Signor and Signora Pizzi of Syracuse, Sicily, began bleeding in 1972. The Pizzis testified that the blood would suddenly appear on the breast of the Christ statuette in the traditional site of the lance wound. According to Dr. S. Rodante, the president of the Catholic Doctors' Association in Sicily, the blood coagulated more quickly than human blood is prone to do.

One of the most recent (as well as one of the best-documented) examples of this miracle occurred in the Philadelphia, Pennsylvania, home of Mrs. Anne Poore. A twenty-eight-inch-tall statue of Christ which had been given to Mrs. Poore in 1974 suddenly began bleeding shortly after Easter of 1975. "I was kneeling before it at my home," Mrs. Poore told reporters in January 1976, "praying about the way people have been going away from religion. Suddenly I looked up at the statue—and my heart stopped beating. Two ruby-red drops of blood had appeared over the plaster wounds in its palms! I was terrified—I could see it was real blood."

Mrs. Poore witnessed several such flows over the next few days, as did the neighbors who had dropped by to observe the statue. When *too* many visitors began showing up, Mrs. Poore turned the effigy over to the Reverend Chester Olszewski, the pastor of St. Luke's Episcopal Church in nearby Eddystone. He, too, later testified to the authenticity of the miracle.

"Hundreds have come to my church to pray before the statue—and it has bled," he told reporters in a statement issued on January 20, 1976. "Yet it stands on a shelf ten feet above the altar, where nobody can touch it. It has bled as long as four hours. I know there can be no trickery. Several times I've seen the palms dry—then minutes later have observed droplets of blood welling out of the wounds."

Another clergyman who has examined the statue is Father Henry Lovett, a Roman Catholic priest from New Jersey who is an authority on miracles. Although at first skeptical of the Eddystone report, Father Lovett changed his mind after examining the statue at St. Luke's. Lovett removed the hands of the statue, which were held in place by wooden dowels, and found no tubes or other punctures which would indicate that Mrs. Poore had been perpetrating a hoax. Father Lovett was also able to observe the blood flows. "I think the purpose of this miraculous bleeding is to call attention to religion again," he told reporters.

A final word on the Eddystone statue came from Joseph Rovita, a prominent Philadelphia physician who analyzed blood samples taken from the effigy. Rovita told reporters that the blood was indeed human, but that it seemed to be in an advanced state of decomposition. Fresh blood contains millions of red blood cells, he explained, yet the blood from the Eddystone statue numbered relatively few such cells. Since the red cell count in a sample of blood diminishes over time, Rovita could only estimate that the blood was "very old"—too old, in fact, to even determine its type.[2]

The bleeding statue of St. Luke's caused a stir in the American press in the early part of 1976, but news of the miracle soon faded, perhaps because the bleedings became less frequent. The last public information about Eddystone's bleeding statue came much later that year, when a *Los Angeles Times* item reported that Father Olszewski had been barred from his church on orders from his superiors. The reason given was that the Episcopal priest had begun celebrating Roman Catholic Mass, apparently in honor of the miracle he had witnessed.

As with most miraculous events, cases of bleeding/weeping effigies often seem to be genuine miracles in that they are physical events that contradict all the laws of nature. They also fit Cardinal Prospero Lambertini's definition of a miracle as the interaction of the supernatural order with the natural order of our terrestrial lives. Bleeding/weeping effigy miracles appear to be events beyond the scope of science and even of parapsychology. It doesn't take a nuclear physicist to know that plaster and wood can't bleed.

On the other hand, as previous discussions in this book have made clear, the independence of the miraculous from time and space is often more apparent than real. The literature on miracles contains several clues pointing to the possibility that the miraculous can only occur through at least the *agency* of the human mind. Sometimes, as in the case of the Remiremont hailstones, it takes a detailed evaluation of the subtle psychological context in which a miracle occurs before this human link becomes obvious. In this respect, miracles are very much like poltergeist effects. When a poltergeist erupts in a home, very rarely (if at all) do the residents realize that *they* are the ones responsible for producing it. In almost *every* case they are certain that they are being plagued by either demons or spirits of the dead.

Psychic phenomena are certainly unusual events. The fact that one can directly perceive the thoughts of another person or make an object move without touching it is a truth that contradicts everything we have been taught—through our formal education and everyday experience—about the world. Yet when we are first born we instinctively believe that our thoughts can control the physical world. (For example, when a child plays "peek-a-boo" he actually thinks that he is destroying and then conjuring his mother back into existence in a magical way.) As we grow older it is disappointing to realize that our thoughts exist only within our minds, and that we can't work "miracles" with them. Through what psychologists call "reality testing," we learn through experimenting with our environment that a dichotomy exists between the world of thought and emotion and the world of physical reality. It's a hard lesson to learn, and one few of us ever get over!

It is for this reason that we become squeamish when confronted by a miracle—be it a poltergeist, a telepathic experience, or a religious wonder. Our everyday, commonsense attitude has told us that the human mind can't influence the world around it, and so we automatically assume that any "supernatural" incidents we may witness are due to the activities of supernatural beings. Just as poltergeist victims attribute their troubles to spirits and demons—which allows their accepting what is happening to them without disrupting the way they have learned to view the world— so do we attribute miracles to divine agencies. It is too difficult, and a little too bizarre, to accept the fact that they are probably the products of our own minds.

Even in those instances in which religious effigies have bled and wept, which seem so contrary to the laws of nature, most of the evidence points right back to the psychic power of the human unconscious. One case that provides just such a clue was reported from France during the hectic years preceding and during World War I. It was extremely well investigated by Everard Feilding, a talented psychic investigator of his day. His report on the miracle constitutes one of the most detailed evaluations of a bleeding/weeping effigy miracle ever published,[3] and Feilding himself described the case as "the strangest in the whole course of my experience."

In 1913 rumors began circulating throughout Europe about a series of miracles occurring at the home of the Abbé Vachère, who was living in retirement in Mirebeau-en-Poitou, near the city of Poitiers. The reports claimed that an oleograph of Christ in his possession had bled, that hosts he had consecrated would drip blood, and that a plaster statue of Christ erected in a nearby grotto had begun to sweat blood. These reports intrigued Feilding, who was a devout Catholic. In May 1914, accompanied by the Irish poet William Butler Yeats, he traveled to Mirebeau and met with the abbé. Vachère turned out to be a kindly sixty-year-old gentleman, highly regarded in his community and held in favor by ecclesiastic authorities in Rome. Living alone in a small house in the

FIRE IMMUNITY

Members of the fundamentalist Free Pentecostal Holiness Church believe that their faith makes them immune to fire. These two photographs show members of a Tennessee branch of the sect holding makeshift kerosene lamps to their hands and feet without suffering any harmful effects. *(Dr. Berthold Schwarz and Van Nostrand Reinhold Company)*

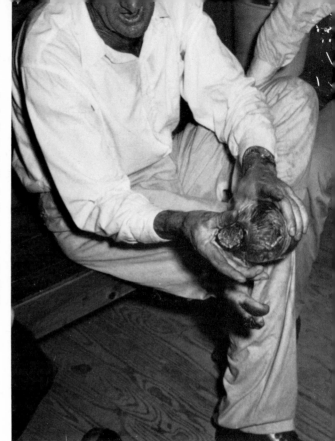

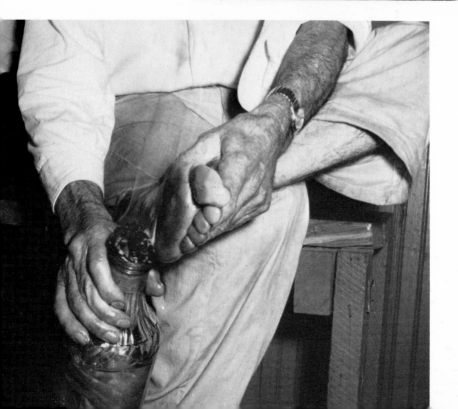

LEVITATION

D. D. Home, one of the best known of all spiritualist mediums, was reported to levitate during his séances. This nineteenth-century illustration, based on eyewitness testimony, is a representation of one of his flights. *(Fortean Picture Library)*

Amedee Zuccarini was an Italian medium who, like Home, was famed for his ability to levitate in the course of his séances. Although it may appear from the photograph that Zuccarini is merely jumping, he often remained elevated for as long as fourteen seconds.

P. T. Plunkett, a British photographer, was able to capture this yogic levitation in India in 1936. The yogi rose into the air after touching his staff, which was not secured to the ground. *(Illustrated London News Picture Library)*

The yogi remained suspended while he was photographed from several angles. *(Right)* After the levitation demonstration, the yogi's staff was uncovered, proving that it had not been fixed to the ground. *(Both Illustrated London News Picture Library)*

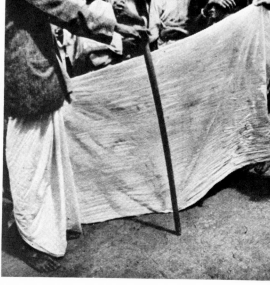

THE STIGMATA

Padre Pio was perhaps the best-known stigmatist of recent times. This photograph clearly shows the wounds on both his palms and the backs of his hands. (Fate *magazine*)

(Below left) Natuzza Evolo, a Calabrian peasant, is another contemporary stigmatist. Her wounds, which were impressed when she was only ten years old, appear in the form of crosses on her hands and feet. *(Valerio Marinelli)* *(Below right)* Blood wiped from Evolo's stigmatic wounds will often rearrange itself from random blots into religious messages and emblems. This phenomenon, which is known as "hemography," is especially unusual in Evolo's case, since she can neither read nor write. *(Valerio Marinelli)*

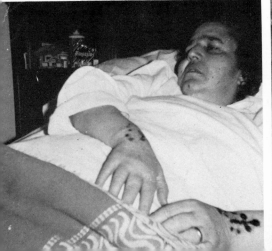

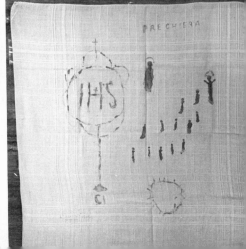

On December 12, 1531, an Aztec Indian named Juan Diego began to see visions of the Blessed Virgin Mary on a small hill just outside Mexico City. When he asked the apparition for proof of its divine nature, she produced this image of herself spontaneously on his mantle. The cactus-fiber cloak, which has shown none of the usual signs of deterioration, is on display in the Mexico City suburb of Villa Madero.

DIVINE IMAGES

(Right) A photograph of Dean Liddell, esteemed rector of Oxford's Christchurch Cathedral, shortly before his death in 1898; (below) a miraculous image of Liddell that gradually formed on one of the walls of the cathedral in the period from 1921 to 1923.

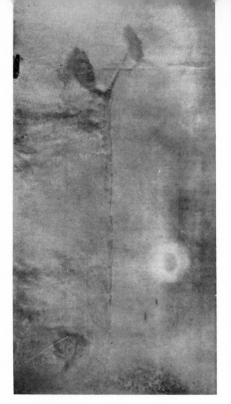

(Above left) A photograph of a miraculous image that appeared on the wall of an English home in 1935. (Above right) A charcoal sketch, drawn by the owner of the home when the image first became visible, shows the figures of a monk, a man's face, and a dog's head as they were seen by the naked eye.

In August 1971, a series of mysterious faces began to appear in the concrete floor of a home in Bélmez, Spain. The photograph below shows the first of these images to materialize. It was later discovered that the house was built over a crypt that contained the remains of Christian martyrs killed by the Moors. (Dr. Hans Bender)

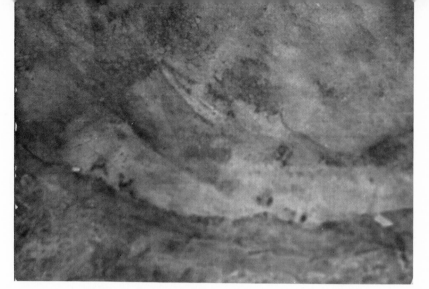

Some of the Bélmez faces appeared in configurations, as in this horizontal grouping of a bearded man, a nun, and a profile. If the photograph is turned upside down, a fourth face is visible at the upper left. *(Dr. Hans Bender)*

During the "Great Cross Flap" of 1971, crosses of light appeared in windows of churches throughout the United States. *(Below left)* In this photograph of a cross that appeared at the Paxon Revival Center in Jacksonville, Florida, images that seem to be human hands can be distinguished at either end of the crossbeam. (Fate *magazine*)

(Below right) The "Great Cross Flap" also saw a number of cross appearances in private homes, such as this image in the window of a Bronx, New York, apartment. (The New York Times)

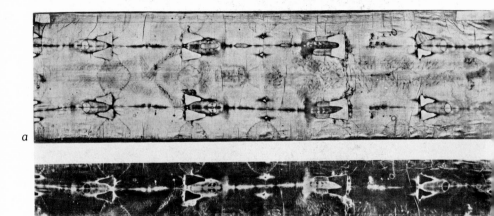

a

b

The Shroud of Turin, the most familiar and controversial of all miraculous images, is widely believed to contain the imprint of the crucified Christ. The photographs show the Shroud at full length, as it appears to the naked eye *(a)* and more clearly as a photographic negative *(b)*. The marks bordering the figure were caused when the Shroud was burned in a fire. *(Holy Shroud Guild)*

A close-up of the face of the figure on the Shroud of Turin reveals, especially in the photographic negative on the right, the clearly discernible features of a bearded young man. *(Holy Shroud Guild)*

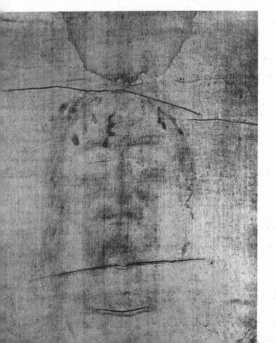

THE MIRACULOUS HAILSTONES OF REMIREMONT

In 1907 the citizens of the town of Remiremont, France, struck a medallion to honor a statue of the Virgin Mary housed in the local church. Soon afterward a mysterious hailstorm hit the town. Some of the stones were impressed with the same figure of the Virgin. The photographs show the medallion and two sketches of the hailstones. *(Society for Psychical Research)*

A case similar to the Remiremont hailstorm occurred in 1503, when a strange "red rain" fell on the German city of Nuremberg. A servant girl who had been caught in the storm found that the liquid had stained her linen shift to form a representation of a crucifixion scene. The image was seen and sketched by Albrecht Dürer, whose reproduction clearly shows a cross, a crucified figure, and mourners. *(Staatliche Museen Preussischer Kulturbesitz, Berlin)*

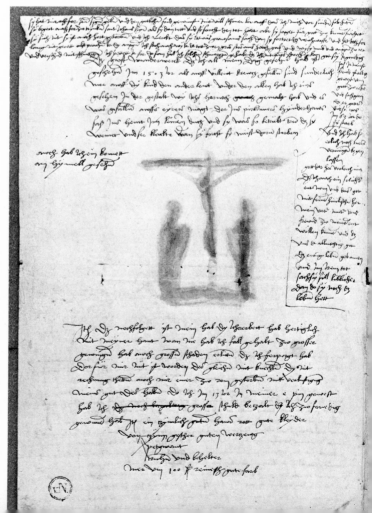

BLEEDING STATUES AND WEEPING MADONNAS

(Left) On January 3, 1971, Giovanbattista Cordiano, an attorney in Maropati, Italy, woke to find his painting of the Madonna dripping blood. As it flowed onto the wall from the picture, the blood formed a group of crosses. (National Enquirer)

(Opposite page, top) Shortly after Easter of 1975, Mrs. Anne Poore, a Philadelphia, Pennsylvania, housewife, discovered that her plaster statue of Christ was bleeding. She later turned the figure over to St. Luke's Episcopal Church in Eddystone, Pennsylvania, where it continued to bleed. *(Religious News Service)*

This rare sequence of photographs, taken in 1911, records an entire episode of the bleeding of an oleograph of Christ. The portrait was owned by the Abbé Vachère, a retired priest who lived near Mirebeau, France. *(Fortean Picture Library)*

Die Blutung am 8. September 1911.

8 Septembre 1911

Décembre 1911

DERNIER SAIGNEMENT

Church officials have on several occasions documented the bleeding of this crucifix, which belongs to Maria Horta, a Portuguese mystic and stigmatist. (National Enquirer)

When Jean Salate, owner of the Hôtel DuVar in Entreveux, France, broke the finger of his statue of St. Anne, thirty drops of human blood flowed from the "wound." *(UPI)*

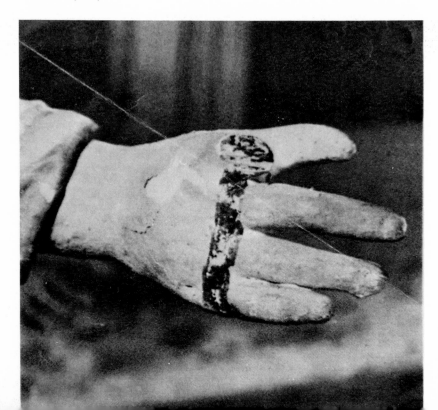

This Japanese bronze owned by Allen Demetrius of Pittsburgh, Pennsylvania, wept on August 6, 1945, the day the atomic bomb was dropped on Hiroshima. The stains produced by the tears can be seen in the photograph. *(Para-Science International and Larry E. Arnold)*

THE MIRACLE OF
ST. JANUARIUS *(below)*

Twice yearly in Naples, Italy, two phials of dried blood—allegedly that of the third-century martyr St. Januarius—are removed from their vault in Naples Cathedral and publicly venerated. During these ceremonies the blood liquefies. No scientific explanation has been offered for this miracle, which has occurred regularly for hundreds of years. This photograph shows the liquefied blood in its case. *(Institute for the Study of Border Areas of Psychology and Psychohygiene)*

MANIFESTATIONS OF THE
BLESSED VIRGIN MARY

On January 17, 1871, a large group of children in the French town of Pontmain saw an apparition of the Virgin Mary in the sky. This representation of the miracle is based on eyewitness accounts.

(Bottom, opposite; this page; and overleaf) These remarkable photographs document appearances of the Virgin Mary witnessed by thousands of people at Zeitoun, Egypt, beginning in 1968. The figure appeared at the top of a church, often in a flash of illumination and surrounded by "doves of light." It would often walk about the central dome of the church and would occasionally hover above it. (Father Jerome Palmer, O.S.B.)

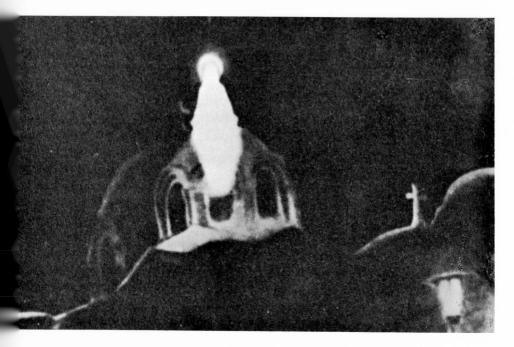

town, he was eager for Feilding to look into the mystery of his bleeding effigies.

The abbé explained to Feilding how on a visit to Rome in 1906 two oleographs of Christ had been given to him by a friend. The abbé hung one of these pictures over the altar of the private chapel of his home when he returned to France. While saying Mass at six thirty on the morning of September 8, 1911, he noticed dark stains on the forehead of the figure. By that afternoon the marks had condensed into a sticky liquid that looked like blood. By September 10 more stains had appeared on the forehead of the image and had formed into a "crown of thorns" configuration. New bleedings began on September 14 and 15, when serum began flowing from the heart area and hands. The blood soon trickled from the effigy daily, and by October, new events began plaguing the abbé's home when tears began to flow from the eyes of the oleograph as well. The abbé also began hearing voices lamenting the decline of religion at about this time. These may have been hallucinations produced by the stress he was under.

Visitors from the neighboring town soon called on the abbé to see the miracles for themselves. Being a devout and obedient clergyman, he thereupon wrote to Monsignor Hembrecht, the bishop of Poitiers, on October 13, and asked for his advice on the matter. He was instructed to deliver the picture to the Catholic seminary in Poitiers, where it could be kept under observation. He complied immediately. (The results of these observations are not, unfortunately, a matter of public record.) The oleograph was returned on December 15, along with strict orders that it was not to be placed on display.

The miracles of Mirebeau took on an added dimension in 1912. While the abbé was consecrating a host in the chapel of his house on May 27, a rent some four or five centimeters long opened in it. Puzzled, the abbé placed the host on the altar and proceeded to consecrate another one. He then noticed that the rent in the first host had begun to issue blood. This so stunned him that he fled from the chapel, leaving the host on the altar. (Feilding personally examined this host in 1914. It was still exactly where it had been left in 1912, and had profusely stained the altar cloth.)

The next development in this strange affair came on March 14, 1914, when the abbé received orders from his superiors to turn the bleeding picture over to his bishop. But this didn't end his troubles. The previous month Vachère had hung a duplicate of the bleeding oleograph in a small cottage he owned in a nearby district of Mirebeau. The cottage, which was near a construction site, was being used as a recreation room by the builders and workmen. On March 19, five days after the abbé had yielded possession of the original painting, some workers reported that this second picture had begun to weep and bleed! Vachère investigated the report that very day and was shocked to see the duplicate picture wet with fresh blood.

It was at this point that Feilding arrived in Mirebeau. Examining this second picture was his first plan of action, since it was the most recent manifestation in the case. After relating the history of the blood miracles, the abbé took him to the cottage where he allowed Feilding to take samples of a dried serum that had congealed into still-sticky pools at the base of the picture. This was all that was left of the blood flows. Feilding also examined the now two-year-old bleeding host that the abbé had left on the altar in his chapel. The host was saturated with a thick substance that resembled human blood. It had become so sticky that the host had become attached to the corporal on which it was lying. A twelve-inch stream of dried blood extended out from the host and over the cloth.

On his return to England, Feilding had the blood samples he had procured analyzed by the Lister Institute in London. The tests revealed that the substance was *not* human blood. The exact composition of the serum remained a mystery, but it contained a microorganism usually found in stagnant water.

Despite a warning from Vachère that he should not come to France (the First World War was raging, and travel was treacherous), Feilding returned to Mirebeau at Easter, 1915, to the priest's considerable consternation. The abbé, who initially greeted Feilding coolly, eventually softened. Skepticism about the miracles had grown, he explained, and the bishop of Poitiers had denounced them without even attempting to investigate the wondrous events. As a result the abbé had been excommunicated by Rome. The controversy over the authenticity of the miracles had also provoked the suspicion of the local civil authorities. Since one of the abbé's most ardent supporters was a French lady of some financial means who had married into a German family, Vachère was therefore suspected of being a German sympathizer and conspirator.

Vachère also told Feilding that the oleograph that had hung in the cottage in 1914 was now situated in his home chapel. In the three days he remained in Mirebeau, Feilding examined the painting during several visits to the abbé's home. It was wet when inspected, though Feilding was never able to see the initiation of a blood flow. He realized, though, that in order to authenticate the miracle he would have to conduct some key experiments. The first would be to dry the picture and seal up the door to the chapel to determine if the blood precipitated even when access to the painting was sealed off. The abbé first refused to sanction this test, feeling that it was an indictment of his personal honor and integrity, but eventually allowed Feilding to lock rather than seal the chapel door. After drying the painting and locking the door, Feilding secretly rigged the hinge with a piece of paper that would dislodge should anyone try to get into the room.

When Feilding returned to the chapel several hours later, he found that the picture was wet once again. He also noticed that the piece of paper had slipped from its position. He informed the abbé of his discovery, and Vachère, duly enraged, suggested that his sacristan might have shaken the door upon finding it locked. Feilding had to admit that this explanation was tenable.

Despite the negative outcome of his investigation to this point, Feilding was becoming more and more impressed with the abbé's good faith in the matter. As he later wrote:

Notwithstanding . . . my own experience with the analysis, the failure of the picture to bleed under observation, and the above incident with the paper I found it increasingly difficult to believe that this simple, almost childish-minded, pious but volcanic old priest could be consciously perpetrating frauds which, associated as they must be with the most sacred and intimate elements of his faith, could not but be repugnant to him.

Since Feilding again had to return to England, in the autumn of 1916 he invited a French woman of his acquaintance, Mlle J. Lichnerowicz, to monitor the Mirebeau affair. Mlle Lichnerowicz kept in touch with the abbé over the next year, but did not reveal that she was acting as Feilding's agent. Mlle Lichnerowicz was able to observe the very phenomenon Feilding had failed to witness— the actual flow of blood from the oleograph—during her first visit to Mirebeau at Christmas, 1916. She was watching the celebration of Mass one morning when, just as Vachère had placed a piece of white linen under the picture (which had been set on a vestment chest in the chapel), blood began to flow from the painting. She was able to make a similar observation during her visit the following May.

Feilding made his final trip to Mirebeau in January 1920. Although excommunicated, the abbé had continued to say Mass in his chapel. His oleograph was still bleeding, but the miracles had by now extended in scope. A statue of the infant Jesus, which had been placed on the steps of the altar in his chapel, had begun to exude blood. Feilding again took samples of blood from the oleograph * and once again turned them over to the Lister Institute. This time, though, tests determined that the liquid *was* human blood.

The concluding history of the Mirebeau miracles is not a happy one. Feilding himself attempted to interest Church officials in France in the case, but to no avail. He also urged the Institut Général Psychologique in Paris to look into the matter, since several researchers there had recently become interested in psychic matters; but nothing came of this proposal, either. In 1920 the abbé finally journeyed to Rome to plead his case personally. Papal officials seemed to be more sympathetic to him than they had been in 1916, but it was too late: The abbé died later that year.

Feilding could never come to a conclusion about this strange affair, and while admitting to the probable authenticity of the Mirebeau miracles, he refused to believe that there was anything divine about them. He believed that the abbé's religious beliefs had somehow produced the miracles, though he wasn't quite sure just how.

---

*Fielding's wife thought she had seen Vachère surreptitiously sprinkle some water on the picture from a nearby vase just before her husband examined it, but wasn't sure of her observation. This charge seems baseless in light of the subsequent findings of the bacteriologist who analyzed the substance.

Today, some sixty years after the Abbé Vachère's death, we can, with our increased knowledge of the powers of the human mind, propose a tentative solution to the Mirebeau miracles: namely, that *the Abbé was a poltergeist agent and that the miracles he witnessed were the result of a poltergeist-type attack manifesting within a religious context.*

This theory may sound farfetched, since the phenomena he witnessed over a nine-year period certainly do not resemble the typical stone-throwing, rapping, and furniture-moving antics of the poltergeist. But one must remember that *poltergeists sometimes choose highly selective methods of attack.* For instance, in July 1979, the electrical system of an industrial plant in downtown Los Angeles began going haywire whenever a young woman who worked there showed up in the building. The company's phone system would malfunction, the call lights on the woman's phone would light up by themselves, the building's paging system would let out a series of ear-shattering whining sounds, and so on. The malfunctions would cease when the woman left the plant. Similar disturbances sometimes occurred in other offices she visited, and broke out in her home as well. Yet the poltergeist never evolved into traditional object-throwings or rappings.*

A poltergeist reported in 1963 in Methuen, Massachusetts, also employed a rather limited range of attack. Mr. and Mrs. Francis Martin were plagued by jets of water that began "popping" out of the walls in their house. The Martins moved to several different places in an attempt to outrun the poltergeist, but the water attacks continued wherever they went. Neither fire nor police officials could find any explanation for the mystery, which lasted several days before ceasing permanently.

In a 1976 case, fire was the only means of attack the poltergeist used during a dramatic one-night siege. A series of mysterious fires broke out in a middle-class home in Simi Valley, about forty miles from Los Angeles, when a young friend of the owner

---

*For more on this case, see Raymond Bayless's report in the *Journal* of the Southern California Society for Psychical Research, 1979, 1, pp. 19–25. This incident is similar to one that struck some law offices in Rosenheim, Germany, in November 1967. Electric equipment, especially the office phone system, went haywire before more traditional poltergeistery broke out. The attack was investigated by Hans Bender and also focused on a young woman working in the office.

had come to visit. Five blazes erupted within a ten-to-fifteen-minute period.

It is clear from these examples that poltergeists don't *always* resort to stereotyped psychokinetic displays, but will sometimes choose a highly selective attack strategy—as it seems they did at Mirebeau. This theory is further supported by the fact that sometimes religious figures would bleed in homes that the abbé merely visited! On June 5, 1920, he paid a call on some Germans who were staying in a private residence in Aix-la-Chapelle, France. Blood started flowing from a picture of Christ hanging in the house on the very day of his arrival. Tears formed in the figure's eyes as well. These flows continued for several days and ceased on June 11—the very day the priest left. Poltergeist phenomena will invariably follow the primary agent wherever he goes, so the abbé's poltergeist was behaving true to form. The mobility of the poltergeist, in fact, is one of its primary characteristics.

Another indication that the Mirebeau miracles may have resulted from a limited form of poltergeist attack is that "bleeding" statues are part and parcel of the poltergeist syndrome and have occurred in more than a few historical cases.

Perhaps the best known of these was reported in August 1920 from the town of Templemore, Ireland. Owing to the many witnesses who observed the antics, the incident received wide press coverage. The poltergeistery broke out in the house of Thomas Dwan, where a devoutly religious sixteen-year-old boy, James Walsh, was lodging. Beginning on August 21, *all* the religious statues and pictures in the house began to bleed or were found smeared with blood. It soon became clear that the events were somehow related to young Walsh. When the boy visited the home of Dwan's sister at the height of the infestation, religious effigies in her home bled, too. More conventional poltergeistery accompanied the miracles in this case. Many visitors to the Dwan residence watched in awe as household furniture moved and shifted position by itself; knickknacks flew from cabinet shelves; and mysterious footsteps began pacing the roof of the house.[4]

It isn't too difficult to determine the cause of the Templemore poltergeist. Ireland was in an uproar in 1920. A separatist government had been elected in 1918, and because the country was still under British rule, civil war continually threatened to break out between pro- and anti-British factions. Religious issues were one cause of the strife. Templemore itself had been the scene of violent street fighting just a few days before the poltergeist first erupted. No doubt these intense emotional and religious circumstances stirred up some conflict deep within Walsh's mind, which erupted in the form of a poltergeist attack that immediately took on religious overtones.

This same thing may have happened in Mirebeau. We know that the Abbé Vachère was deeply religious, almost to the brink of fanaticism. He was also probably psychologically unstable, since after the blood commenced to flow from his oleograph he began hearing hallucinatory voices, which he believed emanated from the painting. These voices, which only he could hear, lamented the decline of the clergy and the sins of France. (The abbé kept detailed notebooks in which he transcribed these messages. The hallucinations apparently lasted for years.) We also know that he was fascinated by the mystery of the stigmata. Before the blood miracles began in 1911, he had been corresponding with a stigmatist in Germany whom he revered as a saint and seeress.

In light of the abbé's unstable mental disposition, his devotion, and his fascination with the stigmata—something was bound to give. It did in 1911, in the form of a poltergeist attack that mimicked the appearance of a religious miracle.*

There is yet another line of evidence that supports the idea that bleeding/weeping effigy miracles may be linked to the mind of the primary witness (or witnesses). Statues or other sacred images in the homes of people already marked with the stigmata have been occasionally known to bleed and/or weep. In these cases it appears that the miracles are extensions of the witnesses' own stigmata.

A case of this very type has recently been reported from Por-

---

* This theory may not seem to account for all cases of bleeding/weeping effigy miracles, since these also occur in homes of people who are only nominally religious. Yet even people who do not ordinarily consider themselves religious in a formal sense often harbor deeply ingrained, though repressed, religious beliefs, which can affect their attitudes and behavior in very subtle ways. Many suffer severe trauma later in life when they try to adjust to life-styles inconsistent with their early religious training and beliefs—even if they have consciously rejected them. For more information on this subject from a psychiatric perspective, see Eli Chesen, *Religion May Be Hazardous to Your Health* (New York: Wyden Books, 1972).

tugal. The subject of the stigmata is forty-nine-year-old Maria Horta, a housewife living in the town of Praia do Pedrogao, who apparently developed psychic powers in 1959 after miraculously recovering from leukemia. In 1972 Maria was attending church and was about to receive communion when she fell to the ground in a faint. A wound miraculously opened in her chest, and blood began to ooze from the host that her priest was about to give her. Wounds of the full stigmata appeared shortly afterward. A crucifix in Maria's home subsequently began to bleed, a miracle witnessed by several visitors to her home as well as by local Church officials.

A more impressive example of this phenomenon was personally investigated by Thurston in 1920. "Lizzie Smith" was a middle-class artisan's wife who lived in a manufacturing city in the north of England. She had converted to Catholicism while a teenager, and suffered a paralytic stroke soon after which left one of her hands gnarled. Years later she was miraculously healed, at which time she apparently developed psychic abilities. Lizzie subsequently began to have religious visions and to see apparitions of the dead, and a huge crucifix in her home began to bleed. Thurston, who never could decide if the case was genuine or fraudulent, devotes four pages to it in *The Physical Phenomena of Mysticism*. As he reports about his visit to Mrs. Smith:

When I saw Lizzie Smith in August 1920, arriving at her house without any notification of my intended visit, she showed me in the palms of her hands slight but quite perceptible traces of a stigmatization which she averred had occurred on the previous Friday. One curious development may be mentioned here, though it has no direct connection with our present subject. In the November of 1919, the soul of a priest from purgatory, so she stated, came to her to ask for prayers. He laid his right hand upon her right arm, and the hand burnt through the blouse which she was wearing and left the impress of the thumb and fingers upon her forearm. There can be no question as to the burning of the sleeve of the blouse, or as to the marks upon her arm. Several persons, some of them quite sceptical as to the supernatural character of these manifestations (her parish priest was one of the latter number), saw the impression when it was quite fresh. They assured me that the imprint, as of four fingers and a thumb, was unmistakable. I myself saw the marks nine months after the event, though at that time they were blurred and fading. Finally, on the afternoon of March 17, 1920, another manifestation occurred.

She declared that the metal figure of a large crucifix, which hung beside her prie-dieu, suddenly began to sweat blood. The whole figure was dripping with blood. She covered the crucifix with a piece of clean linen and next day took it to her director, a priest in another town many miles away. There in his presbytery I saw it five months later, the linen still adhering to the figure and only detached from it with difficulty owing to the coagulation of the blood.

Thurston was suspicious of the case primarily because the date on which the crucifix first began to bleed—March 17, 1920— was the day after a local newspaper had run an account of the Mirebeau miracles. Although it was Thurston's opinion that Lizzie might have faked the miracle after hearing about the Abbé Vachère in France, even he admitted that Lizzie seemed to be genuinely devout. So the Lizzie Smith case may represent a sort of "contagious" miracle. It isn't beyond belief that Lizzie, having heard of the Mirebeau miracles, may have unconsciously produced a comparable miracle of her own.

Similar contagions of bleeding/weeping image miracles have been reported in relatively recent times. One struck Italy in 1953, when several incidents of "weeping Madonnas" were reported from all over the country. This epidemic began in the home of Angelo and Antonietta Janusso, a poor Sicilian couple living in Syracuse, Sicily,[5] who had been married that March. As a wedding present, Angelo's brother Giuseppe had given them a statue of the Blessed Virgin Mary. It was an unusual gift, since the Janussos did not consider themselves religious, even though they were both Catholic in upbringing. The statue, which had been bought at a local gift shop, was made of plaster coated with lacquer and stood about eighteen inches tall.

The Janussos shared a small three-room house with Giuseppe and his wife in the Borgata Santa Lucia, a lower-class district in Syracuse, full of rundown houses and narrow streets. By August it was clear that Antonietta was pregnant, but after suffering epileptiform seizures, attacks of blindness, and fainting spells, she became bedridden. Although from our perspective it seems clear that she was suffering from hysteria, the local doctors couldn't diagnose her problems. The attacks continued for several weeks, and at three in the morning on August 29 she underwent a series of violent fits that left her temporarily blind. Antonietta sensed that she would have another attack at eight thirty that same morning, but the convulsions didn't set in as expected. Instead, she was able to sit up, and her sight was suddenly restored.

The first thing she saw when her vision cleared was the statue of the Madonna that had been her wedding present. Ever since they had moved into the house it had stood over her bed, attached to the wall. Antonietta began screaming when she saw the statue, for tears were forming in its eyes and dripping down onto the bed. Antonietta's sister-in-law, Grazia—as well as another woman who was caring for her at the time—also witnessed the miracle.

Many more people watched the Madonna cry over the next several hours. Grazia couldn't contain herself when she saw the statue crying, and soon rushed to tell her neighbors about it. Other residents of the Borgata Santa Lucia swarmed to the Janusso household to see the miraculous statue for themselves, and though several of them tried to dry the Madonna's tears, the drops of liquid kept reforming as soon as they were wiped away.

One witness to this strange event was Mario Messina, a highly regarded citizen of Syracuse and a neighbor of the Janussos. He visited the house the very day news of the miracle began to spread and has left a detailed and level-headed account of the miracle and how he examined the statue:

> The statue was hanging from the wall and the tears formed slowly. Well aware that among those who stood outside there were skeptics as well as believers, I took the statue down from the wall to have a better look. What is it that causes the moisture? The wall is dry as also the reverse side of the statue. The liquid cannot be seeping down through the roof, for not the slightest trace of moisture is there. More puzzling still—the head of the statue is dry. I had to leave no room for doubt; so I unscrewed the statue and removed the little halo that encircled the head of the Madonna. I noticed that the two small hooks were also dry. I took a cloth and carefully wiped the face and bust of the statue. Instantly two tears, like pearls, glistened on her cheeks, leaving slender traces in their wake. They flowed the length of her face and were followed by many more.

Messina was so impressed by the Madonna that he took it to the window of the bedroom, which looked onto the street, and displayed it to the crowd that had formed there. Giuseppe and Angelo Janusso observed the miracle later that day when they arrived home from work.

Local police officials were the next to be informed of the wonder. Fearing that a riot might break out, they sent a team of Syracuse police to the Janussos' home at ten that evening to impound the statue. It continued to weep even while being transported to police headquarters, where it was inspected before being returned to Angelo later that night.

By the next day, local newspapers were carrying stories about the weeping Madonna. Even *La Sicilia,* which had a reputation for promoting liberal and anticlerical editorial policies, reported favorably on the miracle. "The skeptics have been driven into a corner by hard cold facts which they cannot explain away," stated the paper.

By now, thousands of Sicilians were assembling in the streets surrounding the Borgata Santa Lucia, and buses of sightseers were pouring into the city. The police eventually had to be dispatched to the area to organize the crowd into small groups which were then allowed into the house to see the statue. As *La Sicilia* reported:

All Syracuse has seen the Madonna cry. The entire city is reeling under the impact of this startling event. People everywhere are talking about it—on the street, in the home; there is the constant clash of contradictory theories and comments in an effort to find an explanation for this incredible phenomenon. One thing is beyond dispute—tears are flowing from the eyes of the Madonna of the Via degli Orti; and the miracle, if this astounding and baffling phenomenon can be so styled, has been confirmed by thousands and thousands of people who have incessantly funneled into the home of Antonietta Giusto [sic] to gaze with amazement at the tears of the Madonna. Skepticism, for all its inherent obstinacy and prejudice, must needs bow to reality. The little bust of the Madonnina, mounted on a black plate of glass, has kept up a steady flow of tears all day long except for a few brief intervals. The skeptics themselves, profoundly agitated and trembling pathetically as they pressed their pads of cloth to the face of the Madonna, have yielded to the compelling force of truth. The news which was spread across our early morning edition has been drawing huge crowds; they stand throughout the day hoping to witness the phenomenon and to kneel near the statue which is regarded as miraculous. A great number have had their desires fulfilled and the impression they have carried away baffles description.

At least one visitor to the Janusso home was a trained physician. Dr. Paolo Albani tasted the statue's tears and affirmed that they possessed the salty tang of human tears.

On August 31, the secretary to Ettore Baranzini, the local archbishop, requested the Provincial Health Agency in Syracuse to investigate the matter. So under the direction of Father John Bruno, a commission of priests, police investigators, and medical experts converged on the Janusso home. They witnessed the miracle, took samples of the "tears," and then drew up an official report for the archbishop. They stated:

> With the aid of the police we made our way through the crowd that had gathered in front of the house and were ushered into a bedroom looking out on the Via Corso [sic]. At our request Mrs. Antonietta Junnuso [sic] pulled out a drawer which contained a Madonna. This statue was covered with a cloth and was apparently made of colored plaster and black glass. Several areas of the face and bust were definitely wet. They were carefully wiped with wads of cloth. A drop of liquid still remained in the inner corner of the left eye. It was cleared away by means of a pipette of one tenth of a cubic centimeter. Fresh drops slowly appeared in the same place and these too were collected in the small glass tube. No sooner were the drops collected in the glass tubes than others gushed from the eyes. These were in turn collected. While this operation was taking place it was impossible to wipe all the tears dry. In all, a little more than a cubic centimeter was made available for laboratory analysis. From the moment that the statue was removed from the drawer, the phenomenon lasted a quarter of an hour. It did not recur and that is why we were unable to procure a larger sample for analysis. Reference must be made to the fact that an examination of the inner corner of the eye under a magnifying glass revealed no pore nor even the slightest irregularity on the surface of the plaster. The plaster statue was detached from the black plate of glass to which it had been fastened; the plaster measured two centimeters in thickness. The outside surface was executed in various colors, while the interior presented a rough white surface which, at the time of the inspection, was perfectly dry.

Although the Madonna finally ceased its weeping at 11:15 A.M. on September 1, shortly after the commission had taken its samples, Archbishop Baranzini ordered that the tears be analyzed. Professor Leopoldo Rosa, a Syracuse chemist, was entrusted with this responsibility. He took charge of the sample on September 2, and reported back to the archbishop that the micrography department of the Laboratorio d'Igiene e Profilassi in Syracuse, where three staff chemists had conducted various analyses of the sample, found the solution to be composed of normal human tear elements. No discrepancies between the tears taken from the statue and those taken from a normal adult or child could be found.

Soon even the manufacturer of the statue became involved. Spokesmen for the Industry of Plastic Art, headquartered in Bagni di Lucca, issued a statement in September detailing just how the plastic statue had been produced. Ulisse Viviani, the supervisor of the firm, later traveled to Syracuse to personally inspect the Janusso statue and testified that it had not been tampered with.

Several canonical investigations into the affair followed, and the "miracle" was officially recognized by the Church on December 18, 1953. Shortly after the official proclamation was made, a shrine honoring the statue was erected in Syracuse where the effigy is still venerated to this day.

Although the Church officially acknowledged the miracle of the weeping Madonna of Syracuse as being the direct result of the Virgin Mary's intervention, Antonietta Janusso's role in the miracle was certainly much more important than any of the original investigators cared to admit. Signora Janusso was a very disturbed woman, and her illness—though allegedly brought on by her pregnancy—was undoubtedly hysterical in origin. As we have seen in Chapter Three, hysteria usually results from a deeply repressed conflict hidden in the sufferer's mind. Signora Janusso may have been harboring intense guilt or conflict over her pregnancy and/or the awareness of her sexual maturation that had inevitably been brought about by her marriage.* (The fact that she found herself pregnant soon after her marriage raises the possibility that she had engaged in sexual relations with her fiancé before the wedding, which would have intensified her conflict considerably.)

---

*Sigmund Freud, during the course of his research on the disorder in turn-of-the-century Vienna, was one of the first to recognize the sexual basis of hysteria. He found that guilt over sexual activity or childhood sexual traumas could, later in life, cause the victim to develop any number of complicated hysterical disorders.

It isn't difficult to believe that in such a stressful situation Antonietta could have become a poltergeist agent. Many poltergeist agents are hysterics and seem to be sexually repressed individuals as well.* The weeping Madonna of Syracuse, like the Mirebeau miracles, may in fact have been a limited form of poltergeist attack.

If this theory is true, it should come as no surprise that Signora Janusso's hysterical behavior vanished at the same time that her Madonna began to weep. If Signora Janusso was in fact suffering from guilt over her sexuality, her unconscious mind may have psychically produced the miracle as a divine "sign" of forgiveness, thus alleviating the guilt that tormented her and which had originally caused her hysteria.

The contagion of "imitative" miracles that followed this case began soon after its conclusion and during the next four years eventually spread throughout Italy. The first report came from a housewife in Calabria who stated on December 15 that tears of blood had fallen from several postcard-sized portraits of the Madonna in her possession. On April 3, 1954, Inez Bottazzi of Mezzalombardo claimed that a picture of the Madonna that she had cut from a magazine had begun to shed tears. Several neighbors witnessed the miracle. Reports of similar weeping Madonnas came from the cities of Ango and Casapulla in May 1954 and March 1955 respectively. Finally, in March 1957, a papier-mâché statue of the Madonna owned by a family in Ricca Corneta was said to have wept for several days.

It is worth noting that throughout this entire epidemic not one case of a bleeding effigy of Christ came to light. All the reports were of weeping Madonnas, no doubt spawned by wide press coverage of the Syracuse miracle. While these duplications of the original may have been genuine, some imitative miracles may in fact be hoaxes. The following authentic case and the questionable imitation that followed it will serve as a good corrective to any uncritical belief in miracles.

On the evening of March 16, 1960, Mrs. Pagona Catsounis

---

*For more information on hysteria and the poltergeist, see the chapter on "Psychoneurotic Conditions in Poltergeist Cases" in A.R.G. Owens' Can We Explain the Poltergeist? (New York: Helix Press, 1964). Many poltergeist victims seem to be suffering from sexual traumas. See Nandor Fodor, On the Trail of the Poltergeist (New York: Citadel, 1958), and Hereward Carrington and Nandor Fodor, Haunted People (New York: Dutton, 1951).

of Island Park, New York, discovered that a framed lithograph of the Blessed Virgin Mary stored in her attic was crying. Mrs. Catsounis and her husband called their priest, the Reverend George Papadeus of St. Paul's Greek Orthodox Church in nearby Hempstead, who immediately came to the house to inspect the print.

"When I arrived a tear was drying beneath the left eye," Father Papadeus reported to the press. "Then . . . I saw another tear well up in her left eye. It started as a small, round globule of moisture in the corner of her left eye, and it slowly trickled down her face."

Within a week over four thousand visitors had flocked to the Catsounises' apartment, and several photographs were taken of the lithograph. Father Papadeus blessed the house after the picture had been weeping for a week, and then the tears ceased. The picture was subsequently deposited at St. Paul's on May 23.[6]

Although there is little doubt about the authenticity of the Catsounises' weeping lithograph, the same cannot be said for the case that came to light immediately afterward. No sooner had the Catsounis case hit the press than Father Papadeus received a call from Mrs. Antonia Koulis, Mrs. Catsounis's aunt, who eagerly reported that an icon of the Blessed Virgin Mary that stood in her Oceanside Park, New York, home was also crying! Both Father Papadeus and Archbishop Iakovos, an official of the Greek Orthodox Church, visited the Koulises' home repeatedly over the next few days and were impressed by the miracle occurring there. Mrs. Koulis also called in representatives from the press, who were allowed to take samples of the tears. The substance was discovered not to have the chemical composition of human tears.

The Koulis Madonna was displayed publicly after the miracle was first reported in 1960, and in 1964 it made its way to the Holy Transfiguration Russian Orthodox Church in Los Angeles. There, Raymond Bayless, a well-known local psychic investigator, was allowed to take scrapings from the congealed "tears" that had formed under the figure's eyes. He discovered that they were composed of a solidified sugar solution! Bayless's final judgment was that the case had been a hoax from the start, especially in the light of the suspicious connection between Mrs. Koulis and Mrs. Catsounis.[7]

Despite the occurrence of such cleverly perpetrated hoaxes,

there can be no doubt that a genuine bleeding/weeping image syndrome exists and presents a unique enigma to both science and parapsychology. How can these miracles be explained? Where do the human blood and tears come from? Why do the flows of blood and tears last only a few days in most cases, yet for years in others?

Cases of bleeding or weeping images such as these may be, if not something akin to a poltergeist effect, instances of *externalized stigmata*. Both Antonietta Janusso and the Abbé Vachère had a religious background and hysterical tendencies similar to those possessed by some of the great stigmatists of the Church, such as Domenica Lazzari and Therese Neumann. In Chapter Three it was suggested that the stigmata develops when the victim identifies so closely with the figure of the crucified Christ that he or she develops the wounds of the Passion as a result. Could the liquid that flows during cases of bleeding/weeping effigy miracles actually be the blood and/or tears of the witness that is being transferred to the image through some mysterious process? This theory could be easily tested by comparing the chemical constitution of blood and tear samples taken from the effigies with those procured from the primary witnesses. Unfortunately, there seem to be no cases where such a comparison has been made.

Bleeding/weeping effigies seem to be *the* most common form of miraculous event, with dozens of examples on record. Only a few of the most notable have been summarized in this chapter. John Michell and R. J. M. Rickard list several additional cases reported from England in the 1960s and 1970s in their book *Phenomena: A Book of Wonders;* and Sebastian Robiou Lamarche, a Puerto Rican investigator, chronicles several recent occurrences in the Caribbean islands in his *Manifiesto OVNI de Puerto Rico, Santo Domingo y Cuba.* One of Lamarche's citations is particulatly interesting. He reports that on August 17, 1974, a statue of St. Martin de Porres (see Chapter Four) began to weep blood in the home of forty-year-old Nilda Avila Pagán. The miracle, which was witnessed by both Señora Pagán and her mother, is a rare instance when a religious effigy other than that representing Christ or the Madonna has been the focus of such a miracle.

Several additional cases were presented as part of an article on miracles that appeared in the December 1962 issue of *Esquire* magazine. This report was illustrated by a picture of a small damaged statue of St. Anne belonging to M. Jean Salate, the owner of the Hôtel DuVar in Entreveux, France. In 1954, Salate had broken the plaster figure in a fit of rage and some thirty drops of blood issued from its detached hand over the next twenty-four hours. A chemical analysis of the serum indicated that it actually was human blood.

Cases of more secular bleeding/weeping statues and portraits are reported now and then as well. The Reverend William Rauscher, rector of Christ Episcopal Church in Woodbury, New Jersey, witnessed such a miracle while attending seminary school as a young man. (He reports the story in his autobiography, *The Spiritual Frontier* [1959].) He was visiting the seminary room of his friend Bob Lewis to compare the results of their canonical examinations. Lewis told Rauscher how he wished his grandmother, who had first introduced him to religion, were alive to see him ordained. She had cried for joy, he explained, when he had first entered the seminary.

No sooner had Lewis finished speaking than a framed picture of the woman, which Lewis kept on a dresser in his room, began to cry.

"The photograph of Bob's grandmother was soaking wet, dripping, with a small pool of water spreading on the dresser under it," writes Rauscher. "Examining the picture, we found that it was wet *inside* the glass. That was genuinely puzzling. The back of the picture, made of dyed imitation velvet, was so wet the velvet had streaked and faded.

"Removed from its frame, the photograph didn't dry quickly. When it did dry, the area about the face remained puffed, as though the water had originated there and run downward—from the eyes."[8]

A very different case was reported from Pittsburgh, Pennsylvania, on August 6, 1945—the day the United States dropped the atom bomb on Hiroshima. Mr. Allen Demetrius excitedly told the local press that a bronze statue of a young Japanese maiden in his home had begun to cry: "It was like she was weeping about the bombing. The tears were running down her face." Several of Demetrius's neighbors also observed this bizarre episode.

Today the statue still stands in Allen Demetrius's home, where it recently came to public attention once more. On March 18, 1979—ten days before the nuclear reactor accident at Three Mile Island near Harrisburg, Pennsylvania—the maiden began to cry again.

"It was as though the statue wanted to warn us something was going to happen," Demetrius told newsmen.

Because instances of bleeding/weeping statues and religious paintings *are* so common, they just might be the clue through which science can definitively explore the world of the miraculous. Since these wondrous events generally continue for several days before ebbing, it shouldn't be difficult to make scientific observations and tests during the actual process of the miracle. No other event, in fact, seems so amenable to rigorous examination and exploration. With so many advances in the fields of X-ray photography, chemistry, and physics, there is no telling what a sophisticated analysis of bleeding/weeping images may be able to tell us about the mechanics of these events.

Some supernormal occurrences related to bleeding/weeping effigy miracles, however, threaten to defy *any* scientific explanation. This chapter cannot conclude without at least mentioning a few of these events, no matter how unbelievable they may seem.

In a battle fought during World War I on July 13, 1916, military troops from South Africa valiantly overcame German soldiers in the Delville Woods of pastoral France. It was the end of a four-day confrontation, and the contingent had almost been defeated. Only about one hundred fifty men were left of the nearly three thousand who had originally taken part in the conflict. The survivors constructed a cross from wood taken from the forest and took it back to Pietermaritzburg, the capital of the Natal province of South Africa, at the end of the war. The cross currently stands in a memorial garden dedicated to the fallen soldiers, where a miracle takes place every year on the anniversary of the battle. Beginning in July the cross begins to "cry." Resin exudes from the ends of the crossbeam and develops into a flow of serum that lasts throughout the month. The cross is cleaned by local officials after the flow stops, but each year it begins again.

There is simply no scientific explanation for why the cross "weeps" so regularly. One solution might be that the wood, even after sixty years, is still resinous. "But it is very rare even for slow-growing resinous wood to seep for more than two years," explained Henry Hargh of South Africa's Department of Forestry to Reuters in August 1969.

Another type of miracle that deserves mention concerns those instances in which religious statues have been observed to change position. (Usually they will merely move an arm or change expression.) Such cases are extremely rare and are occasionally (but not invariably) accompanied by traditional weeping and/or bleeding. A few historical cases have been recorded, though their authenticity is not beyond dispute. In 1906 a report from Quito, Ecuador, claimed that several teachers and students at a local Jesuit college had seen a statue of the Madonna open her eyes and smile. A similar case was reported from Assisi in 1948. But these phenomena can often be discounted as optical illusions.

Harder to explain, though, is a case reported from Italy in 1866.[9] The focus of the miracle was a twelve-inch waxen image of the infant Jesus owned by Maria and Marta Parlavecchia, two devoutly religious sisters who lived in a small house in Bari. At some point in 1866 the effigy began to sweat blood. The liquid was collected by the sisters and kept in phials. It exuded an odd cinnamon odor. The sisters eventually converted one of the rooms of the house into a shrine, where the figure was placed in a glass case. Not only did it continue to bleed for two years, but its eyes shifted angle, it would from time to time be found seated in an upright position instead of lying flat, and even its hands would be found outstretched! The case was investigated by a commission set up by Father Francesco Pedicini, the archbishop of Bari, in 1867. Their report was favorable, and later a priest from Bari sent another effigy of the infant Jesus to the Parlavecchia family as a gift. It wasn't long before this statue, too, began to bleed. Unfortunately, it doesn't appear that the blood was ever analyzed.

This case, like so many that have been chronicled in this chapter, must remain unsolved. Fascinating and provocative . . . but just slightly beyond the reach of orthodox science.*

---

*A clue to the nature of this case, and others like it, may be found by studying some recent phenomena that have come to the attention of parapsychology during the last decade. In 1972, the parapsychological world was stunned by the appearance of Uri Geller, a controversial Israeli psychic who had a weird ability to make metal objects (such as spoons and forks) bend or break merely by stroking them. This phenomenon became known as the "Geller effect," and soon other "metal bending" psychics came to public attention in

This chapter will best close with what is probably the most recent report of a bleeding/weeping effigy.

On May 29, 1979, the Santa Monica (California) *Evening Outlook* broke a story of a new case of a bleeding portrait of Christ that had just been reported from the town of Roswell, New Mexico:

Members of the Willie Mae Seymore family think it's a miracle. A local priest calls it "ticklish." In any case, most everyone who has visited the Seymore house the past three days has been mystified.

The object of attention in Roswell, a normally quiet southeastern New Mexico city, is a wallet-sized portrait of Jesus Christ encased in plastic and tucked inside the corner of a larger framed picture at the Seymore residence.

Last Friday, Zack Malott, the husband of Mrs. Seymore's granddaughter, Kathy, glanced at the tiny portrait and noticed what appeared to be a large "tear" of blood just below the right eye of the picture.

Within 1½ hours, Malott said Monday, there was a steady stream of a blood-like substance penetrating through the plastic and coagulating at the base of the frame holding the larger picture.

"The blood was running from the picture just as if I had cut my finger," said Mrs. Seymore.

A newsman, who arrived shortly after the flow stopped, said the red substance was still wet and had flowed directly out of the plastic coating. He said there did not appear to be any cut in the plastic coating and there was nothing behind the picture that could have caused the flow.

At first the family called a priest, but he refused an offer to drive out to the Seymore residence to inspect the picture, calling the incident "ticklish." He said any involvement of the Catholic Church would have to originate from the archbishop.

The family then called the local newspaper, which in turn contacted a medical technician from a local hospital.

Although the portrait has not "bled" since Saturday, tests by the medical technician confirmed the substance at the base of the frame holding the tiny Christ was blood.

---

the United States, England, France, Germany, and Japan. Both the late Dr. Wilbur Franklin of Kent State University in Ohio and Dr. John Hasted of Birkbeck College, England, have made detailed examinations of "Gellerized" metal samples. Franklin found that metal broken by Geller showed signs of intense localized heating, while Hasted determined that localized changes had occurred within the atomic structure of his samples. Perhaps this phenomenon can explain moving-statue miracles. It could be that the minds of the witnesses cause structural changes or heating within the structure of the statues, thus causing them to warp or otherwise change position.

"This is honest-to-gosh, bona fide blood," said the medical official, who asked not to be identified.

The technician left a kit with the family to be used to collect any fresh samples of the substance. Additional tests were also planned on the dried substance in an effort to determine if the blood is human and its type.

By Monday, Malott said about 160 people had viewed the portrait.

The Seymores did not consider themselves especially religious, nor were they attending Church regularly at the time the bleedings began. By now this situation may have changed!

~ VIII ~
THE MIRACLE
OF ST. JANUARIUS

St. NICHOLAS of Tolentino was born in Fermo, Italy, in 1245. He became an Augustinian friar while still a young man, and was eventually posted to a monastery in Tolentino, a city near his birthplace in the central part of the country. For the greater part of his life he dedicated himself to pastoral work and preaching. While many miracles were attributed to him during his lifetime, none of them is as unusual as one that allegedly occurred after his death in 1305. Because Nicholas had so impressed the superiors of his order with his holiness, they exhumed his miraculously incorrupt body in 1345 so that portions of it could be sent to other monasteries as relics. A legend claims that during the exhumation, a lay brother detached the right arm of the body, and a stupendous flow of fresh blood issued from the wound. The arm was thereafter enshrined in Tolentino in a reliquary deposited at the monastery where he had served.

Most hagiographers consider this story to be more fiction that fact. Thurston, for example, notes that "the evidence for the original prodigy at the severing of the limb is certainly not satisfactory"[1] However, the sequel to the legend of St. Nicholas is truly mystifying. Apart from what *really* happened when the limb was first severed, the arm has continued to bleed sporadically *ever since*. Blood was seen to drip from the amputated arm in 1671 and 1676, and then continuously for some three months in 1699, from May 29 until September 1. The bleedings have occurred some twenty times in all.

The relic of St. Nicholas of Tolentino is typical of an entire class of miracles that involve the issuance of blood from disinterred bodies or the sudden liquefaction, many years later, of dried samples of blood taken from the bodies of the great saints. There are even cases in which blood has issued from the skeletal remains of a saint. These macabre stories deserve to be taken seriously, for they reveal yet another aspect of the miraculous.

A good example of this phenomenon is the miracle of St. Pacifico di San Severino. Pacifico was born in 1653, entered a monastery when he was seventeen, and was ordained eight years later. When he was thirty-five, he was crippled and blinded by an illness, after which he was transferred to a friary in San Severino, where he remained until his death in 1721. The brothers of the monastery were amazed when a strange and beautiful perfume exuded from his body as it was being prepared for burial, and when no rigor mortis set in. Four years later, monastery officials ordered that the body be unearthed and moved to a site within the chapel. The brothers who disinterred the body accidentally jarred it while it was being transported, severing the head of St. Pacifico and splattering fresh blood over the carriers. Today, the blood-smeared shift of one of the brothers is still preserved in San Severino.

A similar story concerns St. Francis di Geronimo, a Jesuit friar born near the town of Taranto in 1642. He ministered in the city of his birth for most of his life, and especially enjoyed preaching to the outcasts of society, often visiting prisons and brothels. He soon developed a reputation for being a wonder worker, and was so beloved that large numbers of his spiritual children attended his funeral in 1716.

Church officials entrusted John de Giore, a lay brother serving in Naples, with the job of preparing St. Francis's body for the funeral. The saint had died at ten in the morning and had been laid in state in a church where de Giore was to carry out the preparations. As part of the preliminaries de Giore decided to remove two corns from the feet of the holy man to save as relics. "In cutting the first corn," he writes, "blood began to flow, bright crimson blood, in such quantities that we had to use a number of cloths to mop it up, besides collecting an ounce of it in a little basin." But the blood refused to behave according to the laws of biology. "It would not stop running, for all the efforts made to check it by bathing it with *aquavita fslemmata*," he continued. "In fact, as I have said, it went on flowing from about half-past ten to seven in the evening." [2]

The blood flows from St. Francis's body were certainly unnatural, since blood usually doesn't issue from a body that has been dead for more than a few hours.

This same miracle occurs in the hagiography of St. Catherine of Bologna. Catherine was born in 1413 and served as maid of honor in the ducal court of Nicholas d'Este in Ferrara, Italy, before becoming a nun. From 1456 to 1463 she was abbess of a convent in Bologna. When she died on March 9, 1463, she was buried without a coffin on the grounds of the convent. Soon afterward a wondrous perfume emitted from the ground where she was interred. Her body was duly exhumed and, though over two weeks had elapsed, showed no signs of corruption. According to the eyewitness testimony of Sister Illuminati Bembi, who had become abbess upon St. Catherine's death, the body was still fresh with blood. Sister Illuminati herself supervised the preparations that were made for reburial. She later testified that one of the nuns who was dressing the body noticed a piece of skin peeling away from St. Catherine's foot. The nun pulled on it, and fresh blood began dripping from the spot "as if it were alive," according to the abbess.

The body of St. Catherine of Bologna was put on display in a sepulcher, where it bled from the nose some three months later. The incorrupt body was later placed in a special chapel built in the saint's honor in Bologna in 1688. It remains there today, seated on a throne. Though it has apparently not bled again, the body shows no sign of desiccation.

Similar miracles have been documented recently. On May 10, 1970, the Worcester (Illinois) Telegram reported that the body of St. Maximina, housed in St. Adrian's Church in Chicago, Illinois, had begun to ooze a bloodlike solution. What distinguishes this miracle is the fact that the "body" is actually a wax figure that was molded around pieces of the seventeen-hundred-year-old bones of the saint. Only the bones of the hands and feet were left intact and remain skeletal. The figure, which is preserved in a glass coffin in the church, oozed a sticky red serum from its neck, hands, and feet for several days.

Another version of this form of miracle is even more bizarre and apparently supernatural. During the Middle Ages it was customary, especially in Italy, to collect blood from the deceased bodies of holy persons as relics. The samples were usually preserved in small phials, where they eventually dried. These blood relics, which are currently enshrined in reliquaries deposited at monasteries, convents, and churches throughout Italy, have been known to liquefy, and occasionally even to bubble and foam as they desolidify!

This miracle, colorfully called the "ebullition of blood," occurs several times yearly in Naples, where two small phials containing the blood of St. Januarius, a legendary fourth-century martyr, are preserved in Naples Cathedral. Although not very well known in this country, the miracle of St. Januarius is famous in Italy. It is a scientific puzzle as well as a religious one, and more reports have been written about it than any other miracle of the Church.

Historians actually know very little about St. Januarius. He was born near the end of the third century, and eventually became bishop of Benevento. He traveled throughout Italy, preaching relentlessly and arousing the ire of Diocletian, the Roman emperor and a fierce persecutor of Christians. Januarius was eventually arrested in Naples in 305 A.D. along with several companions and thrown to the lions during a public execution held at the city's amphitheatre. The lions, according to legend, refused to attack; so on September 19, the band of Christians was taken to a forum near the city of Pozzuoli and beheaded.

Januarius's body was buried near the town of Marciano, on a road leading from Pozzuoli to Naples. Around 420 A.D. the bishop of Naples ordered the body exhumed and brought to his city, where ceremonies in April and September were instituted in the saint's honor. In 831 A.D. the bones of the martyr were seized by a nobleman of Benevento, but for some reason the skull of the saint was allowed to remain in Naples. The relics were sent throughout Italy over the next several hundred years and were finally returned to Naples only at the end of the thirteenth century. It was then that Charles II, king of Naples, ordered a cathedral built in the saint's honor, where the skull of the martyr could be permanently enshrined.

At about this time two phials of dried blood were added to the relics. The tale of the saint's blood appears to have been added to the legend many centuries after his death, perhaps as late as the Middle Ages. A servingwoman had purportedly collected the blood from the stone where Januarius had been executed, and the two phials containing it were buried with his body in the catacombs near Naples. A small altar was later erected there to his memory, and the phials were placed in a small urn. The blood eventually dried, but then began to liquefy periodically in a miraculous way, and has been doing so ever since. It is not known whether the phials traveled with the other relics, or even whether they were part of the material returned to Naples. In any case, toward the end of the thirteenth century two phials of blood, allegedly that of the martyr, found their way to the city and were considered genuine relics.

In 1608 a chapel was constructed adjacent to the cathedral as a final resting place for the martyr's skull. It was finished in 1646 and since that time has enshrined the skull, which is currently preserved in a silver reliquary. Today the chapel is the center of festivals in honor of St. Januarius's relics. These ceremonies were first formalized in 1337 by Giovanni Orsini, the archbishop of Naples. His original declaration outlined the ceremonies that were to be held, and they are still being faithfully observed twice a year. It is interesting to note, though, that in this declaration *Orsini made no mention of the two mysterious phials of blood.* Because they are not mentioned in any other contemporary Church chronicles either, it is highly likely that the phials of blood were deposited in Naples Cathedral after that time.

The phials and the miracle of Januarius's blood were first documented in 1389, when an anonymous traveler published a tract in which he told about the periodic liquefaction of the blood. Further mention of the relic and the miracle associated with it was made by several other travelers to Naples over the next two centuries. In his *Mirouer historical de France* (1536), Robert Gaguin, a French historian, reported that Charles V had gone to Naples to be crowned as king: "On Sunday, the third day in the month of May, the king heard a mass to St. Januarius in the great cathedral of Naples. They brought some of the precious blood of that saint in a great glass phial . . . hard as stone, but after it had set on the altar awhile, it began forthwith to warm up and to soften as if it were blood taken from a living man." Since 1659 the ritual liquefaction of the blood has been carefully documented by the Church.

Today the blood is installed in a chapel within Naples Cathedral. It is usually locked away in a special vault and kept under constant guard by Church and civil authorities. It is preserved in two glass phials which are held in a small cylindrical silver-and-glass case. This case is several centuries old (the exact date of its origin is unknown) and measures about twelve centimeters in diameter. It in turn is attached to a large silver monstrance to which a handle is affixed. One of the phials is larger than the other and is about two-thirds filled with dried blood. The second contains only a few drops of the substance, which apparently do not liquefy during the miracle. Unfortunately, these phials are permanently sealed to their case by putty, which has become so hardened that the case cannot be opened without breaking them. This makes a chemical analysis of the blood impossible.*

However, the substance stored in the phials is definitely blood. Several scientists at the University of Naples examined the phials in 1902. By shining a beam of light through the glass case they were able to make a spectroscopic analysis of the relics. This analysis verified that the phials contain blood, though it is possible that it has been contaminated by a foreign substance.

Although the blood enclosed in the phials is quite ancient, it usually liquefies—and frequently bubbles and foams—several times a year during public ceremonies held in Januarius's honor. The first of these ceremonies is held on the first Sunday in May (in commemoration of the entry of the relics into Naples); the second occurs on September 19 (the anniversary of the martyr's death). The blood has also been known to liquefy during other rituals and celebrations. The blood relics are occasionally exhibited publicly on December 16 to commemorate a miracle that occurred at the time of the eruption of Mt. Vesuvius in 1631, when the blood stayed liquefied for thirty days. They are also paraded through Naples Cathedral—just like the "Notre Dame du Trésor" in Remiremont—to ward off natural disasters when they threaten the city.

---

*Only one attempt has been made to open the phials. In 1956 Church officials decided to clean out some sawdust that had made its way into the case when the relics were packed away for safekeeping during the war. The project had to be abandoned when it was realized that opening the case would probably destroy the relics.

The blood has even been known to liquefy spontaneously when the case has been taken from its vault for cleaning or special examination.

The blood doesn't always liquefy on schedule, however, and although this occurs only rarely, such a failure is usually considered to be a bad omen by the citizens of Naples. For instance, it did not liquefy in May 1976, just before the worst earthquake in Italian history struck. Previous failures had been chronicled in 1835 and 1944.

The traditional miracle occurs in the context of an elaborate festival. The ceremony begins at nine in the morning, when throngs of people crowd into Naples Cathedral in anticipation. Most of them try to position themselves near the small chapel where the relics of the saint are enshrined. Close to the chapel altar is a silver bust that contains the skull of St. Januarius. Because the room can accommodate only about a hundred people, most of the participants must remain in the cathedral proper, though they can look into the chapel without too much difficulty. Only officials of the city and Church and specially invited guests are able to watch as the blood is taken from the vault in the chapel at the beginning of the ceremony. Included among these guests, however, are a special group of elderly women known as the "relatives of St. Januarius" who "help" the miracle along. They line up at the side of the altar and literally act as "cheerleaders." As soon as the phials are removed from the vault and are raised into the air in full view of the crowd, the relatives of St. Januarius begin their work. They begin to scream and beseech the saint to liquefy his blood, which at this point is usually dry and crusty. They will even shout obscenities if the miracle doesn't occur quickly enough! Soon the crowd joins in with cries and worship.

Several minutes usually pass before the next stage of the ceremony. Eventually the Church dignitaries entrusted with holding the phials will wave a red handkerchief to signify that the blood has begun to liquefy. Another specially delegated Church official will then hold a candle near the phials so that the crowd can see the liquefaction in the dim church. The case is then kissed by all the officials present and by the relatives of St. Januarius. Finally it is paraded through the aisles of the cathedral in a magnificent procession. A Te Deum is played during the procession, and the phials are subsequently locked away again in the chapel. Sometimes the blood will remain in a liquid state throughout the procession; on other occasions it will resolidify as it is carried about.

A very good eyewitness report on the miracle itself was made in 1970 by Dr. Giorgio Giorgi, a physician from Naples who was allowed to observe the event at close range. He published his account as part of a ten-page report in the Italian parapsychology journal *Quaderni di parapsicologia.*[3] During the ceremony, which on this occasion was being officiated by the archbishop of Naples, Dr. Giorgi was able to stand only about a yard or so from the glass case holding the phials. He described how the archbishop held the case in full view of the crowd and then began to rotate it slowly while invoking the saint, beseeching him to produce the miracle:

> After about four minutes, certainly no longer, I was disconcerted to see just in front of my nose, at a distance of little over three feet, that the clot of blood had suddenly changed from the solid state into that of a liquid. The transformation from solid into liquid happened suddenly and unexpectedly. The liquid itself had become much brighter, more shining; so many gaseous bubbles appeared inside the liquid (shall we call it blood?) that it seemed to be in a state of ebullition.

Dr. Giorgi was able to kiss the case immediately after the miracle had occurred. He found it was cool, thus proving that the blood had not been heated to cause the liquefaction. He also saw that the blood had increased in volume during the process.

The liquefaction of the dried blood is only one of many mysteries surrounding this miracle, which have been documented in over a thousand books, articles, and studies written in Italian. David Guerdon, a French writer, was asked to make an investigative report of the miracle in 1978 by the French magazine *Psi International.* After visiting Naples, witnessing the miracle, and studying the existing literature on it, Guerdon published a lengthy report on the many paranormal aspects of the event. He was able to document three additional mysteries that would seem to authenticate its miraculous nature:[4]

(1) *The miracle is completely independent of the temperature within the Cathedral.* It would appear that the blood liquefies no matter how warm or cold Naples Cathedral is at the time. There

also seems to be no set period of time required for the blood to turn to a solution after it is first exhibited. For example, in May 1879 it took two hours for the liquefaction to occur, while the blood bubbled up within fifteen minutes at the ceremony held the following September. On occasion the blood will already be liquefied when it is taken from the vault; at other times it won't dissolve for over twenty-four hours. There seems to be no correlation between the temperature inside the cathedral and the duration of the wait.

(2) *The liquefied blood shows alterations in volume.* Although two thirds of the larger phial is filled with dried blood, the volume frequently either increases or decreases as the clot liquefies. During the May ceremony, for instance, the blood will usually increase in volume until it fills the entire phial. In September, however, the volume usually decreases. For some reason the volume tends to *increase* when the liquefaction takes place slowly and to *decrease* when it occurs shortly after the ceremony begins. The extreme differences in volume can range from twenty to twenty-four cubic centimeters, which, considering the size of the phial, is an enormous amount.

These variations must be considered miraculous, since they violate basic laws of chemistry. The volume of any solidified substance will either increase or decrease when that substance passes to a liquid state—it can't do both.

A related mystery is that even the weight of the phials will change. Amazingly enough, the weight of the phial sometimes increases when the volume *decreases* and vice versa! This discovery was first made by a group of Italian scientists who attempted to study the miracle in 1902 and was confirmed in 1904. No purely scientific explanation can account for this phenomenon, especially since these alterations in weight range over several grams.

(3) *The blood does not simply liquefy.* During the course of the miracle the color of the substance goes through several stages. Dark brown when dry, the blood turns lighter when the miracle commences. It then turns yellowish red and finally scarlet. Its viscosity also goes through a sequence of variations, becoming abnormally pasty just before liquefying and then much more viscous than normal blood. Occasionally not *all* of the matter will

liquefy, but a central "ball" or clot will remain solid and bob about in the middle of the blood. This central clot is one of the more peculiar aspects of the manifestation. Witnesses have testified that it will actually exude liquefied blood—and absorb the blood as it resolidifies—as though serving as a sort of "filter" for the miracle.

As has been discussed, the blood can also liquefy in two different ways. While it usually simply "melts" into a liquid state, it has been known to bubble and foam during the miracle.

It is unfortunate that because the phials are permanently sealed in the case, no current analysis can be made of the blood. "We must certainly regret that the scientific analyses of the blood of St. Januarius . . . date from the beginning of the century," writes Guerdon in his report. He continues:

The Church does not wish to have the integrity of the relics compromised, and we understand this, for to open the one phial still containing the blood would be to risk losing forever so precious a vestige. To be sure, the analysis of the substance would permit us to resolve all sorts of questions. But at what price? The hardened putty would oblige us to break the phial in order to open it—at the risk of annihilating its contents. On the other hand we could try to penetrate the glass by means of a trephine and to extract a drop from the phial. Among other things, this would allow spectrographic study on a flat glass slide (rather than on the curved glass of the phial), and chromatographic study (the examination of the substance by the differences in the absorption of its components on blotting paper).

Even if the phials could be opened, any serious attempt to analyze the blood, or even a cursory examination, could destroy whatever chemical or psychic equilibrium exists within the clotted blood and allows it to liquefy. A carbon 14 test could determine the age of the blood and possibly verify that it dates back to the time of St. Januarius's death. But such a test would require the sacrifice of at least half of the blood, which would never be tolerated by Church officials.

Another mystery associated with the blood, perhaps the weirdest of all, occurs about nine miles from Naples in the town of Pozzuoli. It was here that Januarius was beheaded in a forum located near some sulphur pits outside the town. The city is presently the site of a Capuchin monastery, which houses the stone on which the saint was beheaded. Enshrined in a church attached to the monastery, the stone is actually a block of marble that has been hollowed out in the center. A Greek cross is carved into the upper part of it. The block measures three feet tall by about two feet wide and *turns deep red when celebrations in honor of St. Januarius are held in Naples.* Sometimes it will even drip blood.

These blood flows have been thoroughly documented, even though they have occurred only on rare occasions. On February 22, 1860, for instance, the stone bled when a church in Naples dedicated to St. Januarius caught fire. Samples of the blood were personally collected by Monsignor Purpo, the bishop of Pozzuoli at the time. Another blood seepage commenced on September 19, 1894. Samples of this liquid were preserved on pieces of cotton by church officials. These were sent to the Laboratory of Forensic Medicine in Naples in May 1926 for analysis. It proved to be human blood.

The present century has brought a decline in these blood flows, but the marble slab still changes color when celebrations honoring St. Januarius are held in Naples. One explanation for this synchronous miracle might be that the discolorations result from heat and humidity fluctuations in the church where it is kept. But when Church officials, working along with a team of interested scientists, tested the theory in September 1902 and again in September 1927, they found no indication that the change was related to any known atmospheric condition.

So we are left with a host of inexplicable phenomena—blood that liquefies, stones that bleed, and a number of other supernatural events—surrounding the two mysterious phials of blood in Naples. Although neither science nor parapsychology can offer a total solution to the mystery, several theories about the nature of the miracle of St. Januarius's blood have been proposed.

There have been occasional unsuccessful attempts to explain the miracle along conventional scientific lines. Some skeptics have even proposed that the miracle is a fraud perpetuated by Church authorities in Naples. This is a preposterous idea when one considers that the miracle has been enacted over and over again for some six hundred years and that the phials of blood cannot be opened. Other theories speculate that the liquefaction is a heat effect generated by the crowds who jam the cathedral when the miracle is about to take place or by the daylight that strikes the phials during the subsequent procession. Yet another theory is that the miracle is a result of the constant jarring the blood undergoes. Yet each of these possible solutions can be rejected. We know the liquefaction is independent of the temperature inside the cathedral, and Dr. Giorgi noted in his 1970 report that the case holding the phials was cool when he kissed it. It might also be pointed out that heating tends to accelerate the coagulation of blood, not its lique-faction. And the fact that the blood has been known to liquefy while still in its vault rules out the notion that the clotted mass is sensitive to light or jarring.

A favorite theory of some religious skeptics is that the blood is somehow mixed with a chemical agent that causes the liquefac-tion. A few scientists have even attempted to replicate the miracle artificially and thereby "expose" the Naples enigma. One such attempt was made by Professor A. Albini of the University of Naples in 1880. Albini discovered that a solution of chocolate powder, sugar, casein, whey, salt, and water remains solid when left undisturbed but liquefies when agitated. But his explanation could not account for the fact that the blood is able to liquefy while the phial is resting quietly in its vault. It was totally invali-dated in 1902 when a spectroscopic examination of the phial showed that it did contain genuine blood. A more interesting attempt to discredit the miracle was made on December 22, 1906, when Professor Guido Podrecci, an Italian scientist, gave a public demonstration at a theater in Rome that promised to be an expo-sure of a fraud. For his rather comical performance, Dr. Podrecci showed that a phial of calf's blood mixed with a specially prepared chemical solution would liquefy when heat was applied to it. But once again the performance was only a weak imitation of the Naples prodigy. It took Podrecci's solution over an hour to liquefy, and it required violent shaking over an open candle!

Whatever the nature of the miracle, it is doubtful whether the answer to its puzzle will be found by drawing solely on the knowl-edge of conventional science. A supernatural and psychic interpre-tation is also necessary. Cardinal Lambertini, the great authority on the miraculous, came to this realization in the early 1700s while conducting research for his *De canonizatione*. The future Pope Benedict XIV was so fascinated by the miracle of St. Januarius that he went so far as to procure samples of dried blood and experimented with various processes to try to make it liquefy. He was unable to do so, and argued in his treatise that the liquefying blood of St. Januarius could well be a genuine miracle. Similar views have been expressed by the few parapsychologists who have studied the phenomenon.

Chief among these is Hans Bender, whose research has been mentioned several times in this book. Bender traveled to Italy in the 1960s to witness the miracle and was able to photograph it. (These photographs are currently in the archives of the Institute for the Study of Border Areas of Psychology and Psychohygiene in Freiburg.) Bender has adopted a basically parapsychological explanation for the miracle. He believes that the liquefaction is caused by a process similar to that which apparently influences traditional "haunted houses."

Haunted houses have been chronicled down through the ages from every corner of the globe. They are characterized by a recurring set of symptoms: Ghosts are seen marching about, the sound of mysterious footsteps is heard at night, furniture may move by itself, odd odors are noticed, "presences" may be felt, and so on. By legend, a place—a house, church, cemetery—becomes haunted when some tragedy occurs there. In his book *Fenomeni d'infestazione* (1919), Ernesto Bozzano, who was one of Italy's foremost parapsychologists, collected and analyzed some 374 cases of haunted houses and was able to show that a tragic death such as an accident or murder had occurred in 180 of them. In twenty-seven other cases there was circumstantial evidence—such as the discovery of bones buried near the house—that suggested that some foul deed had transpired and had been covered up. Deaths had occurred in ninety-seven additional cases, but these were not tragic or unusual in any way. Bozzano's findings therefore suggest that the *emotions* linked to these sites caused them to become haunted, not the deaths themselves.

Many parapsychologists believe that a house that has been the scene of violent or intense emotion may become "charged" with a psychic force. This "field" may permanently affect the house and "discharges" itself, much like a tea kettle releasing steam, over and over again. One might say that a haunted house is charged with a "psychic ether" that is very sensitive to the human mind. When a person enters a haunted house, his mind may become attuned to this ether and he might therefore "see" and experience events that occurred there years earlier. He might "see" the people who once lived there (as ghosts) or hear them (as disembodied voices, footsteps, or other mysterious noises). On occasion, the force or psychic field affecting the house may actually cause furniture to move.

Dr. Bender's theory, then, is that the violent emotions that accompanied the beheading of St. Januarius in 305 A.D. paranormally charged the blood with a psychic field that somehow regulates its liquefaction. The blood is, in his opinion, a "haunted" object.

Convincing as Bender's ideas may seem, they are to some degree incomplete. Many researchers who have studied hauntings or have lived in haunted houses have made two rather consistent observations about these places. First, hauntings tend to deactivate over time: the symptoms occur less and less frequently. Second, haunted houses seem to "act up" cyclically—ghosts will be seen and mysterious noises will be heard for a while, but then the houses will go into a period of quiescence that may last several months before the ruckus begins again. Yet whatever the psychic factors are that cause the miracle of St. Januarius, they don't follow these rules. Not only does the miracle occur on schedule every year, it is occurring just as miraculously today as it did six-hundred years ago. And while Bender's theory may be correct in principle, it does not take into consideration another important factor.

This factor is the emotions of the crowd that takes part in the biannual celebrations at Naples Cathedral. It has been proposed earlier in this book that many miracles may be mass psychic effects produced by the worshipers who are witnessing them. The miraculous hailstones of Remiremont and the psychic portrait of Dean Liddell that appeared in Christchurch Cathedral are two cases in point. *The intense religious fervor of the crowds gathered to witness the miracle in Naples might catalyze a preexisting psychic field dormant in the blood, thus causing the clot to liquefy.*

The celebrations in honor of St. Januarius are hardly dignified affairs. The crowds often become boisterous and even unruly as they shout and invoke the saint. When the phials are taken from their vault in the chapel, the participants become nearly hysterical.

This violent emotion, continuously focused directly onto the phials of blood as they are held in public view, may be a prime ingredient of the miracle.

It is also worth noting that the "relatives of St. Januarius," who seem so crucial to the miracle, *inherit* this honor and position from their forebears. The post has been handed down from mother to daughter for centuries. Could the original "relatives" have been especially psychic women who were chosen by Church officials in Naples years ago because they were gifted with the psychic ability to catalyze the miracle? Could they have passed on this power genetically to the women who currently serve in this peculiar capacity?

Because the emotions of the crowds are probably simply a catalyst, and not the actual *cause* of the liquefaction, it is also possible that whatever field is affecting the blood may, on occasion, cause it to liquefy quite spontaneously. This general theory could also explain the bleeding stone of Pozzuoli. Through years of public veneration, the stone may be psychically enveloped by a field similar to that which affects the blood in Naples. When the blood liquefies in Naples, the psychic field affecting the stone in Pozzuoli might be catalyzed through some sort of long-distance sympathetic action.

This psychic interpretation might also explain the great historical puzzle about the miracle of St. Januarius—i.e., why didn't it manifest itself until 1389, long after the relics of the saint had been placed in Naples Cathedral? The phials of blood may have indeed accompanied the relics of St. Januarius on their travels throughout Italy. But they may never have been recognized for what they were until in 1389, when the blood spontaneously liquefied for the first time, bringing the miracle to public attention. The veneration of the phials, which dates from about that time, may have caused the further liquefactions.

There are some indications that in the not too distant future a more concerted effort may be made by either the Italian scientific community or the parapsychological world to explore the miracle more fully. Dr. Hubert Larcher, an Austrian parapsychologist, wrote a book on the miracle in 1966 in which he called for the creation of a scientific commission entrusted with the job of impartially studying the phenomenon. Two scientists at the University of

Naples suggested in 1972 that a center for the study of the miracle be founded and that the archives of Naples Cathedral (which house pertinent historical documents) be opened to the public and properly catalogued. This idea has recently been echoed by Bender. He has proposed that a commission be formed—composed of physicians, chemists, theologians, psychologists, and parapsychologists—to study the miracle and explore its mysteries.[5] At the present time several scientists at the University of Naples are showing some interest in renewing study of the miracle. Just what course of action such an investigation is likely to take has not been determined.

In the meantime, Church officials are taking a neutral attitude. Cardinal Ursi, the archbishop of Naples, recently released a public statement about the miracle in response to the publicity the events there have been receiving:

> The periodic liquefaction of the blood held in two phials kept in the chapel of St. Januarius in the cathedral of Naples is a very remarkable phenomenon which has always aroused keen interest and, at the same time, discussions and polemics.
>
> This extraordinary matter, strengthened by rigorous documentation for at least six centuries, goes outside the ordinary natural laws and is for that reason considered miraculous.
>
> Nevertheless the Church, while consenting to the cult, has never made an official pronouncement on the miraculous nature of the event, leaving to scholars every chance for research, providing that the integrity of the relics is granted.

Any final evaluation of the miracle of St. Januarius must take into consideration that the Naples prodigy is *not* unique. A number of other cases of "liquefying blood" miracles have been documented, though none of them have received as great an amount of coverage and publicity as the Naples phenomenon.

Several churches in southern Italy house relics of various saints, including phials filled with samples of their dried blood. These samples, too, are known to liquefy periodically. These miracles usually occur only once a year, and most often on the anniversaries of the saints' deaths or on their feast days. A typical case is the blood relic of St. Bernardino Realino, whose feats of levitation were discussed in Chapter Two. St. Bernardino died in 1616 in the town of Lecce, near Naples. A phial of his blood was kept in a Naples church for two hundred years, during which time it periodically liquefied. Eyewitnesses testified that the dried blood would become ebullient and increase in volume as it turned to liquid. The miracle apparently ceased some time in the eighteenth century. A similar phenomenon occurs at the cathedral in Ravello in the southern part of the country. The cathedral houses a phial of blood allegedly taken from the body of St. Pantaleon, who was beheaded in 304 A.D. by order of Diocletian, the same Roman emperor responsible for the martyrdom of St. Januarius a year later. The blood has been known to liquefy on July 27, the saint's feast day. Still another phial of dried blood attributed to St. Pantaleon is currently enshrined in the Church of San Severino in Naples; it, too, liquefies on occasion. In all, there are twenty such cases in southern Italy.

Another interesting example is that of the Venerable Passitea Grogi, a Capuchin nun born in 1564. She showed religious tendencies from an early age and began experiencing religious ecstasies when she was twenty-five years old. It was at about this time that she was impressed with the full stigmata, which bled copiously from her hands, feet, and breast. She eventually became a nun, and in 1599 she founded her own convent in Siena and became its abbess. She was reputed to have the ability to bilocate, and her stigmata remained fully visible on her body even after her death in 1615.[6]

Since the wounds of the stigmata bled profusely during her ecstasies, many of the sisters at the convent collected it in phials. These are still preserved in Siena and sometimes spontaneously liquefy.

What makes this case unique is that Siena is located near the central part of Italy, while the great majority of liquefying blood miracles occur in the south of Italy, in or around Naples. This geographical quirk, and the fact that none of these miracles predate the miracle of St. Januarius, may provide a clue to the nature of the phenomenon. Could it be that the news of St. Januarius's miracle in Naples which spread throughout southern Italy sometime in the fourteenth century caused congregations in *other* churches that housed blood relics to pray for or expect similar wonders?

Part Three

~⸘~

MIRACULOUS INTERVENTIONS

The major theme of this book has been that the human mind is ultimately responsible for creating the world of the miraculous.

We will now confront the most difficult of all miracles to explain by this theory: instances in which the course of human events has actually been *altered* by the appearances and actions of spiritual beings. The most notable of these miracles is the appearance on earth of the Blessed Virgin Mary. These generally date from the mid–nineteenth century and have been occurring to the present. Our second area of concern will be instances of miraculous healings—i.e., healings that defy all medical, biological, and physiological laws.

Can we explain these extraordinary events as the psychic creations of the human mind, or must they be traced to an infinite, ineffable intelligence?

～ IX ～
MANIFESTATIONS OF THE BLESSED VIRGIN MARY

WHEN Juan Diego encountered the Blessed Virgin Mary at Tepeyacac in 1531, he had what might be considered a "religious vision." Was the apparition "real," or was it the product of his overzealously religious mind? If a passerby had chanced upon Juan Diego while traveling that same road, would he have seen the figure, too? Or would he have seen only the bewildered Indian, perhaps entranced, staring into blank space?

Religious visions are not unique to Christianity. The mystics, shamans, and holy men of all religions and cultures have told of visions during which they confronted and spoke with angels, spirits of the dead, or other heavenly ambassadors. The world of visionary experience is a definite personal reality for the mystic: Therese Neumann did not merely watch the Passion during her visions, but seemed to be taking an active part in it. But are religious visions "real" in the sense that we normally define the term? Were the "angels" and "spirits of the dead" so often seen by such mystics as Gemma Galgani (see Chapter Two) or Therese Neumann figments of their imaginations, or were these apparitions real beings which only they—through some psychic or mystic gift—were able to perceive?

The difficulty in differentiating between psychological experience and preternatural revelation is the chief problem we encounter when discussing the appearances down through the ages of the Blessed Virgin Mary (or BVM for short). The miracle of Guadalupe established as a tenet of the Roman Catholic Church that Mary, the mother of Jesus, is a living presence in the world today and that throughout history she has intervened in human affairs by appearing to selected mortals. These appearances have usually been in times of great social turmoil: for example, had the manifestation at Guadalupe and the miracles it wrought not occurred, it is likely that a bloody civil war between the indigenous Indian population and its Spanish conquerors would have taken place. The apparition was therefore *meaningful* within the social context of Mexico's domestic problems of that era. While it could be argued that Juan Diego suffered a series of pathological hallucinations, this theory cannot account for the fact that the apparition correctly foretold that Diego's dying uncle would miraculously recover from his grave illness, or for the miraculous flowers at the site of her visitation, or for the portrait of the Virgin that spontaneously appeared on Juan Diego's mantle. The same holds true for the revelations that were made during many other cases of Marian visitations, especially those which were seen by more than one person at the same time!

A typical example of a Marian appearance at a time of political unrest took place on the evening of July 18, 1830.[1] At the motherhouse of the Daughters of Charity in Paris, a young postulant named Zoé Catherine Labouré awoke to see the figure of a young child about four or five years old at her bedside. He beckoned Catherine to rise and follow him to the chapel. She obediently accompanied the apparition to the church, where at the altar stood a glowing figure of the Virgin Mary. Catherine threw herself to the floor, and the gentle apparition imparted a series of messages to her. Catherine was given to understand that some of these prophecies would be fulfilled shortly, while others would come to pass in 1870. After issuing its revelations, the apparition vanished "like a cloud that had evaporated," and Catherine returned to her room. She told no one but her confessor about her experience, and related to him only those parts of the messages that she felt safe to disclose. (She would later reveal warnings that terrible calamities would befall the world, that the throne of France was about to fall, and that the Church would be victimized.) The priest considered the encounter and warnings nothing more than the product of an overactive imagination.

He had to reevaluate his rash opinion a few days later when a bloody revolution broke out in Paris, just as Catherine had foretold. The target of the uprising was not only the established government, but the Church as well. The civil unrest was the product of a wave of anticlerical sentiment that had been spreading throughout France for some time.

To grasp the importance of the BVM's messages to Catherine in 1830, one must understand France's religious and political background at that time. A cordial liaison had existed between France and Rome since 1516, when King Francis I agreed to allow papal investitures an influence in the political appointments of the French monarchy. But anti-Rome feelings had begun to arise among the French aristocracy around the time of the 1789 revolution, and had resulted in widespread political attacks on the Church even before the fall of the monarchy. Attempts to reestablish relations with the Church were made in 1801 by Napoleon Bonaparte, who was willing to allow Roman Catholicism to become the unofficial state religion. However, he limited its influence in the decision-making policies of the government. When the Bourbons returned to power after Napoleon's fall, Louis XVIII (reigned 1814–24) tried to solidify a relationship with Rome by creating within France's political machinery an influence of the sort the Church had enjoyed during the sixteenth century. This plan, which Louis initiated in 1817, failed, and resulted in the instigation of a renewed antimonarchist and anticlerical movement among the French people. Louis's effort to appease Rome was matched by a genuine attempt to reduce the power of the monarchy by setting up a representational form of government. However, his successor—his brother, Charles X—had a much more conservative approach to government. His plan was to reinstate the absolute rule of the monarchy, which included even stronger ties with the religious establishment. Resistance to this scheme took the form of a three-day uprising that struck Paris in 1830. Charles had to flee to England, and a more populist government came to rule. Though the country remained nominally a monarchy, it was now a monarchy with only limited power.

The BVM revealed herself to Catherine a second time on November 27, 1830. The postulant was visiting the convent church when she saw the apparition floating over the altar. The figure stood on an orb representing the world, surrounded by an oval frame which began to glow and then formed the words *O Mary, conceived without sin, pray for us who have recourse to thee.* The apparition requested that a medal be struck in the form of this appearance and then departed. A third manifestation was made in December, at which time the request was repeated.

Catherine lived to see the fulfillment of the Virgin's prophecies for 1870. A bloody insurrection broke out in France in 1871 when a fierce political struggle between royalist and republican factions erupted after the country's humiliating defeat in the Franco-Prussian War, which had begun the previous year. This insurrection, like that of 1830, was anticlerical in nature. Many priests were murdered by marauding street gangs, who were strongly influenced by the new and revolutionary writings of Karl Marx. (In the years to come the Virgin Mary would often appear during times of political upheaval instigated by Socialist or Communist activities.) Catherine Labouré died in 1876 and was canonized in 1947.

The appearances of the Virgin Mary in 1830 are prototypical of the BVM visitations in a number of respects:

(1) *The witness was young.* Catherine Labouré was only twenty-four when she first saw the apparition.

(2) *The apparition was concerned with world affairs and made several accurate predictions.* The basic intention of the apparition seemed to have been to warn Catherine of coming political and social crises. Upheavals were not unexpected in the politically torn France of 1830, but the apparition made several rather specific prophecies. For instance, Catherine was told that the coming crisis would cause the death of the archbishop of Paris. During the Paris uprisings of 1871, he was indeed brutally murdered by the insurrectionists. The prediction that the French throne would fall was realized when Charles X fled to England in 1830, ending the absolute rule of the monarchy.

(3) *The apparition meant for some of its messages to remain secret.* While telling her confessor of much that transpired between the apparition and herself, Catherine Labouré never revealed everything that had been told to her. She understood that some of the revelations were to be kept confidential.

The image of the BVM that appeared to Catherine Labouré in 1830 proved by its accurate predictions of the future that it was no hallucination. While it is therefore hard to believe that the visions were solely a product of the young woman's mind, no one other than Catherine saw the apparition during its three visits. Had another witness seen the figure, the case for its authenticity would be that much stronger.

A Marian apparition that was witnessed by more than one observer *did* occur in 1846, when an image of the Virgin Mary appeared several times to two young children in La Salette, France.[2] These appearances were almost identical in purpose and type to Mary's previous visitations sixteen years before.

La Salette is a small village in the southeast of France, populated during the nineteenth century mostly by peasants and country folk. On September 19, 1846—the eve of a festival in honor of Mary known throughout France as the feast of Our Lady of the Seven Sorrows—two children were tending a herd of cows on the slopes of Mount Gargas, which lies behind the town. Maximin Giraud (age eleven) and Melanie Mathieu (age fifteen) were playing when suddenly they saw a large orb of glowing light approaching them from the heavens. As it neared a small stream bed, it opened to reveal the figure of a beautiful woman. Though the children were frightened that the apparition would hurt them, their fears vanished when the lady spoke to them in a sweet, musical voice that immediately put them at ease. She bade them come closer to her and told them she had important messages. The figure was so radiant that the children found it difficult to look directly at her, but they could discern that she wore white shoes encircled by roses and a white cape bordered with the same flower. A crucifix hung from her neck.

The apparition told the children that unless the Christian world submitted to God, her Son would unleash a vengeance upon it. She also warned that, due to the prevalence of sin throughout the world, France's harvest would fail. She specifically mentioned the potato crop, which was so vital to France's economy. The apparition further predicted that a great famine would result from the failure of the wheat and grape crops, which would cause the death of children throughout the country. The apparition then spoke to the children individually, giving each a secret. Before leaving, the Virgin promised that the world could be spared if it repented. The apparition then floated up the hill and disappeared.

It should be noted that despite their religious upbringing, the children had no idea what the visitation meant, nor did they associate the woman they saw with the Blessed Virgin Mary. When the apparition spoke figuratively of the "heavy hand of her Son," they merely thought she was referring to a boy who had beaten her! Because the religious education of children in France during this period was extremely rudimentary, the naïveté of these two young witnesses is not difficult to accept; furthermore, neither child seems to have been particularly bright.

The children duly reported what had happened to Church officials in La Salette. And when the dry stream by which the BVM had appeared began to miraculously flow shortly after the visitation, the area became a place of pilgrimage.

The apparition's warnings came true as well. The great potato famine which would eventually cause widespread starvation in Europe had already begun its deadly damage in Ireland in 1845. By 1846 it had spread to the Continent. France's wheat crop also failed, and its grape crop was decimated by an especially virulent disease later the same year. It is estimated that over a thousand people died in Europe as a result. Infant mortality was especially high.

Some writers on La Salette have also theorized that the BVM's apparition may have served as a veiled warning about future convulsions on the French political scene. Two years after this visitation, France underwent a series of civil insurrections spurred on by activists influenced by the writings of Marx. Don Sharkey, an authority on Marian apparitions, points out in his classic *The Woman Shall Conquer* (1954) that the apparition's messages may have been a direct warning against the rise of communism, thus linking the La Salette miracle to the Paris visitations in 1830.

In 1851 Pope Pius IX personally requested that Church officials in La Salette procure statements from the children about the "secrets" they had been given by the apparition. The children agreed, on condition that the messages be placed in sealed envelopes and delivered directly to the Pope by the priests who collected them.*

---

*These documents were released between 1879 and 1915. Melanie Mathieu published hers in a brochure issued in 1879 with the approval of the bishop of Lecce. Versions of Maximin Giraud's messages were published in 1878 and 1915. Both accounts are concerned with future turmoil in Europe and prophecies about the rise of the Antichrist. They are, however, so cryptic that it would be difficult to offer an objective or concise evaluation of them.

If one chooses to reject the testimony of Catherine Labouré as the hallucinations of a religiously disturbed mind, such a theory cannot be used as an explanation for the La Salette mystery. It is hard to believe that the two children could have shared a pathological hallucination. The vision that appeared to them on September 19, 1846, was perceived by each child in exactly the same way. The children never wavered in their story or altered it during subsequent retellings. When they were questioned independently, they invariably agreed about what they had seen—even down to the smallest detail.

The figure at La Salette was therefore in some sense (though perhaps only spiritually) "real." It is unlikely, though, that anyone else would have seen the apparition had he chanced upon that meadow near La Salette while the visitation was taking place. Marian visitations seem to appear only to select individuals or to small groups of people while remaining invisible to others who may be present. This phenomenon, which might be called "perceptual selection," was most notable during the BVM's appearances in Pontmain, France (1871); Fatima, Portugal (1917); and Garabandal, Spain (1961). In each case the BVM appeared to small groups of children, yet remained unseen by the many adults who accompanied the children to the sites of the miraculous visitations.

Visions of the BVM have altered in appearance through the years, and seem to adapt themselves in order to best "fit in" with the culture in which they are revealing themselves. The BVM who appeared near Mexico City in 1531 was a dark-complexioned Indian maiden; yet during her French visitations of 1830 and 1846 she seemed European. In no case did she appear Semitic, as the historical Mary must have looked. This tendency indicates that the appearances are somehow at least partially generated (as were the "divine image" miracles explored in Chapter Five) *by the culture itself.* This phenomenon has not gone unnoticed by Catholic writers. In her history of Marian worship in the Catholic Church, *Alone of All Her Sex* (1976), Marina Warner describes the alteration in the appearance of the Virgin Mary down through the ages and as our conception of her has changed.

Yet there can be no doubt that Marian visitations follow a rather concise pattern. They seem to be cosmic reactions to threats against the religious and social status quo of the time. Her appearance in Mexico apparently quelled a potential Indian uprising while her French appearances anticipated threats against that country's political and social systems. In this respect, the apparitions seem to be intelligently planned by some spiritual presence which is independent of our own minds but which is concerned with our welfare.

One could, of course, argue that times of crisis are those when Mary (if one accepts her literal spiritual existence) *would* choose to visit earth to offer us her guidance. And it would be difficult, in view of the accurate predictions so often made by Marian apparitions, to find fault with this traditional Catholic viewpoint. But the altered appearance of the Virgin seems to contradict traditional Catholic theology, which states that Mary was taken into heaven in bodily form. Consequently, her appearance should not change from visitation to visitation.

But while Marian apparitions may essentially be what they purport to be—the appearances of an actual being existing in some spiritual level of reality who is concerned with our welfare—it is also possible that they are projections of *images* latent in our minds which literally become temporarily *real* on rare occasions.

It was the great Swiss psychologist Carl Jung (1875–1961) who first developed the concept of the *archetype*. While studying the rich folklore of a number of different cultures, Jung was struck by the fact that many societies throughout the world have developed similar symbols and legends. For instance, most cultures associate "darkness" with evil and "light" with good. Likewise, the bird is often used as the symbol of the soul.

Jung eventually discovered that human beings, no matter in what country they live or during what period of time, seem to share a common, unconscious, symbolic "language." He called these shared symbols *archetypes,* and considered them to have been genetically inherited from the beginnings of mankind. Related to the concept of the archetype is what Jung called the collective unconscious, which is one of the most misunderstood of all his theories. The "collective unconscious" does *not* actually refer to a supermind to which we are all connected on some cosmic level, nor is it a "universal unconscious." By "collective unconscious" Jung meant a primitive level of mind in which we all *think* in the same way by the use of similar symbols or archetypes.

It is conceivable that linked to these universal archetypes are culturally determined religious "images" that become limited archetypes in societies that share a common religious background. In Western culture, for instance, we invariably imagine God to be a bearded old man seated on a throne, Jesus as a bearded man about the age of thirty, and Mary as a radiant queen. We can therefore construct a theory about the nature of Marian apparitions by uniting the concept of culturally determined archetypes with the theory (held by many parapsychologists) that all of us are telepathically linked to one another at some subliminal level of mind.

The key to understanding Marian apparitions may be in their tendency to occur at times of social and/or political crisis. At such times of stress, some form of mass telepathic communication may occur in the collective unconscious of the threatened culture. This may lead to the formation of a "group mind," which, in turn, results in the projection of a Marian visitation—a process similar to the one that may have produced the Guadalupe miracle of 1531. Most Marian apparitions have occurred in traditionally Catholic cultures, which view Mary as the protectress of the world. This concept, shared at some level of mind by all Catholics, has probably become an archetypal image for members of this faith. In times of crisis, Catholic cultures could therefore literally *project* this image into the real world of the five senses. The apparition, which might be compared to a thought form, merely echoes back the concerns of the people who have projected it. Note that when examined carefully, the world catastrophes or social turmoil so often predicted by Marian apparitions were events any astute person could possibly have foretold.

Marian apparitions, as we have seen, are most often witnessed by small groups of children. Experimental evidence suggests that children may be inherently more psychic than adults, and therefore more naturally sensitive to spiritual presences projected by the group mind. This is certainly the view of Dr. Arthur Guirdham, a British psychiatrist who has studied psychic phenomena for several years. In his book *Obsession—Psychic Forces and Evil in the Causation of Disease,* he suggests that children have no natural immunity against spiritual forces and so naturally tune in on them. Dr. Ernesto Spinelli of the University of Surrey has even collected experimental evidence that children are remarkably psychic but lose this power as they grow older. Spinelli tested young children for ESP, and after running the same tests with progressively older children, found a gradual decline in their scoring.[3]

Children were directly involved in the La Salette visitation, and were also the sole witnesses to the Virgin's appearances in Pontmain in 1871, one of the most astonishing of Marian visitations of all time.[4]

Pontmain is a small village lying in the northwest part of France near Le Mans, and during the nineteenth century its population was predominantly Roman Catholic. At the time of the visitation, the town church was in the center of the village. It was surrounded by houses and barns. In 1871 one of these houses was the residence of the Barbadette family. The principal witnesses to the Pontmain visitation were two of the Barbadette children, Eugene (age twelve) and Joseph (age ten). The date of the miracle was January 17. France was at war with Prussia.

The day had begun uneventfully. M. Barbadette, a farmer by vocation, had wakened his boys at six that morning to do their chores and attend school. At six in the evening, M. Barbadette, Eugene, and Joseph had gone to work in the barn when a neighbor dropped by. Her visit interrupted what was surely a monotonous routine for the boys, so Eugene decided to take the opportunity to leave the barn and get some fresh air, or "just to see the weather," as he later would recall. The sky was clear, and the brilliant stars that shone from the heavens also sparkled on the snow-covered houses and grounds. Entranced by the scene, Eugene suddenly noticed an apparition hovering about twenty feet above a neighboring house. It was of a tall, beautiful woman dressed in a blue robe studded with stars. A blue veil hid her hair and forehead. Her hands were lowered and spread as if in supplication. Eugene's first thought was that the vision was heralding the death of his elder brother, who was in the army fighting the Prussians. But he rejected this initial impression when he saw that the apparition was smiling.

Eugene was still staring at the figure when moments later the neighbor, Jeanette Detais, emerged from the barn. Eugene asked her to look over to where he was staring and describe what she saw. Mme Detais was perplexed; she couldn't see anything at all. The subsequent exchange between Eugene and Mme Detais soon attracted M. Barbadette and Joseph. M. Barbadette saw nothing, but Joseph startled everyone by stating that he, too, could see the apparition of the wondrous woman. The adults looked on in confusion as the two boys began to compare what they were seeing. Finally M. Barbadette angrily ordered the boys back into the barn. The children dutifully obeyed, and M. Barbadette and Mme Detais agreed not to mention the incident to anyone.

A few minutes later M. Barbadette began to have second thoughts about his rash behavior; so he thoughtfully asked Eugene to go outside to see if the apparition was still in the sky. The boy ran to the barn door and reported back that it was. M. Barbadette instructed his son to fetch his mother, but warned him to say nothing about the apparition either to her or to her maid.

Mme Barbadette was shocked by what greeted her when she finally arrived. Joseph had left the barn and was staring at the sky, clapping his hands, and repeatedly shouting, "Oh, how beautiful she is!" Mme Barbadette's only response was to give the boy a quick slap for causing so much commotion! At Eugene's request she looked up to the sky; but, like her husband and neighbor, she seemed immune to the apparition. When the two boys continued to describe the miraculous vision, Mme Barbadette urged the family to pray.

Within a short time a small crowd formed in the streets around the Barbadettes' house and barn. M. Barbadette tried to quell matters by ushering the family into the barn to pray. Meanwhile, Mme Barbadette ran back to the house to fetch her maid. But the maid couldn't see the figure either, and Mme Barbadette's only conclusion was that her children were lying. It was now six fifteen.

The Barbadettes kept their two sons indoors for a short while, first by making them pray and then by serving them dinner. Afterward, though, the boys ran outside to see if the apparition was still floating in the sky. It was. The children had now become so insistent in their claims that M. Barbadette began to wonder if some spiritual manifestation really *was* taking place, which only the children were being allowed to see. He thereupon took Joseph into the house, while Mme Barbadette took Eugene across the street to a convent house to talk with Sister Vitaline, a well-loved nun who lived in the community. Sister Vitaline was surprised by the visit, but followed Mme Barbadette back to the barnyard as Eugene continued to relate the vision he was seeing. The nun looked to the sky in vain. "I opened my eyes widely," she later testified, "and saw absolutely nothing."

Eugene carefully pointed at three stars in the sky and described how they outlined the BVM's figure. But the adults still couldn't see a thing.*

Sister Vitaline, however, was intrigued by the boys' claim. She quickly returned to the convent and fetched two young girls who were staying there, Françoise Richer (age eleven) and Jeanne-Marie Lebosse (age nine). Without giving any hint as to what was happening outside, the nun urged the girls to follow her out into the street. Without any prompting from Eugene they immediately began to describe to Sister Vitaline *the apparition of a woman floating high in the sky, dressed in a blue robe with golden stars.* Joseph emerged from the Barbadette house at about this time as well and joined in the collective vision. The adults were awestruck and soon rushed through the neighborhood gathering up other children. These children, too, could see the apparition!

By this time the image had begun to change in appearance. Although the Virgin remained motionless, the village children described how an oval frame containing four candles had formed around her. The countenance of the apparition also began to change; from joy, her face turned to sorrow. The entire tableau began to grow, and words slowly formed under the figure. Each letter appeared separately, until a brief message had been spelled out: *"Mais priez, Dieu vous exaucera en peu de temps. Mon Fils se laisse toucher."* (An approximate translation would be: "But pray, God will hear your prayers in a short time. My Son allows himself to be moved.") Many of the little witnesses had been separated from one another by the townsfolk during the formation of the message, yet they all saw the same words.

The message at first made little sense to the fifty or so adults now gathered in the streets of Pontmain. But during the formation

---

*Some accounts of the Pontmain miracle state that the adults did see the triangle of stars and noted that they were shining with an unusual brilliance. This claim is not made in the Abbé M. Richard's booklet on the miracle (translated as "What Happened at Pontmain"), which was drawn up in 1871 from the witnesses' own testimonies.

of the message, one of the villagers rushed up to the crowd to announce that Prussian troops were marching toward Pontmain. The time was now seven thirty.

The words of the Virgin's message were still forming when this news was relayed. As the townspeople became aware of the gravity of the situation, the children reported that the apparition was moving for the first time. The message was now complete, and the figure was raising its hands in benediction. A smile came over its face as well. Although the message then faded, the apparition remained distinct. The children next reported that the face of the BVM had taken on a sullen expression and that a crucifix had formed over her breast. Crosses also appeared on her shoulders. Finally, as a veil began to cover the figure, it faded away. The vision had remained in the sky for two hours.

As is true of most Marian manifestations, the Pontmain miracle occurred at a time of upheaval. France was at war with Prussia, and the citizens of Pontmain knew full well that they were in danger of imminent invasion. Yet at the very time the Virgin appeared over Pontmain, German military officials—having already advanced on Laval, a city close to Pontmain—inexplicably decided not to continue any farther into the west of France. It is the belief of many Catholic writers on Pontmain that the Virgin Mary was announcing that she had divinely intervened in the war, causing the German high command to spare the village. The war itself ended shortly after. An armistice was signed on July 17, and defeated France was forced to surrender both territory and indemnities to Prussia.

Today a basilica stands beneath the site where the apparition was seen. It was begun in 1872 and consecrated in 1900. On February 2, 1875, the bishop of Laval, under whose jurisdiction Pontmain falls, decreed the genuineness of the BVM's visit to the town.

The Pontmain affair supports the "archetype theory" of Marian apparitions which was formulated earlier in this chapter. At some deep level of mind, the residents of Pontmain must have been aware of the threat posed to their town by the advancing Prussian troops. This danger could have caused a vivid unconscious preoccupation with the Virgin Mother in her archetypal image as protectress and intermediary between Man and God. This may ultimately have produced a mass psychic effect (similar to the one responsible for the miraculous hailstones of Remiremont in 1905) that resulted in the projection of an image of the BVM into the night sky. (Note that the figure was more a projection or holograph-like image than any living presence.) The unconscious minds of the villagers may then have telepathically picked up the information that the Prussian high command had decided to spare Pontmain, and the figure adjusted her appearance and message accordingly.

Projection-type appearances of the Virgin Mary are not restricted to France. A Marian apparition in Knock, Ireland, in 1879 must rank as one of the most bizarre incidents in the history of the miraculous.[5]

Knock is a small village in County Mayo, Ireland. August 21, 1879, had been a dismal day. It had rained for hours, and the dreariness had lingered into the night. At about seven P.M. a young girl from the town, Margaret Beirne, was carrying out her evening chore of locking up the town church. She noticed an odd brightness illuminating the top of the building as she approached, but paid it little attention. This illumination was also seen at seven thirty by Mary McLaughlin, the housekeeper for the village priest, who was passing the church on her way to visit the Beirne family. She noticed that the glow was emanating from the south gable of the building. It was illuminating a tableau at the side of the church depicting Mary, St. Joseph, and a bishop standing by an altar. The figures didn't move, and Mrs. McLaughlin merely thought that the priest had bought some new religious statues for the church.

At about eight fifteen, though, after her visit to the Beirnes, Mrs. McLaughlin again passed the church. She was now accompanied by Mary Beirne, Margaret's older sister. Both of the witnesses found their attention drawn to the figures by the eerie light emanating from the building. Then the figures moved!

By the end of the evening a small group of fourteen Knock residents had congregated in front of the church to observe the mysterious tableau.* Everyone present could see it, and they all agreed as to its appearance. The Virgin Mary was dressed in white and wore a glimmering gown. Her hands were raised in benedic-

---

*A fifteenth witness, Patrick Walsh, lived a half-mile from the church. He had seen an orb of gold light shining from it while working in his fields, but not the figures. Although puzzled by the light, he didn't investigate the matter or learn about the apparitions until the next day.

tion. The figure of St. Joseph appeared to her right, with a gray beard and hair. The third figure seemed to represent St. John the Evangelist dressed as a bishop, holding a book and sermonizing. The altar stood to the left of the figures, and a cross and lamb rested upon it. The whole tableau seemed to stand out from the gable wall and to float about a foot and a half above the ground. The gable itself was enveloped in light the entire duration of the vision. Rain continued to fall during the two hours the apparitions remained in sight, yet the spot at which they appeared stayed dry.

A perceptive account of the apparitions was later recorded by Patrick Hill, who was fourteen years old at the time of the miracle. He testified to a Church inquiry that "the figures were full round as if they had body and life. They said nothing; but as we approached them they seemed to go back a little towards the gable." Yet the apparitions were obviously ephemeral: "I was up very near. One old woman went up and embraced the Virgin's feet, and she found nothing in her arms or hands." Despite the fact that the forms were immaterial, they were so lifelike that Hill could even read the lettering in the book the figure of St. John was holding.

The appearance of the BVM in Ireland in 1879 is not surprising if we accept the theory that apparitions tend to occur in times of national stress. The country was undergoing one of the worst periods in its history. The potato crop had failed in both 1877 and 1878, and was bound to fail again in 1879. Many who were spared death by the resulting famine were stricken by an epidemic of typhus that swept through the country that same year. In these hard times, the thoughts of the Knock community no doubt often turned to religion, especially on this special day—for the date of the visitation was the eve of the octave of the Assumption, a feast of special importance in the worship of Mary.

The subsequent history of the Knock apparitions is also interesting. The Reverend John MacHale, the local archbishop, sent a commission of inquiry to Knock soon after the news of the miracle spread throughout the locality. The commission was composed of three priests, who interviewed all the witnesses separately and found that their combined testimony was mutually corroborative. A second investigation was made in 1936. The last two surviving witnesses were again questioned, including the now quite elderly

Mary Beirne. Both confirmed the accuracy of their earlier testimony. Knock itself eventually became the site of numerous pilgrimages, and soon miraculous cures were claimed by many of those who visited the little church where the tableau had appeared. (A medical commission was established in 1936 to investigate these cures.) Today the little town of Knock still plays host to thousands of pilgrims yearly.

The apparitions of Knock are unusual in that they were visible to a relatively large number of witnesses. They neither spoke nor delivered a message, which is typical of "collectively" seen apparitions of the Virgin Mary.* Similar manifestations were later reported from Italy in 1888 and from Zeitoun, Egypt, in 1968. The Blessed Virgin's 1888 appearance occurred sometime in September near the town of Castelpetroso, where two young women saw her form standing within some rocky fissures by the side of a hill. The witnesses were herding sheep at the time, and their attention was drawn to the fissures by an odd light that was illuminating the area. This apparition was eventually seen by some five hundred spectators, including several priests and a bishop. During the Zeitoun apparitions of 1968–69, the BVM was seen by thousands of witnesses and photographed repeatedly. But this is a lengthy story which will be told in the following chapter.

The appearances of the Virgin Mary in Paris, La Salette, Pontmain, and Knock were visionary in nature. Even though the apparitions were collectively seen in the latter two cases, the figure of the Virgin was more ghostlike than real. But what of those cases in which a Marian apparition is able to act physically upon the real world? If such an apparition could move a physical object, such as open a door or pick up a book, the figure would have to be considered in some sense objective—that is, as a three-dimensional object occupying physical space. But the study of apparitions is not so clear-cut, and many of these ephemeral visitors tend to walk that slim yet infinite boundary between visionary existence and material reality. "Ghosts" and apparitions—including Marian apparitions—often possess characteristics that indicate that they are simultaneously material and immaterial.

---

*Parapsychologists call an apparition that is seen by more than one person at the same time a "collective" apparition or "collective" hallucination.

This paradox can best be illustrated by an example. You and a friend are sitting at home when you suddenly notice an apparition in the room. You both see it, and by comparing notes realize that you are seeing it in proper perspective vis-à-vis where each of you is sitting. Then the apparition places its hands on a book lying on your coffee table, turns around, opens your front door, and departs, yet leaves the door open. It vanishes into thin air as you and your startled friend look on. You then run to your coffee table to find that the apparition has left a handprint scorched into the surface of the book. But a second glance to the front door shows that it is closed—and has presumably never really been opened.

This visitation, which is a composite drawn from several well-authenticated cases, contains three puzzling elements. The apparition was (1) material, since it left its handprint on a book; yet it was (2) immaterial, since it vanished into thin air, and (3) hallucinatory, since it gave you the illusion that it had opened a door that in fact had never been touched. This hypothetical incident is a good example of the great difficulties parapsychologists have faced while studying apparitions. These phantoms seem capable of creating their own laws when they appear; laws very different from those that govern the material world.

The same obstacles apply to Marian apparitions as well, where it often becomes equally impossible to determine whether these phantoms are merely visions or genuine material beings. Probably the most celebrated and bewildering of all these material Marian manifestations is the Blessed Virgin's visit to Fatima, Portugal.[6]

The wonderful story of Fatima began in May 1917. This was a troubled period for Portugal and for Europe in general. Portugal was split by political factionalism. Its last king had been deposed in 1910 by a revolution which had set up a republican form of government. A more formal government, roughly modeled after that of the United States, had been organized in 1915. With the fall of the monarchy there came a decline in religion—for while the Portuguese people remained dutifully Roman Catholic, the government was openly hostile to the Church and had severed relations with Rome in 1913. Church property was confiscated, and the clergy were treated almost as second-class citizens. In the meantime, the First World War was blazing on the Continent. The seeds of the Bolshevik revolution were already germinating in Russia, where in 1918 a thoroughly antireligion government would come to power.

Portugal, hidden away on the Iberian peninsula and protected from most of Europe, was too preoccupied with her own internal strife to be deeply involved in world politics. She had joined World War I on the side of England, but was generally immune to the attacks and devastation her allies were suffering at the hands of the Germans. In trying to stabilize the country's economy and social structure, the new government had spread a great deal of anti-Catholic propaganda. But this scheme had done little to turn people in the countryside from their deeply ingrained religious convictions.

One spring day in 1916 in Fatima, a small town near Ourem, Lucia dos Santos (age nine), Francesco Marto (age eight), and his sister Jacinta (age six) were playing near the Cova da Iria, a hollow outside the town where the village children often took their sheep to graze. All three were illiterate but religious. Lucia's parents were landowners; but, like the parents of the other two children, they were very poor. The three were tending sheep on a nearby hill when an apparition of a boy aged about fifteen suddenly materialized and exhorted them to pray. The "angel" appeared to the children on two other occasions in 1916, once while they were playing at Lucia's house and another time again on the slopes. These angelic visitations heralded the appearance of the Virgin Mary in Fatima.

The date normally associated with the beginning of the Fatima story is May 13, 1917, quite a few months after the children first saw the apparition that had diligently instructed them to pray. The three children were tending sheep at the Cova da Iria as usual. They had just knelt in prayer when a flash of lightning pierced the otherwise cloudless sky. Lucia, Francesco, and Jacinta were frightened by the lightning, fearing that a storm was brewing. They quickly drove the sheep down the slopes of the hollow, but were again shaken by a bolt of lightning. They immediately ran farther down the slope. Reaching the bottom, Lucia and Jacinta beheld a remarkable sight. Before them was the figure of a beautiful and dazzling woman standing within the foliage of a small oak tree. The woman appeared to be about eighteen years old and wore a white veil bordered with gold. A rosary hung from her neck. Only Lucia ventured to talk to the figure, who told them that she was from heaven and wished them to return to the Cova on the thirteenth of every month for a period of six months. The figure then promised that the children would go to heaven, but that Francesco, who was unable to see the apparition, would have to say many Rosaries. The woman finally instructed Lucia to tell Francesco to recite the Rosary. The boy complied, and the apparition then became visible to him, though he could still not hear it speak. The woman went on to inform the children of the spiritual fate of several recently deceased Fatima villagers, and also warned them that they would suffer much in the coming months. The apparition then glided toward the east and disappeared.

After the woman had vanished, the children agreed that it would be best not to discuss what they had seen with anyone in the village. But little Jacinta couldn't contain herself. That very evening she told her parents what had happened at the Cova. She specifically said that she had seen the Virgin Mary. This was a premature claim to make, since the apparition had revealed neither her identity nor what her mission entailed during her talk with Lucia. The woman promised to inform the children of her identity only at the end of six months.

The sequel to Jacinta's confession was predictable. News of the visitation spread throughout the village within hours. The rumors that began to fly about angered Lucia's parents, and her mother was soon accusing the children of lying. When the story reached the pastor of Fatima, he wasted no time in interviewing Lucia. He was unimpressed by her testimony, but advised Lucia's mother to allow the girl to return to the Cova in one month. Secretly, though, he told her to forbid her daughter to go there again should the vision actually reappear.

The children soon became the center of attention in the small town. As they walked the streets over the next several days, they were constantly mocked by the skeptical townsfolk. A few residents, though, came to believe that the children were telling the truth and treated them as saints. Despite the accusations of their neighbors, none of the children wavered in their story, and all three exhorted the townsfolk to hold fast to their faith.

June 13 was the date that the apparition had promised to

return to the Cova. No one in Fatima really expected the children to go there, since the thirteenth was the feast day of St. Anthony, the town's patron saint, and a celebration had been planned. All the villagers were eagerly planning to attend. Nonetheless, the youngsters shunned the festivities and went directly to the Cova around midday, accompanied by about fifty devout residents of the town. The children began their vigil by praying before the oak tree upon which the vision had previously appeared. Soon Lucia pointed to the sky, and the three children saw the apparition of the Virgin gliding toward them. The spectators saw nothing. After arriving at the oak tree, the beautiful apparition imparted several messages to Lucia. She encouraged the girl to learn to read and write and delivered the first of several "secrets" to her. Then the apparition departed.

Although the visitation was invisible to the villagers, several of them did observe manifestations of the BVM's presence. According to the Reverend V. Dacruz, a Spanish priest who made a study of the Fatima miracle, several supernatural occurrences highlighted the BVM's June 13 appearance:[7]

Besides the three little seers, none of those present had seen the mysterious Lady. But several marvelous facts confirmed their impression that something extraordinary was taking place. The day was bright and hot as it usually is in Portugal in the month of June. Now, during the entire period of the apparition the light of the sun was dimmed in an exceptional manner, without any apparent cause. At the same time, the topmost branches of the tree were bent in the form of a parasol, and remained thus as if an invisible weight had come to rest upon them. Those nearest the tree heard quite distinctly Lucy's [Lucia's] words, and also perceived in the form of an indistinct whispering, or the loud humming of a bee, the sound of the Lady's answer, alternating regularly with the girl's voice.

At the end of the apparition, there was heard near the tree a loud report which the witnesses compared to the explosion of a rocket, and Lucy cried:

"There! She is going away."

At the same time the onlookers saw rise from the tree a beautiful white cloud which they could follow with their eyes for quite a while as it moved in the direction of the East. Further, at the Lady's departure, the upper branches of the tree, without losing the curved shape of a parasol, leaned towards the East, as if in going away the Lady's dress had trailed over them. And this double pressure which had bent the branches, first into a curve and then towards the East, was so great that the branches remained like this for long hours, and only slowly resumed their normal position.*

As a result of this second appearance, all of Portugal began to hear about the supernatural events at Fatima. Lucia's mother still remained unconvinced that her daughter was telling the truth, and the village priest even suggested to the girl that perhaps the devil was responsible for the apparition.

After much self-questioning and reflection, Lucia decided to return to the Cova on July 13. Jacinta and Francesco accompanied her, and the little trio of visionaries arrived at the Cova that afternoon. Some four or five thousand onlookers assembled there as well.

When the apparition appeared at the oak tree, it once again addressed its messages to Lucia. She urged the girl to pray every day so that the war would come to an end. Lucia, in turn, asked the apparition to perform a miracle so that the onlookers would all be converted. The apparition readily complied, setting the date for October 13 and once again promising to reveal her identity at that time. She then imparted several more secrets to Lucia, who requested the apparition to cure some infirm residents of the town. But the apparition agreed to help them only if they prayed. Then she departed. Although the vision again remained invisible to the crowd, several signs of its presence were apparent. Once again the sun seemed to lose its brilliance; many of the spectators saw a white orb of light form over the tree where the apparition stood, and heard a whispering voice emanating from it.

This vision had now appeared three times, and Fatima was quickly becoming the center of a religious and political storm. The anticlerical government in Lisbon was beginning to worry about the political repercussions should the Fatima affair result in a

---

*In researching his authoritative book *Our Lady of Fatima* (1947), William Thomas Walsh was also able to confirm that many of the spectators had witnessed these eerie events. Walsh's book contains interviews with some of the Fatima residents who witnessed the visitations as well as an interview with Lucia dos Santos herself.

renewed wave of religious sentiment throughout the country.* So by August, Portugal's political leaders felt compelled to act. The job of investigating and discrediting the Fatima affair was entrusted to Arthur d'Oliveira Santos, the subprefect of Ourem, under whose political jurisdiction Fatima fell. On August 11 Santos journeyed to Fatima and personally interviewed Lucia, Jacinta, and Francesco. He hoped to obtain a confession from them, but despite his threats, the children refused to admit that they had lied or that they had been put up to a hoax by their village priest. Santos became enraged when Lucia resolutely refused to tell him the secrets that the Virgin Mary had imparted to her. So two days later, on the day the apparition was due to appear for the fourth time, he had the children abducted and taken to Ourem.

There the children were questioned even more brutally than they had been in Fatima. In the intimidating setting of a government administration building, Santos interrogated each of the children separately, hoping to force them to retract their claims. He went so far as to threaten them with death if they failed to cooperate. He even led each child to believe that his playmates had already been put to death for refusing to confess and for conspiring against the state. But still none of the children would admit that they had lied. Frustrated and embarrassed, Santos finally returned them to Fatima.

In spite of the children's abduction, thousands of pilgrims and local townsfolk gathered at the Cova da Iria on August 13, hoping that the apparition would somehow make her presence known. Indeed, the crowd heard a loud detonation and a flash of lightning illuminated the sky at the very time the woman should have appeared. The sun dimmed, and a kaleidoscope of colors bathed the Cova. A white cloud appeared by the oak tree, remained for an instant, and then rose and moved quickly away.

Although the children were devastated when they realized that they had missed the apparition, they had a surprise visit from her on August 19 while tending their sheep outside the village of Valinhos. She told the children that the October miracle would be

---

*The government's fears were actually unsupported. The religious authorities in and about Fatima had to this point adopted a "hands off" policy toward the matter. Ecclesiastical officials in Lisbon had explicitly forbidden any priests to take part in the Fatima gatherings once the appearances there became generally known.

less magnificent now, and urged them not to miss any future meetings. She again begged them to pray for sinners and to make sacrifices for them.

The abduction of the children had accomplished very little, and actually backfired on the government. Once the story became known, even more people became interested in the commotion at Fatima. When September 13 finally arrived, an estimated thirty thousand pilgrims were in attendance at the Cova da Iria. They waited there patiently, anticipating that the children would reveal to them the apparition's latest messages.

When the children arrived, the crowd began to calm. The sun began to dim mysteriously around noon, stars could be seen in the sky, and an orb of white light appeared and settled on the tree. One of the witnesses that day was Monsignor John Quareman, the vice-general of Leiria, who attended the gathering incognito with a fellow priest. He was one of many observers who actually saw the mysterious orb of light that had often appeared when Lucia claimed the apparition was arriving at the oak tree. "To my surprise," he later testified, "I saw clearly and distinctly a globe of light advancing from east to west, gliding slowly and majestically through the air." He later noted, "My friend looked also, and he had the good fortune to see the same unexpected vision. Suddenly the globe with the wonderful light dropped from sight."

The orb apparently disappeared as it came to rest on the oak tree before which the three children were praying. Then another miracle occurred. The Cova was inundated with a rain of white flower petals. The petals were clearly seen by the crowd, though they disintegrated before reaching the ground. This "rain of flowers" was even photographed by a government official, Antonio Robelo Martins, who published the pictures in a small book, *Fatima, Espérance du Mond,* shortly after the war. (This miraculous rain was repeated at the Cova on May 13, 1924, on the anniversary of the first manifestation of the figure.) The apparition's September message to Lucia was similar to those she had delivered on her previous visits: More prayer was needed before the war would come to an end. She once again promised a miracle for October 13.

The anticipated miracle was generating political, religious, and social controversy throughout Portugal. Lucia had first made a public announcement about the miracle two months earlier, after eliciting the promise from the apparition. There was never any doubt in the minds of the children that the miracle would actually take place, and they were apparently quite unaware of the immense stir the announcement had caused in Fatima. The political regime in Ourem and Lisbon (and especially the disgraced Santos) was delighted with the news. The government officials were convinced that no miracle would take place. The failure of the miracle to occur, they hoped, would permanently expose the children and put an end to the Fatima affair once and for all. They also planned to use the affair as an excuse to spread another rash of anticlerical propaganda throughout the country. Meanwhile, as the date approached, the parents of the three children grew more and more anxious. If the miracle failed to come off, they feared, the crowd present at the Cova to witness the event might turn vicious and harm the children.

October 13 finally arrived. It was raining, and the many pilgrims who had come from all over Portugal and beyond were drenched by the time they arrived. As one newspaper poignantly reported:

Nearly all, men and women, have bare feet, the women carrying their footwear in bags on their heads, the men leaning on great staves and carefully grasping umbrellas also. One would say that they were all oblivious to what was going on about them, with a great lack of interest in their journey and in other travelers, as if lost in a dream, reciting their Rosary in a sad rhythmic chant. A woman says the first part [of] the Hail Mary; her companions in chorus say the second part of the prayer. With sure and rhythmical steps they tread the dusty road which runs between the pine woods and the olive groves, so that they may arrive before night at the place of the apparition, where, under the severe and cold light of the stars, they hope they can sleep, keeping the first places near the blessed azinheira so that today they can see better.

Several religious officials from Lisbon and Ourem attended the gathering, and government officials swarmed there to see what might happen. They had brought along military troops in case the crowd turned into a violent mob. Representatives from all the major newspapers, including the viciously anticlerical *O Seculo,* were present, ready to expose the whole Fatima affair.

It was about noon when the children arrived at the Cova. By now about seventy thousand people had assembled, and it was still pouring rain. Once again kneeling before the little oak tree, Lucia, Jacinta, and Francesco began to pray. Lucia ordered the spectators to lower their umbrellas. The crowd obeyed instantly and joined in prayer. Soon afterward the children announced that the apparition was coming, and the rain began to turn to a meager drizzle.

During the next several moments, the apparition spoke directly only to Lucia, as usual. As she had promised on May 13, she now revealed her identity and purpose, calling herself Our Lady of the Rosary and requesting that a chapel be built in her honor at the Cova. She then predicted that the war was about to end. Having completed her message, she showed the children a series of visions. She then spread her arms, and beams of light shone from them. Lucia, dazzled by the sight, cried out for everyone to look at the sun. The great miracle was about to begin.

Since a cloud bank had hidden it the entire day, the sun had not yet appeared in the sky. Yet as the crowd followed Lucia's eyes to the heavens, the clouds parted and a huge silver disc— which everyone took to be the sun—was seen floating in the sky.* Although glistening with light, it did not blind those who looked at it. The disc began to gyrate by turning on itself, throwing off colored flames in all directions simultaneously. The Cova was bathed in a fantasy of colored shadows. The disc stopped and repeated its gyrations twice; the entire aerial ballet lasted about twelve minutes. Then it began to plunge toward the earth in a zigzag motion. The heat caused by its descent was so intense that the crowd began to panic. It seemed as if the world were coming to an end. But before crashing to earth, the disc suddenly stopped and returned to the sky by retracing its path. The storm had now dis-

---

*Most writers on Fatima claim that the disc *was* the sun. But judging by the descriptions we have of the miracle, the disc was at the wrong elevation and azimuth to have actually been the sun. The object seems to have been an immense UFO-like silver disc.

sipated, and the spectators discovered that the ground and their clothing were completely dry.

It cannot be emphasized too strongly that this great miracle, called "the dance of the sun" by Fatima scholars, was *not* a vision. It was seen by all seventy thousand spectators. Even *O Seculo,* which had long maintained an anticlerical editorial policy, reported on the miracle in its October 15 issue. Most other newspapers in Portugal reported the event as well.

The miracle made a great impact on the crowd. While researching his book on Fatima, Walsh spoke with several witnesses who had journeyed to the Cova that day. Their testimonies agree uniformly about the sequence of events.* A brief dispassionate description of the miracle was provided by Dr. Almeida Garrete, a professor at the University of Coimbra in Portugal, who had witnessed the events as a young man:

I was at a distance of little more than a hundred yards away. The rain was pouring down on our heads and, streaming down our clothes, soaked them completely. At last it came along to 2 o'clock P.M. (official time—really corresponding to noon, solar time). Some instants previously, the radiant sun had pierced the thick curtain of clouds which held it veiled. All eyes were raised towards it as if drawn by a magnet. I myself tried to look straight at it, and saw it looking like a well-defined disc, bright but not blinding. I heard people around me comparing it to a dull silver plate. The comparison did not seem to me exact. Its appearance was of a sharp and changing clarity, like the "orient" of a pearl. It did not resemble in any way the moon on a fine night. It had neither its colour nor its shadows. You might compare it rather to a polished wheel cut in the silvery valves of a shell. This is not poetry, I saw it thus with my own eyes.

Neither would you confuse it with the sun seen through a fog. Of fog there was no trace, and besides, the solar disc was neither blurred nor veiled in any way, but shone clearly at its centre and at its circumference.

This chequered shining disc seemed to possess a giddy motion. It

---

* A more recent attempt to track down living witnesses to the Fatima miracle was made by John Haffent, a Catholic writer, in the late 1950s. Their testimonies and interviews were published in 1961.

See John Haffent, *Meet the Witnesses* (Washington, New Jersey: Ave Maria Institute, 1961).

was not the twinkling of a star. It turned on itself with an astonishing rapidity.

Suddenly a great cry, like a cry of anguish, arose from all this vast throng. The sun while keeping its swiftness of rotation, detached itself from the firmament and, blood-red in colour, rushed towards the earth, threatening to crush us under the immense weight of its mass of fire. There were moments of dreadful tension.

All these phenomena, which I have described, I have witnessed personally, coldly and calmly, without the slightest agitation of mind.

The miracle was also seen by many residents in outlying districts. Father Ignatius Lawrence Pereira testified in 1931 that he had seen the miracle as a boy while attending school some nine miles from Fatima.[8] He was nine years old at the time, and his schoolhouse was perched on a hill overlooking the town. It was two in the afternoon when he and his schoolmates heard cries and shouts outside:

Our teacher rushed out, and the children all ran after her. In the public square people wept and shouted, pointing to the sun, without paying the slightest heed to the questions of our teacher . . . it was the great solar prodigy with all its wonderful phenomena which was seen distinctly even from the hill on which my village was situated. This miracle I feel incapable of describing such as I saw it at that moment. I looked fixedly at the sun, which appeared pale and did not dazzle. It looked like a ball of snow turning on itself. . . . Then suddenly it seemed to become detached from the sky, and rolled right and left, as if it were falling upon the earth. Terrified, absolutely terrified, I ran towards the crowd of people. All were weeping, expecting at any moment the end of the world.

All around him people were praying and falling to their knees. Pereira continues:

During the long minutes of the solar phenomena, the objects around us reflected all the colours of the rainbow. Looking at each other, one appeared blue, another yellow, a third red, etc., and all these strange phenomena only increased the terror of the people. After about ten minutes the sun climbed back into its place, as it had descended, still quite pale and without brilliance.

When the people were convinced that the danger had passed, there was an outburst of joy.

Because of the large number of witnesses, the great miracle of October 13 cannot be explained as a mass hallucination or as the product of hysteria. It was a genuinely paranormal occurrence.

One of the most fascinating aspects of the Fatima case is the "secrets" that were purportedly revealed there. Their content and meaning became known only many years later, long after Lucia dos Santos entered a convent in the city of Porto in 1921. (She was later moved to a convent in Coimbra, where she has lived since 1948.) Acceding to a request from her bishop in 1941, Lucia wrote out a description of her conversations with the Virgin Mary. It was at this time that she publicly revealed several of the secrets that had been imparted to her and admitted for the first time that she and her friends had been prepared for the Virgin's visit by the angel that had appeared to them on three occasions in 1916. The first secret given to Lucia (during the BVM's June appearance) was that Jacinta and Francesco would soon die and join her in heaven. This prediction came to pass. Both children died of influenza, Francesco in 1919 and Jacinta in 1920. The Virgin's primary secrets were delivered to Lucia on July 13. They were delivered in three parts, of which only the first two have been revealed. The first was a vision of hell, which thoroughly terrified Lucia.

The second part of the message was that another world war might scourge the earth if man did not stop offending God. The Blessed Mother revealed that this war would be heralded by a mysterious light in the sky. (This prediction also came to pass. On January 25, 1938, shortly before the onset of World War II, the aurora borealis put on a spectacular and unprecedented display. The northern lights were seen all over Europe, and newspapers throughout the world reported this rare natural phenomenon.) Concomitant with the BVM's warning was a plea for the world to pray for Russia, or that country would spread her errors throughout the world. (It is interesting to note that the date of the Virgin's first appearance in Fatima coincided with a bloody raid on a Moscow church which had been organized by Lenin. The event spearheaded the Russian Revolution.)

The last part of the Fatima secret has never been publicly revealed. Though disclosed to Pope Pius XII, he never released its contents. Lucia noted in her 1941 account that the message could be made public in 1960, but Church officials in Rome decided against it.*

While the BVM's Fatima appearances of 1917 may represent the greatest of all Marian manifestations, several significant visitations have occurred since that time. The Virgin appeared to a group of children in Beauraing, Belgium, in 1932, though there is some evidence that in this instance the witnesses might have been lying about their experiences.† A more interesting case occurred a year later in Banneux, a town of about three hundred inhabitants in Belgium south of Liège.⁹ What makes the Banneux visitations so unusual is that the primary witness, eleven-year-old Mariette Beco, was not particularly religious. She and her family lived in a small house outside of town. Mariette had not gone to church or engaged in any religious activities for two months prior to the BVM's first appearance to her on Sunday, January 15. It was a cold winter day, and Mariette was playing at home. She had just gone to a kitchen window and was looking out into the family's garden when she saw a luminous figure. It was draped in a white gown and wore a crucifix. The girl was so startled by the apparition that she called her mother to the window. Mme Beco couldn't actually see the figure, but she perceived a white luminous form walking in the garden. Mariette wanted to go into the garden to have a better look, but her mother, afraid that the phantom was something evil, forbade her to leave the house.

Mariette encountered the apparition again on January 18. She had come home from school and was working at her household chores when she had a sudden urge to go out to the garden and pray. Suddenly she saw the apparition rushing toward her from the sky. She became entranced as the figure spoke to her. By this time her father had gone outside in search of the girl, and finding her almost dazed, rushed off to fetch the village priest. The apparition then began to move, and Mariette followed it through

---

*There has been much speculation about the nature of the last Fatima prophecy, known today to only a few Vatican officials. In his booklet *Fatima Secret* (Rockford, Illinois: Tan Books, 1967) Emmett Culligan cites circumstantial evidence that the last prophecy concerns a third—and final—world war.

†See the chapter "Authentic Miracles and Doubtful Miracles—The Beauraing 'Epidemic' " in Jean Hallé, *Miracles* (New York: David McKay, 1952).

the garden to a nearby stream. The Virgin told Mariette that the stream was "reserved for me" and then floated away into the sky. Mariette encountered the apparition again on January 19, January 20 (during which she asked that a chapel be built in her honor), February 11, February 15 (during which she imparted a "secret" to her), February 20, and March 2 (when she revealed her identity as the "Mother of the Saviour, Mother of God").

As we have seen, there are really only two basic theories that can account for Marian visitations. The first is that these apparitions are psychic projections, something akin to thought forms, which are produced by the minds of the spectators or by the Catholic community at large in the countries in which they appear. The alternative is that they represent actual visitations by a spiritual being or presence deliberately sent here to instruct us. The first of these seems to be the more cogent. It was suggested earlier that Marian apparitions might be the result of a projected archetype that occasionally emerges from a universal collective unconscious in times of spiritual crisis. The apparitions at Pontmain in 1871 and Knock in 1879 can certainly be explained by this theory, since these particular images showed no awareness, self-identity, or intelligence. They seem therefore to have been visions that, perhaps psychically charged by their onlookers, took on a semblance of temporary reality.

This general theory about the nature of the Marian apparitions is supported by two additional lines of evidence. First, the classic Marian apparitions of history *have all occurred in traditionally Roman Catholic countries.* Sharkey's historical study, *The Woman Shall Conquer,* shows that Marian apparitions have occurred primarily in France, Italy, and Portugal. None of the classic Marian apparition cases have been reported from such Protestant strongholds as Germany, the United States, or Scandinavia.

Second, apparitions of the Virgin Mary *often tend to appear at times when Mary's role in the Church is being reevaluated, or when the Roman Catholic society in a particular country or village is preoccupied with her cult.* The apparitions of Knock occurred on the eve of a festival in honor of the Assumption, and the miracle at La Salette also coincided with a traditional Marian festival. Fatima represents an even more striking case. The Virgin Mary continually exhorted Lucia, Francesco, and Jacinta to recite the

Rosary, the importance of which was one of her primary concerns. On May 5, 1917—only a week before the apparition revealed itself for the first time—Pope Benedict XV had issued a statement to the effect that only the Blessed Virgin could intercede to end the First World War, and he urged the world to pray to her. This "echoing" of a statement issued in Rome also occurred in 1858, when Mary appeared to Bernadette Soubirous near the town of Lourdes and referred to herself as "the Immaculate Conception" for the very first time. The doctrine of the Immaculate Conception, which holds that Mary was born without the stain of original sin, had been made a dogma of the Church only four years earlier, in December 1854.

In light of these data, it is almost possible to *predict* when a Marian apparition is likely to occur. These miracles generally transpire in times of fierce world problems and/or social turmoil, especially when the role of Mary is being reevaluated by the Church or is at the forefront of popular interest. These conditions lead the citizens of a traditionally Roman Catholic country to *create*—at some psychic level—the figure of their adoration. The *people* of Knock created the Virgin's appearance there in 1879, just as the *people* of La Salette produced her previous manifestations in 1846.

But can this theory account for the perplexing Marian manifestations at Fatima? How could a mental projection predict the future so accurately and produce physical miracles?

A tentative explanation for the miracle of Fatima is that there may actually have existed two distinctive forces—one that gave rise to the apparition and another that produced the miracles that took place before thousands of onlookers. The figure of the Virgin Mary may indeed have been an archetype projected either by the children themselves or by the entire Portuguese people in response to overwhelming national chaos. Influenced perhaps by the Pope's recent declaration concerning Mary, their collective thoughts virtually created the figure of the Virgin. This creation then may have taken on a temporary life of its own. Why it appeared in Fatima—and why only Lucia, Jacinta, and Francesco could see it—remains a mystery. Perhaps these children had just the unique psychic constitutions needed to see the apparition.

The buzzing sounds and other supernatural signs witnessed

by the worshipers who so devoutly gathered at the Cova da Iria between June 13 and October 13, 1917, could likewise have been produced by the crowds themselves. Their belief in the Virgin's appearance at the Cova may have been so great that they literally brought about these phenomena as a setting for the visions of the children. *Or the figure may have drawn some sort of psychic energy from the throngs in order to produce the effects.*

This argument can be extended to the great miracle that terminated the series of appearances. The crowds may have psychically produced this effect themselves, or the apparition may have tapped the crowd's psychic energy to manufacture it. Despite the awesomeness of the Fatima miracle, *it is not unique.* It is a fact that mysterious orbs of lights play a conspicuous role in the history of the miraculous. There are several recorded cases of high-pitched religious gatherings culminating in the sudden and mysterious appearance of lights in the sky. In 1905 north Wales was the scene of a revival movement, and outdoor meetings were held daily as a rash of religious mania ran through the country.[10] The spectators at these gatherings often noted that orbs of light would suddenly appear in the sky and zigzag about. When the movement petered out toward the end of that year, the mysterious UFOs vanished as well.

A more specific Fatimalike miracle recently occurred in the Dominican Republic. On March 29, 1972, a public Mass attended by more than a thousand people was held in the courtyard of Arroyo Hondo College. During the ceremony a dark cloud appeared and opened in the sky, revealing a glowing disc that illuminated the entire courtyard. The cloud then folded up and the object vanished.[11]

In light of these similar cases, it seems that Fatima's "dance of the sun" was merely a very heightened version of a form of miracle that sometimes occurs when large groups of people gather for religious purposes. The participants are actually responsible for the creation of these glowing discs. One might call these lights a form of "psychic fallout" produced by the psychically energized emotions of the crowds.

Fatima and Banneux are not the last of the uncanny manifestations of the Blessed Virgin on earth. Another series of visitations occurred in Garabandal, Spain, beginning in 1961. Here again the

Virgin appeared to a group of children, and her visitations culminated in a miracle witnessed by dozens of spectators. The other great recent Marian apparition was seen hovering near a Coptic Church in a Cairo suburb by thousands of witnesses night after night. These two sets of visitations are so complex, and so filled with hints about the nature of Marian apparitions, that they deserve a chapter to themselves.

~~ X ~~

MIRACLES AT
GARABANDAL, SPAIN;
AND ZEITOUN, EGYPT

SAN Sebastian de Garabandal is a small village wedged among the mountains of northeastern Spain. It doesn't appear on most maps of the area, and fewer than a hundred families make their homes there. Most of the residents live in buildings roughly constructed of rock and tile. It is a primitive place where such facilities as indoor plumbing and heating are rare. The only access to the town is via a narrow dirt road.

Until 1961 hardly anyone outside of Spain had ever heard of Garabandal. But that year the world's Catholic community began to focus its attention on the village when news spread across Europe that four young visionaries were seeing repeated apparitions of the Virgin Mary.

The story, one of the most complex Marian visitations ever recorded, began on Sunday, June 18, 1961. Mass had been said that morning by a visiting priest from the neighboring town of Cosio, since Garabandal had no cleric of its own. After church services, the townspeople customarily gather in the village square, where the adults usually spend the day socializing while their children play and dance. That day was bound to be different. Having become bored with the recreational opportunities afforded by the village square, eleven-year-old Conchita Gonzales (the daughter of one of the poorer families in town) decided to steal away to engage in some mischief. She quickly enlisted her playmate, twelve-year-old Mary Cruz Gonzales, to aid in her plot. The plan was to sneak away from the square, visit the vegetable patch adjoining the home of the village schoolmaster, and steal fruit from his apple tree. Mary Cruz readily agreed to join her.

The young mischief makers didn't vanish unobserved, however. Two other village girls, Mary Loly Mazon and Jacinta Gonzales (both twelve years old) saw them leave and decided to follow. They, too, were bored and were hoping to find some adventure outside of town. When they arrived at the schoolmaster's house, the other girls were already stuffing apples in their pockets. Mary Loly and Jacinta surprised them in the act and threatened to turn them in to the schoolmaster, but soon they realized that joining in the fun would be more enjoyable than putting an end to it. All four were soon stalking away from the garden loaded with their booty. It was now eight thirty in the evening.

As the children made their way down a rubble road back to town, they heard a roll of thunder. They weren't too concerned about an impending storm, so they sat down in the road and began eating the stolen fruit while playing a game of marbles. Their game was interrupted when Conchita noticed that a figure had appeared at the side of the road. The apparition seemed to be an angel. It wore a blue robe, had pink wings, and was about eight years old. He was, according to Conchita, "surrounded by a great light that did not dazzle my eyes." Since they were facing away from the apparition, the other three children saw nothing at first; only when they noticed that Conchita seemed entranced did they realize that something strange was occurring. When they turned around to see what she was staring at, they, too, saw the angelic visitation. The figure said nothing, and as the children looked on in amazement, it disappeared. The girls were so shocked that they immediately ran back to town, where they told the schoolmistress what they had seen. By later that evening, news of the children's adventure had spread. Although the visiting priest from Cosio interviewed the children the next day, he could come to no conclusion about the incident. He merely advised the girls to ask the apparition about its mission should they see it again.

The next day the four children returned to the roadside where the apparition had materialized. There they held vigil, hoping that the figure would return. A small group of villagers accompanied them, mostly to mock and harass them. But when nothing happened, everyone went home a little disappointed. That night, however, Conchita had a startling experience while preparing for bed. As she prayed, she suddenly heard a voice say, "Do not worry.

You will see me again." She would later learn that at exactly nine forty-five Mary Cruz, Mary Loly, and Jacinta—all at their respective homes and all preparing for bed—had heard the same voice and message.

On June 20 the children once again went to the site of the angel's appearance. They prayed, said the Rosary, and waited. When again nothing happened, they turned to go home, but found that an intense screen of light suddenly blocked the path. The girls screamed in terror, and the light dimmed.

The children reluctantly decided to return to the roadside the next day, but on this occasion they asked a neighbor to join them. Though Señora Clementine Gonzales was skeptical of the girls' claim, she agreed to accompany them. They were joined by several other villagers, who were becoming increasingly interested in the children's experience. No sooner had the troop arrived at the roadside than the angel appeared once more. Only the four girls could see the apparition, and the villagers were startled to see the children enter into a deep trance as they stared at the side of the road. The children remained in this state for several minutes, and when they revived, they dolefully reported that the angel had refused to respond to any of their questions.

Father Valentin Marichalan, the priest from Cosio, accompanied the children to the roadside himself on June 22. Having become more and more disturbed by the stories coming out of Garabandal, he felt a responsibility to look into the matter personally. The Garabandal visitations had become widely known throughout the district, and small crowds were beginning to form at the roadside daily. The four children arrived at the spot at eight fifteen that evening and promptly went into trance. As the priest looked on, the townsfolk tested the girls during their absorption. "The most painful pinpricks, the roughest shaking, even burns and so on [were] quite incapable of arousing them from their rapture,"[1] one witness subsequently reported. Some of the villagers tried shining bright lights into the children's eyes, but the visionaries didn't even blink.

The visions and ecstasies were reenacted at the roadside almost daily from June 23 until July 1, even though the angel failed to appear on June 26, 29, and 30. By now larger crowds were forming at the site. On July 1, the angel told the children that the Blessed Virgin Mary would appear to them the very next day.

July 2 marked the beginning of the second phase of the Gar-abandal miracle. The whole town had been alerted to the immi-nent arrival of the Virgin Mary by Conchita, who had announced her coming on the previous day. A Rosary was said in the town church at three, and then almost the entire village paraded to the road where the angel had originally appeared and where a stone enclosure had been constructed to protect the children from the crowds.

The children were still walking up the road to the likely site of the visitation when they suddenly fell into trance. The BVM appeared to them, accompanied by two angels. The apparition showed the children a chalice, into which either blood or tears were falling. She proceeded to tell them that the "cup" was "already filling" (meaning that the world was filling with too much sin) and then instructed them in the proper recitation of the Rosary. After a brief conversation with the children, the BVM van-ished, and the girls awakened from their trances. The villagers sur-rounded them eagerly, hoping to learn of the Virgin's message.

From this point onward, the trances and visions of the chil-dren become too numerous to summarize individually. So instead of following a concise chronology of the Garabandal visitations, it would be more instructive to investigate only a few of the appari-tions with special emphasis on the miracles that accompanied them. These events will help us to analyze the *nature* of the Gar-abandal visitations.

The Virgin's first appearances seemed to sensitize the children to her, and after July 2, the history of the Garabandal visitations takes on many added complexities. Many of these are unprece-dented in the annals of Marian manifestations. July 2 marked the last time the children voluntarily journeyed to the site of the appar-itions to hold vigil. Now, no matter where they were or what they were doing, they would suddenly receive a "mental command" when the BVM wished to speak with them. Even if they were in different places, each of the children would receive the "sum-mons" at the very same time. They would then independently go to the roadside, usually arriving there almost simultaneously, and subsequently fall into trance.

When the villagers learned of this strange new phenomenon,

they tested it over the next several weeks by separating the children from one another and keeping each one under strict observation. They took careful note of when each child reported hearing the "summons." These times tallied to a remarkable degree. On at least one occasion Conchita was taken by Church officials to the neighboring town of Santander. There she spontaneously entered a trance at the very same time Mary Cruz, Jacinta, and Mary Loly went into ecstasy in Garabandal.

It was also during these weeks that the site of the appearances changed. Instead of at the roadside, they began taking place in a small pine grove at the top of a small hill next to the village church. The ecstasies also became more violent. Sometimes the girls would fall to the ground and would become so heavy that they could not be lifted by the villagers. Conchita especially would sometimes rise from this prone position by her shoulders as though she were beginning to levitate. Rosaries and religious medals the girls had been given during the trances occasionally smelled of roses when handed back to their owners.*

During these bizarre ecstasies the girls often spoke at great length with the Virgin Mary, whose message at Garabandal was similar to those she had given in her many appearances elsewhere. She despaired of the spread of sin in the world, urged the world to repent, and promised to eventually perform a great miracle at Garabandal. (To date, this miracle has not occurred, although believers in the Garabandal visitation—including Conchita herself—are still firmly convinced that it will come to pass.) She also criticized the clergy for not following the strictures of the Church more closely.

These ecstasies continued through July with little change. But on August 4 a new development shocked the town and added a new—and possibly supernatural—dimension to the case.

A detailed report on the August 4 "miracle" is given by F. Sanchez-Ventura y Pascual, a Spanish attorney and economics

---

*In their book on the Garabandal visitations, *Star on the Mountain* (Newtonville, New York: Our Lady of Mount Carmel of Garabandal; 1968), M. Laffineur and M. T. Le Pelletier report on a trip made to the village by several American tourists in September 1965. The visitors found the entire area of the pine grove saturated with the odor of roses, though none were growing there. Pieces of bark and roots taken from the trees retained this odd perfume even after being transported back to the United States.

professor, in his history of the Garabandal visitations.[2] That day, Mary Loly and Jacinta had gone to the pine grove to confer with the Virgin. Their trances continued to follow the pattern of the earlier ones. A crowd of villagers looked on during the girls' ecstasies and handed them religious medals and other tokens, hoping that the BVM would bless them. One of the bystanders had brought a tape recorder to record the mumblings the children often made as they spoke with the Virgin. The spectator showed the girls the tape machine after they had come out of trance, and was explaining its use, when Mary Loly suddenly slipped back into trance. She was holding the recording microphone at the time. The villagers and visitors could hear the girl asking the Virgin to speak into the microphone. Then, just as suddenly, she awoke from her brief ecstasy. The observers eagerly waited for the tape to be rewound. At the point where Mary Loly had asked the Virgin to speak, the crowd could *clearly* hear a sweet female voice say, "I shall not speak." The assembly became tremendously excited when the discovery was made, and the recording had to be replayed several times. The mysterious voice was heard twice more, but then vanished from the tape.

After August 4, the girls would sometimes become spontaneously entranced either at home or while walking in the village streets. These "ecstatic walks," as they were called, often lasted several minutes and were filmed on a number of occasions. They were very bizarre to behold. Although the girls would often merely walk forward, at other times they would literally *run backward at incredible speeds without tripping or falling.* All the while their eyes would remain glued to the sky, as though following a beckoning figure. The walks would often begin in town and end in the pine grove, where the children would commune with the BVM. At other times they would trance-walk from the grove back into the village.

The girls also apparently became brilliantly psychic when entranced, and many witnesses have testified that the children seemed able to read minds. One such incident, which took place on August 31, is documented by Sanchez-Ventura y Pascual. The children were in ecstasy at the pine grove. After the trance ended, Jacinta announced to the crowd that the BVM had told her that a priest was present among them, but that he was wearing his cas-

sock tucked up beneath a trench coat in an effort to hide his sta-
tion. The amazed priest stepped forward after Jacinta made her
announcement, and opened his coat to reveal his clerical garb.
The priest then gave the girl a crucifix to kiss, and Jacinta immediately told him that the cross came from Rome and had been a
gift from the Pope. The priest admitted that this was true.

Many reports tell how the children could carry out specific
acts if a priest silently willed them to. Sanchez-Ventura y Pascual
has recorded an incident in which a priest from Asturias arrived
incognito at one of the girls' homes on October 16:

> He watched one of the children approach him. She offered him a
> crucifix to kiss several times. "If this is genuine," he thought to himself,
> "let the child come to." In an instant the visionary emerged from her
> ecstasy, smiled at the priest and turned to go home. Hardly had she
> taken a few steps, when she again went into a trance. The priest then
> said to himself: "If you've just made the Sign of the Cross over me with
> your crucifix because I am a priest, I want you to prove it to me again,
> giving me the crucifix to kiss and crossing me several times." This was a
> thing that the visionary had not yet done to anyone.
>
> No sooner had this request formed in his mind than the child turned
> round, came to him, "smiled and besides proffering me the crucifix to
> kiss, made the Sign of the Cross over me three times in succession."

What is probably the most mysterious aspect of the Garabandal story concerns a visit made to the town on August 8, 1961, by
Father Luis Andréu, a young priest who was apparently skeptical
about the stories he had heard. When the priest from Cosio
couldn't make his regular trip to Garabandal that day, he asked
Father Luis to conduct the scheduled religious services. On arriving in town, Father Luis went immediately to the village church,
where he said Mass and met Conchita, Jacinta, and Mary Loly,
who received communion from him. He gave Mary Loly a small
crucifix, and she, in turn, told him that there would be a visitation
from the Virgin at two that afternoon.

As it happened, though, the children went into ecstasy at ten
after twelve while still in the town church, which was filled with
villagers who had come to hear Mass. Conchita was heard to petition the BVM repeatedly to perform a public miracle, while the
others asked why so long a time had passed since they had seen
the little angel who had heralded the visitations. After waking from

trance, the girls announced to Father Luis and the villagers that the Virgin would appear to them again that evening.

A large assembly of Garabandal residents were waiting in the church when the girls arrived at nine thirty-five. The children soon fell into a trance, left the church, and scaled the hill next to it. Father Luis and the townsfolk followed. There at the pine grove the children communed once more with the Virgin Mary. Father Luis observed them unemotionally, but then, according to bystanders, appeared to fall into a momentary trance himself. He stood quiet for a moment and mumbled "a miracle, a miracle . . ." four times before coming back to himself. No one asked him what had happened, for by this time the girls were dashing down the hill back to the church. In the course of this ecstatic run, Mary Loly lost Father Luis's crucifix. He was never to see it again.

At the end of the day, Father Luis drove back to his home in Aguilar del Campo with several friends who had accompanied him to Garabandal. During the last leg of the exhausting trip he sat in the backseat of the car. He was very excited and kept repeating that the day had been the "most happy" of his life. This puzzled the other passengers, since the happiest day in the life of a priest is generally his day of ordination. Father Luis would not elaborate on the reason for his elation, but decided to take a nap. According to the driver of the car, he lowered his head and coughed a bit, then lapsed into unconsciousness. A few minutes later he was dead. No cause was ever discovered for his sudden passing away.

On August 16, while the children and a group of villagers were at the pine grove, the Virgin appeared as usual . . . but now she was accompanied by the spirit of Father Luis! He told the children about his death and funeral and gave them several particulars about his surviving relatives. He appeared with the BVM on several other occasions, some of which were witnessed by Father Ramon Andréu, the brother of the deceased priest. Father Ramon was able to overhear Conchita's conversations with Father Luis and to talk with the girl after her trances had ended. He was constantly astounded by the confidential information Conchita revealed to him:

. . . I was truly stupefied: the little girls repeated in my presence the words of their vision and I heard them relate the death of my brother and the description of the funeral. They gave a certain number of very precise details concerning the special rites of the burial of a priest. They even knew that Father Luis's burial had involved a few exceptions regarding the traditional rules for the dressing of the deceased: for example, they had not placed a biretta on my brother's head and the chalice which he should have held in his hands had been replaced by a crucifix. The girls also gave the reasons for these variations.

On another occasion, I heard the children say in ecstasy that my brother Luis died without having made his profession [of religious vows]. They also talked about me and my vows: they knew the precise date, the exact place where they had been pronounced and the name of the Jesuit who had taken them at the same time I did. You will understand my astonishment, my stupefaction in the face of this unchallengeable array of rigorously exact details, when I knew pertinently that the children could not have learned about them, at least through purely human means. . . . There is no doubt that all this is truly astonishing, and I would even say, bewildering, incomprehensible. . . .[3]

The ecstasies and experiences of Conchita, Mary Cruz, Mary Loly, and Jacinta lasted into 1965, though they were most frequent in 1961 and 1962 when they occurred almost daily. Conchita's detailed diaries of the Virgin's appearances during the first two years of the visitations have been published by Father Joseph Pelletier, an expert on Marian studies, in his *Our Lady Comes to Garabandal* (1971). This book offers a precise chronology of the case during the period from October 1961 to July 1962, when the affair came to a dramatic climax with a minor miracle that has become legend among followers of Marian manifestations. It is considered the definitive "proof" of the Garabandal case by those who have studied it and support its authenticity.

Throughout the previous June, Conchita had been announcing that the Virgin had promised a miracle for July 18. She claimed that a host would miraculously appear on her tongue during one of her ecstasies on that day.* This message apparently had been given to Conchita both during her ecstasies and by a mysterious voice she often heard within her mind. She never doubted

---

*This miracle, called the "divine communion," has occurred several times in the course of Catholic history. Thurston devotes a chapter to the subject in *The Physical Phenomena of Mysticism,* citing examples from the fifteenth century to the present.

the truth of the message and during June and July made certain that news of the impending miracle was made known throughout Garabandal and the surrounding district.

On July 18 villagers and tourists loitered about the streets surrounding the Gonzales house, waiting for the miracle to transpire. Since no time had been specified, no one knew exactly when to expect the prodigy. The day passed, uneventfully, and it began to appear that the miracle wouldn't take place after all. Meanwhile, a strange drama was occurring inside the home. At ten that night Conchita received a summons from the Virgin Mary. It was repeated a second time at midnight. The miracle was beginning. At about one twenty-five it finally took place just as Conchita had predicted, though perhaps a little tardy.

Alejandro Damians, a photographer from Barcelona, was able to film part of the event. He had been allowed inside the house earlier that day and followed the progress of the miracle from its inception. As he has written in his detailed account: [4]

Conchita was upstairs, in company with a cousin and an uncle, I think, when she was seized into an ecstasy. The first I knew was when I saw her descend the stairs very fast, wearing that classic expression which softens and embellishes [her] features.

As she crossed the threshold, the crowd waiting before the house opened in just sufficient time to let her pass, and then the multitude was milling around her, like a river that has burst its banks and sweeps away everything in its path. I saw people falling to the ground and trampled by others. As far as I know, nobody was hurt. But the sight of that fantastic mob on the run, shoving and elbowing one another, could not be more terrifying.

I attempted to follow Conchita, but a crowd, fifteen or twenty deep separated us. I sometimes caught a vague glimpse of her. She turned left along the lane formed by the side of her house and a low wall. She turned left again, and there, right in the middle of the alley, which is fairly wide at that spot, she suddenly fell to her knees.

Her fall was so unexpected that the avalanche of people were carried past on either side of her by the weight of their own numbers. I was fortunate in not being carried past with them, and before I knew it, I unexpectedly found myself to her right, with her face a mere eighteen inches from mine. I staunchly withstood the pushing of those behind me, striving with all my might not to be wrenched from my vantage point. I succeeded.

The shoves gradually ceased and relative calm ensued.

Shortly before midnight, the clouds obscuring the sky had slowly drifted away, and the blue mantle of the heavens had become studded with stars shining about the moon.

In their light, and that of an infinite number of torches in the alley, I could see quite plainly that Conchita's mouth was open and her tongue out in the position customary when going to Communion. She was prettier than ever. Far from causing laughter or looking the slightest bit ridiculous, her expression and attitude had about them an awesome, moving mysticism.

Suddenly, without my knowing quite how, without really realizing it, without Conchita changing her expression in the slightest, the Sacred Host appeared on her tongue. It was totally unexpected. It did not seem to have been deposited there, but might be described rather as having materialized there, faster than the human eye could see.

Conchita kept her head in full view of the villagers for several minutes before swallowing the Host. She continued to remain in ecstasy for over an hour.

Although Conchita continued to experience raptures until 1965, they became less and less frequent after the July 18 miracle. The other three girls stopped experiencing them altogether. Between December 8, 1963, and July 18, 1965, however, the BVM delivered a series of messages to Conchita, which included her continued affirmation that she would perform a great miracle. She also confided a number of "secrets" about the political/social future of the world. These, however, have never been revealed. A third topic was the world's spiritual fate, which was also the dominant subject of the Virgin's final appearance to Conchita on November 13, 1965.

Since the Garabandal episode ended in 1965, three of the visionaries—Jacinta, Mary Cruz, and Mary Loly—have remained in Spain where they now live relatively normal lives. Jacinta Gonzales eventually entered a convent. Only Mary Cruz Gonzales later tried to cast doubt on the authenticity of the Garabandal affair by asserting to interviewers that *some* of the trances were faked. She claimed that she and her friends had used them as a means of getting away from town to play!

Conchita has remained steadfast in her devotion to the Virgin Mary and to the cause of Garabandal. She eventually married a physician and moved to New York, where she continues to publicize the Garabandal messages. (She maintains that she did not enter a convent because, during their frequent talks together, the Virgin had specifically instructed her not to do so.) Today there are Garabandal information centers in several cities in the United States, including Lindenhurst, New York, and Pasadena, California.

What can we conclude about the apparitions at Garabandal? In some respects the case is very similar to other Marian visitations—only the children could see the apparition, a series of secrets was entrusted to one of them, and an authentic miracle apparently took place. But the Garabandal appearances differ from the majority of historical Marian manifestations in several critical ways. The most notable of these is the unusual duration of the affair. Conchita's ecstasies and meetings with the BVM lasted over four years, and virtually the same is true of the other three children. Yet even at Fatima the BVM appeared for only a period of six months.

Another questionable facet of the case at Garabandal concerns the prophecies the Virgin made there. Perhaps the most impressive feature of Marian apparitions in general is their accuracy in making correct predictions. Yet even the most ardent believers in the Garabandal visitations have trouble explaining the fact that the "great miracle," promised over and over again, never came to pass.

Finally, the attitudes of the children involved in the Garabandal miracle are open to question. None of them seemed to be characterized by the almost superhuman humility and moral perfection many other witnesses to Marian visitations either possessed or subsequently developed. The fact that at least one of the witnesses claims to have faked some of the trances places the entire Garabandal incident on a different footing from Fatima or La Salette.

Yet these considerations have to be matched against the testimony of such critical witnesses as Father Ramon Andréu and many other priests who went to Garabandal as skeptics but left as believers. Certainly their eyewitness investigations must be considered as being more valuable than anything we can infer today by merely reading the vast literature on the subject. One must also take into account the many paranormal aspects of the case, such as the girls' telepathic displays during their trances and the veridical material they received from Father Luis.

The story of Garabandal is a chronicle without an ending and a mystery without a solution. The case is still controversial in Spain, and Church leaders there have made no official or final pronouncement about its authenticity.

Anyone trying to analyze the Garabandal affair is forced to confront a twofold problem. Not only must the nature of the messages delivered by the BVM be evaluated, but value judgments must constantly be made about the credibility of the four children who claimed to have seen her. The validity of any "selective perception" apparitions can be determined only by questioning the motivations, veracity, and moral integrity of the limited number of direct witnesses to the visitations.

These problems do *not* arise, however, in the evaluation of what is undoubtedly the most spectacular and important series of Marian apparitions documented in modern times. These visitations took place in Zeitoun, Egypt, and lasted well over three years, during which they were seen by thousands of witnesses.[5]

Zeitoun is a poor suburb of Cairo, a city whose population is predominantly Moslem. Yet it is legend that Mary and Joseph, the parents of Jesus, hid in Zeitoun after fleeing their homeland when Herod, the tetrarch of Judea, ordered all firstborn Jewish children killed after learning that the Messiah's birth had been foretold. The Catholic tradition of Zeitoun is still evident today, as the suburb is populated by both Moslems and Coptic Catholics.

The Coptic Church is a sect closely allied to the Roman Catholic Church. It broke away from orthodox Catholicism in 1054 A.D. and is strongly represented in several Near Eastern countries. Despite a number of affinities, the Coptic Church recognizes its own Pope, who has historically resided in Constantinople, and its own synod of bishops. The patriarch of the Coptic Church at the time of the Zeitoun manifestations was Pope Kryllos VI, who rose to leadership in 1959 after years of internal strife had almost devastated the sect.

Zeitoun is also the site of a beautiful Coptic church known as St. Mary's Church of Zeitoun, which stands directly across the street from some buildings that then served as an auto mechanic's garage. On April 2, 1968, two Moslem mechanics had been working well into the late hours of the night in this garage and had decided to go outside for some fresh air. No sooner had they done so than they noticed a white figure standing at the top of the church, silhouetted near the large central dome of the structure. The mechanics first thought the figure was a nun, who they feared was about to leap from the building. One of the men immediately ran to fetch the church's pastor, while the other hurriedly called an emergency rescue squad. The figure remained in sight for several minutes before disappearing. No one knew quite what to make of the phenomenon, but during the next several days rumors began to spread throughout Cairo that the figure was the Blessed Virgin Mary herself. Small crowds of Zeitoun residents began to form in the streets surrounding the church, hoping that the figure would reappear.

On Tuesday, April 9, the apparition materialized near the dome, just as it had done a week before. It was glowing white and radiated an aura.

After this second appearance, the figure soon began to be seen at frequent, though unpredictable, intervals. It would usually appear two or three times a week and often materialized surrounded by radiant light. Several Egyptian newspapers carried stories about the manifestations, and large crowds waited nightly outside the church. On April 13 a photographer from Cairo was able to photograph the figure. Mr. Wagih Pizk Matta had heard about the apparition through the media and visited the church on the night of April 12. The Virgin did not appear until 3:55 A.M., and though she remained in view for only ten minutes, Matta was able to take several pictures of her from a street adjoining the church. The resulting pictures were not of very high quality, but they were the first of what would eventually be many spectacular photographs of the apparition.

The figure appeared dozens of times during April and May. Most witnesses who saw it agreed that it glowed with a soft but intense radiance. "The first time I saw the apparition," Matta later testified, "the light cloud of the Mary was so bright that the light blinded my eyes."[6] On May 5 the figure stayed in full view for several hours before disappearing. All of Cairo had now learned of the materializations, and the crowds eventually became so large that city officials had to tear down some old buildings near the church so that an open "lot" could be set aside to accommodate them.

The apparition revealed itself in a variety of ways. Before the actual appearances, flashes of light would often be seen darting about the top of the church. Occasionally the central dome would become eerily luminescent as well. At other times, meteoric lights would rush down toward the church as though sent from the heavens themselves. The figure always appeared in a brilliant flash of light. The apparition would at first appear somewhat amorphous, but would eventually form into a more defined human shape. It would initially be seen either in the air above or before the center dome or pacing back and forth on the rooftop. The figure would usually acknowledge the crowds by bowing to them, and on rare occasions it would even appear as a "Madonna with Child." The apparition never spoke, and its manifestations were unpredictable. It might appear only once on a particular evening, or else it would disappear and reappear repeatedly during the span of a night. While usually seen at the top of the church, on rare occasions it would materialize in the courtyard of the building. The figure was most often white in color, but sometimes appeared bluish white. It always seemed to be wearing flowing robes of light.

An especially bizarre aspect of this apparition was the way its appearances would often be heralded or accompanied by "doves of light." These were images of light resembling pigeons or doves that would fly about the dome either during the apparition or shortly beforehand. At times they even flew on nights when the BVM failed to appear. They seemed formed of pure light, and although they soared through the air for considerable distances, they never seemed to flap their wings. These phenomena, too, were repeatedly photographed.

A brief description of one of the appearances at Zeitoun has been placed on record by Bishop Samuel, an official of the Coptic Church, who saw the apparition repeatedly in early April 1968 after journeying to Zeitoun to investigate the matter. On his first visit, he had to wait until well into the morning hours before the apparition finally materialized:

At 2:45 in the morning the Blessed Virgin Mary appeared in a complete luminous body as a radiant phosphorescent statue. After a short while the apparition vanished. It reappeared at four o'clock and remained until five o'clock—dawn. The scene was overwhelming and magnificent. The apparition walked toward the west, sometimes moving its hands in blessing, and sometimes bowing repeatedly. A halo of light surrounded its head. I saw some glittering beings around the apparition. They looked like stars, rather blue in color. . . .

A more detailed account was prepared by Bishop Athanasius, another official of the Coptic Church, who traveled to Zeitoun from his home in the city of Beni Soueiff at the direct request of Kryllos VI. Bishop Athanasius reported his observations to Pope Kryllos and to the Reverend Jerome Palmer, an American priest who has become an authority on the Zeitoun affair. In 1969 Father Palmer went to Egypt specifically to interview witnesses to the Marian visitations there. He eventually published the collected testimony in his book *Our Lady Returns to Egypt* (1969).[7]

Bishop Athanasius made a first visit to the church on April 6, and obtained his first good look at the apparition at three forty-five the next morning from a street near the building:

The crowd was tremendous. It was too difficult to move among the people. But I tried and worked my way in front of the figure. There she was, five or six meters above the dome, high in the sky, full figure, like a phosphorous statue, but not so stiff as a statue. There was movement of the body and of the clothing. It was very difficult for me to stand all the time before the figure, as human waves were pushing me from all sides. One would estimate the crowd at 100,000. In an hour or so I think I stood before the figure eight or nine times. I began to tire and thought it was sufficient for me.

The bishop then entered a small building to the south of the church, where he was able to watch the apparition through a window:

I stood inside for one hour, from four to five o'clock, looking at the figure. It never disappeared. Our Lady looked to the north; she waved her hand; she blessed the people, sometimes in the direction where we stood. Her garments swayed in the wind. She was very quiet, full of glory. It was something really supernatural, very, very heavenly.

I saw a large strange pigeon. It came from behind us—I don't know where—proceeded to the church and returned. Several bright spotlights moved quickly over us. Some people were reciting verses from the Koran. Some (Greeks) were praying in Greek; others were singing Coptic hymns. It was something really above human experience that attracted and captivated us.

I stood there and tried to distinguish the face and features. I can say there was something about the eyes and mouth I could see, but I could not make out the features. That continued until about five minutes before five. The apparition then began to grow fainter, little by little. The light gave way to a cloud, bright at first, then less and less bright until it disappeared. I went there many times later, but that was the appearance that left the greatest impression on me.

A good description of the way in which the apparition would initially materialize was given to Father Palmer by Mr. Wadie Tadros Shumbo. Mr. Shumbo was a Protestant who was then working for the Mobil Oil Company in Egypt. He visited the church several times before finally observing the apparition from the lot that had been prepared near the church for the convenience of the crowds:

We picked what we thought was the best place from which to watch and sat there. At about 9:50 we saw lighting over the church, much stronger that one could make with a flashlight. I had a feeling something was about to happen. A thin line or edge of light appeared like the light you see when you open the door to a lighted room. Within seconds it formed itself into the shape of the Virgin. I could not speak. All who were with me said, "It is impossible!"

The Moslems all started to cry. This sight lasted for five minutes, when the figure rose and vanished. I could distinguish only a difference in color between the skin in the face and hands and the veil. There was some color in the face and hands. It was evident when St. Mary walked back and forth. When she disappeared from our side of the church, the people from the other side shouted they were seeing her. Then she returned to our side for five minutes.

When I returned to the car for something I found it impossible to get back to the church because of the crowd. I could hear the people shouting. Above the center dome I saw Mary in full body, standing before the cross. I cannot describe what I felt. There were some "pigeons"—six or seven of them—over the church.

Other signs and wonders often occurred at St. Mary's Church on those nights when the figure didn't appear. Mrs. Pearl Zaki, a New York housewife who visited Zeitoun in August 1968, has described these phenomena in a diary of her trip which she published in the booklet *Our Lord's Mother Visits Egypt.*[8]

Mrs. Zaki arrived in Zeitoun on August 7 and waited all through the nights of August 8, 9, and 10 to see the apparition. On two occasions she saw mysterious flashes of light over the church, but the figure failed to materialize. Mrs. Zaki decided not to go to the church on August 11. That night the apparition materialized at one forty but quickly vanished. Disappointed at having missed the Virgin's appearance, Mrs. Zaki came to the church once again on the night of the twelfth. Some four thousand people had gathered. After a considerable wait, she was startled to see a series of brilliant flashes of light over the church. Then, according to Mrs. Zaki, "the large dome [of the church] became engulfed in a brilliant blue white light, as if it were melting, and the edges of light on top of the lighted dome appeared to roll inward so that one's eyes were directed to the very center. . . ." The light then vanished, but reappeared momentarily. When it did, Mrs. Zaki could plainly see the outline of the BVM against the dome. The figure stood immobile like a statue, but then began to move its arms. "They moved slowly upwards," writes Mrs. Zaki. "This lasted a few seconds only. Two flashes of light like meteors or shooting stars came from behind the dome to form a cross over her head and then all became dark. She was gone." The apparition didn't appear again that night, nor did it materialize the next night.

Mrs. Zaki kept a day-by-day account of the Zeitoun miracles from April 1968 to September 1970, during which time the figure appeared at increasingly longer intervals. By the summer of 1968 the apparitions were already waning, though the flashing lights and "doves" continued to be seen. In 1969, for example, the full-form figure of the Virgin was seen only on January 3; March 16 and 23; April 2, 13, and 20; May 4 and 10; September 13; October 11; and December 6. The luminescent doves and eerie flashes of light were seen atop the church at least twice a week during these same months, or in their place, a smoky "fog" would infrequently emit from the top of the building.

The apparitions became even more sporadic in 1970 and finally ceased entirely in 1971.

From the standpoint of the available evidence, the Zeitoun miracle is probably the greatest of all Marian visitations. It represents the strongest proof ever obtained demonstrating the existence of the miraculous. We have detailed testimony on the apparition from Church officials, bystanders, and newspaper reporters. The total number of witnesses to the event is well over hundreds of thousands. We also have a great deal of photographic documentation of the apparition's authenticity.

But although the Zeitoun apparition was certainly authentic, there is also considerable evidence available to support the theory that the apparition was actually a kind of thought form—i.e., only a temporarily "real" figure produced by human thought.

The strongest support for the theory can be found in the background of St. Mary's Church itself. The land upon which the structure was built was donated to the Coptic Church in 1920 by the Khalil Ibrahim family after one of its members had experienced a strange dream. The Virgin appeared and urged him to build a church on the property. St. Mary's was built in 1925, at which time the same family member had another dream. This time the Virgin promised to appear at the church the following year. Even before the Zeitoun miracle of 1968–71, then, *there existed a forty-year-old tradition that a Marian visitation would eventually take place at the church.* Remember, too, that Zeitoun is steeped in a rich Marian tradition. It was to here that the Holy Family is said to have fled after leaving Judea, and of course the church built on the land donated by the Ibrahim family is specifically devoted to the worship of the Virgin Mary.

Taking these factors into consideration, what happened at Zeitoun in 1968 becomes clear. During the years between 1925 and 1968, many of the visitors to St. Mary's Church were probably either consciously or unconsciously preoccupied with the role of the Blessed Virgin in the building of the church. They probably held firm expectations that she would eventually appear at the site. These preoccupations may have gradually built up a psychic "blueprint" of the Virgin within the church itself—i.e., an ever-increasing pool of psychic energy created by the thoughts of the

Zeitounians which in 1968 became so high-pitched that an image of the Virgin Mary burst into physical reality!

This explanation of the Zeitoun apparition can also explain the frequency of its appearances. Though common in April and May, the first months of the sighting, the figure's materializations became less and less so during the months that followed. It seemed that the power that had generated the form was gradually ebbing. The infrequency of the Marian appearances in 1969—sometimes only once or twice a month—seems to indicate that the figure had to slowly reenergize itself after each manifestation before it could materialize again. The flashing lights and other related phenomena seen so often over the church may have been abortive apparitions during which the thought form was actually *attempting* to appear.

This theory can also explain the longevity of the apparition's visitation to Zeitoun. Once the thought form became a physical reality, it is likely that it was constantly being reenergized by the crowds that came nightly to the church to view it. The power they donated to the figure, through their intense emotions and prayers, may have increased its longevity, which under other conditions might have been only a few hours or days.

Whatever the truth of the Blessed Virgin Mary's appearances in Zeitoun, they rank with the collectively perceived Marian visitation to Knock, Ireland, in 1879 as one of the most spectacular chapters in the often *un*natural history of the miraculous.

∾ XI ∾
MIRACULOUS HEALINGS

DR. LERRAC looked at young Marie Ferrand with little hope that she would live much longer. Her once youthful body, now emaciated and distended simultaneously by tubercular peritonitis, was a mass of diseased tissue, cancerous lumps, and pockets of fluid.

"In five minutes the pain will be gone," he said reassuringly as he gently inserted a morphine-filled syringe into her withered arm.

Why, Lerrac wondered, was this poor creature even trying to make the journey to the healing springs at Lourdes? Here they were, doctor and patient, aboard a train heading for the famous shrine, but the young doctor knew in his heart that his charge would never survive the journey. Both her parents had died from similar cancers and the hospital where she had been treated had given her case up as untreatable. This journey to Lourdes was Marie Ferrand's last hope; a hope that was now the only thing sustaining her life.

Only a few hours later the train carrying Marie, Lerrac, and scores of other patients who hoped to be healed at Lourdes came to a halt. They had arrived at their destination, the world-famous sanctuary of healing. Even as early as 1903, when Lerrac made this journey, there were hundreds of tales of incurables who had been miraculously healed by bathing in the waters of the Lourdes spring. Although a compassionate man, Lerrac was also cynical about the value of the journey—especially when he thought about Marie Ferrand.

"If such a case as hers is cured . . . I would become a monk!" he complained to a fellow physician.

The day after their arrival, Lerrac walked down the street from his hotel to the Our Lady of the Seven Graces Hospital, where all the Lourdes-bound patients were huddled together, waiting for a hospital car to transport them to the spring. Lerrac's job was to examine them before they bathed at the shrine that day, so that a medical report could be filed if any healings took place. Lerrac went about his job dolorously; he couldn't believe that the sick and twisted bodies before him could possibly be cured by the Lourdes waters. However, a friend of his, another doctor who had made the journey, took the reports of miracle healings more seriously.

"But I saw a miracle at the Grotto," Lerrac's medical colleague told him that afternoon. "I was walking near the pools when an old nun hobbled up on crutches. She let a little of the water run into a cup, made a large sign of the cross, and drank the water. Her whole face lighted with joy, she threw aside her crutches and almost ran to the Grotto, where she kneeled before the Blessed Virgin. She was cured. I am told that, as a result of a sprain six months ago, she had developed an incurable disease in her foot."

"Her cure is an interesting example of autosuggestion," Lerrac replied coldly, for he had in fact once examined this very patient and had found the leg quite healed, although the nun refused to believe it.

Lerrac argued with his colleague for hours.

"Lourdes is powerless against organic disease," he finally maintained.

"What kind of disease would you have to see cured to convince you that miracles exist?"

"I would have to see an organic disease cured," replied Lerrac in an instant. "A leg growing back after amputation, a cancer disappearing, a congenital dislocation suddenly vanishing. If such things could be scientifically observed, they would mean the collapse of all the laws we now accept, and then and there it would be permissible to admit to the intervention of a supernatural process."

As Lerrac argued against Lourdes, he thought of Marie Ferrand.

"This unfortunate girl is in the last stages of tubercular peritonitis," he confided to his friend. "I know her history. Her whole family died of tuberculosis. She has had tubercular sores, lesions of the lungs, and now for the last few months a peritonitis diagnosed by both a general practitioner and the Bordeaux surgeon, Bromiloux. Her condition is grave; I had to give her morphine on the journey. She may die any moment right under my nose. If she could be cured, it would indeed be a miracle."

Lerrac returned to the hospital later that day accompanied by his friend and called upon Marie. He was dismayed by what he saw.

"Our patient is worse than ever," Marie's companion sobbed. "I don't know what to do. She can hardly speak. I'm afraid she is sinking fast."

Marie's heart was racing at 150 beats a minute and was about to give out. Her entire body was swollen, her stomach distended. Lerrac could do little but give her an injection of caffeine.

"Death is very near," he whispered to his fellow doctor.

Although Marie's distraught companion begged that the girl be taken to the pools at Lourdes, Lerrac was pessimistic. What if she died on the way, he thought to himself? The girl was in such a pitiful physical condition that even trying to transport her might kill her. The Mother Superior of the hospital, who had overheard the companion's pleas, stepped in at this point.

"The girl has nothing to lose," she said. "It makes little difference whether she dies today or tomorrow. It would be cruel to deprive her of the supreme happiness of being taken to the Grotto, though I fear she may never live to reach it. We shall take her there now, in a few minutes."

Lerrac was still hesitant to approve the venture, but bowed to the Mother Superior's authority.

"I will be at the pools myself, in any case. If she goes into a coma, send for me," he said rather brusquely, though secretly intrigued by these unexpected developments.

Later that day, Lerrac, his friend and Marie Ferrand traveled to the Grotto. Marie Ferrand's almost lifeless body was resting on a stretcher, and as Lerrac looked at her he could only think that here was a girl who was going to die before even having had a chance to live.

Because Marie was obviously too sick to be immersed in the pool, the attendants at Lourdes instead sprinkled drops of water over her bloated abdomen. She was then carried away to another part of the Lourdes facilities. Once again Lerrac examined her, but it now seemed to him as if her skin was less ashen. He pointed out the change to his friend.

"All I can see is that she is no worse," replied his colleague.

"Look at her abdomen!" shouted Lerrac in surprise only moments later.

The blanket covering Marie's distended abdomen was sinking, and it looked as though her body was returning to normal. As the doctors watched on in amazement, the girl's heartbeat stabilized and she began to speak. She was soon sitting up and began to move around. After a few days, her body was totally and inexplicably cured. Her sores, lumps and pockets of fluid vanished. She had been brought back from the very brink of death. Lerrac had seen the very miracle he had disdained.

The story told above is not really about Dr. Lerrac at all. If you read the doctor's name backward, it spells "Carrel." Dr. Lerrac was, in fact, the Nobel prize-winning physician Dr. Alexis Carrel, who visited Lourdes as a young man. Toward the end of his life he sketched out a short case study of Marie Ferrand (her real name was Marie Bailly), entitled *The Voyage to Lourdes,* in which he refers to himself as Dr. Lerrac. The material was found in his files after his death and was eventually published in 1950 with a foreword by Charles Lindbergh, who had been a long-time friend of the physician's.[1] The narrative that begins this chapter is a brief condensation of Carrel's work.

Lourdes had an impact on the skeptical young doctor that profoundly affected the rest of his life. Carrel was born in 1873 and was educated at the University of Lyons, but emigrated to the United States in 1905, where he worked at the University of Chicago. Later he conducted research at the Rockefeller Institute for Medical Research in New York. Because Carrel's work was always innovative, he was subject to constant criticism from his more orthodox medical colleagues—and not least for his vocal support of the Lourdes healings. He focused much of his research on such pioneering areas of medicine as blood transfusion techniques and vein and organ transplantation, and introduced novel methods for healing severe wounds. He received a Nobel prize for his work in 1912, and in 1935 wrote his magnum opus, *Man the Unknown.* He died in 1944.

Carrel was always guided in his work by the principles of science, but because he also believed in the existence of the miraculous, he tried to apply scientific rigor to the study of religion. "I pray that God will grant me another ten years of work," he said shortly before his death. "With what I have learned, and with what I have experienced, I believe I shall succeed in establishing, scientifically, certain objective relationships between the spiritual and the natural and thereby show the truth of the beneficence of Christianity."

Carrel was able to achieve at least part of this goal in *The Voyage to Lourdes* by providing the medical world with strong circumstantial evidence that the miraculous can be observed and studied by means of conventional science.

But can the case of Marie Bailly actually be considered a miraculous healing? Just when can a healing be considered medically inexplicable?

Anyone who tries to evaluate cases of miraculous healing faces a fundamental problem, for even modern medicine knows relatively little about the restorative and regenerative powers of the human body. Doctors frequently see cases of what they call

"spontaneous remissions," instances in which terminal patients—
suffering anything from cancer to tuberculosis—will suddenly take
a surprising turn for the better and sometimes even totally recover.
Cases of terminal cancer, leukemia, and even malignant anemia
have been known to remit abruptly for no apparent medical reason.

Because of the possibility of spontaneous remission, a healing
must meet several strict and extraordinary medical requirements
before it can be considered genuinely miraculous. Perhaps the
best codification of these criteria was first set forth by Lambertini
in *De canonizatione*. Lambertini was keenly aware of the problem
of verifying the miraculous nature of a sudden cure, and therefore
established several guidelines that he felt should be adopted in
determining whether a healing was genuinely divine:

(1) *The disability or malady should be serious.* That is, the condition
should be one that is difficult or impossible to cure through conventional
treatment. Cases that usually carry a fatal prognosis would especially fall
into this category.

(2) *The patient should not have already been improving at the time
of the healing, nor suffering from a condition that normally might be
expected to improve.* It is not clear what role the body's own immune
system plays in the "cure" of a condition that is known occasionally to
remit.

(3) *The patient should not have been under orthodox medical treatment at the time.* Lambertini was aware that medication could sometimes
have latent or long-lasting effects in or on the human body. He went so
far as to suggest that the investigator should procure sworn statements
from the patient's doctor and pharmacist as to what treatment was
administered and when it was terminated before evaluating the miraculous nature of a healing. He also stipulated that if a patient was receiving
treatment at the time of his cure, it must positively be shown that it had
produced no beneficial effect.

(4) *The healing should be sudden and instantaneous.* The body's
own immune system requires time to combat an infection, a wound, or
a cancer. One true sign of a miraculous cure is that it is instantaneous;
i.e., the healing occurs much too fast to have been the result of any
biological activity within the body.

(5) *The cure must be perfect and complete.* Even very sick patients
often go through periods when they feel better, or when their illnesses go
into temporary remission. A cure cannot be considered miraculous if a

patient merely becomes less ill. The affliction must clear up totally before a healing can be considered supernatural.

(6) *The cure should not occur at a time when a crisis due to natural causes has affected the patient or the illness.* Even in the eighteenth century Lambertini realized that a nexus exists between the mind and the body and that a sudden shock to one might affect the other. He constantly sought to determine the effect of trauma on human illness. He was also aware that certain medications might produce a gross effect on a patient's condition that might seem to make him worse while actually making him better.

(7) *The cure must be permanent.* A patient has to be free from all symptoms of his illness for at least a year before a miracle is declared.

Although Lambertini's sound advice about how miraculous cures should be studied is as cogent today as when it was originally outlined, a great many other principles could be added to it, since today we have a better understanding of pathology than did the Church of two hundred years ago. In the September–October 1977 issue of the *Parapsychology Review,* Renée Haynes, a Catholic writer who is well versed in parapsychology, proposed some further conditions that might help to differentiate between a genuinely miraculous cure and a normal, though perhaps baffling, medical anomaly. Her first provision for a miracle is that the natural healing abilities of the human body must seem to be supernormally accelerated: "In miraculous healing events which would ordinarily take weeks to come about may happen within hours or even minutes." So the *speed* of the cure, and not necessarily its instantaneous implementation, should be considered a mitigating factor.

Ms. Haynes's second proposed basis for identifying a supernatural healing is that, while the normal duration of a "spontaneous remission" can be quite long, most miraculous cures are completed quickly, or even suddenly. (Lambertini believed that a cure had to be completed within ten days of its inception before being considered miraculous.)

Finally, she suggests that if a patient is suffering from an infirmity that *should* have cleared up normally but has not, he might consider himself miraculously healed if he finds himself suddenly and inexplicably cured.[2] Ms. Haynes cites the case of Jack Traynor, a British soldier badly wounded during World War I, as an example of such a case. Traynor returned home to Liverpool so infirm that he received a total disability pension from the government. A bullet had ripped through his skull and the wound had refused to heal. His arm had become atrophied due to another wound that had damaged the brachial nerve center and left the limb paralyzed. The head wound apparently also triggered an epileptic condition. Surgery was performed but failed to rectify any of the handicaps. In July 1923 Traynor made a pilgrimage to the Lourdes shrine. He was so ill when he arrived that officials there didn't want him to undergo the ordeal of immersion in the waters. Despite their objection he insisted on being taken to the pool. The next morning he awoke totally cured. He leaped from his bed at the hospice in town, walked about, shaved, and ultimately returned home to live a normal life for several more years—he even retained his pension. For, in the words of Ms. Haynes, "The Ministry of Pensions, incidentally, thought this impossible, mislaid the papers, and obstinately continued to pay his disability pension."

Though many different types of miraculous healings have been documented, we will be concerned with only four in this chapter: (1) Healings that occur spontaneously when a patient (or a friend or relative) directly petitions a saint to implement the cure. (2) Cures that occur at healing shrines, such as at Lourdes. (3) Cures implemented through the spiritual powers of a religious leader or figure. (4) Cures that include biologically impossible feats, such as the total regeneration of a limb or organ that has been irreparably damaged.

Many recorded miraculous cures have been attributed to the direct intervention of the great Roman Catholic saints. A Catholic can be sainted only when the Church has determined that the candidate has lived a life of "heroic virtue." The ability to perform miracles *in itself* is not sufficient grounds for canonization, but it does serve as secondary evidence that the candidate lived a particularly holy life. Church inquiries have usually attempted not only to secure eyewitness accounts about the miraculous feats of its mystics and ascetics. It has also tried to determine whether a candidate performed miracles both before and *after* his death.

Although belief in miracles is not actually a dogma of the Catholic Church, Catholics generally accept that a very holy person can directly intervene in human affairs, through the grace of God, even after his death. Many of these alleged postmortem miracles have been miraculous cures and healings. They are widely reported in the canonization processes of the saints, and some of these defy all medical explanation.

St. Martin de Porres, who has already been mentioned in the discussion of bilocation, is a good case in point, since his postmortem healings were carefully recorded and scrutinized by the Church. Although various commissions were sent to study the life of this Peruvian holy man during the years 1659–64, his initial beatification came only in 1837, and was based more on the healings he had allegedly brought about after his death than on those he had performed while alive. Two miraculous cures attributed to him were decreed valid by the Vatican in 1836. The first of these concerned a Lima housewife who had sustained an eye injury when a sliver of an earthenware jar she had broken had lodged in her eye. The fluid normally present in the eye leaked out, leaving the eye incurably blind. The master of a nearby monastery, however, sent the woman a small bone fragment, a relic of Martin de Porres, and instructed her to hold it to the damaged eye. She did as she was directed and woke the next morning to find her eye and sight totally restored. Though this was medically impossible, the cure was authenticated by the woman's own doctor, who had examined the original wound.

The second healing that led to St. Martin's beatification concerned the two-year-old son of a slave who worked in an aristocratic home in Lima. One day the child fell eighteen feet from a balcony and split open his head. Convulsions soon set in and a doctor was summoned. He considered the case hopeless and could only confine the child to bed. With no other recourse available, the child's mother prayed to Martin de Porres. The woman's employer, a noble Spanish woman, joined in her prayers and placed a portrait of the saint under the boy's head. Three hours later the boy left the bed, completely recovered.

The evidence supporting these two cures was sent to Rome and was approved by Pope Gregory XVI on March 19, 1836, paving the way for Martin's beatification on October 29, 1837.

Healing miracles attributed to the intervention of St. Martin have been reported within recent years as well. Dorothy Caballero

Escalante was an eighty-seven-year-old widow who had led a normal and healthy life in Asunción, Paraguay, until September 8, 1948, when she fell ill with an intestinal disorder. An X ray revealed that an obstruction was blocking the passageway and could only be rectified through surgery. This course of action was impossible, though, since the patient had a bad heart. By the end of the week, Sra. Escalante's condition had so deteriorated that death was expected at any time. The woman's doctors duly notified her daughter, who lived in Buenos Aires. She immediately began praying to St. Martin and continued to pray, she later testified, throughout the entire plane flight from Argentina to Paraguay. Her prayers were apparently answered, for Sra. Escalante awoke the next day completely cured and led a normal life for several more years.

An even more startling healing ascribed to St. Martin's intercession was reported in 1956 from Tenerife in the Canary Islands. On August 25, a four-and-a-half-year-old boy named Anthony Cabrera Perez, fell from a wall at a construction site. A block of cement weighing some seventy pounds, which had broken from the wall when the boy lost his balance, landed directly on his leg. The limb had been crushed, and later gangrene set in. The child had been sent to St. Eulalia's Hospital in Tenerife, where no fewer than four doctors examined him and agreed that the leg had to be amputated in order to save his life. They had initially attempted to treat the gangrene with medication, but the boy had not responded.

On September 1, a friend of the Perez family flew to the Canary Islands from Madrid and gave the distraught parents a picture of St. Martin and urged them to pray to the saint. The next morning, the doctors found that the boy's gangrene had completely disappeared during the night and that blood had begun circulating normally through the leg. Anthony was soon completely cured.

These two cures were examined in Rome in January and October 1961 by the medical college of the Sacred Congregation of Rites, a Vatican body charged with investigating reports of miracles. The cures were officially approved as miraculous in March 1962 by Pope John XXIII.[3]

Another very well documented healing miracle was instrumental in the canonization of Blessed John Ogilvie, a Scottish holy man who was executed in 1614 on the order of Protestant authorities in Glasgow. John Ogilvie was canonized in 1976 by Pope Paul VI, due in large measure to a miraculous cure allegedly performed by him in 1969.[4]

The subject of the healing was John Fagan, a middle-aged Glasgow dock worker. He had first become ill on April 26, 1967, when he woke up violently sick and vomiting blood. He was admitted to Glasgow Royal Infirmary later that day, where medical tests were completed by May 5. The results, especially the X rays, were not good. Fagan was informed on May 14 that his condition necessitated stomach surgery, but the doctors refrained from telling him that he was suffering from cancer. The resulting surgery revealed that the cancer had eaten through the stomach and into the transverse colon. The stomach was greatly ulcerated, and the cancer had apparently spread far by the time of the operation. The cancerous tissue could not be completely removed, and the doctors duly advised Mrs. Fagan that her husband had only from six months to a year to live. Again, Fagan was not told of this prognosis.

Fagan's condition began to worsen gradually after his surgery. By the end of the summer he was very weak and had totally lost his appetite. His wife was so concerned by his continued deterioration that she took him back to the hospital on December 21. The doctor in charge of his case noted at that time that secondary malignant tumors had developed, just as had been predicted. The secondary growths were inoperable and, as far as the doctors were concerned, terminal. They informed Mrs. Fagan that there was nothing they could do to help other than administer pain-reducing medication.

Fagan remained bedridden from that day onward. His strength, vigor, and enthusiasm paled and he began to realize that he was dying. He attempted to go back to work only once during these months, but couldn't manage the exertion. Mrs. Fagan cared for him at home during the terminal phase of his illness, even though his doctors had suggested that he be placed in a hospice for the dying.

The Fagans had few visitors during these bleak days. But one who did come to visit the dying man was Father John Fitzgibbon, the assistant pastor at the Church of Blessed John Ogilvie in Glasgow. Since the Fagans were Catholic, Father Fitzgibbon became a source of spiritual support to them. Fagan's condition became so bad by January that the priest even administered last rites. Before leaving that day, though, he gave Mrs. Fagan a medal of Blessed John Ogilvie and suggested that she pray to the martyr for her husband's recovery and pin the medal to his bedclothes. She followed his advice and gave the medal to her husband.

By March, Fagan was so weak that he could neither get up from bed, eat, or even talk. He could only vomit repeatedly, since by now his stomach was literally dissolving itself. Then on March 5 several religious friends of the Fagans visited and held a prayer session around Fagan's bed. Although they beseeched Blessed John Ogilvie repeatedly to intercede in the dying man's behalf, the situation didn't look very encouraging. The Fagans' doctor, Archibald MacDonald, arrived the next day and was so shaken by his patient's condition that he could do nothing but advise Mrs. Fagan that he would return after the weekend to sign the death certificate. He gave her husband a pain killer and left. Fagan then fell into a deep sleep, delivered at least momentarily from his constant pain.

Mrs. Fagan entered her husband's room the next morning expecting to find a corpse, and was shocked at what seemed to be his partial recovery. Fagan was hungry! He hadn't eaten in weeks, and was trying to tell his wife that he now felt "different." She frantically called Dr. MacDonald, who arrived later that day and was equally amazed by Fagan's condition. His pain was completely gone and the vomiting had suddenly stopped. He soon recovered completely.

When John Fagan's cure became common knowledge, Church officials in Scotland acted swiftly to examine it. They hoped that the miracle—if it was a miracle—would help in their long effort to have John Ogilvie canonized.

The story of Blessed John Ogilvie's life is known to every Catholic in Scotland. A Calvinist by upbringing, he had converted to Catholicism while studying in Europe as a young man. These were difficult times for Catholics in Scotland. Anti-Catholic sentiment had been growing since 1540, when Henry VIII abolished the influence of the Catholic Church there. By the 1560s Catholicism was banned and the activity of Catholic missionaries was prohibited. Ogilvie returned to Scotland from his studies in 1613 a zealous Catholic, and in spite of the prohibition, immediately began missionary activities. He was arrested in 1614 and tried for treason. When he refused to admit that the king of England had religious authority over the Pope, he was executed. Ever since that time, Roman Catholics in Scotland have revered John Ogilvie not only as a hero, but as a saint. He was beatified in 1886, but his cause for canonization had never been completed. Scottish Catholic leaders had since then diligently petitioned to have the martyr's cause reexamined.

Before they could promote Fagan's cure as a miracle, the Church hierarchy realized that it would have to prove beyond a doubt that Fagan had in fact been *miraculously* healed. The result of their subsequent investigation was that the recovery of John Fagan, a victim of terminal cancer, became one of the most thoroughly documented healings reported in modern times.

The case was first considered in October 1967 by a group of priests in Glasgow under the direction of Father Thomas Reilly of the Church of Blessed John Ogilvie. The panel procured a statement from Dr. MacDonald about the nature and course of Fagan's cancer and then selected three local doctors to act as a medical committee charged with examining the case in detail. These included Dr. John Fitzsimmons, a general practitioner in Glasgow; Dr. Andrew Curran, a lecturer in medicine at Glasgow University; and Dr. Aloysius Dunne, an expert in geriatrics. The committee initially met in the presbytery of Father Reilly's church in May 1968, and after spending over two years evaluating the evidence, came to the general conclusion that no medical explanation could be found for Fagan's cure. Of the three, only Dr. Curran still harbored doubts as to the genuinely miraculous nature of the cure.

The investigation of the case was continued in 1971 by a medical expert sent to Scotland from Rome. Professor Livio Capacaccia, a professor of gastroenterology at the University of Rome and an advisor to the Vatican on reported cases of miraculous healings, was selected to make the trip. Although Capacaccia was initially impressed by the Fagan cure after meeting with the medical panel, his conversation with Father Reilly in February convinced him that the data had to be reexamined in order to rule out several possible normal explanations that might have accounted for the cure. Capacaccia advised Father Reilly that his panel had to consider specifically whether the cure could have been due to spontaneous remission or to the dissolution of post-operative adhesions (and not cancer), which had caused a "relapse." He also questioned whether Fagan's problems had been caused by growths unrelated to the original stomach cancer and which had been cured by the patient's own immune system.

The doctors met a number of additional times and, after considerable discussion, rejected all three of Capacaccia's theories. The cancer seemed too advanced to have been able to undergo remission, and they were reasonably sure that John Fagan's relapse really was due to a metastasis from the original cancer. The only dissenting voice was that of Dr. Gerard Crean, an expert in gastrointestinal disorders from Edinburgh, who had been invited to act as a consultant to the panel. His theory was that Fagan's relapse was due to an abscess that had subsequently discharged itself, and not to a secondary cancer. Crean's theory was finally rejected on the basis that (1) Fagan was too near death to have been suffering from a simple abscess; (2) the original surgeon was ready to confirm that not all of Fagan's cancer had been removed during the surgery; and (3) Fagan's decline was consistent with his doctors' original diagnosis and prognosis. The panel could find no alternative explanation and concluded that Fagan was suffering from a secondary malignant cancer that had—for no apparent medical reason—suddenly healed of its own accord.

In May 1971, John Fagan was asked to submit to a new series of medical tests at Western General Hospital in Edinburgh. The results of these tests corroborated the panel's primary conclusions that Fagan's relapse was, according to the hospital's report, "entirely consistent with the natural history of a patient with recurrent gastric carcinoma" and that there was "no satisfactory explanation" for his recovery. The tests also showed that Fagan was now completely free from cancer.

Professor Capacaccia returned to Glasgow in October to re-evaluate personally all the evidence accumulated and speak once again with the doctors involved in the lengthy investigation. His judgment that the healing was in fact miraculous was sent to Rome. There it was analyzed yet again by authorities at the Vatican concerned with the canonization of Blessed John Ogilvie—which now rested almost solely on the documentation of the Fagan case. Pope Paul VI finally issued a decree on February 12, 1976, in which Fagan's cure was declared a miracle due to the intercession of the Scottish martyr. On October 17, 1976, John Ogilvie's name was entered onto the calendar of saints of the Roman Catholic Church.

There seems little doubt that John Fagan, Anthony Perez, and the other cases mentioned in this chapter were indeed miraculous cures. Because these healings resulted from the petitionary prayers offered by the patients' friends and relatives, it is a moot point whether the cures were brought about by the saints whose intercession was sought or whether they were actually produced by the friends and relatives themselves.

Parapsychologists have long been interested in whether such mind-over-matter powers as psychokinesis might be used to heal and have attempted to explore this question experimentally. The results of this research bear significantly on the subject of miraculous healing in general.

Pioneering research in the area has been conducted by Dr. Bernard Grad, a morphologist working at McGill University in Canada. In the late 1950s and early 1960s he implemented a series of experiments which were meant to explore the nature of so-called psychic healing. Grad undertook this project after meeting a psychic healer named Oskar Estebany, a retired Hungarian military officer who claimed that he could relieve pain and produce cures through the ancient art of the "laying on of hands." Grad was sufficiently intrigued by Estebany that he recruited him for a series of laboratory tests.

Grad's first experiment was designed to test Estebany's ability to heal goiters in mice. Grad began by feeding several mice on iodine-deficient diets, which caused goiters to develop. The mice were then housed in special cages (eight or ten mice per cage). He asked Estebany to "heal" them by merely holding the cages and concentrating on the animals. Estebany was allowed to treat the mice for only fifteen minutes per session, and only five sessions were held per week. At the end of several weeks, the goiters of the target mice were measured and compared to those of two other groups of mice fed with the same iodine-deficient diet. One group had received no treatment whatsoever, while the other had been periodically subjected to mild heat. (This was intended as a control in case Estebany accidentally warmed the target mice with heat from his hands while holding their cages. Such an application might have had a beneficial effect on the mice.)

The results of the experiment bore out Estebany's claim. Grad was able to determine that the goiters of the mice treated by Estebany had not grown as much as those afflicting the control mice. In other words, Estebany had somehow retarded the growth of the goiters merely by concentrating on them.

Grad's second experiment tested his subject's ability to heal a physical wound. He began by surgically "wounding" a number of mice by removing small patches of skin from their backs. It was Grad's theory that Estebany should be able to accelerate the process of healing, so that the target mice would heal more quickly than another group of control mice. Several wounded mice were placed in a cage, while others were isolated and left untreated. Estebany was once again allowed to hold the cages of the target mice but was permitted no direct contact with them. After each session, Grad placed pieces of cellophane over the wounds and traced them. In this way he was able to keep a day-to-day record of the progress of each mouse's wound as it healed.

It was apparent after only several days that Estebany had once again had an effect on the mice. The wounds of the target animals were all clearly healing (i.e., reducing in size) faster than those on the control group.

Grad now repeated this experiment with three hundred test animals. After they were surgically wounded, the mice were divided into three groups. One third were treated by Estebany; a skeptical medical student of Dr. Grad's played "healer" for a second third; and the remainder were left as a control group. The protocol for the experiment was roughly that of the prior study. The "healers" were allowed only to hold their hands over selected cages of mice and were told to send healing energy to the animals. Though they were occasionally allowed to hold the cages, they were at no time allowed any direct contact with the mice.

The results of the experiment were intriguing. The mice treated by Estebany again healed more quickly than the control mice. But the mice treated by the skeptical medical student healed *more slowly* than either Estebany's or the control animals. This suggested to Grad that, perhaps because of his attitude toward the experiment, the student had somehow interfered with the healing process and had actually retarded it! He had apparently used some sort of psychic power to interfere with the immune systems of the mice.

Grad was not willing to terminate his research in the face of his discomfiting findings, and soon designed yet another experiment that would deliberately consider the nature of this malign form of psychic ability. Barley seeds were planted in a series of plots and were watered with a 1 percent saline solution. Under normal conditions, this will inhibit plant growth. Tap water was substituted for one group after the seeds had germinated. The other was watered with saline solution that Estebany had treated by simply holding the beakers in which it was being stored. The results were consistent with Grad's earlier findings about Estebany's powers. The seeds that had been watered with the solution treated by Estebany grew much fuller and larger than the control plants.

Having established that a healer can influence a plant's growth rate, Grad was ready to begin his formal experiment. Three subjects were used. The first was a lab technician at McGill who Grad believed might possess healing abilities. The other two subjects were mental patients being treated in the psychiatry department of the university. Grad believed that these subjects, because of their negative or depressed personalities, might actually retard the development of the plants while attempting to treat them.

The structure of the experiment closely followed that of the pilot study Grad had run with Estebany. Barley seeds were planted and fed with a saline solution that had been carefully bottled in sealed beakers. The subjects treated several of these beakers by holding them for short periods of time.

The results of the experiment were again surprising. The plants fed water from the beakers treated by the lab assistant gave the best results and outgrew the controls. But the plants watered from the beakers held by the two mental patients showed an unusual effect. One group of plants had grown poorly—and even worse than the control plants. Those of the other patient had grown better than the controls! Grad was finally able to solve the mystery. As he reported in the *International Journal of Parapsychology* in 1964, his second mental patient had had a curious reaction when she discovered the nature of the study in which she was participating. She became elated! This positive attitude toward the experiment, believes Grad, may have released the woman's healing powers, which helped her to tend her plants.

Grad presented his conclusions about the nature of the healing process at a symposium sponsored by the American Society for Psychical Research in New York on March 18, 1974.[5] He began by dismissing the idea that the healing force is an energy unique to some people. He argued instead that a number of people, perhaps even all of us, possess the ability to *channel* some sort of cosmic life force—perhaps existing everywhere in the universe—and direct it for the purpose of healing. A healer, then, does not use his own psychic ability when he implements a cure. Grad believes he or she acts as a conduit for an omnipresent cosmic energy that is necessary for the sustenance of life on this planet.

In essence, Grad's conclusions are similar to the claims that faith healers have been making for years.* Most Christian faith healers do not believe that they possess any particular spiritual powers, but only that they are channels through which God projects his love and power. Although the nomenclature used by Grad and the faith healers may be different, the basic process they are describing is not.

Probably the best-known contemporary Christian faith healer was Kathryn Kuhlman, a Pittsburgh-based evangelist who had a worldwide reputation and following before her death a few years ago. Miss Kuhlman was born circa 1915 (she would never reveal her age) and began her career as a child evangelist in Pennsylvania. Her meetings, which were held in church and assembly halls throughout the East and Midwest, soon attracted large audiences. Her healing ministry apparently began in 1946 in Franklin, Pennsylvania, where she was conducting one of her regular services. A

---

*Grad's experiments are typical of the research parapsychologists have undertaken to test the abilities of the many psychic healers practicing in this country. These psychics have been able to alter electrical and magnetic fields, affect plant and bacterial growth, rebond water molecules, and change the blood pressure in laboratory animals. For a report on these experiments, see Stanley Krippner and Alberto Villoldo, *The Realms of Healing* (Millbrae, California: Celestial Arts, 1976).

man in the congregation stood up and testified that he had been cured of a tumor while attending the service the day before. From that day to the time of her death, prayers for cures and healings were a significant element of the Kuhlman ministry and eventually became the most important aspect of her crusade.

Miss Kuhlman often came to Los Angeles during the 1960s and 1970s, where she preached at the huge Shrine Auditorium, an assembly hall near the campus of the University of Southern California. The form of her services rarely changed. They would begin with hymn singing. The emotional pitch would grow as the singing proceeded and as assistant ministers spoke to the audiences about the ministry and the wonders that sometimes occurred during her services. When the audience had been duly warmed up, Miss Kuhlman would stride out onto the stage. In a cool, studied, and low-pitched voice, she would then begin to preach. She would usually talk about God's love, the nature of healing, and how she—Kathryn Kuhlman—was only a channel for God's love and not a miracle worker. Prayers and invocations for healing would follow as the evangelist would seem to enter a trance. She would pray intensely for healings, and would soon begin to point to specific areas in the auditorium where she intuitively felt a healing was taking place. It wouldn't be long before several people in the auditorium would jump up to announce that they had indeed been healed. Miss Kuhlman would then invite them up to the stage to testify to the audience. A physician would usually be in attendance to conduct an on-the-spot (though admittedly cursory) examination.

Dr. William Nolen, a doctor who attended several of these meetings in the early 1970s subsequently interviewed several people who felt that they had been healed through her ministry. He devotes some fifty pages to Kuhlman's cures in his skeptical book *Healing: A Doctor in Search of a Miracle* (1974).[6] After interviewing twenty-three people who claimed cures as a result of attending Miss Kuhlman's meetings, Nolen discovered that while many of them said that they subsequently felt better, no true healings could be medically documented. For example, one of Nolen's subjects, an eighteen-year-old girl whom he calls Marilyn Rogers, had developed multiple sclerosis. She subsequently attended a Kathryn Kuhlman meeting and believed that she had received a divine healing. When Nolen investigated the case he found that, while the girl was indeed feeling better, the illness was still in effect. Multiple sclerosis often tends to go into temporary remission and can also be affected by the mental state of the sufferer. Marilyn Rogers felt better after she attended the Kuhlman meeting, maintains Nolen, because she expected to. The change was unfortunately destined to be only temporary.

While Nolen was unable to find any proof of the authenticity of Kuhlman's abilities, another impartial investigation into her claims and cures had a very different outcome. In the late 1960s a reporter from the Toronto *Star* began to document Miss Kuhlman's healings. Allen Spraggett started his professional career as a minister, but left in order to turn to journalism. He subsequently became the religion editor for the *Star* and developed a strong interest in parapsychology. It was during this time that he became interested in Kathryn Kuhlman's work. Spraggett was able to track down several people who had been healed through Miss Kuhlman's ministry and who were willing to give him full access to their medical records. The results of his lengthy inquiry were published in 1970.[7]

Probably the most remarkable of these healings is that of George Orr, who was cured of an eye injury on May 4, 1947, while attending one of Miss Kuhlman's meetings in Franklin. Orr had had almost no vision in his right eye since 1925 as a result of an industrial accident. He had been working for the Laurence Foundry Co. in Grove City, Pennsylvania, where his job entailed casting molds of molten iron. A bit of the iron splashed into his eye one day and severely burned it. The injury was examined by Dr. C. E. Imbrie, who found the eye so damaged by a scar that had formed over the cornea that it was virtually nonfunctional. Orr could see only a bit over and under the scar. He petitioned the state's Department of Labor and Industry for compensation, and in 1927 the department issued an evaluation supporting the petition. Their report stated that the workman's injury was "equivalent to the loss of the use of the member for industrial use" and that "the claimant is entitled to complete compensation . . . for the loss of an eye." Dr. Imbrie testified personally at the hearing and confirmed that the damage to Orr's eye was permanent, since the burn had produced a scar that even surgery could not correct.

In March 1947 Orr and his wife drove to Franklin to attend one of Miss Kuhlman's services. They were impressed by the young evangelist and returned to hear her many times. They drove to Franklin again on May 4 with some family friends. It was at this meeting that Orr finally became convinced that spiritual healing was possible and, for the first time, actually began to pray for a healing. Within moments, he felt a tingling in his eye as though an electrical current were being passed through it. Then the eye began to tear. Orr couldn't stop the watering and was embarrassed at the tears falling onto his jacket. It wasn't until he was driving home, however, that he realized what had happened. He suddenly could see completely! When he arrived home he discovered that the scar across his eye had simply disappeared. Dr. Imbrie, who examined the eye two years later, was astonished at Orr's condition.

The Orr case is particularly significant because the healing could not have been due to any normal cause. Most of the healings that have been discussed in this chapter seem to have been the result of a paranormal acceleration of the body's own restorative powers. Such healings, while certainly inexplicable, may not be genuinely "supernatural." Because scar tissue on the eye does not simply vanish or dissolve, George Orr's cure must be considered a legitimate miracle, one that meets every criterion demanded by Lambertini in the eighteenth century. It was not of a sort that might occur naturally, Orr was under no medical treatment at the time, and the healing was instantaneous, complete, and permanent.

Another impressive cure apparently produced by Kathryn Kuhlman is that of Karen George, who was born in Conway, Pennsylvania, in 1948 with a clubfoot. The bottom of her left foot faced upward and a walnut-sized ball of flesh was embedded in its surface. The toes were pushed together as well, and the kneecap was twisted over to the side of the leg. The girl's parents were heartbroken by the deformity and received little comfort from their doctor's assessment that Karen would need several years of medical care before the condition could be corrected.

For the next five months, the Georges drove Karen to their family doctor twice a week for treatment. The foot was bandaged into place during each visit, but the treatment had no effect whatsoever. When Karen was about three months old, a brace was placed on her leg. This was only the first of several such braces, but none of them rectified the condition. The Georges went from doctor to doctor, but none of them could successfully treat the girl. Surgery was contemplated, but there was no guarantee that even that would help.

In the middle of 1948 the Georges heard about Kathryn Kuhlman and attended one of her meetings in Pittsburgh.

"During the healing part of the service," Mrs. George later told Spraggett, "Kathryn came down and asked if there was something wrong with the baby. Karen's foot was covered by a blanket so the deformity wasn't visible, but I rolled the blanket back and said she had a clubfoot.

"Kathryn took the baby in her arms and told the congregation what was wrong with her and asked them all to pray for the healing of the foot. You could see she was deeply touched. It was wonderful. After praying, she gave Karen back to me and said she was going to be all right."

Mrs. George noticed that the girl's leg began to straighten on the trip home after the service, and within two days the cure was completed. The foot assumed a normal position, the lump of flesh disappeared, and the foot grew healthily from that day forward. No further medical treatment was ever needed.

Even if the majority of Miss Kuhlman's "cures" can be dismissed, the existence of cases such as those of George Orr and Karen George prove that genuine miracles did take place during her services.

In addition to her healing powers, Kuhlman seems to have had an ability to discover clairvoyantly who in her audience was being healed. During her services she would often suddenly point to a particular area in the hall and announce that a cure was taking place there. She would even highlight these pronouncements with an occasionally detailed diagnosis of what condition was being cured and would offer a description of the recipient as well.

Dr. E. B. Henry, a physician from Pittsburgh, attended one of Kuhlman's meetings at Faith Temple in Franklin on November 19, 1950. He was skeptical and had gone only at the insistence of his wife. Henry was suffering at the time from a chronic and painful sinus condition. He was also almost totally deaf in one ear and was recovering from a broken collarbone, which after ten months had failed to heal properly. An X ray confirmed that the bone had been broken and had produced a large fleshy lump under the skin at the site of the break.

Henry sat through the service amused at the theatrics on stage. But then the evangelist entered into what appeared to be a light trance, looked directly into the area of the temple where the Henrys were sitting, and announced that a healing was taking place there. She described how "a sinus [was] opening up" and said that someone was "regaining hearing in an ear." She went on to tell of seeing a "lump the size of a walnut beginning to dissolve," and stated that the recipient of the cure was a man. Mrs. Henry immediately recognized that Miss Kuhlman was describing her husband's afflictions in detail and urged him to acknowledge the cure. But he was still skeptical and too shy to humor his wife.

During the eighty-five-mile drive back to Pittsburgh after the service, Henry suddenly realized that he could hear and breathe normally for the first time in ages. His sinus condition had cleared, and the deafness in his right ear had been corrected. Even his collarbone gradually healed, though it had stubbornly resisted more conventional treatment for many months.

This case was thoroughly documented not only by Henry himself, but also by his son-in-law, Dr. Don Gross, a psychologist and an Episcopal priest in Pittsburgh. Gross collected all the medical documents pertinent to the case and published them as part of an article that appeared in the Spring 1955 issue of *Tomorrow* magazine.

The experiences of George Orr, Karen George, and E. B. Henry make a convincing case for the existence of miracle healings. George Orr was cured of a permanent and irreversible condition. Karen George was only an infant, so her cure could not have been brought about by "the power of suggestion." And E. B. Henry was a physician himself and therefore in a perfect position to determine whether his cure was miraculous.

Not all successful spiritual healers are as untrained in formal theology and religion as Kathryn Kuhlman was, however. Perhaps the most remarkable healer today is Father Ralph Anthony DiOrio, a Catholic priest presently serving in Worcester, Massachusetts. His healing ministry began only a few years ago, but it has aroused considerable commotion within East Coast ecclesiastical circles. Many spectacular cures have been credited to him, and some are as incredible as any cases recorded in the historical literature on the subject.

Father DiOrio was born in Providence, Rhode Island, in 1930 and was ordained a Roman Catholic priest in 1957. Aside from his theology degree, he holds a B.A. in philosophy and an M.A. in education. He is a certified school psychologist, and speaks six languages. Father DiOrio approached religion from a strictly orthodox perspective until 1972. Because of his fluency in Spanish, he was assigned that year to a Hispanic congregation in the Worcester area. The congregation was dissatisfied with the traditional austerities of the Catholic ritual and service, and so they asked Father DiOrio if they could convert their services from the traditional Catholic ceremony to a more charismatic one. The charismatic movement, which was becoming popular in the Catholic Church at the time, encourages spontaneity and the expression of emotion. Charismatic services often resemble old-fashioned revival meetings more than they do conventional church ceremonies. Father DiOrio was at first taken aback by this request, but assented after receiving approval from his bishop. These new services were immensely popular, and even Father DiOrio took spirited part in them. He began performing the laying on of hands during the ceremonies and publicly called for healings. Soon healings at the church were reported.

Today Father DiOrio is the director of the Apostolate of Healing and Christian Renewal, which is formally under the auspices of the Diocese of Worcester and conducts its work with the full approval of the bishop's own board of directors. The priest holds regular healing services at St. John's Church in Worcester and also travels to other local parishes, where he heads outreach programs modeled after his St. John's meetings.

Some of the astonishing healings that have occurred at Father DiOrio's meetings have been thoroughly documented. One such cure was reported by NBC-TV's *That's Incredible* series and was aired as part of its September 29, 1980 broadcast. The feature included an impressive interview with Mr. Leo Perras from Easthampton, Massachusetts, who had been a hopeless cripple for years before meeting Father DiOrio. Perras had suffered severe back injuries as a result of an industrial accident when he was only eighteen years old. Surgery was performed to rectify the damage to his back, but the operation left him paralyzed from the waist down and confined to a wheelchair. The muscles of his legs soon atrophied as a result, and arthritis set in. Perras's condition caused him a great deal of pain, and to control it he had to take regular doses of Demerol and Percodan. Since nothing could be done for him, Perras was advised by his doctor to attend one of Father DiOrio's services. Perras was at first reluctant, but finally made the trip. By then he had been in a wheelchair for twenty-one years.

Father DiOrio took a special interest in Perras when he met him at the service, and prayed over him. The results were instantaneous. Perras told television reporters that he immediately left his wheelchair and was able to walk out of the church! All pain left him as well, and he stopped taking the medication that had been a regular part of his life for so long.

The program also contacted Perras's family doctor, Dr. Mitchell Tenerowicz, who is chief-of-staff at Cooley Dickinson Hospital in Northampton, Massachusetts. Perras had visited him soon after his healing, and the doctor was amazed that his patient was walking. He examined him and found that Perras's legs were still atrophied. There was no way, he said, that Perras was physically capable of walking. Yet there he was.

Perras's legs gradually strengthened and healed over the next few weeks. There have been no complications since the healing occurred.

That's Incredible had also researched (but did not air) another of DiOrio's remarkable cures. Mrs. David Paquin of Southbridge, Massachusetts, gave birth to a baby girl in 1976. The child was born blind in one eye, a condition due to poxiplasmosis, a disease that her mother had contracted during her pregnancy. An ophthalmologist who examined Kelly shortly after her birth told her parents that their daughter would never have vision in that eye.

During the summer of 1978, the Paquins decided to pay a call on Father DiOrio. They had heard about his ministry and found that he was visiting St. Anne's Church in Worcester at the time. They arrived at the church on a day when no healing services were planned, but Father DiOrio saw the family loitering on the walkway to the church and asked if he could be of help to them. They explained why they had come, and the priest decided to see what he could do. He began by asking Kelly if he could pray over her. The little girl said yes, and DiOrio attempted a "healing through prayer" where they stood.

The healing was almost instantaneous. Kelly regained at least some sight in her eye at that moment, and it continued to improve over the next few days. The Paquins eventually took their daughter back to their family doctor. Kelly had by this time achieved 20/40 vision in her right eye. Though the girl could clearly see, the doctor discovered that her eye was still so scarred that—medically speaking—she should have been totally blind in that eye.

These healings are notable for several reasons. In both instances the patients recovered the use of organs that should have remained useless according to the laws of biology. The healings were also either instantaneous or completed within a phenomenally short amount of time, and they cured conditions that were long-standing and considered untreatable.*

Despite the attestations of such wonder workers as Kathryn Kuhlman and Father DiOrio, it seems unlikely that the power they are able to channel in their healings is in any sense truly divine. Some psychic healers have achieved similar cures through the laying on of hands. Yet they rarely credit God as the architect of these healings and readily accept the fact that they themselves are responsible for them. As has been the case with other miracles discussed in this book, the difference between paranormal and miraculous healing is in the degree—and not the nature—of the effect. Although the miraculous may merely be a different *order* of event than the purely psychic, both are probably of the same intrinsic nature. It seems likely that healers such as Father DiOrio and Kathryn Kuhlman possess a healing capability similar to Oskar Estebany's, but to an infinitely greater degree.

A good deal has been written on the subject of psychic heal-

---

*The case of Kelly Paquin is reminiscent of an equally fascinating healing reported from Italy in 1947, when Padre Pio (see Chapters Three and Four) was asked to bless a child who had been born without pupils in her eyes. The girl was brought to Padre Pio's monastery, where he stroked her eyes. She was able to see instantly, even though to this day she still possesses no pupils. How she can see is a medical mystery. The case was widely documented by physicians in Italy at the time and created a great controversy when it was first reported.[8]

ing and healers, since these practitioners seem to be relatively common in this country.* Yet admittedly the results achieved by the majority of them differ significantly from those achieved by healers working from within a religious context. First, divine healing is often spontaneous and sudden. Psychic healing usually occurs over an extended period of time and may be fully implemented only after the patient has made several visits to a healer. Second, some miraculous healings produce "medically impossible" results. The cases of George Orr and Kelly Paquin are typical in this regard. This sort of spectacular effect is generally absent from the literature dealing with psychic healing. Third, miraculous healings are often characterized by the patient's complete recovery. Psychic healers typically report only partial recovery.

But how can one explain these differences? Why should a psychic who possesses the ability to heal produce less powerful results than a religious healer?

One solution might be that paranormal healing can come about in one of two ways. In the first instance, it can be effected by the healer himself. People such as Father DiOrio may be "superpsychics" whose powers far outreach any that parapsychologists have observed during the course of their work with more conventional psychics. Because parapsychologists have no conception of how powerful psychic powers can be when stretched to their limits, the idea that superendowed psychics exist in the world today is not beyond reason.

On the other hand, it is also conceivable that religious healers utilize a source of energy or power quite different from that tapped by more conventional psychic healers. Most psychic healers tend to believe that their powers come from within themselves and that ultimately everyone possesses the potential to heal. Yet most religious healers say that they are in no way responsible for their healings but are merely the channels for God's power. This claim may, in fact, have some truth to it. Most of the healings during Kathryn Kuhlman's and Father DiOrio's meetings have occurred spontaneously *within the setting of a large, emotional religious assembly.*

---

*See Sally Hammond, *We Are All Healers* (New York: Harper & Row, 1973), and Bill Schul, *The Psychic Frontiers of Medicine* (New York: Fawcett, 1976).

The recipients of the healings were simply "faces in the crowd." It is therefore possible that such healers do not really cure by using some power of their own, but only act as channels for some sort of spiritual energy generated by the faith of the crowds who attend their meetings. The healings performed by such religious figures as Kathryn Kuhlman may be so extraordinary simply because these healers draw and direct the enormous amount of healing energy generated by the entire assembly. This may be a force that possesses a potential far beyond that available in or to a single person.

This theory might also provide a clue to another enigma one confronts while studying religious healing. Probably more miracles are reported from healing shrines, such as Lourdes in France, than from all the world's psychic healers combined. Could it be that such shrines are conducive to healing because they have become saturated with the accumulated healing energy of the thousands of people who continually visit and pray there?

Before exploring this possibility any further, it would be best to examine in detail the history of one of these shrines. The most famous of all healing centers is the spring at Lourdes, the miraculous result of a Marian apparition over a hundred years ago.

On February 11, 1858, three little girls left the confines of the town of Lourdes in southwestern France to hunt for firewood. One of these children was Bernadette Soubirous, the illiterate daughter of an impoverished family who were long-time residents of the town. Her sister and a playmate had joined her that day. During the search the girls eventually arrived at a nearly dry mill stream. Bernadette's sister and friend quickly crossed it, but Bernadette remained behind since she was afraid of catching cold. A few moments later, as she watched her companions leave her behind, she felt a sudden gust of wind on her face. She was confused when she noticed that the wind caused no ripples in the water of the mill stream. She was even more puzzled when she saw a golden light radiating from the mouth of a rock grotto on the far side of the stream. When a white-clad apparition emerged from the grotto, Bernadette immediately fell to her knees in prayer, but the figure did not speak to her. Her companions, who had returned at about this time, were unable to see the apparition, but could only see Bernadette kneeling in front of the grotto. After she had emerged from her trance, Bernadette quickly told her playmates what had happened, but urged them not to repeat the story to anyone.

The girls couldn't contain their excitement, though, and by that night most of Lourdes was speaking of the news of the Virgin's appearance. But Bernadette's story was not taken very seriously, and even her parents considered the apparition to have been an illusion.

After the incident, Bernadette soon began to feel irresistibly drawn to return to the grotto. (She later described this feeling as a compulsion—as though she were being summoned peremptorily.) The girl returned to the scene of the apparition on February 14, followed by some of her curious neighbors. Once again she saw the figure, but the villagers couldn't see a thing and began to tease her. Though it was apparent that only Bernadette could see the apparition, the Lourdes grotto nevertheless began to attract pilgrims.

At dawn on February 18, Bernadette went there for a third time. The apparition duly revealed itself to her and spoke for the first time. The figure instructed Bernadette to continue to return to the grotto for a fortnight, and promised the girl happiness in "the next world." During the delivery of these messages, the villagers could only see Bernadette replying, and it soon became clear that the girl had entered a trance when the figure appeared. The observers became more sympathetic when they realized that Bernadette actually believed in the reality of the apparition.

The figure next appeared to Bernadette on February 20. On this occasion she taught the girl a "secret" prayer and advised her never to reveal it. By February 23, huge crowds were converging on the grotto, where a climax to the visitations came on February 25. During her ecstasy in front of the grotto that day, Bernadette suddenly rose from her knees, walked a short distance, and fell to the ground. She began to dig fervidly at the ground until a small puddle of water broke through. Over the next few days the puddle gradually formed into a pool and eventually became a spring. The discovery of the spring was generally acclaimed as a miracle in Lourdes, where now more than ever it was believed that the Virgin Mary was visiting the humble village. This belief was strengthened a week later when the apparition instructed Bernadette to tell Lourdes officials to build a chapel at the grotto.

The figure continued to appear to Bernadette even after March 4, but now less frequently. On March 25, she finally identified herself as "the Immaculate Conception."

Meanwhile, the water that was now freely flowing from the spring had become the center of another controversy. The local residents would often take flasks of it home to use as a remedy for any illness that struck them. It was soon claimed that the water possessed the power to heal.

Today the Lourdes grotto is a shrine known throughout the entire Catholic world. A church stands where the Virgin Mary originally appeared, and the water in the grotto has been channeled into a piscine where the ill may come to bathe. Public visits are regulated by officials at the shrine, who also try to keep careful records of all healing that takes place there. The organization reponsible for validating and following up any reports of such healings is the Bureau des Constatations Médicales, which is composed of physicians interested in the Lourdes cures. The BCM is interdenominational and currently maintains offices near the shrine. It also maintains an advisory committee in Paris, which sometimes goes over the records of any inexplicable cures that come to its attention. Since its founding in 1884, the BCM has periodically narrowed the criteria it uses to evaluate reports of miraculous cures.

The process leading to the pronouncement of a miracle at Lourdes is a lengthy one. When a Lourdes pilgrim believes that he has been cured, he is taken immediately to the BCM's offices where he is examined by a physician, who also takes possession of all pertinent medical data and documents the patient may have brought with him. This initial evaluation at the BCM is intended to determine whether the patient was actually sick or injured at the time of his journey, was actually cured at the shrine, and was cured in a medically inexplicable way. If the healing seems to meet these three tests, a doctor registered with the bureau in the patient's hometown or district is contacted. The patient is sent home, and the doctor there is given the responsibility of observing him for one year. This procedure serves as a precaution against the occurrence of a relapse that might not otherwise come to the attention of Lourdes officials. The doctor is also expected to interview the patient's own physician and collect any medical records from him that may bear on the case. The patient is then asked to return to Lourdes after the year has expired, at which time he is once again examined by the BCM. Only when all the doctors involved in this evaluation agree that the cure seems inexplicable is the case given candidate status as a miracle.

In making its final evaluation, the BCM looks for several characteristics that they consider differentiate a miraculous healing from a biological one. They verify that the cure was instantaneous, that it led to the termination of the patient's convalescence, that it wasn't consistent with the normal process the condition in question undergoes while healing biologically, and that it occurred at a time when the patient was no longer receiving any conventional treatment. Also subject to this careful analysis are cases in which a damaged limb or organ—such as a permanently damaged eye—is miraculously restored to use.

The discrimination of the BCM is evident when one examines some of its statistics. Seventy-five cures were accepted by the bureau in 1947 as being possibly due to paranormal causes, but only eleven of them were reevaluated at the end of a year. Six were ultimately selected for further study and possible documentation. In 1948 only eighty-three cases met the BCM's initial criteria; fifteen of these were reevaluated at the end of twelve months. Six cases were rejected at that time.[9]

Probably the most authoritative study in English of the Lourdes cures has been made by Ruth Cranston, a Protestant writer who made repeated visits to the shrine and was given full access to the BCM's files. These records served as the basis for her book *The Miracle of Lourdes* (1955).[10]

A typical case documented by Cranston is that of Charles McDonald of Dublin. McDonald, who had been healthy and athletically inclined all his life, fell ill in 1924. He suddenly became tired and irritable, and a chronic cough slowly set in. A subsequent X-ray examination showed that he was suffering from tuberculosis. He was sent to a sanatorium in April 1925, where he stayed for five weeks and where his condition seemed to improve. He emigrated to South Africa and became ill again in 1931. A medical examination made at that point revealed that his previous condition had flared up again and that he was now suffering from tuberculosis of the twelfth thoracic vertebra. McDonald returned to

Dublin in June 1932 and learned that surgery couldn't relieve his problem. His health gradually worsened. Gross complications and secondary ailments set in, and by November 1935 his condition was so bad that he entered a hospice for the dying.

With no hope left, McDonald turned to religion, and in September 1936 he made a pilgrimage to Lourdes. He was so ill that he had to travel on a stretcher. Any movement caused him intense pain, and his chances for recovery seemed nil. His medical diagnosis at this time was Pott's disease of the twelfth dorsal vertebra, nephritis, and tubercular arthritis of the left shoulder.

McDonald arrived in Lourdes on September 5, and the next morning was taken to the shrine, where he was immersed in the piscine. He immediately felt greater mobility than he had during the last several months of his illness. Although he was up and about by the next day, his lack of exercise made walking difficult. All pain eventually ceased and McDonald returned to Ireland, where an examination revealed that his tuberculosis, nephritis, and arthritis had all cleared up.

McDonald returned to Lourdes in September 1937, and he and his medical files were scrutinized by thirty-two doctors at the BCM. Among the records was a statement from the patient's own doctor testifying that there could be no doubt that McDonald had gone to Lourdes suffering from an advanced tubercular condition with complications. The conclusions of the bureau on the case of Charles McDonald was based on the opinion that it met four of their five criteria for a miraculous healing. (Their fifth criterion, concerning the restoration of an irreparably damaged organ or limb, was irrelevant.) Their report read, in part:

> Charles McDonald has been afflicted with (1) tuberculosis of the left shoulder with three fistulas; (2) tuberculosis of the dorsal spine with two fistulas; (3) chronic nephritis characterized by the presence of pus, blood, albumin. These three conditions were in full evolution at the moment of the pilgrimage to Lourdes, the five fistulas giving off pus.
>
> They were abruptly halted in their evolution on September 7. An immediate functional healing after a bath in the piscine was followed in less than four days by a definite cicatrization of the five fistulas, of return of normal urinary secretion rid of its infectious germs; cessation of pain, return of partial movements of the left arm and lumbar region.
>
> This healing, obtained without the use of medicaments or of any

therapeutic agent whatever is confirmed by one year of excellent health and work. . . . No medical explanation, in the present state of science, can be given; considering the extraordinary rapidity of the healing of these tuberculous affections, judged incurable by the specialists called in to treat him, and whose beginning was noted by general infection, later by bony localizations. This healing is written down as on the margin of the laws of biology.

McDonald's healing was exceptional. However, the most unusual cures reported from Lourdes are those in which a diseased organ—such as an eye, an ear, a paralyzed limb—will suddenly begin to function again *while remaining damaged to such an extent that it couldn't possibly perform physiologically.* Several such instances have been documented within recent years.

A fairly recent example of the phenomenon is the strange case of Gerard Baillie, an eight-year-old who was cured of blindness at Lourdes in September 1947. Gerard had been left sightless at the age of two from a condition known as bilateral chorioretinitis with double optic atrophy. His optic nerves, which were incapable of regeneration, were completely deteriorated. His condition was therefore irreversible. His parents had even placed him in the Institute for Blind Children in Arras, a town in the south of France. Despite the hopelessness of the case, Mme Baillie brought the boy to Lourdes. Although nothing happened when Gerard was first immersed in the healing waters of the shrine, he suddenly regained sight in both eyes a day later. The boy was immersed in the Lourdes water again the day after his cure, and his sight continued to improve. The Lourdes medical bureau was so impressed with the case that they had the boy examined by an ophthalmologist in the city of Tarbles in order to study the healing further. The ophthalmologist certified that the boy's optic nerves were still atrophied and could not understand how the child could see. Yet it was quite apparent that he *could see*—and quite well at that! Gerard ultimately left the home for the blind, went to school, and still leads a normal life today.

An even more astonishing case is that of Guy Leydet, a pathetic French five-year-old who had been stricken with infantile encephalopathy. This disease of the brain had left him a quadraplegic, subject to convulsions, and so brain damaged that he was unable to speak, recognize people around him, or care for himself. He was taken to Lourdes by his family and was bathed at the shrine on October 6, 1946. Immediately after his immersion, Guy began to speak intelligibly. His condition steadily improved over the next several days; he regained the use of his limbs, and even his intelligence reached a normal level.

Despite the BCM's certification that the cases of Gerard Baillie and Guy Leydet were medically inexplicable, neither was ever declared a miracle by the Church. Gerard's cure was rejected since it was neither complete nor spontaneous. (His eyesight functioned adequately, but never became perfect.) In the Leydet case, Guy's family doctor would not release crucial records needed for documentation. That neither of these cases was formally declared "miraculous" does not alter the fact that the healings actually took place. In fact, one doctor at BCM said of the Leydet healing that he would pledge "never again to sign a Lourdes dossier" if any of his colleagues had "ever once in his whole career seen a cure of such a case."

The incidence of such remarkable cures has not prevented the development of a heated controversy over Lourdes within the medical establishment, however. Because not all the cures declared medically inexplicable by the BCM are as clear-cut as the Baillie and Leydet examples, some medical experts have questioned the validity of many of them. One such skeptic is Dr. Donald J. West, a British psychiatrist and parapsychologist. In his 1957 study of many of the Lourdes healings, *Eleven Lourdes Miracles,* West concluded that most of the cures were of conditions that are extremely sensitive to psychosomatic influences. Cancer and tuberculosis were chief among them. These diseases can easily be affected by the patient's moods and emotional well-being.[11] West therefore argues that because improvement and complete remission can result from such changes in mood,* many of the Lourdes cures might actually be due solely to the positive feelings a patient experiences after a visit there. He also found that the

---

*For strong evidence supporting the holistic theory of healing, refer to *Getting Well Again* (Los Angeles: Tarcher, 1978) by O. Carl Simonton, Stephanie Mathews-Simonton, and James Creighton. The authors cite medical evidence that many diseases, especially cancer, may be triggered by psychological trauma and can be cured or remitted through the psychotherapeutic treatment of the patient.

original diagnoses of many subsequently cured visitors to Lourdes may have been based either on conjecture or on possible error.

West analyzed eleven recent Lourdes miracles in his report and was able to reject all on a medical basis alone. While admitting that some of the cures might be considered "faith healings" of a sort, he did not consider any of them to be miraculous or even medically inexplicable.

It is fascinating to compare West's findings with Ruth Cranston's, which were published only two years earlier, since both authors cite some of the same alleged healings in their opposing arguments.

One such case was that of Rose Martin, a Frenchwoman from Nice who was diagnosed as suffering from cancer of the uterus in November 1945. A hysterectomy was performed the following February at the Pasteur Hospital in Nice, and a biopsy made at the time confirmed the malignant nature of the condition. Mme Martin was reexamined at the hospital in April 1947 when she began to show what appeared to be complications arising from her cancer. She was suffering acute constipation, and a growth the size of a small orange was found within her rectum. Her health deteriorated so quickly that she was soon confined to her bed. By this time she was emitting fetid discharges from the rectum. Mme Martin's doctors diagnosed the problem as a metastasis of the original uterine cancer into the rectum. They declared her case untreatable, gave her repeated injections of morphine to control her constant pain, and waited for her to die.

Though she was totally bedridden, Mme Martin undertook a trip to Lourdes in June 1947. She was bathed at the piscine three times, and after the last visit on July 3, she took a remarkable turn for the better and was soon capable of walking about. The fetid discharges stopped and her appetite returned to normal. A medical examination undertaken by her physician in Nice showed that the growth in her rectum had completely disappeared and that her rectal and vaginal tissues were completely normal. The BCM, which reviewed the case at a meeting of its medical panel on February 27, 1949, issued a report stating, in part, that they were "in agreement with the *rapporteur*, that this case has no natural scientific explanation."

While researching the Lourdes cures, Mrs. Cranston was able

to locate Rose Martin in Nice. Rose told her that doctors had given her only three months to live and that her husband had been trained to give her constant injections of painkiller. She weighed only seventy pounds at the time of her trip, although her normal weight was about eighty pounds more! Rose said that she could actually feel herself being cured during her third immersion at Lourdes, and described it as feeling like something "moving inside" her body. Mrs. Cranston also located Rose's doctor, who verified that his former patient had been suffering from an inoperable condition at the time of her pilgrimage.

The same evidence for Rose Martin's cure is assessed negatively by West. He points out that because no formal biopsy was made when Rose returned to the Pasteur Hospital in 1947, her relapse may in fact have been due to a postoperative infection that gradually cleared of its own accord. He also cites the pertinent fact, overlooked by Mrs. Cranston, that a nurse at Lourdes had surreptitiously given Rose harmless camphor injections instead of morphine to reduce her pain. Rose had responded positively to the placebo, indicating that she was highly suggestible and probably in much better health than she thought. Withholding the morphine may even have resulted in the sudden alleviation of the patient's constipation.

Did Rose Martin receive a miraculous healing? As one analyzes the medical controversy over the healings at Lourdes, this question seems less of an issue than whether the cures are really backed by irreproachable documentation. Although West has certainly shown that many cases declared "medically inexplicable" by the BCM can *sometimes* be explained medically, it is also true that his study is *very* selective. West limits himself to an examination of only a handful of cases. He then extends his conclusions to discredit all reported miracles that have occurred at Lourdes. In so doing he overlooks some of the famous historical cures reported from the shrine. He neglects, for instance, such crucial cases as the Baillie and Leydet healings and similar cures that involved a miraculous restoration of a permanently damaged and useless limb or organ. Yet these are the most important cases upon which an argument can be made for Lourdes and for miraculous healings in general. What West has shown most convincingly is that many spontaneous cures at Lourdes are extremely difficult to document adequately—not that the mystery of the Lourdes healings can be "explained away."

Cases of miraculous restorations are admittedly rare, but no study of divine healing is complete without them. Had the case of Pierre de Rudder come to Dr. West's attention, his attitude toward the subject may have been modified.

The healing of Pierre de Rudder is perhaps the best documented of all the cures related to Lourdes. While the healing did not actually take place at the Lourdes shrine, it is directly relevant to the Lourdes controversy.

Pierre de Rudder was a Belgian peasant who lived in Jabbeke, a town near Bruges. In 1868 he fell from a tree and broke his leg so badly that bone fragments had to be taken from the wound. The leg was so damaged that it couldn't be set back together, and the break was so complete that over an inch separated the upper and lower parts of the bone at the site of the injury. The lower portion of the leg dangled freely, held in place only by skin and muscle tissue. The condition was extremely painful. The only recourse was amputation, but de Rudder refused to consider it. He lived with his pain for eight years before deciding to make a pilgrimage to Oostacker, a city near Ghent where a statue in honor of Our Lady of Lourdes had been erected. Before making this journey, he was once again examined by a physician in his hometown, Dr. van Hoestenberghe, who found that an open wound was still unhealed at the site of the original break and that one could actually see that the two sections of bone were separated by over three centimeters. The doctor found no sign of healing, and his patient was still in great pain. The lower portion of the leg could be freely gyrated in all directions and could even be folded upward.

The train ride to Ghent caused de Rudder no end of agony. He had to be lifted onto the train by three helpers, and the discharge of blood and pus from his wound was so offensive that he was almost removed from the omnibus going from Ghent to Oostacker.

Though de Rudder was in a terrible state by the time he arrived in Oostacker, he began to pray earnestly before the statue. He asked that his sins be forgiven and, should he be unable to provide for his family, that his children be able to manage without having to rely on charity. While rapt in prayer, de Rudder felt a sudden change come over him. In a fit of ecstasy he stood up without the aid of his crutches and began to walk toward the statue! It was only then that he realized that he had been cured. His leg bone had immediately and quite inexplicably fused together and the wound had healed. De Rudder was able to return to his home a healed man.

Everyone in Jabbeke was shocked at de Rudder's condition. Not the least was Dr. van Hoestenberghe. He subsequently wrote a letter to officials in Lourdes in which he testified:

Pierre is undoubtedly cured. I have seen him many times during the last eight years, and my medical knowledge tells me that such a cure is absolutely inexplicable. Again, he has been cured completely, suddenly, and instantaneously, without any period of convalescence. Not only have the bones been suddenly united, but a portion of bone would seem to have been actually created to take the place of those fragments I myself have seen come out of the wound. But if a miracle, then there is something beyond law—a God exists, and surely He must have given some revelation of Himself.

Dr. van Hoestenberghe did not have an opportunity to explore fully the nature of de Rudder's cure until 1900. De Rudder had died of pneumonia in 1898, and van Hoestenberghe was given permission to exhume his body two years later. He amputated both of de Rudder's legs and photographed them. These photos clearly show that the two parts of de Rudder's leg bone had been fused together by *a new piece of healthy bone over an inch long that had formed, apparently instantaneously, over its broken ends.* Such growth or regeneration of bone is medically unprecedented. The normal formation of bone is a very slow process, and since van Hoestenberghe had examined de Rudder's leg shortly before his pilgrimage, its new segment could not have formed normally.[12]

Today de Rudder's leg bones are preserved at the University of Louvain in Belgium. Copper molds of them are also preserved at the BCM's offices in Lourdes. The case caused a sensation in

Europe when it was originally reported and has never been medically explained.*

Another shrine where miraculous cures have been known to occur is a healing center dedicated to Our Lady of Lourdes in Istanbul, Turkey. Supernatural cures were also reported by witnesses who traveled to St. Mary's Church in Zeitoun when apparitions of the Virgin Mary started occurring there in 1968. Some of these healings were documented by a special investigatory commission sent to Zeitoun by Coptic Church officials in Egypt and Turkey. The church in Knock, Ireland, where an apparition of the Virgin was seen in 1879, is also visited by the infirm and ill. A medical bureau modeled after the one at Lourdes has been established to investigate cures there.

Once again, there seems to be nothing truly divine about the healings that take place at these centers, though the cures are certainly "miraculous" in every sense of the word. It is likely that shrines such as Lourdes have become so spiritually charged over the years by the prayers of the pilgrims who have visited them, that they have become dynamos of healing power. Anyone who visits these shrines and who is sensitive to the psychic forces generating there may well receive a cure.

This suggestion was also made in the 1950s by Dr. Leslie Weatherhead, a noted British psychologist and Methodist clergyman, to account for the Lourdes cures. It was his theory that through their faith and prayers the many pilgrims who regularly visit Lourdes have created a "spiritual atmosphere" there which possesses the power to heal. Dr. Weatherhead also theorized that if this atmosphere could be recreated at another such shrine, healings would probably take place there as well.[13]

---

*The de Rudder case is similar to one reported anecdotally by Kathryn Kuhlman in her book I Believe in Miracles. James McCutcheon, whose thighbone had been damaged in a railroad accident, had undergone surgery on five occasions, during which doctors unsuccessfully tried to fasten the femur to the shaft. A decalcification of the bone eventually set in. Sometime later McCutcheon attended a healing service conducted by Miss Kuhlman. In the course of the service he experienced a tingling and burning sensation in his hip which jolted him upright. Then he stood without his crutches! Subsequent X rays showed that new bone, which apparently formed instantaneously, had fused over the shaft and femur and had reconnected the bones.

CONCLUSION

~ XII ~
PSYCHE
AND THE MIRACULOUS

MIRACLES come in so many different guises, forms, and manifestations that it is difficult to make any purely general closing comments about them. It certainly isn't feasible to explain the actual physical mechanisms by which miracles occur in the material world of our five senses. It is highly unlikely that orthodox science and technology are sophisticated enough to explain the physics of the miraculous.

It would instead be more useful to review the major themes that have been presented during the course of this book. One of these is that most religious miracles have purely secular analogues that occur within the world of psychic phenomena. The phantom faces of Dean Liddell and Dean Vaughan that appeared on the walls of their respective churches do not seem too dissimilar from the puzzling faces that appeared on the floor of Señora Pereira's "haunted house" in Bélmez, Spain. The bilocating feats of Padre Pio and Natuzza Evolo closely resemble the exploits of such gifted astral travelers as Blue Harary and Mrs. Lucian Landau. And the levitations of such great saints as Joseph of Copertino and Teresa of Avila are comparable to the feats of the equally great fakirs of the East and some of the famous mediums of the Victorian age.

Relatively few "miraculous" talents actually seem by nature to be exclusively religious. The only exception might be the stigmata, a miracle that remains strictly Christian because of its historical connection with veneration of the figure of the crucified Christ. The majority of the other gifts of the saints are usually forms of phenomena that have been observed and studied by psychical researchers for many years. In *The Physical Phenomena of Mysticism,* Thurston provides a codification of several of these supernatural religious abilities. He includes such miracles as levitation, the stigmata, fire immunity, the emission of light from the body, inedia, the multiplication of food, and the emission of the "odor of sanctity." Yet if one were to catalogue the feats being performed by psychics living today as well as those produced by the great Victorian mediums, a very similar list would result. Thurston was himself aware of this fact, which explains his reluctance to believe that anything truly supernatural (as opposed to simply psychic or paranormal) was responsible for many of these "miraculous" talents.

Even some rare abilities which are commonly attributed solely to the saints and mystics of the Church have been demonstrated by psychics here in the West in recent years. The "odor of sanctity," for example, is a phenomenon that has been recorded all through the history of Catholicism. Teresa of Avila was known to impregnate her habit and other clothing she wore with a delightful perfume that apparently exuded from her body. St. Veronica Giuliani was a stigmatic and mistress of novices at a Capuchin convent in Umbria. When her stigmatic wounds opened, many of her sister nuns testified that the resulting blood was scented with a beautiful aroma. A similar perfume apparently emanated from Padre Pio's stigmata. The priest was famous for his "odor of sanctity," and many people who met him during his years at San Giovanni Rotondo reported smelling this fragrance when visiting him. Sometimes this aroma would suddenly permeate a room he was in, would then vanish just as mysteriously. On some occasions it smelled like violets, while on others it had the fragrance of fine incense. Sister Giovanna Maria della Croce was a seventeenth-century nun who lived much of her life at a convent in Rovedero, Italy. Her companions could often discern that one of her fingers emanated a wonderful aroma which would imbue anything with which it came into contact. On rarer occasions the odor would be produced by her entire body, especially just after she had taken communion. Blessed Maria degli Angeli, an eighteenth-century Carmelite nun who lived and died in Turin, emitted a perfume that would linger for days in any house in which she lived or even visited.[1]

But to describe this emanation as an "odor of sanctity" is a complete misnomer, since the phenomenon probably has little to do with sanctity. It can even occur in homes plagued by poltergeist attacks. Nandor Fodor encountered one such odoriferous spirit in 1938 during one of his poltergeist hunts in England. The poltergeist focused on an extremely neurotic and unhappy housewife whom he called Mrs. Forbes in all his reports on the case. Mrs. Forbes lived with her husband in the Thornton Heath suburb of London. The case had first come to public attention when stories about the "haunted house of Thornton Heath" were reported in several London newspapers. Fodor investigated the matter while the poltergeist was still active. It was of the typical "object-throwing" variety, and he was able to witness a great deal of its mischief. The unusual aspect of this case was that a rather strong or even violent aroma of violets would sometimes waft through the house. (Fodor suspected that Mrs. Forbes might have counterfeited it, but never accumulated any evidence to support the idea.) In his investigation into the psychological cause of the outbreak, Fodor came to believe that Mrs. Forbes herself was psychically producing the attacks in a desperate attempt to vent deeply repressed hostility against her husband. This hostility seems to have originated in a sexual trauma she had experienced as a child at the hands of her father.[2]

A phenomenon similar to the "odor of sanctity" is also noted in traditional yogic literature. In his book *The Other Side of Death*, Raymond Bayless reports the case of Attila von Szalay, a psychic whose powers didn't fully develop until he began studying yoga. Von Szalay was born in New York but moved to Los Angeles during the 1940s. Bayless met him in 1949 and spent several years studying his abilities. Von Szalay was undergoing out-of-body experiences, seeing apparitions, and even spontaneously entering altered states of consciousness and reality. He also found himself experiencing wondrous perfumes. These odors would either precipitate in the rooms or public places he was visiting or would seem to exude from his own body. The odors were intensely sweet, though on occasion they could be less appealing.

One of the incidents Bayless recounts concerns an unusual visit he paid to von Szalay in 1952:

On one occasion we were sitting in his studio discussing psychism when a great outpouring of a sweet scent occurred. It continued for perhaps a few minutes and, in searching for the source of the scent, I dis-

covered that it actually came from Mr. von Szalay's chest. He opened his
shirt at my request, and I was able to determine that it was pouring from
a small area on his chest exactly as though a faucet which provided scent
had been turned on. The odor became so powerful that his entire studio
became saturated with it. Then, as suddenly as it came, it ceased.[3]

While von Szalay is certainly gifted with psychic abilities, it
would be inaccurate to consider him holy or ascetic. His "odor of
sanctity" appears instead to be a byproduct of his yogic training,
just as the "odor of sanctity" displayed by the great mystics of the
Church may be more a result of *their* psychic abilities than a grace
specifically granted because of their holiness.

The same explanation can be offered to account for one of
the most unusual of all miracles recorded in the history of Christianity—the multiplication of food. This is an extremely rare phenomenon, and even Thurston could find only a handful of
documented cases in the hagiographic records of the Catholic
Church. (His chapter on the subject in *The Physical Phenomena
of Mysticism*—the shortest in the book—spans only twelve pages.)
Even the ordinarily reserved Lambertini considered this great miracle to be genuinely divine. He was able to cite examples of the
miracle by drawing upon the lives of St. Teresa of Avila, St. Rose
of Lima, and St. Clare of Assisi, among others.

Perhaps the best-documented multiplication of food witnessed within relatively modern times was recorded during the life
of St. John Bosco (1815–88), who was canonized in 1934.[4] He
is best remembered today for his ministry among the underprivi-
leged children in Turin, which paved the way for important
changes in Italy's educational system. Don Bosco was atypical
among the great saints of the Church in that he was not naturally
prone to ecstasies or visions. Although he may have been more
interested in social reform than in mystical contemplation, he was
apparently intensely psychic and performed many miracles during
his lifetime.

The incident in question occurred in 1860, by which time
Don Bosco had founded a boardinghouse for wayward youths in
Turin which he ran with the help of his mother. A young boy
named Francisco Dalmazzo, who was staying at the house, later
testified to Church officials that Don Bosco was informed one

morning that there weren't enough rolls to provide breakfast for the three hundred children under his care. Don Bosco was hearing Dalmazzo's confession when the news was delivered to him, but he appeared unperturbed and merely instructed the house matrons to gather up all the food that was available. He promised to come personally to the refectory to distribute it.

Dalmazzo sensed that something unusual was going to happen and went to the refectory after his confession:

I found a place where I could overlook the scene, just behind Don Bosco, who was preparing to distribute the rolls (*pagnottelle*) to the 300 lads as they came up. I fixed my eyes upon the basket at once, and I saw that it contained fifteen or twenty rolls at the most. Meanwhile, Don Bosco carried out the distribution, and to my great surprise, I saw the same quantity remain which had been there from the first, though no other rolls had been brought and the basket had not been changed.

Dalmazzo watched in amazement as Don Bosco distributed some three hundred rolls from the little basket. It is quite clear from his deposition that the boy had observed this miracle for a lengthy period of time and was most impressed by it.

It is difficult to believe that Don Bosco performed this miracle, which certainly seems to have been supernatural, merely through the agency of his own psychic abilities. Yet in fact a similar "miracle" was performed in San Francisco in the 1930s by a man who made no claim whatsoever about possessing divine gifts. He apparently did, however, have the ability to multiply food, and even demonstrated his gift to several friends and acquaintances.

Dr. Philip S. Haley, a dentist who later became a prominent amateur psychic investigator in the Bay Area, issued a privately printed book entitled *Modern Loaves and Fishes—and Other Studies in Psychic Phenomena* (1935; revised 1960), which describes his experiments. Haley begins his chapter on the multiplication of food by describing how he originally became interested in the subject. He had studied both religion and psychical research for some years and had apparently succeeded in developing his own psychic powers. He had also come to believe that the various miracles described in the Bible were true and had been produced through the psychic powers of Jesus and the great prophets. Since by this time he considered himself psychic, Haley began to investigate whether he could perform a miracle as elaborate as the multiplication of food.

His fascination with the psychic replication of food was further aroused when food in his home began to regenerate itself spontaneously as his interest in the subject increased. First, some oranges he had carefully stored away in a cupboard suddenly increased their number. Then new pieces of lighter-colored wood would appear in his cache of firewood, one after another.

Haley soon realized that he had to find a way to control his apparent ability to multiply food so that he could produce the phenomenon under experimental conditions. In the early 1930s he started a series of short tests along these lines. It is not clear how long he experimented before achieving any successful results, but the following extract from Haley's book will give an idea of how these tests were conducted. The account is drawn from an experiment conducted on May 22, 1933, in which Haley, his wife, and an anonymous friend took part:

We had decided to fast before attempting this experiment, and did so, Mrs. Haley and "X" having eaten nothing since the evening meal on the previous day. I had taken three cups of coffee during the preceding thirty-six hours, omitting all other food. Not being accustomed to fasting, my two sitters had slight headaches, so they reclined on a couch at the northeast corner of the dining room.

I prepared ten slices of apple and seven slices of bread in the kitchen, placed them on a plate, and carried them into the dining room. I had counted them most carefully, two or three times as I prepared them, so that I was sure of the number. I purposely cut the pieces thick, from firm food, to prevent fracturing. When I reached the couch where my sitters were, we counted again, and to my amazement I noted that the bread had increased to eight pieces! We counted together carefully, and checked this fact, so that we agreed on the amount of food to start with.

We then read briefly from the Bhagavad Gita and recited the Lord's Prayer, after which we began to eat, except for myself, since I meant to continue my fast until the following morning. Both sitters ate two pieces of apple, and in addition Mrs. Haley ate two pieces of bread. We counted the food remaining after the repast, repeating, as usual, until quite sure of the amount, and noted nine pieces of apple and seven of bread.

Haley conducted over twenty successful experiments between 1933 and 1934, some of which were witnessed by as many as five friends. Stewart Edward White, a famous novelist who later turned to psychic research when his wife developed psychic abilities, observed several of these replications.

Was Philip Haley actually able to multiply food? Since he died recently, it is no longer possible to test his abilities under scientifically controlled conditions. However, there seems good reason to believe that he was absolutely sincere about his claims. Haley never tried to reap any benefits from his experiments. He made no money from them, and did not lecture about them. His book itself is scientifically written. His experiments are described to the point of tedium, and he even included statements from several witnesses who had verified his observations, as well as graphs, weight indexes of the multiplied food, and photographs of it. This rigorous attention to detail suggests that he expected his book to be read only by serious students of the psychic field, and not necessarily by the public. During the 1930s, Haley also sent private reports of his experiments to the American Society for Psychical Research in New York. He did not submit these for publication, but merely to inform other researchers about his work. Taking all these factors into consideration, it seems reasonable to conclude that Haley was a sincere experimenter who fully believed in his work.

The second theme in this book was to show that the talent to perform a miracle may be a natural human potential, not just the province of saints and mystics. A complementary theme is that while the great saints of the Catholic Church were probably genuinely psychic, no single world religion has a franchise on the miraculous. Catholicism's saints; the fakirs and holy men of the East; the shamans of Alaska, Africa, and Mongolia; the witch doctors of the American Indians—all possess similar abilities. The occurrence of miracles within a particular religious tradition does not therefore prove the ultimate and exclusive truth of that belief system. The bilocations of Natuzza Evolo and Padre Pio no more establish the superiority of Christianity than do the bilocations of Satya Sai Baba and Dadaji demonstrate the preeminence of Hinduism. In fact, the miraculous talents of the saints seem to be almost indistinguishable from those of the holy men of other religions and cultures.

For example, although this book has included little discussion of the miracles of Islam, its traditions in this area closely parallel those of Christianity. Each claims that its founder worked miracles, and each subsequently produced saints who have been credited with performing similar feats.

Islam was founded in the seventh century by Mohammed (570—632 A.D.), who was born in Mecca and was originally a businessman who conducted caravans for a living. He led a respectable life as a merchant for several years. His first religious revelation came when he was about forty years old. He was meditating in a cave outside Mecca when he had a mystical experience during which he found himself in direct contact with God. Mohammed returned to the cave several times and decided to enter upon the life of a prophet. He began preaching in Mecca, but his message—that his people should give up their licentious ways and adopt an extreme form of monotheism—was not at all popular. He was harassed, imprisoned, and finally expelled by the city's political authorities. Despite this suppression, Mohammed was able to bring together a great number of converts, whom he took to Yasbith, a city some two hundred miles from Mecca, in 622 A.D. Mohammed soon proved himself to be an able political leader, and a rivalry developed between the Moslems in Yasbith and the political establishment in Mecca for control of Arabia. After several years of military confrontations, the Moslems gained control of the country.

Mohammed was claimed to be both a prophet and a miracle worker, and the miracles attributed to him are taken on faith by Moslems today just as the miracles recorded in the New Testament are accepted by many Christians. Moslem tradition teaches that Mohammed possessed the ability to know clairvoyantly when someone had died, discern a person's name without asking it, open the flesh of his body, and heal the sick.[5] In short, Mohammed was credited with performing many of the same miracles that Jesus and his disciples reputedly performed, and which later became the miraculous talents of the saints.

Unlike the miracles of the New Testament, however, those of Mohammed rest on a verbal tradition, which was not set down until circa 720 A.D. and was made formal only circa 775 A.D., almost 150 years after Mohammed's death. This delay in transcription has led some theologians who accept the miracles of the New Testament to question the authenticity of Mohammed's miracles. Father Robert D. Smith's objections are typical:

It was not until a full century later [after the eighth century] that complete written collections were to be made of all traditions including those reporting signs worked by Mohammed.

Thus, two and one half centuries after the beginning of the Moslem Era, the work of collecting, in writing, all the accepted traditions containing reports of miracles was finally completed. There is not even a single tradition or group of traditions of which we can affirm with any degree of likelihood that it was written before the end of the first century A.H. [anno hegirae] Nor is there any document dating from the first century of Islam which verifies any of the miraculous facts in the traditions. We cannot show that any of these reports were written and circulated in a fixed form while the witnesses of the events were still alive. Because of this, we can have no assurance that any of them were actually checked with and verified by these alleged witnesses.[6]

Although Smith's criticisms about the unreliability of Moslem oral tradition are cogent, he overlooks the important and obvious point that the miracles reported in the Christian and early Moslem traditions are extremely similar. If the tales of Mohammed's alleged miracles are merely based on legend or folklore, why would they parallel so closely the documented miracles of the Catholic Church and the very type of effects studied today by parapsychologists? The best explanation for this resemblance is that miracles of a similar sort *did* occur during the early years of both religions.

The similarity between the Christian and Islamic supernatural tradition becomes even greater when one studies the wonders allegedly performed by the saints and visionaries of the Moslem faith. Clément Huart, a French anthropologist, made a major study of the miracles allegedly performed by the Islamic holy men of Iran in his two-volume work *Les Saints des Derviches tourneurs: Recits traduits du persan* (1918–22). After examining the hagiographic records of the Moslem saints, Huart listed the following miracles that they were known to perform:

(1) an awareness of events occurring in a distant place
(2) the emanation of a radiance from their bodies
(3) fire immunity
(4) an ability to disappear from one area and turn up in another instantaneously
(5) becoming invisible at will
(6) bilocation
(7) levitation

Each of these miracles has been similarly chronicled in Catholic hagiography. Thurston specifically discusses divine radiance, fire immunity, levitation, and, to a lesser degree, bilocation in *The Physical Phenomena of Mysticism*. Such contemporary mystics as Padre Pio, Therese Neumann, Natuzza Evolo, and others have been known to display telepathic and clairvoyant powers. Even the ability to become invisible is mentioned now and then in Catholic literature. In his biography of Padre Pio, Father Charles Carty cites at least one case in which the priest used this gift to avoid some visitors he didn't want to see! [7]

It should be clear from these comparisons that it would be fruitless to argue that the miracles of Jesus and the saints demonstrate the supremacy of Christianity, since adherents of other world religions could make equally valid claims for the divinity of their own revered sacred individuals.

Now we come to the third theme that has been emphasized in this book. If we accept that an individual human mind can indeed produce miracles, then the psychic capabilities of a whole group of minds acting in consort must be immense. Miracles may potentially occur when large crowds of people who share a common religious background and a similar world view come together to worship. Their combined faith and emotion may somehow become psychokinetically linked to the world around them. Miracles may be the result. Religious revivals—especially energetic and emotional ones—may be especially susceptible to the production of signs and wonders.

A recent miracle of this sort occurred in the Dominican Republic on March 29, 1972, during a highly emotional open-air Mass that was being held in the courtyard of Arroyo Hondo College. The meeting had been instigated by Sra. Luciana Pelaéz de

Suero, a forty-year-old Catholic charismatic leader and healer whose work has been highly regarded in her country. The service, which began at about 5:00 P.M., was attended by over a thousand people. The priest saying Mass opened the ceremony by beseeching the crowd to pray for healings. At the very moment Sra. de Suero fell into a trance during the communion service, a huge glowing disc appeared in the sky. The disc resembled the moon, but was yellow and seemed to pulsate. Since the moon appeared in the sky at the same time, there can be no doubt that the disc was an independent object. It had emerged from behind a large dark cloud, behind which it sank and ultimately disappeared.

Sebastian Robiou Lamarche, a ufologist from Puerto Rico, traveled to the Dominican Republic shortly after learning of the occurrence and interviewed several people who had witnessed the event. In 1972 he published a report on the incident in which he quoted eyewitness testimony, including that of the priest who performed the Mass.[8]

The glowing disc in the Dominican Republic may have been related to a "cloud of fire" that was seen in Ireland in 1859 at an open-air revival meeting being held in a small country town. About six hundred to one thousand people were assembled when a curious radiant cloud suddenly appeared in the sky and floated above the congregation. It hovered for quite some time and then quickly ascended and drifted away. The brightness of the cloud filled the revivalists with awe.[9]

Similar lights were seen all over Wales in 1904 and 1905, a period when a religious revival movement was spreading across the country. The revival was the result of widespread social degeneration which had occurred in the wake of the decline of the established church. One of the most popular evangelists of the Great Welsh Revival was Mary Jones, a thirty-five-year-old housewife who had been converted in 1904. She began preaching in her hometown of Egryn in North Wales, and during her very first service mysterious lights were seen near the church. These lights continued to appear near or above other churches in which she sermonized. They often resembled bright stars or fireballs and "bobbed" and "zigzagged" as they moved. The lights were seen by hundreds of witnesses, including many British journalists who were covering the revival for their papers.

The following is a report that was sent to the London *Daily Mail* by one of its correpsondents, who had traveled to Egryn to cover Mary Jones's ministry:

. . . At 8:14 P.M. I was on the hillside, walking from Dyffryn to Egryn. In the distance, about a mile away, I could see the three lighted windows of the tiny Egryn chapel, where service was going on. It was the only touch of light in the miles of countryside. Suddenly at 8:20 P.M. I saw what appeared to be a ball of fire above the roof of the chapel. It came from nowhere, and sprang into existence instantaneously. It had a steady, intense yellow brilliance, and did not move.

Not sure whether or not I was deceiving myself, I called to a man 100 [yards] down the road, and asked him if he could see anything. He came running to me excitedly, and said "Yes, yes, above the chapel. The great light." He was a countryman, and was trembling with emotion.

We watched the light together. It seemed to me to be at twice the height of the chapel, say fifty feet, and it stood out with electric vividness against the encircling hills behind. Suddenly it disappeared, having lasted about a minute and a half.

I leaned against the stone wall by the wayside, and waited for further developments, the countryman leaving me and making his way alone. Again the chapel windows were the only lights in all the countryside. The minutes crept by and it was 8:35 P.M. before I saw anything else. Then two lights flashed out, one on each side of the chapel. They seemed about 100 feet apart, and considerably higher in the air than the first one. In the night it was difficult to judge distance, but I made a rough guess that they were 100 feet above the roof of the chapel. They shone out brilliantly and steadily for a space of thirty seconds. Then they both began to flicker like a defective arc-lamp.

They were flickering like that while one could count ten. Then they became steady again. In the distance they looked like large and brilliant motor-car lights. They disappeared within a couple of seconds of each other.

The lights ebbed when popular support for the revival waned toward the end of 1905, and ultimately vanished from the Welsh skies.[10]

Many writers on the Welsh Revival have argued that this phenomenon was associated only with Mary Jones, implying that she individually was somehow responsible for it. But since appearances of the lights were also reported in towns that Mary Jones had already left, it seems likely that at least some of them were produced by the people who attended her meetings. This was certainly the view of Nandor Fodor, who wrote in 1932 that the Welsh lights seemed "to be the result of an outpouring of combined psychic forces which religious ecstasy generates." [11]

Now that we have reviewed the three underlying themes of this book, can we use these principles to explain the entire range of miraculous events as merely the result of our own psychic capabilities? Or would this lead to a form of "psychic" reductionism, in which all the mysteries and wonders of the universe can be reduced to products generated by human thought? Can attributing the miraculous to a human agency be considered a form of overstated materialism in which life itself is stripped of its spiritual purpose and meaning? These disquieting implications could easily arise from the studies and the evidence that have been presented here.

Yet recent research in another area of the parasciences suggests that a vast spiritual realm *does* exist in the universe, and may manifest itself to us in the form of UFOs and related mysteries . . . including the miraculous.

Although the study of UFOs may at first seem far removed from religion and religious issues, it really has a unique bearing on them. This is perhaps truer today than it was twenty years ago, when UFO research was in its infancy and investigators in the field took it for granted that UFOs were attempts by extraterrestrials to visit our planet. But most ufologists have now abandoned this theory for a number of reasons. One concerns the number of sightings reported. If UFOs were reconnaissance craft from another world, their visits to us would be infrequent. In fact, hundreds of sightings are filed monthly. UFOs have also altered in shape and appearance over the years, as though conforming to the technology of the culture in which they are appearing. They also tend to appear to a witness at a psychologically meaningful point in his life. Finally, many people who have close encounters with UFOs and their occupants have subsequently developed psychic abilities.

These considerations have led many ufologists—including myself—to believe that UFO phenomena are produced by some "X" intelligence that exists in the universe but which is symbiotically linked to our minds and to our planet. For lack of a better term, this supermind or intelligence might simply be called *The Phenomenon*. This term was first introduced by Jerome Clark in a book written jointly with the present author entitled *Earth's Secret Inhabitants* (1979). It was suggested that *The Phenomenon* might be a force and an intelligence beyond our ability to comprehend, but to which all of us are linked at some cosmic level. *The Phenomenon* may be sending us "signs and wonders"—such as the UFO mystery—that are reflections of our cultural and technological concerns.*

This theory has its origins in the proposals of such ufologists as Jacques Vallee, a computer expert and astrophysicist in Stanford, California. Vallee believes that UFOs are created by a "control system" that exists somewhere in the universe. It attempts to benignly manipulate our cultural and spiritual evolution by presenting us with bewildering enigmas that cause us to reevaluate the way we normally view reality. In his book *The Invisible College* (1975), Vallee suggests that some religious miracles—such as Marian apparitions—might also have their origins in this "control system." One might say that *The Phenomenon* is attempting to educate us spiritually through the production of such mysteries.

Another tenable theory is that *The Phenomenon* is not directly responsible for the creation of miracles, but rather *generates some sort of spiritual realm that can be tapped into on rare occasions* and that possesses the power to produce wonders and signs. It might also be the ultimate source of the visions and apparitions seen by the mystics and saints of all religions, past and present. But how can this theory be reconciled with the evidence that miracles seem to be the direct result of human thought? Miracles might occur when a human mind makes contact with this realm.

A vast spiritual realm may have come into being at the same time that life evolved on this planet, and as our views about the existence of such a realm took shape. It would be fruitless to argue whether our thoughts created this spiritual dimension or whether

---

*In the concluding chapter of my *The Tujunga Canyon Contacts* (Englewood Cliffs, New Jersey: Prentice-Hall, 1980), which I co-authored with Ann Druffel, and in my anthology *UFO Abductions* (New York: New American Library, 1980), I revised this theory and suggested that it might be possible for an individual human mind to make direct contact with this supermind. Such a link might well endow that person with formidable psychic powers.

the spiritual realm sparked the evolution of man. All one might propose is that the physical world and the spiritual world developed mutually, each dynamically interacting with the other. As human thought and faith evolved, they generated a system of beliefs that became realities within the spiritual realm. Once created, these realities became independent of the minds and beliefs that gave birth to them.

What this theory is stating is relatively simple. When a group of people or an entire society shares a common religious world view, their ideology is eventually translated into a literal spiritual reality. The world of Jesus, the Virgin Mary, and the angels actually does exist in this reality, and will continue to do so as long as Christian beliefs are held by millions of people. The realm of the Hindu devas and the many heavens and hells that constitute the spiritual realm of Buddhist belief may likewise exist within this dimension.

This hypothesis can certainly help explain some of the mysteries we confront in studying the lives of the mystics of the Church. It is difficult to read their biographies without acknowledging that the visions and spiritual adventures they experienced during their ecstasies were more than merely hallucinations brought about by their pious beliefs. During their trances, such mystics as Teresa of Avila, Catherine Emmerich, Therese Neumann, and many others were probably entering into a spiritual dimension just as real to them as the world of the five senses is to us. The same could hold true of the spiritual worlds to which the shamans of primitive cultures travel during their trances and out-of-body experiences.

This spiritual realm may not exist as a personal reality purely for the benefit of these mystics. Once a belief system or a world view becomes a reality in the spiritual realm, *it becomes a reality for the entire culture that supports it.* Though most of its members may not contact it during their earthly lives, it exists in the universe nonetheless.

This general theory may also provide a clue to the remarkable "superpsychic" powers of such wonder workers as St. Joseph of Copertino, St. Anthony of Padua, Padre Pio, and Teresa Higginson, whose abilities seem to be so much greater and more consistent than those of the many psychics who have come to the attention of parapsychology over the decades.

The saints and mystics of all religions are wonder workers precisely because of their sensitivity to this spiritual realm. Whether their psychic powers bring them into contact with the spiritual world or whether closeness to the spiritual world causes them to become psychic is debatable. Whatever the case, perhaps these psychic individuals can draw upon vast reservoirs of spiritual power generated by this spiritual realm in order to intensify their capabilities. They may be so attuned to the creative forces of the universe that they can tap its creative energy to disrupt the patterns of reality. When they do so, a miracle takes place. For instance, St. John Bosco's thoughts and faith probably brought about the multiplication of food that occurred at his boardinghouse in 1860. It was not produced by God. The saint's own psychic talents gave him the *ability* to perform the miracle, but he could accomplish it and alter reality only by drawing upon the spiritual realm. In other words, the mind of St. John Bosco was responsible for the miracle, but some spiritual force in the universe was the source of power through which the miracle occurred.

As pointed out earlier, *The Phenomenon* might also exist in this great spiritual realm, regulating or perhaps acting as a mediator between it and the physical world. *The Phenomenon* might even be the source of the universe's creative energy and the mastermind that produces any alterations generated within the spiritual realm through human belief and thought. Likewise, it may endow anyone attuned to it with psychic powers far beyond those possessed by even the greatest psychics in the world.

Now, one could reasonably point out that this might well be a description of God. That would indeed be a fascinating point of discussion.

BIBLIOGRAPHY

I. *Science, Psi, and the Miraculous*

1. Seymour Mauskopf. *The Reception of Unconventional Science.* Boulder, Colorado: Westrien Press, 1979.
2. Gino Simi and Mario Segreti. *Saint Francis of Paolo.* Rockford, Illinois: Tan Books, 1977.
3. Berthold Schwarz. "Ordeals by serpents, fire, and strychnine." *Psychiatric Quarterly* 34 (1960): 405−29.
4. Mircea Eliade. *Shamanism.* Princeton, New Jersey: Princeton University Press, 1964.
5. Hereward Carrington. *Loaves and Fishes.* New York: Charles Scribner's Sons, 1935.
6. Redmond Mullin. "The evidence for miracles." In *Mysteries of the World,* edited by Christopher Pick. Secaucus, New Jersey: Chartwell Books, 1979.
7. Renée Haynes. *Philosopher King: The Humanist Pope Benedict XIV.* London: Nicolson and Weidenfeld, 1971.

II. *Levitation*

1. F. Fielding-Ould. *The Wonders of the Saints.* London: Watkins, 1919.
2. Herbert Thurston. *The Physical Phenomena of Mysticism.* London: Burns Oates, 1952.
3. St. Teresa of Avila. *Collected Works.* Washington, D.C.: ICS Publications, 1976.
4. M. Mir. *Vida de Santa Teresa.* Madrid: 1912.
5. *Beatifatimis et canonizationes V.S.D. Bernardino Realino.* Rome: 1828.
6. Eric Dingwall. *Some Human Oddities.* London: Home & Van Thal, 1947.
7. W. Franklin Prince. "Some coincidental dreams." *Journal* of the American Society for Psychical Research 13 (1919): 61−93.

8. Ian Stevenson. "The substantiality of spontaneous cases." *Proceedings* of the Parapsychological Association 5 (1968): 91–128.
9. W. J. Evans-Wentz. *Tibet's Great Yogi Milarepa*. London: Oxford University Press, 1951.
10. Dingwall, op. cit.
11. Louis Jacolliot. *Occult Science in India and Among the Ancients*. London: Rider, 1884.
12. Sri Swami Rama. *Living with Himalayan Masters*. Honesdale, Pennsylvania: Himalayan International Institute, 1978.
13. Lord Adare. *Experiences in Spiritualism with D. D. Home*. Reprint. London: Society for Psychical Research, 1924.
14. John Nicola. *Diabolical Possession and Exorcism*. Rockford, Illinois: Tan Books, 1974.
15. Steve Erdmann. "The truth behind 'The Exorcist.'" *Fate* 28 (1975): 50–59.
16. Adolf Rodewyk. *Possessed by Satan*. Garden City, New York: Doubleday, 1975.
17. Herbert Thurston. *Surprising Mystics*. London: Burns Oates, 1955.
18. Thurston, *The Physical Phenomena of Mysticism*. London: Burns Oates, 1955.

III. *The Stigmata*

1. Thomas of Celano. *Vita prima*, 1229. Cited in Herbert Thurston, *The Physical Phenomena of Mysticism*. London: Burns Oates, 1955.
2. St. Bonaventura. *Legenda Major*. Cited in Thurston, ibid.
3. Thurston, ibid.
4. Montague Summers. *The Physical Phenomena of Mysticism*. New York: Barnes & Noble, 1950.
5. Padre Germano. *The Life of Gemma Galgani*. London: Sands, 1914.
6. Thurston, op. cit.
7. Cited in Charles Carty. *Who Is Therese Neumann?* Rockford, Illinois: Tan Books, 1974.
8. Fritz Gerlich. *Therese Neumann von Konnersreuth*. Munich: Verlag Joseph Kusel und Friedrich Pastet, 1929.
9. Reported in *Berliner Hefte* 4: September 1940.
10. Cited in Thurston, op. cit.
11. Cited in John Schug. *Padre Pio*. Huntington, Indiana: Our Sunday Visitor, 1976.
12. Ibid.

13. Robert Rickard. "Stigmata." In *Mysteries of the World,* edited by Christopher Pick. Secaucus, New Jersey: Chartwell Books, 1979.
14. Lauritz Miller. "10-year-old girl bleeds like crucified Christ." *National Enquirer,* July 16, 1972.

IV. *Bilocation*

1. Montague Summers. *The Physical Phenomena of Mysticism.* New York: Barnes & Noble, 1950.
2. Herbert Thurston. *Surprising Mystics.* London: Burns Oates, 1955.
3. Cecil Kerr. *Teresa Helena Higginson—Servant of God.* Reprint. Rockford, Illinois: Tan Books, 1978.
4. Karlis Osis and Erlendur Haraldsson. "OOBE's in Indian swamis: Satya Sai Baba and Dadaji." In *Research in Parapsychology 1975,* edited by Joanna Morris, Robert Morris, and W. G. Roll. Metuchen, New Jersey: Scarecrow Press, 1976.
5. Lucian Landau. "An unusual out-of-the-body experience." *Journal of the Society for Psychical Research* 42 (1963): 126−8.
6. Eleanor Sidgwick. "On the evidence for clairvoyance." *Proceedings of the Society for Psychical Research* 9 (1891): 30−99.
7. D. Scott Rogo. "Experiments with Blue Harary." In *Mind Beyond the Body,* edited by D. Scott Rogo. New York: Penguin Books, 1978.
8. Charles Carty. *Padre Pio—the Stigmatist.* St. Paul, Minnesota: Radio Replies Press, 1955.
9. Ibid.
10. Albert Freiherr von Schrenck—Notzing. Reported in *Gesammelte Aufsätze zur Parapsychologie.* Stuttgart: 1929.
11. Joseph Lapponi. *Hypnotism and Spiritism.* New York: Longmans, Green & Co., 1907.
12. Vicente Maliwanag. "Manila's disappearing boy." *Fate* 18 (1965): 37−42.

V. *Divine Images*

1. Ian Wilson. *The Shroud of Turin.* Garden City, New York: Doubleday, 1978.
2. Ibid.
3. Donald Damerest and Coley Taylor (eds.). *The Dark Virgin.* New York: Coley Taylor Inc., n.d.
4. D. Scott Rogo. *The Haunted Universe.* New York: New American Library, 1977.

5. Barbara McKenzie. "Faces in the wall of Christchurch Cathedral." *Psychic Science* 10 (1931): 84–89.
6. Nandor Fodor. *Between Two Worlds*. West Nyack, New York: Parker, 1964.
7. Barbara McKenzie. "Faces on the wall." *Psychic Science* 18 (1939): 35–42.
8. David Techter. "A flap of glowing crosses." *Fate* 25 (1972): 52–59.
9. Benson Herbert. "The Padfield effect." *International Journal of Paraphysics* 8 (1974): 136–50.
10. Anna Sproule. "The Turin Shroud." In *Mysteries of the World,* edited by Christopher Pick. Secaucus, New Jersey: Chartwell Books, 1979.
11. Paul Vignon. *The Shroud of Christ*. Reprint. New Hyde Park, New York: University Books, 1970.
12. Wilson, op. cit.

VI. *The Miraculous Hailstones of Remiremont*

1. Cited in English by Charles Fort. *Wild Talents*. New York: Ace, n.d.
2. M. Sage. "The alleged miraculous hailstones of Remiremont." *Proceedings* of the Society for Psychical Research 21 (1908–9): 405–435.
3. M. J. Vuillemin. "Report on the 'Hailstone Medallions.' " Summary in English, reprinted in *Annals of Psychical Science* 7 (1908): 426–428.
4. D. Scott Rogo. "Psychic weather control." *Fate* 33 (1980): 79–85.
5. D. Scott Rogo. *The Poltergeist Experience*. New York: Penguin, 1979.
6. Nandor Fodor. *Between Two Worlds*. West Nyack, New York: Parker, 1964.
7. Frances Russell. *The World of Dürer*. New York: Time-Life Books, 1967.

VII. *Bleeding Statues and Weeping Madonnas*

1. Lloyd Mallan. "Vatican investigates claim that painting weeps human blood." *National Enquirer*, September 5, 1971.
2. Paul Bannister. "Statue of Christ drips human blood." *National Enquirer*, January 20, 1976.
3. Everard Feilding. "The Case of Abbé Vachère." In *Sittings with*

Eusapia Palladino and Other Studies. New Hyde Park, New York: University Books, 1963.

4. Charles Fort. *Lo!* New York: Ace, n.d.

5. H. Jongen. *Look!—the Madonna is Weeping.* Bayshore, New Jersey: Montfort Publications, 1959.

6. Nandor Fodor. *Between Two Worlds.* West Nyack, New York: Parker, 1964.

7. Raymond Bayless. "Investigating a weeping icon." *Fate* 19 (1966): 59–64.

8. William Rauscher (with Allen Spraggett). *The Spiritual Frontier.* Garden City, New York: Doubleday, 1975.

9. Eric Dingwall. *Some Human Oddities.* London: Home & Van Thal, 1947.

VIII. *The Miracle of St. Januarius*

1. Herbert Thurston. *The Physical Phenomena of Mysticism.* London: Burns Oates, 1952.

2. A. Mazzarelli. *Raccolta di documenti spettanti alla vita del B. Francesco di Geronimo.* Rome: 1806.

3. Giorgio Giorgi. "Fede, scienze, parapsicologia di fronta al miracolo di Gennero." *Quaderni di parapsicologia* 1 (1970): 18–28.

4. David Guerdon. "Le sang de Saint Janvier se liquéfie et se coagule depuis des siècles." *Psi International* Bimestrial #5 (1978): 9–29.

5. Cited in Guerdon, ibid.

6. Montague Summers. *The Physical Phenomena of Mysticism.* New York: Barnes & Noble, 1950.

IX. *Manifestations of the Blessed Virgin Mary*

1. Don Sharkey. *The Woman Shall Conquer.* Kenosha, Wisconsin: Prow Books/Franciscan Marytown Press, 1954.

2. William Ullathorne. *The Holy Mountain of La Salette.* Altamont, New York: La Salette Press, 1942.

3. M. Richard. *What Happened at Pontmain.* Reprint. Washington, New Jersey: Ave Maria Institute, 1971.

4. Ernesto Spinelli. "The effects of chronological age on GESP ability." In *Research in Parapsychology—1976*, edited by J. D. Morris, W. G. Roll, and R. L. Morris. Metuchen, New Jersey: Scarecrow Press, 1977.

5. William Coyne. *Our Lady of Knock.* New York: Catholic Book Publishing Co., 1948.

6. William T. Walsh. *Our Lady of Fatima*. New York: Macmillan, 1947.
7. V. Montes de Oca. *More About Fatima*. No publisher listed, 1945.
8. Montes de Oca, op. cit.
9. John Beevers. *Virgin of the Poor*. St. Meinrad, Indiana: Abbey Press, 1975.
10. Kevin and Sue McClure. *Stars, and Rumours of Stars*. Privately printed by the authors, 1980.
11. Sebastian Robiou Lamarche. "El estrano caso de Arroyo Hondo." *Stendek* 3:10 (1972): 17–20.

X. *Miracles at Garabandal, Spain; and Zeitoun, Egypt*

1. F. Sanchez-Ventura y Pascual. *The Apparitions of Garabandal*. Detroit, Michigan: San Miguel Publishing Co., 1966.
2. Ibid.
3. Joseph Pelletier. *Our Lady Comes to Garabandal*. Worcester, Massachusetts: Assumption Publications, 1971.
4. Sanchez-Ventura y Pascual, op. cit.
5. Jerome Palmer. *Our Lady Returns to Egypt*. San Bernardino, California: Culligan Publications, 1969.
6. Hans Werner Bartsch. "Pentecost and the light cloud from Cairo. Visit from the world beyond?" *Stern*, June 2, 1968.
7. Palmer, op. cit.
8. Pearl Zaki. *Our Lord's Mother Visits Egypt*. Cairo: Privately printed by the author, 1971.

XI. *Miraculous Healings*

1. Alexis Carrel. *The Voyage to Lourdes*. New York: Harper & Brothers, 1950.
2. Renée Haynes. "Miracles and paranormal healing." *Parapsychology Review* 8:5 (1977): 25–28.
3. Giuliana Cavallini. *Saint Martin de Porres*. Rockford, Illinois: Tan Books, 1979.
4. Des Hickey and Gus Smith. *Miracle*. London: Hodder & Stoughton, 1978.
5. Bernard Grad. "The biological effects of the 'laying on of hands' on animals and plants: Implications for biology." In *Parapsychology: Its Relation to Physics, Biology, Psychology and Psychiatry*, edited by Gertrude Schmeidler. Metuchen, New Jersey: Scarecrow Press, 1976.

6. William Nolen. *Healing: A Doctor in Search of a Miracle.* New York: Random House, 1974.
7. Allen Spraggett. *Kathryn Kuhlman—the Woman Who Believes in Miracles.* New York: Crowell, 1970.
8. Charles Carty. *Padre Pio—the Stigmatist.* St. Paul, Minnesota: Radio Replies Press, 1955.
9. Ruth Cranston. *The Miracle of Lourdes.* New York: McGraw-Hill, 1955.
10. Ibid.
11. Donald J. West. *Eleven Lourdes Miracles.* New York: Helix Press, 1957.
12. Cranston, op. cit.
13. Leslie Weatherhead. *Psychology, Religion and Healing.* New York/Nashville: Abington Press, 1951.

XII. *Psyche and the Miraculous*

1. Herbert Thurston. *The Physical Phenomena of Mysticism.* London: Burns Oates, 1952.
2. Nandor Fodor. *On the Trail of the Poltergeist.* New York: Citadel Press, 1955.
3. Raymond Bayless. *The Other Side of Death.* New Hyde Park, New York: University Books, 1971.
4. F. A. Forbes. *St. John Bosco—The Friend of Youth.* New Rochelle, New York: Salesiana Publishers, 1962.
5. A. Wensinck. *Handbook of Early Mohammedan Tradition.* Leiden: E. Brill, 1927.
6. Robert D. Smith. *Comparative Miracles.* St. Louis, Missouri: B. Herder Book Co., 1965.
7. Charles Carty. *Padre Pio—the Stigmatist.* St. Paul, Minnesota: Radio Replies Press, 1955.
8. Sebastian Robiou Lamarche. "El estrano caso de Arroyo Hondo." *Stendek* 3:10 (1972): 17–20.
9. Nandor Fodor. *The Encyclopaedia of Psychic Science.* London: Author's Press, n.d.
10. Kevin and Sue McClure. *Stars, and Rumours of Stars.* Privately printed by the authors, 1980.
11. Fodor, op. cit.

INDEX

ABOUT THE AUTHOR

D. Scott Rogo, one of this country's most widely published experts on psychic phenomena and related subjects, has written nearly twenty books on the field, as well as over a hundred magazine and journal reports and articles. A researcher and educator as well as an author, Mr. Rogo served as a visiting research consultant for the Durham, North Carolina–based Psychical Research Foundation in 1973, and in 1975 was simultaneously a visiting researcher at the Maimonides Medical Center's division of parapsychology and psychophysics (in Brooklyn, New York) and director of research for the Society for Psychic Research in Beverly Hills, California. Since 1979 he has held the position of lecturer in parapsychology at John F. Kennedy University in Orinda, California. He is also consulting editor for *Fate* magazine.

Mr. Rogo is a lifelong resident of Los Angeles, where he makes his present home.